THE AGE OF DISCONTINUITY

'The book is in four parts. In the first, the author decries the ageing industries of agriculture, steel and automobiles. Instead he sees four new industrial areas emerging, namely information, oceans, materials and those activities which react to "megalopolis", all based on knowledge as developed in the twentieth century ... this penetrating book is sufficiently novel to jolt the thinking public out of its present complacency.'

Institute of Office Management

'What makes this such a fascinating book is Drucker's deep knowledge of Central Europe, Britain, US and Japan, from which he draws numerous practical examples.' *The Financial Times*

'Drucker's most ambitious book. The world's best-read business author draws on his whole experience ... sanguine and highly informative.'

European Business

'Stimulating, instructive and well worth studying.'
Advertisers' Weekly

'You may disagree but you cannot afford to ignore it.' *The Times Educational Supplement*

Also available in this series

CONDITIONS OF SALE

Management Series

THE AGE OF DISCONTINUITY

Guidelines to our Changing Society

PETER F. DRUCKER

UNABRIDGED

PAN BOOKS LTD : LONDON

First published in Great Britain 1969 by William Heinemann Ltd.
This edition published 1971 by Pan Books Ltd,
33 Tothill Street, London, S.W.1

ISBN 0 330 02693 3

Printed in Great Britain by
Richard Clay (The Chaucer Press), Ltd, Bungay, Suffolk

CONTENTS

Contents

6

Preface

IN GUERRILLA COUNTRY a hand-car, light and expendable, rides ahead of the big, lumbering freight train to detonate whatever explosives might have been placed on the track. This book is such a 'hand-car'. For the future is, of course, always 'guerrilla country' in which the unsuspected and apparently insignificant derails the massive and seemingly invincible trends of today. Or, to change the metaphor, this book may be looked at as an 'early-warning system', reporting discontinuities which, while still below the visible horizon, are already changing the structure and meaning of economy, polity, and society. These discontinuities, rather than the massive momentum of the apparent trends, are likely to mould and shape our tomorrow, the closing decades of the twentieth century. These discontinuities are, so to speak, our 'recent future' – both already accomplished fact and challenge to come.

Major discontinuities exist in four areas.

(1) Genuinely new technologies are upon us. They are almost certain to create new major industries and brand-new major businesses, and to render obsolete at the same time existing major industries and big businesses. The growth industries of the last half-century derived from the scientific discoveries of the mid- and late-nineteenth century. The growth industries of the last decades of the twentieth century are likely to emerge from the knowledge discoveries of the first fifty and sixty years of this century: quantum physics, the understanding of atomic and molecular structure, biochemistry, psychology, symbolic logic. The coming decades in technology are more likely to re-

7

semble the closing decades of the last century, in which a major industry based on new technology surfaced every few years, than they will resemble the technological and industrial continuity of the last fifty years.

(2) We face major changes in the world's economy. In economic policies and theories, we still act as if we live in an 'international' economy, in which separate nations are the units, dealing with each other primarily through international trade and fundamentally as different from one another in their economy as they are different from one another in language or laws or cultural tradition. But imperceptibly there has emerged a world economy in which common information generates the same economic appetites, aspirations, and demands – cutting across national boundaries and languages and largely disregarding political ideologies as well. The world has become, in other words, *one market*, one global shopping centre. Yet this world economy almost entirely lacks economic institutions; the only – though important – exception is the multi-national corporation. We are also totally without economic policy and economic theory for a world economy.

It is not yet a viable economy. The failure of new major economies to join the ranks of 'advanced' and 'developed' nations has created a fissure between rich – and largely white, and poor – and largely coloured, nations that may swallow up both. The next decades must see drastic change. Either we learn how to restore the capacity for development that the nineteenth century possessed in such ample measure – under conditions for development that are quite different – or the twentieth century will make true, as Mao and Castro expect, the prophecy of class war which to have sidetracked was the proudest achievement of the generation before World War I. Only the war now would be between races rather than classes.

(3) The political matrix of social and economic life is changing fast. Today's society and polity are pluralistic. Every single social task of importance today is entrusted to

a large institution organized for perpetuity and run by managers. Where the assumptions that govern what we expect and see are still those of the individualistic society of eighteenth-century liberal theory, the reality that governs our behaviour is that of organized, indeed over-organized, power concentrations.

Yet we are also approaching a turning-point in this trend. Everywhere there is rapid disenchantment with the biggest and fastest-growing of these institutions, modern government, as well as cynicism regarding its ability to perform. We are becoming equally critical of the other organized institutions; revolt is occurring simultaneously in the Catholic Church and in the big universities. The young everywhere are, indeed, rejecting *all* institutions with equal hostility.

We have created a new socio-political reality without so far understanding it; without, indeed, thinking much about it. This new pluralist society of institutions poses political, philosophical, and spiritual challenges that go far beyond this book (or the author's competence).

(4) But the most important of the changes is the last one. Knowledge, during the last few decades, has become the central capital, the cost centre and the crucial resource of the economy. This changes labour forces and work; teaching and learning; and the meaning of knowledge and its politics. But it also raises the problem of the responsibilities of the new men of power, the men of knowledge.

Yet neither economics nor technology, neither political structure nor knowledge and education, is the theme of this book. The unifying common theme is the *discontinuities* that even a cursory glance at reality reveals. They are very different, perhaps, from what the forecasts predict. But they are even more different from what most of us still perceive as 'today'.

Every single one of the views which this book records will be familiar. Yet the social landscape that emerges when they are put together into one picture bears little resemblance to what all of us still see when we look around us. Or, to change the metaphor, we, the actors, still believe we are playing Ibsen or Bernard Shaw – while it is the 'Theatre of the Absurd' in which we actually appear (and on TV rather than 'live' on Broadway).

It is high fashion today to predict 'The Year 2000'. We suddenly realize that we are closer to this milestone than we are to that fateful year 1933, when both Hitler and Roosevelt came to power. And yet anyone middle-aged today still experiences 1933 as 'current events'.

I envy the courage of the seers who tell us what 2000 may look like; but I have no desire to emulate them. I remember too well what the future looked like in 1933. No forecaster could then have imagined our reality of 1969. Nor could anyone, a generation earlier in 1900, have anticipated or forecast the realities of 1933.

All we can ever predict is continuity which extends yesterday's trends into tomorrow. What has already happened is the only thing we can protect and the only thing that can be quantified. But these continuing trends, however important, are only one dimension of the future, only one aspect of reality.

The most accurate quantitative projection never predicts the truly important: the meaning of the facts and figures in the context of a different tomorrow.

It would have been highly optimistic in 1950, less than twenty years ago, to predict that the United States could in this century reduce poverty to where fewer than one-tenth of white families and fewer than one-third of Negro families live below the 'poverty threshold'. Yet we had achieved this by 1966. Even in 1959, in the closing years of the Eisenhower administration, it would have been considered almost Utopian to predict a reduction within one decade of almost half in the number of families in poverty, from more than eight million to fewer than five million – the concrete achievement of the Sixties. Yet during this period the income level that defines 'poverty' was sharply raised.

The correct figures could perhaps have been forecast; but what today, only ten years later, controls America's mood and shapes its policies – not to mention its picture of itself – would have been quite unpredictable to any statistical, projective method: there has been a change in the meaning, the quality, the perception of our experience. In 1959 the accent was all on our affluence. In 1969 it is all on the poor.

This book tries to look at these other dimensions, at the qualitative and the structural, the perceptions, the meaning and the values, the opportunities and the priorities. It is limited in its subject matter to the social scene. But there it takes a broad view, looking at economics and politics, at social issues, at technology and at the universe of learning and knowledge. Only incidentally does it concern itself, however, with those great realms of individual experience, the arts and man's spiritual life.

This book does not project trends; it examines discontinuities. It does not forecast tomorrow; it looks at today. It does not ask: 'What will tomorrow look like?' It asks instead: 'What do we have to tackle today to make tomorrow?'

PETER F. DRUCKER

Montclair, New Jersey

PART ONE

The Knowledge Technologies

1. The End of Continuity

No ONE knowing only the *economic* facts and figures of 1968 and of 1913 – and ignorant both of the years in between and of anything but economic figures – would even suspect the cataclysmic events of this century such as two world wars, the Russian and Chinese Revolutions, or the Hitler régime. They seem to have left no trace in the statistics. The tremendous economic expansion throughout the industrial world in the last two decades has by and large only made up for the three decades of stagnation between the two world wars. And the expansion has in the main been confined to nations that were already 'advanced' industrial nations by 1913 – or were at least rapidly advancing.

Our time, all of us would agree, is a time of momentous changes – in politics and in science, in world view and in *mores*, in the arts and in warfare. But in the one area where most people think the changes have been the greatest, the last half-century has in reality been a period of amazing and almost unparalleled continuity: the economy.

The economic expansion of the last twenty years has been very fast, but it has been carried largely by industries that were already 'big business' before World War I. It has been based on technologies that were firmly established by 1913 to exploit inventions made in the half-century before. Technologically, the last fifty years have been the fulfilment of the promises bequeathed to us by our Victorian grandparents rather than the years of revolutionary change the Sunday supplements talk about.

Imagine a good economist who fell asleep in July 1914, just before 'the Guns of August' shattered the world of the

15

Victorians. He wakes up now, more than fifty years later, and being a good economist he immediately reaches for the latest economic reports and figures. This Rip van Winkle would be a very surprised man; not because the economy has changed so much, but because it has changed so very much less than any economist (let alone a good one) would have expected during fifty years.

The figures would show that by the mid-Sixties all economically advanced countries had, on the whole, reached the levels of production and income they would have attained had the economic trends of the thirty or so years *before* 1914 continued, basically unchanged, for another fifty years.

The one important exception to this might be Russia, where production and income today are probably well *below* what the pre-1914 growth rates had promised. We know the reason, of course. It is the political straitjacket into which the Communists forced Russian agriculture just when the technological revolution got going on the farm. As a result Russia, in 1913 one of the world's largest food exporters, now can barely feed her own population. Yet she still keeps nearly half her people on the land – at least twice as many as would be needed had Russian farm productivity been allowed to grow at the rate at which it grew between 1900 and 1913.

All other countries that had reached by 1913 what is now called the 'take-off point' in economic development – the United States, Western and Central Europe, and Japan – are today roughly where a long-range projection of the growth trends of the years between 1885 and 1913 would have put them half a century later, that is, today. This is true even of Britain; by 1913 her growth had already slowed to a crawl.

Even more amazing: our Rip van Winkle economist would find the economic geography of the world quite unchanged in its structure. Every single area that is today a major industrial power was already well along the road to industrial leadership in 1913. No major new industrial country has joined the club since. Brazil, at least in its central region, may be on the threshold of emergence, but she is not there yet. Otherwise, only areas that are, in effect, extensions of the old industrial regions, such as Canada, Mexico, and Australia, have grown to industrial stature, and mainly as satellite economies at that.

In the half-century before 1913, the economic map of the world had been changing as fast and as drastically as the physical map of the world had changed during the age of discovery in the fifteenth and sixteenth centuries. Between 1810 and 1870 both the United States and Germany had surfaced as new, big industrial powers and rapidly forged ahead of the old champion, Great Britain. Twenty years later, Russia, Japan, the present Czechoslovakia, and the present Austria had soared aloft, with Northern Italy following closely behind. The economic development which seemed so easy and effortless then, even for a non-Western country like Japan, has since World War I become so difficult as to be apparently unattainable. This is not only a fundamental economic contrast between our era and that of the Victorians and Edwardians; it is also the greatest political threat today – comparable only to the threat of class war inside industrial society before 1913.

Should he turn to industrial structure and technology, our Rip van Winkle economist would find himself equally (and equally unexpectedly) on familiar ground. Of course, there are hundreds of products around that would be unfamiliar to him: electric appliances, TV sets, jet planes, antibiotics, the computer. But in terms of economic structure and growth the load is still being carried by the same industries and largely by the same technologies that carried it in 1913.

The main engine of economic growth in the developed

countries during the last twenty years has been agriculture. In all these countries (excepting only Russia and her European satellites), productivity on the farm has been increasing faster than in the manufacturing industry. Yet the technological revolution in agriculture had begun well before 1913. Most of the 'new' agricultural technology – tractors, fertilizers, improved seeds and breeds – had been around for many years. The 'good' farmer of today has just about reached the productivity and output of the 'model farm' of 1913.

Second only to farming, as a moving force behind our recent economic expansion, comes steel.

World steel capacity has grown five-fold since 1946 with Russia and Japan in the lead. But steel production had become synonymous with economic muscle well before World War I. Almost all the steel mills built since World War II use processes that date back to the 1860s and were already considered obsolescent fifty years ago. The automobile industry – probably number three in the growth parade today – was also well advanced when World War I started. Henry Ford turned out a quarter of a million Model Ts in 1913 – more than the Soviet Union has yet produced in any one year. And there is not one feature on any car anywhere today that could not have been found on some commercially available make in 1913.

The electrical apparatus, the telephone, and the organic-chemical industries were already giants fifty years ago. General Electric, Westinghouse, Siemens, the Bell Telephone System, and the German chemical companies were by then well-established 'blue chips', Rockefeller's Standard Oil Company and British Shell were scarcely struggling infants – indeed they were the 'octopuses' of 1913 with tentacles into every country in the world. And though electronics was just beginning its growth then, it was already large enough to spawn in the

British 'Marconi Affairs' of 1912 a scandal so big and juicy as to threaten the political life of the first of the new breed of 'democratic' leaders, Lloyd George.

Of course, all around us there are new industries and new technologies. But as the economist defines 'importance', that is, by contribution to gross national product, personal income, and employment, these new industries are still almost negligible, at least to the civilian economy.

The aeroplane began to make an economic impact only with the coming of jets in the 1960s. Airfreight is only now growing at a phenomenal rate. With the advent of big 'jumbo jets' the freight plane may well, within a few years, make obsolete the ocean-going cargo ship as the truck has broken the railway monopoly on land in the last thirty years. So far, however, airfreight is still a lesser factor in world transportation than bullock or burro.

Only now, when IBM is turning out computers at a rate of a thousand a month, are they starting to have substantial economic impact.

The pharmaceutical industry has all but revolutionized the practice of medicine in the last thirty years. Thanks to new drugs, health care has become the 'best buy' on the market and a universal demand; as a result health services and their financing are everywhere becoming a governmental concern – just as schooling went public 150 years ago when literacy first became a profitable investment for the individual. Yet economically – that is, in terms of employment or of direct contribution to national product – the pharmaceutical industry is still hardly visible to the naked eye, and a pygmy next to such traditional industries as food processing, railways, or textiles.

Indeed of all the new industries only one has, so far, attained major economic importance as the economist measures importance: it is plastics.

Plastics were looked upon until a very few years ago as

19

'substitutes' – *ersatz* – rather than a major new industry and technology in their own right. And even the plastics industry today is only a faint premonition of what the 'materials' industry of tomorrow is likely to be, both economically and technologically.

The new industries with their new technologies loom much larger in our eyes than the old familiar steel mills and automobile assembly plants. They capture our imagination and furnish the 'glamour' stocks in our investment portfolios. But if all of them (except plastics), with all their output and all their jobs, were taken out of the figures for the civilian economy, the difference would hardly show in national income or total employment; that is, in the figures by which the economist measures economic strength and growth.

An economist of 1913 could, therefore, have forecast the industry structure of the 1960s with reasonable accuracy. Only no sane economist of that time would have dreamed of forecasting continuity. The relative stability in technologies and industries during the last fifty years is in the sharpest imaginable contrast to the turbulence of the half-century before. The fifty years that came to an end with World War I produced most of the inventions that underlie our modern industrial civilization. Synthetic dyes (and with them the organic-chemical industry), the Bessemer steel process, and the Siemens electrical generator came in the late 1850s and 1860s. The electric light bulb and the phonograph were invented (both by Edison) in the 1870s. In the same decade appeared the typewriter and the telephone, which together took respectable women out of the home and into the office and thus led, in another half-century, to female emancipation and the vote for women. In the 1880s came the automobile, and in the same decade aluminium – together with the slightly older vulcanized rubber, the first truly new material since the Chinese had first made paper in about the time of Christ. Marconi's wireless, and aspirin (the first effective synthetic drug and the beginning of the pharmaceutical industry) were developed in the 1890s; the Wright Brothers' aeroplane in 1903; and the electronic tube (de Forrest and Armstrong) in 1912.

Most industrial technology is an extension and modification of the inventions and technologies of that remarkable half-century before World War I.

This continuity, in turn, has made for a stable industrial structure. Every one of the great nineteenth-century inventions gave birth, almost overnight, to a new major industry and to new big businesses. These are still the major industries and big businesses of today.

The best example is the rebuilding of industrial Germany after World War II. The same companies dominate the German economy today, and are the 'blue chips' of the Frankfurt Stock Exchange, that dominated the German economy and stock exchanges in 1913. Their names are unchanged; their product scopes, their markets, their technologies are largely unchanged – they are only much, much bigger.

To be sure, this faithful, almost antiquarian, restoration of pre-World War I German industry overdid it; the Krupp concern rebuilt by the last bearer of the name to look as much as possible like the empire his grandfather had left behind in about 1900 – an empire of coal mines, steel mills, and shipyards – had to be taken over by the banks under a government guarantee in 1967. But the reason for failure was that old and familiar nemesis of industrial empire builders, financial over-extension, rather than the ancestor-worship of the last Krupp.

Even the techno-economic 'catastrophes' that are so widely threatened are still future rather than present. The 'population explosion' has not, so far, caused large-scale famine and pestilence. We would actually still worry a good deal about 'unsaleable surpluses' of farm crops if Russia had continued to increase farm productivity at the pre-World War I rate (let alone if Russian farm productivity had shown anything like the explosive growth of American agriculture). While we have the technological means to control population, not even the 'pill' has so far had a major impact in the poor countries of rapid population growth.

The world of the 'New Left' and of the 'Hippies', of 'Op Art' and of Mao Tse-tung's 'Cultural Revolution', of H-bombs and moon rockets seems further removed from the certainties and perceptions of the Victorians and Edwardians than they were from the Age of the Migration at the end of Antiquity. But in the economy, in industrial geography, industrial structure, and industrial technology we are still very much the heirs of the Victorians.

Measured by the yardsticks of the economist, the last half-century has been an *Age of Continuity* – the period of least change in 300 years or so, that is, since world commerce and systematic agriculture first became dominant economic factors in the closing decades of the seventeenth century.

The growth during this period of continuity has been great, especially in the countries that were already well advanced before 1913. But the growth has been largely along lines that had been laid down well and truly in those distant days of our grandparents and great-grandparents.

What is amazing is perhaps not that it took half a century for the work and thought of those earlier generations to come to fruition; it is that the generation of 1900, which we tend today to look down on as stodgy stick-in-the-muds, laid down economic foundations of such strength and excellence that they have prevailed over all the wickedness, criminal insanity, and suicidal violence of the last fifty years. The towering economic achievements of today, the affluent, mass-consumption economies of the advanced countries, their productivity and their technological powers, are built four-square on Victorian and Edwardian foundations and out of building blocks quarried then. They are, above all, a fulfilment of the economic and technological promises of the Victorian and Edwardian eras and testimony to their economic vision.

Now, however, we face an *Age of Discontinuity* in world economy and technology. We might succeed in making it an age of great economic growth as well. But the one thing that is certain so far is that it will be a period of change – in technology and in economic policy, in industrial structures and in economic theory, in the knowledge needed to govern and to manage, and in economic issues.

While we have been busy finishing the great nineteenth-century economic edifice, the foundations have shifted under our feet.

2. The New Industries and their Dynamics

FORECASTING 'TECHNOLOGICAL marvels' is highly fashionable these days. Hardly a month goes by without the well-publicized appearance of a new list of future 'miracle' products and processes. But no matter how persuasive these forecasts* may be, they rarely mention the most important qualitative and structural features of the technology ahead for the last third of the twentieth century – even though these are infinitely more important than any invention, product, or process.

First, major expansion of the economies of the industrially developed countries, both those of the West and those of the Communist world, cannot be carried any further by the industries and technologies that have provided the dynamics of growth for the last one hundred years. In the developed countries these industries have become 'mature' industries – the economist's euphemism for incipient senility. Only in underdeveloped or developing nations can these industries still provide the technological foundation for rapid and extensive economic growth.

Between 1850 and 1870 the centre of economic gravity shifted from the industries of the 'Industrial Revolution', coal and steam, textiles and machine tools, to new and

* Most persuasive perhaps is a list of *One Hundred technical innovations likely in the next 33 years*, devised by Herman Kahn and Anthony J. Wiener of the Hudson Institute. See their article 'The Next Thirty-three Years: A Framework for Speculation' (*Daedalus*; Summer, 1967).

different industries: steel and electricity, organic chemicals, and the internal combustion engine. Now, a hundred years later, we are in the early stages of a similar and equally drastic shift to industries based not only on new and different technologies, but on different science, different logic, and different perception. They are also different in their work force for they demand knowledge workers rather than manual workers.

These industries are capable of providing rapid economic growth in jobs, opportunities, income, standards of living, and aspirations for many decades, if not for another century, and they are most unlikely to emerge except in countries that have a solid industrial and educational foundation – that is, in the developed countries.

THE AGEING 'MODERN' INDUSTRIES

Technologically, the established 'modern' industries may still enjoy a long period of growth and advance. Financially, that is, as investment channels, they may be highly attractive and offer rich returns. They may even grow at a good pace in the years ahead. But in respect to their ability to provide the thrust for further substantial growth of the developed economies they are mature, if not stagnant. No matter how much they themselves grow and prosper, they will lose increasingly the capacity to contribute to rising national incomes, to increased employment, and career opportunities. They will increasingly be unable to provide economic dynamics for the developed countries.

To clarify – but also to illustrate – this conclusion, I shall take a brief look at the three industries that, together, have powered the tremendous growth of the developed economies of the West (and of Japan) in the last twenty years: agriculture, steel, and automobiles.

(1) Agriculture has been the most spectacular performer in the growth parade. In the United States, ten out of every twenty members of the labour force were working on the

land in 1900. At the end of World War II, in 1945, we still had almost one-third of the population on the farm. Now fewer than one-tenth of the labour force work as farmers. They produce, however, infinitely more food and farm crops than the much larger number produced sixty years ago. The indirect contribution of agriculture to national product, to incomes, and the standard of living may be greater still. The people no longer needed to work on the land have provided the labour force for an expanding manufacturing industry, for the services, and for the rapidly growing information and knowledge employments. The transfer of marginal farmers and farm workers to urban employment has by itself probably been the largest single fact in the rise of national productivity. A good many of these farm workers moving from the land to the city did not go into very productive employment; but since in many cases they had had no productivity at all on the marginal farm, even employment as waiters or as handymen represented a sharp increase in their productivity, in their incomes, and in the economy altogether.

In Japan, too, the tremendous economic expansion of the last twenty years was fuelled, above all, by a sharp shift of labour resources from farm jobs with marginal productivity to city jobs with higher productivity. Farm population in Japan was almost 60 per cent of total population at the end of World War II. It is barely 20 per cent now. In Germany and France farm population is still quite high, though a great deal lower than it was only twenty years ago. But in Germany and France (and also in Northern Italy and Switzerland) a tremendous increase in productivity resulted from the importation of formerly non-productive farm dwellers from Southern Italy and Sicily, from Greece, Turkey, Spain, and Portugal into urban jobs in the industrialized areas.

One of the main reasons for Britain's economic difficulties during the last twenty years has been the lack of such a reserve of marginal farmers to move into new industries;

this shift from country to city had taken place in Britain a hundred years before. There simply were no people left in Britain who could leave the land in the last two decades. This explains in large measure why the new highly productive industries in Britain have been plagued by constant labour shortages. As a result, Great Britain lacked the built-in almost automatic increase in the productivity of the whole economy which galvanized the rest of the industrialized West.

In Soviet Russia the underemployed reservoir of rural labour is tremendous. But the collective farm has served to retain people on the land, thus both holding down farm productivity and creating labour shortages in the cities, especially in the service industries. New industries could, therefore, grow in Russia only by withholding from the consumer the benefits of economic growth.

The available figures are not too helpful, but it seems probable that one-half or more of the total increase in productivity – ranging from an average of 3 per cent a year in the United States in the two decades after World War II, to an average of 6 or 7 per cent in Japan for the same period – can be attributed to this shift in population. Better performance in the existing industries is rarely the main cause of rising productivity. The central cause is usually a change in the 'mix' as new industries with high productivity grow faster than old industries with low productivity. This change in the 'mix' was brought about, in the last twenty years, largely by a shift of workers from farm work with very low productivity to more productive urban employments. This, in turn, was made possible by the rapid expansion of agricultural technology which made it increasingly possible for a very small number of highly trained, highly equipped 'commercial' farmers to produce very large outputs.

Farm technology is still advancing. A period of very fast increase in farm productivity for the developed countries may be just ahead. Many already available technologies are not yet in general use. The 'systems approach' is just beginning to be applied to the farm crops with the highest value – fruits, vegetables, and meat animals – which still, in many ways, are being produced by yesterday's labour – intensive methods with fairly low productivity.

We are now, for instance, for the first time, developing 'systems' for cultivating tomatoes from the planting of the seedlings to the packaging of the ripe fruit for shipment. And we do this by developing in parallel genetic selection of new varieties of tomatoes suitable for machine cultivation, and machines suitable for tomato growing.

It is not at all unlikely that agricultural productivity, which has been growing by and large at twice the rate of increase of manufacturing productivity, will grow at three times that rate during the next decade.

Yet this expansion would have little impact on the developed industrial economies. The agricultural population by now has simply become too small. Even if the American farmer doubled his productivity in ten years – an almost unprecedented feat in economic history – he would add only 4 or 5 percentage points to national product – especially as such an increase would be confined to the even smaller number of 'commercial' farmers, no more than a million perhaps, who produce practically the entire farm output that goes to market. Things are not much different in the other developed countries. There, too, the number of productive 'commercial' farmers is by now so small that even a sharp increase in their productivity, while undoubtedly highly beneficial to them, is unlikely to have great impact on the total national economy.

At the same time, the reservoir of employable people in low-productivity jobs on the farm has almost disappeared. In the United States, this is one of the reasons for the problem of the 'unemployable' young man in the city who has moved off the farm during the last few years. He comes from a background of no productivity to be sure, but he is also not prepared by schooling nor trained by habit for any work. Even for the simplest jobs of minimal productivity, he needs highly expensive training in habits, elementary literacy, and skills. What is left, in other words, as 'marginal' farmers are people who need to be rehabilitated first before they can be productively employed at all. Similarly, in Japan, too, a substantial part of the remaining small farmers are old people or young children still at school.

In Western Europe the reservoir might seem a good deal larger. There are still many able-bodied men and women working on uneconomically small farms with outmoded tools and obsolete methods – in the Bavarian mountains, for instance, or on the stony acres of Brittany. But there, the social resistance to a shift from a farm which is as much a 'way of life' as it is a 'living' is tremendous. As General de Gaulle has learned, any government has to preserve the wine growers who grow few grapes and the dairy farmers who produce little milk, no matter how beneficial it would be for the national economy if this reservoir of able-bodied labour were to be tapped for productive employment in industry.

There is still huge unemployment in Southern Italy and Sicily. But again the manpower that has stayed behind during these years of mass migration into the industrial North consists largely of older people, women, and children. The young men and women are gone in the main; what is left behind is not easily employable. Instead of a resource, these remaining rural people are a social problem. It would require a large investment in education, in health, and in skills before they could be moved into any employment. This explains why Italian industry is becoming reluctant to put any more factories into the South despite the grave labour shortage in the industrial North.

Of all the industrially developed areas, only European Russia and Russia's European satellites are exceptions.

There the farm population is still almost as large as it was at about the time of World War I, with low productivity, even of the best 'commercial farmers', and a large reservoir of able-bodied, intelligent, and motivated people. But to tap this reservoir would require political changes which no Communist régime is likely to risk. At the least, the country would first have to pump tremendous investment into the farm economy – in housing, credit, education, health, and so on – before it could modernize agriculture and sharply reduce the farm population. Economically, this would appear to be the most intelligent thing the Communist countries could do, but, politically, it would demand a complete reversal of policies that are the foundation of the Soviet régime and essential to its staying in power.

In the developed countries, therefore, it seems likely that from now on even substantial advances in farm technology and farm productivity will not have a major impact on the overall economy. On the contrary, to the extent to which such advances force off the land the remaining non-productive rural people (the people whom the census calls 'farmers' even though, as a rule, they produce no farm products), rising farm productivity might even retard economic growth. The social problem of a farm proletariat that is unemployable in the city might well cause such a drag on the overall economy as to upset whatever boost is supplied by rising farm productivity – at least for a decade or two.

Agriculture in the developed countries has become the most productive, the most capital intensive, the most highly mechanized, and altogether the most 'industrial' of all modern industries. It is an 'industry' with a very high input of scientific knowledge per unit of production. From being the most traditional sector, agriculture in the developed countries has become the most progressive sector. Modern agriculture is capable of producing a great deal more than it produces today. In fact, ten years hence, every developed country should be able to raise considerably more farm produce than it can consume itself. This is true not only of

North America and Western Europe, but also of Japan, even though the best agricultural economists, Japanese as well as Americans, predicted incurable chronic starvation conditions for the country only twenty years ago. There is, in other words, good reason for the apparent schizophrenia of all ministries of agriculture in the developed countries which predict worldwide famine while fighting desperately for markets for their own farm surpluses. But even a star performance of agriculture and agricultural productivity could not provide the thrust to the economy of the developed countries which agricultural expansion has provided in the last two decades.

(2) During World War II, the second and third largest steel industries of the time, those of Germany and Russia were completely destroyed. Yet the world has now about five times the steel-making capacity it had in 1939. In terms of tonnage the greatest increase has been in the United States and in other old steel countries. But the greatest relative growth among the developed nations has been in the two countries that, measured against their populations and the size of their economy, were still 'underdeveloped' in steel twenty-five years ago: Russia and Japan. Japan, almost negligible as a steel-making country before World War II, now ranks ahead of Germany and Great Britain as the third largest producer. Even more spectacular has been the development of the steel industries in countries that did not make any steel at all twenty-five years ago, that is, in the developing countries such as Latin America, where even small nations now have their own sizeable steel mill.

This expansion of steel capacity in countries which only recently had little or no such capacity, underlies the growth and prosperity of the steel industries of the old steel-making countries, and above all of the United States. For a steel-making plant is first and foremost a steel-consuming plant. It takes a great many tons of steel to build capacity to make one single ton a year; before steel can be produced, it, therefore, has to be consumed in large quantities. These, of

31

course, could only come from the existing mills; and for the first ten years after the war, the United States was the only country that had an undamaged steel industry capable of volume production and of supplying the steel needed to rebuild destroyed plants in Germany and to build new ones all over the globe.

But this boom resulting from the explosive expansion of steel capacity all over the world masked a wasting sickness of the industry. In the advanced countries, and above all in the United States, steel, since World War II, has lost a full quarter of its traditional markets and uses to competitive materials such as glass, plastics, concrete, or paper. Such losses have occurred in containers and packaging, where plastic-impregnated paper is being increasingly used to make heavy containers – oil drums, for instance – for which, only a few decades ago, steel was used exclusively. Increasingly, plastics, aluminium, and paper are being used to make the traditional 'tin' can, again a steel monopoly only a few years ago. Pre-stressed concrete has become a serious competitor to steel in bridges as well as in building construction, and so on. Steel is still the most widely used and most versatile material but there are few uses any more in which it is the exclusive material. For every single application there is at least one other material that does the specific job at least as well, and often better.

Three of the four major industries which carried the early 'Industrial Revolution', cotton, coal, and railways, have declined sharply in this century. Iron and steel, the fourth old industry, was saved by the technological innovations of the mid-nineteenth century, especially the Bessemer and Siemens-Martin processes, which produced cheap steels to take the place of the irons of the first century of industrialization. But during the last twenty-five years, steel has come closer and closer to being marginal and to sinking into the same chronic crisis that has overtaken the other foundation industries of the modern world.

The reason for this has been known for at least fifty

years. The steel-making process, invented more than a century ago and basically unchanged until recently, is a grossly uneconomical process. Nothing is more expensive, whether in terms of physics or of economics, than creating temperatures. Yet the steel-making process creates high temperatures three times, only to quench them immediately – which is just as expensive as heating. Equally expensive in terms of cost and effort is moving weight. Yet in the steel-making process, hot melted steel in highly corrosive form is moved again and again over considerable distances. No amount of ingenuity can make such a process economical; it has inherently high costs. For steel to recapture its traditional capacity to grow faster than the economy, or at least as fast, it would have to come out of a process with much lower costs. Steel to regain its growth dynamics would probably have to cost at least one-third less than it costs now.

Such a technological revolution in steel-making has now begun.

The new oxygen process, developed during World War II in Austria and made capable of handling large tonnages in the last ten years, is a major step towards converting steel-making from a mechanical to a chemical industry. Equally important are such changes in process as 'continuous casting' which eliminates wastes of temperature and substitutes gravity flow of raw steel to and through the finishing equipment for the expensive and dangerous lifting, hauling, and moving of individual batches. There are also such new and still experimental methods as an English spray process which would do away with practically the entire steel mill and replace it by a continuous chemical flow producing finished steel directly from the raw materials.

If steel, by means of these new processes, becomes economically competitive again, it might well be once more a major growth industry, even in the industrially developed countries. But the steel industry would first have to go through a severe financial crisis. Almost all the steel mills at work today are based on old processes and would have to be scrapped or completely rebuilt. In fact, a great many of tomorrow's mills, based on new processes, would not be built where today's mills are, but rather at deep-water ports where iron ore can be unloaded easily. The European steel industry in particular is in the wrong location. And so, it would seem, is a good deal of Russia's, as well as America's oldest mills in Pittsburgh.

Even without physical relocation, the shift from the old technology, with its tremendous investment in huge mills, to tomorrow's technology, requiring equally large investments (even though the individual units might be a good deal smaller), would be long and painful. The underdeveloped and developing countries might be able to escape it. Firstly, they still have little steel capacity individually, so that they could shift to new technology for their future mills. Secondly, their mills do not have to be competitive and could be justified, despite high costs, in terms of the savings in foreign exchange they produce (though this is a dubious argument). But in the developed countries, the steel industry has to be competitive. Even if protected against imports, it has to be able to supply its own industries at the lowest possible cost. In the developed countries the users can switch to other materials in abundant supply. Hence no amount of protectionism – something the steel industry has always believed in everywhere – can really change the basic situation.

Even with lower costs brought about by new and expensive technology, steel, in the developed countries, can only hope to regain some of the ground it has lost. It cannot expect a repetition of the world steel demand to build steel capacity in the developing countries such as largely underlay the last two decades of steel boom. In India, in Latin America, in China apparently, in South Africa, the steel industry has reached the point that America had reached in about 1885. It no longer needs to import steel to build additional steel plants. The imports of the steel-makers of the poor countries are likely from now on to be specialized machinery and equipment rather than steel itself.

Despite technological change and despite much lower costs, steel may therefore still, within the next ten or twenty years, become a chronically depressed industry. None of the other traditional materials is so vulnerable to the threat of the new 'materials' industry (discussed in the next section).

(3) Third in importance as a generator of rapid growth in the industrially developed countries during the last twenty years stands the automobile industry. It played a major part – perhaps *the* major part – in the rapid growth of Western Europe and Japan. But it also grew considerably in the United States. There may still be fair growth opportunities for the automobile industry in the developed countries. In Russia, where the geographic conditions are much like those of the United States, the automobile boom has barely begun. Above all, the secondary impact of the automobile on the economy and society – roads, service stations, tourist travel, and hotels – is still ahead in Russia. In the underdeveloped countries, the automobile industry is certain to be *the* major growth industry if there is any growth.

The automobile represents a major value choice of modern man. It represents mobility and freedom. It is also one of the main energizers of modern society and in itself a propellant towards economic growth and development. It knits together a nation. It makes possible the movement of people from marginal, unproductive rural work towards productive employment. Without the automobile, the large-scale shift of manpower from marginal farming into urban jobs would not have taken place, at least not at the same speed. And, perhaps its most important impact, the automobile creates demand, simply because here is one economic possession which even the most self-sufficient tribesman in the most remote village covets. That Brazil within the last few years has built and can support a substantial automobile industry of its own is impressive evidence that the country is approaching, and may indeed have reached, the 'take-off point' in economic development at which economic and industrial growth become self-sustaining.

But in the developed countries (outside Russia) the automobile, no matter how much growth it still has ahead, is clearly on the defensive. The increasing congestion of the cities makes the automobile less and less serviceable as transportation.

We have to put our emphasis increasingly on alternative methods of mass transportation for people as well as for goods. Otherwise congestion will choke our cities to death and asphyxiate all of us through air pollution. It is only a matter of time before the internal combustion engine, if not the automobile itself, will be banned from the central city. A few years ago the mere mention of this would have produced an uproar from an indignant citizenry. But when New York's Commissioner of Air Pollution recently stated that the automobile would soon have to be banned permanently from four or five of the city's most important thoroughfares, such as Times Square, everybody accepted this as obvious, if not as overdue; and though the proposals of the ministers of transport in Great Britain and Germany to shift the transport of heavy goods back from the lorry to the railway had to be modified when the truckers protested, the population in general, and especially the respective parliaments, apparently acquiesced.

It is even possible that Western Europe – and to a lesser

extent Japan – are already close to automotive saturation.
In number of cars per square mile, Western Europe is as
highly motorized as any part of the United States; and even
if the proper measurement is the number of automobiles
per family, Western Europe – and with a few years' lag,
Japan – have increased automotive density so fast during
the last twenty years that progress from now on must be
substantially slower.

In the developing countries, the love affair between man
and the automobile is perhaps only just beginning – this is
certainly the case in Russia. The young everywhere want to
be on wheels. But in the developed countries, and specially
among adults, the automobile from having been a passion
is turning into a convenience and a utility. It is a necessity
but no longer the great ego need and 'status symbol'. The
uproar over road safety in the United States during the last
few years was, in all likelihood, the violent quarrel that
always accompanies the end of a long liaison.

It is entirely conceivable, to repeat, that these 'modern
industries' still have substantial growth ahead. Certainly
they should provide the fastest growth in the developing
countries – India and Pakistan, South America, and South-
East Asia. Indeed these are the industries on which the
development of these countries has to be based. For their
technology can be imported, ready-made, from the
developed countries; and developing countries need so
much creative energy for social and cultural innovation that
they cannot afford the risky, dangerous, and demanding
process of technological innovation on top of it.

Moreover, the main 'modern' industries, such as agriculture, automobiles, and petrochemicals, are the ideal foundation for rapid economic growth in a developing economy.
They combine high immediate economic impact with great
multiplier effect. A rapidly modernizing agriculture not
only produces the food without which an economy cannot
possibly grow, it also creates demands for a great many
new industries – from fertilizers to farm equipment, from

repair shops to farm credit, from transportation and roads to food processing – which, in turn, give high and well-paid employment. The automotive industry similarly creates about eight jobs for every worker in the manufacturing plants themselves – in road-building and road mainten-ance; in petrol stations, repair stations, and dealerships, and so on. At the same time, these industries produce high satisfaction for the consumer. They, therefore, generate great development energy throughout the population.

Their rapid expansion in the poor developing countries would also generate economic opportunities for the de-veloped countries by creating export markets in the way that the building of steel mills throughout the world brought boom to the steel mills of the developed countries.

Even if there were no new industries on the horizon, there need, therefore, be no depression in the developed countries. There could be a period of high-level economic activity, high employment and great affluence, based on the demands of the developing countries for equipment, sup-plies, and advanced products.

Still, while comfortable, this is too much like the kind of prosperity Britain has had during the last thirty or forty years. The British have learned that what looked like afflu-ence and ease was really slow but steady weakening. It is vitally important that the developing countries build their economies rapidly; and they can only do so around these 'modern' industries of the last fifty years. But while this may be enough for the developing countries – and it is more than they have been able to do these last twenty years by and large – it is not enough for the developed countries. They need a dynamism of their own. They need growth, and this the ageing 'modern' industries can no longer supply.

Small wonder then, that we hear predictions of 'tech-nological maturity' or 'technological stagnation'. The most widely discussed economic tract of the last few years, John

The New Industries and their Dynamics

Kenneth Galbraith's *The New Industrial State*,* is squarely based on this prediction.

We heard a similar prediction in the late Thirties when all the talk among economists was of the 'economic maturity' of the West – the United States in particular – and of the resulting economic stagnation. This prediction was almost immediately followed by the greatest economic expansion the Western world has ever experienced in a comparable time span. Today, too, there is a good chance that the prediction of technological maturity and resulting stagnation will be followed by tremendous technological change and economic expansion. Of course, even the most glowing prospects can be aborted by human stupidity – we have shown our capacity for crippling ourselves only too often in this century. But unless we engage in the criminal folly of another major war or another major depression we can anticipate the rapid rise of major new industries based on major new technologies.

WHAT'S ON THE HORIZON?

Four new industries are already in sight:

(1) The information industry. There is a great deal more to information and data processing than the computer. Now the computer is to the information industry roughly what the central power station was to the electrical industry.

The electrical industry became a certainty when Werner von Siemens in 1856 invented the first practical generator. But the electrical industry only became a reality twenty-three years later, in 1879, when Edison designed the electric light bulb. In between there was furious activity with a host of highly talented inventors at

* (Hamish Hamilton, London, 1967; Houghton Mifflin, New York and Boston, 1967.)

work. If it had been fashionable then to speak of 'first generation', 'second generation', or 'third generation' generators, as it is now fashionable to speak of 'first generation', 'second generation', or 'third generation' computers, there would have been a 'fifth generation' or a 'sixth generation' generator before there really was any widespread use of electric power. Practically every single one of the major electric-apparatus companies (eg, Westinghouse) that are still household words today, was already founded by 1879 in every industrial country, including such small ones as Sweden, Switzerland, and Hungary. But it was only Edison's light bulb that made possible the use of electricity as a universal form of energy.

Without the central power station there would be no electrical industry; without the computer there would be no information industry; and yet most of the money in the electrical industry – and most of the engineering and technical ingenuity as well – has been invested in the equipment to transmit and to apply, whether power lines, lights, motors, or appliances. Similarly, most of the money and most of the ingenuity of the information industry will go into the transmission and application of information rather than into its generation and storage, that is, into the computer. And most of the profit will come from transmission and application too.

Since the computer first appeared in the late 1940s the information industry has been a certainty. But we do not have it yet. We still do not have the effective means to build an 'information system'. This is where the work is going on, however. The tools to create information systems may already exist: the communications satellite and other means of transmitting information; microfilm and the TV tube to display and store it; rapid printers to reduce it to permanent record, and so on. There is no technical reason why someone like Sears Roebuck should not come out tomorrow with an appliance selling for less than a TV set, capable of being plugged in wherever there is electricity, and giving immediate access to all the information needed for school work from first grade through college.

Yet though IBM is now shipping computers at the rate of a thousand a month, we do not have the equivalent of Edison's light bulb. What is lacking is not a piece of hardware as was the light bulb. What still has to be created is the conceptual understanding of information. As long as every set of data has to be laboriously translated into a separate 'programme', we do not understand information. We have to be capable of classifying information according to its characteristics. We have to have a 'notation' – comparable to the one St Ambrose invented 1,600 years ago to record music – that can express words and thoughts in symbols appropriate to electronic pulses rather than in the clumsy computer language of today. Then each person could, with very little training, store his own data within a general system, that is, in what the computer engineers call a 'routine'. Then we shall have true 'information systems'.

Twenty years hence it may be as unlikely for individual users, even big companies, to have their own large computers as it is today unlikely for an individual manufacturing plant to have its own power station. Sixty years ago, a plant had to have its own power station if it wanted electricity; now it gets power through 'time-sharing' from a central station. Similarly, information a few years hence may be primarily on some 'time-sharing' basis, in which a great many users have their data on one and the same computer, with complete privacy, but also with complete and immediate access at all times. Already the cost of information is going down drastically. A few years ago one hour of computer time cost several thousand dollars. It now costs perhaps one hundred to two hundred dollars. Ten years hence it may cost as little as a dollar or two. Eventually it should cost no more than an hour of lighting, that is, a penny or less.

In one important respect the computer differs greatly from the electric generator: an information industry can function without a computer. This shows clearly in the field of education.

Learning and teaching are going to be more deeply affected by the new availability of information than any other area of human life. There is great need for a new approach, new methods and new tools in teaching, man's oldest and most reactionary craft. There is great need for a rapid increase in the productivity of learning. There is, above all, great need for methods that will make the teacher effective and multiply his or her efforts and competence. Teaching is the only traditional craft in which we have not yet fashioned the tools that make an ordinary person capable of superior performance. In this respect, teaching is far behind medicine where the tools first became available a century or more ago. It is, of course, infinitely behind the mechanical crafts where we have had effective apprenticeship for thousands and thousands of years.

A new concept of information and a new understanding of learning and of teaching is needed (on this see Chapter 15 below). But while the 'information revolution' will have its most dramatic impact on education, teaching and learning may not use computers at all, or may use them only marginally. The materials, while certainly quite different from what we have been using – as different as was the printed book of 500 years ago from the oral tradition of the earlier schools – probably do not need to be big machines with huge memories. The amount of information needed throughout all the years of formal schooling is actually quite limited and hardly requires anything as complex as an electronic memory. 'Programmes' can be a great deal simpler than anything the computer uses. An ordinary desk calendar is, after all, also a 'programme', and a highly effective one. Information systems without a computer, in other words, are perfectly possible and may indeed be as important as the systems built around the computer.

Yet without the computer we would not have understood that information, like electricity, is a form of energy. Electricity is the cheapest, most plentiful, and most versatile energy for mechanical work. But information is energy for mind work. This is the first era when energy for mind work has been available. Information through the ages has been all but completely lacking. At best it has been expensive, late, and totally unreliable. Most people in responsible positions today, whether in government, in hospitals, in research laboratories, or in business, spend most of their time scratching to get a little incorrect and unreliable information on what happened yesterday.

The impact of cheap, reliable, fast, and universally available information will easily be as great as was the impact of electricity. Certainly young people, a few years hence, will use information systems as their normal tools much as they now use the typewriter or the telephone. Yet the telephone eighty years ago evoked somewhat the same panic the computer now does. In another generation, it is safe to predict, people will have learned that the computer is their tool and not their master, and that it enables them to do the mind work they want to do and are unable to do today for want of cheap, reliable, and fast information.

The information industry will create tremendous employment opportunities. We need, for instance, in the United States about 1 million computer programmers between now and 1975 – as against 150,000 to 200,000 to date. The computer programmer is to the information industry what the worker on the assembly line was to the mass-production industry of yesterday: the semi-skilled but highly paid, highly productive worker. But at the same

43

time, the information technology also creates a great many more highly skilled and demanding jobs – systems engineers, for instance, of whom we might need up to half a million or so within the next ten years. Yet these are only beginnings.

(2) *The Oceans.* Our shift from being nomads, hunters, and gatherers to explorers and exploiters of the oceans may have an equally great impact, and perhaps we are moving even faster here.

Seven thousand years ago or so, not long after our ancestors had become settlers and exploiters on the land, two great technological feats were accomplished by the Egyptians of the Old Kingdom at almost the same time, perhaps even within the same generation: first, the building of the Great Pyramids and, secondly, the invention of the plough. The pyramids had momentous impact on the imagination of the West, on its world view, its philosophy, its mathematics, and its science (even though the impact was on the Greek rather than the Egyptian imagination). Few contemporaries paid attention to the plough, yet within a century or two it had multiplied farm yields twenty to fifty times, providing the food that made possible the first cities of man.

I suspect that space exploration is our 'pyramids' and the exploration of the oceans our 'plough'. Certainly the ocean is a virtually untapped reservoir of material resources, infinitely richer than the land. As yet we know almost nothing about the ocean. In fact, our remote ancestors of the early Bronze Age knew where the game was and where it was going much better than we know the location and movement of fish in the seas. We pick and gather whatever comes our way. This is now changing rapidly – with respect to the food resources of the ocean, especially its fish, where we are about to turn into fish-farmers rather than fish-hunters; with respect to the mineral and hydrocarbon resources in ocean water; and, above all, with respect to the mineral resources on and under the bottom of the sea.

There is little economic reason for settling on or under the seas. Unlike transportation on land, transportation on the sea is easy and cheap so that there is little reason for moving the sites of settlement to the oceanic resources. But the development of the oceans is about to be tackled systematically as the greatest economic resource to be found on this earth. With this will come new supplies of food and materials. With it will come new technologies, new major industries, and of course entirely new major business enterprises (together with a host of new problems such as those of law in an area that historically has always been considered *res nullius* and outside the control of any territorial government).

(3) *Materials.* We are similarly deep into another major technology, that of materials. Plastics, I have said before, can be considered the only major industry which is rooted in twentieth- rather than in nineteenth-century science. Its foundation is X-ray diffraction – one of the early fruits of the discovery of radiation. Plastics is the first of the new 'materials' industries, the industries which create materials for specific purposes and with specific qualities, rather than exploit nature's substances as they occur.

It is rarely realized how old our basic materials are. Glass, iron, steel, and the non-ferrous metals, ceramics, concrete, and timber all existed four or five thousand years ago, that is, before the beginning of the Greek era. Paper was invented by the Chinese at about the time of the birth of Christ. Only rubber and aluminium are 'modern' – and now, the plastics.

It is realized even less often how well the ancients wrought. The materials developed first in the Fertile Crescent at the dawn of civilization have not been changed or improved since. The city of Cologne in Germany is still being supplied with water through a concrete aqueduct laid down by the Romans 2,000 years ago and never since repaired. No one has made better steel than the Damascene or Japanese swordsmiths of old. And Phoenician glass still holds secrets of colour and texture we have not been able to penetrate.

Small wonder, then, that for thousands of years, right down to our own day, it was axiomatic that a certain material could be made only from one resource, eg, ore, and that it could only be used for certain purposes, on which, however, it had practically a monopoly. The material streams were determined both at the source and at their final application and ran, so to speak, in parallel without ever touching. As a result, no one had to know anything about any other material than his own speciality. And in his speciality, the applications of his materials were, so to speak, protected, as if by natural immutable law.

Aluminium was the first challenger, but for a long time aluminium was seen as a 'substitute' – until it established itself as the preferred material in a number of areas during World War II. The plastics also began as 'substitutes', but they were soon seen as being different. For one, they were not to be found in nature nor were they the result of refining a natural raw material. They were man-made. Moreover, since the work done during World War I in Germany, they were clearly seen as designed by man and as 'structures of matter', that is, as molecular arrangements developed for a specific purpose and out of an understanding of the fundamental characteristics of matter. From their early days, therefore, the plastics contradicted the axiom that a material could be made from one source only and that in turn it had specific applications which 'belonged' to it. The plastics were the first example of what we now mean by 'materials', that is structures of matter rather than specific substances; and 'open-ended', that is, capable of being fashioned according to the intended end-use.

Yet the plastics, technologically, are only the beginning of the new 'materials' technology, and a limited beginning at that, for they are still based on the old idea of one discrete substance which serves as the 'material'. What we are realizing more and more is our ability to design composite materials in which different structural elements serve different purposes – just as in building a house, timber may carry the load while brick provides the insulation. 'Composites' are now increasingly being designed combining, for instance, the great strength of pure crystals of metals with the elasticity of organic compounds. We are designing structures which combine the electric conductivity of certain atomic configurations with the electrical resistance of others, eg, the 'impurities' with which a transistor crystal is purposefully 'doped', and so on. The result of these composite designs is one new material which has specific and totally new properties. The starting point is not a substance but a specific micro-structure of atoms and molecules and the physical, chemical, and electrical characteristics of such a structure under the laws of quantum mechanics.

This has been carried furthest in space technology, if only because the need for specific performances is greatest there, while the penalties for excess weight or excess bulk are highest. Hence, 'materials' is one area where one can expect a 'fall-out' from space technology into the civilian peacetime economy.

General Schriever, the former head of the United States Air Force's space and design work, has called the new space materials 'the greatest single advance that has been made in the last three thousand years' – and his enthusiasm seems only slightly exaggerated.

One of the new materials developed for use in advanced aeroplane design is, for instance, twice as strong and two and a half times as stiff as aluminium, yet weighs 25 per cent less and should, eventually, be considerably less expensive. It is a composite in which tiny fibres made from pure boron crystal are embedded in a plastic resin. There are many similar materials, usually

47

combining a metal in pure crystal form with some organic material such as a plastic (but also with inorganic materials such as silicones and glass) all of which are stronger than anything found in nature, or capable of greater resistance to heat or to chemicals – and yet lighter and cheaper – than traditional metals.

More important than any one new material or any one new application is the new 'materials' concept itself. It marks a shift from concern with substances to concern with structure, a shift from artisan to scientist as man's artificer, a shift from chemistry to physics as the basic discipline, and a shift, above all, from the concrete experience of the workshop to abstract mathematics, a· shift from starting with what nature provides to what man wants to accomplish.

Economically this may have the greatest impact on those materials that have always been multi-purpose – that is, above all, for modern steel. (Actually modern steel is metallurgically a form of iron rather than what has traditionally been meant by 'steel' – but this is irrelevant here.)

Specific-purpose materials – concrete is probably the most specific – are unlikely soon to be seriously affected by the new 'materials' technology. Within their range they have exceedingly high performance characteristics. Economically it would be difficult to substitute for them a new material, since its cost is unlikely to be compensated for by new performance capabilities (except in such new and demanding surroundings as space or the depths of the sea with demands as to weight, bulk, resistance to temperature, corrosion, and pressures which materials on earth are never called upon to meet). Steel, on the other hand, has been the 'universal' material of modern civilization rather than (as the steel of the swordsmith used to be) a special-purpose material fashioned for one specific application. It is of the nature of a 'multi-purpose material', that is, it is not the best possible material for any one use but a compromise in which cheapness makes up for lack of specific performance capability. But if we can raise specific-performance capability of any one material way beyond what has been possible in the past, the 'multi-purpose' material, in turn, has to be a great deal cheaper to be competitive.

The advent of the new materials technology, which assumes that a structure of matter ideally suited for any single purpose can be built at moderate cost, may, therefore, put even more pressure on steel than its economically obsolete process has already done. Even if steel succeeds in developing an economically rational chemical flow process that will lower steel costs materially, it may still find itself under pressure in a vast variety of end-uses and applications in which new, specially designed materials, while more expensive by weight, may be more economical in performance.

But all materials will from now on have to be considered as potentially competing with all others. All of them will from now on have to be considered as part of one and the same materials stream with the end-user capable of specifying performance rather than settling for this or that substance.

Yet they will not alter the fact that nothing comes out of a petroleum cracking tower but the distillates found in crude oil, and nothing out of a glass oven but glass. The end-user who wants a container may be able to choose between a dozen materials, some existing ones such as paper, plastics, glass, tin cans, and so on; some as yet unknown ones; or some composites of known and unknown ones. The container manufacturer, however, will have to obtain substances out of specific processes rather than produce 'packaging materials'. The 'materials revolution' will predictably make countries less and less dependent on natural

49

resources, since the same end-use can be satisfied by starting with almost any natural resource, organic or inorganic. It will make end-users increasingly independent of specific substances. It will make possible an enormous number of new products, new satisfactions, and new markets. But it will greatly disturb existing industry structures and challenge traditional industrial organization and existing economic alignments.

One of the largest tin-can makers, the American Can Company, has in the last few years added a paper company, a glass company, and a very large plastics capacity, while the world's largest glass bottle-maker – Owens Illinois in Toledo, Ohio – has gone into the plastics and paper business in a big way.

There may also be the emergence of entirely new industries which start out with end-uses and then become specialists in providing end-materials which the builder, for instance, might want; or any material one might need, for another instance, in the storage and processing of food. As a result, we are almost certain to see great, rapid, and disturbing changes in the industrial sector that for hundreds of years has been the most clearly defined and the most clearly delineated one, the 'heavy' industries such as mining and lumbering, or industries producing large quantities of specific materials, such as steel, brick, copper, glass, or paper.

(4) *The Megalopolis.* Finally, man's new habitat, the megalopolis,* is likely to spawn a clutch of new technologies and of new major industries based on them.

One reason for the misery and disorganization of the megalopolis is that it has outgrown what are still considered modern technologies – in transportation and in

---

* The term was coined by the French geographer, Jean Gottesmann, and is fast gaining general acceptance.

housing, in water supply and sewerage, and above all, in conserving the fundamental necessities of life such as clean air, clean water, and the total natural environment. At the same time, there is little doubt that we will continue to live in metropolitan areas, and that more and more of mankind will make the megalopolis its home. Only worldwide nuclear catastrophe or a pestilence beyond any recorded in history could reverse this trend in the foreseeable future.

A hundred years ago or more the industrial city arose, though only the Germans coined a word for it – they called it *Grosstadt* – it was distinct and different from the traditional city of Western man. Paris, London, New York, or Vienna were in 1800 still what the city had always been: the political, craft, and trading centres of a rural society and an agricultural economy. Fifty years later they were industrial cities, with the factory chimney rather than the town house of the nobility their distinctive feature, and with the factory worker the dominant resident. Just as the megalopolis of today is not organized and does not represent an integrated community, the *Grosstadt* of 1850 was disorganized and disintegrated. Rioting was endemic and rebellion just below the surface – breaking out, for instance, in 1848 all over Europe and in the 'draft riots' of the Civil War in New York City. Indeed, the more 'organized' the early nineteenth-century *Grosstadt* looked, the less organized it really was. The least disturbed of the cities were those industrial wastelands, Liverpool, Birmingham, Essen, or the Franco-Belgian *Borinage*, where the new industrial concentration had not grown up around a pre-industrial city.

If the *Grosstadt* never became beautiful, it did become organized. This required, however, a new perception of what a city is – best exemplified in Haussmann's great plan of the *Grands Boulevards* which created modern Paris. Haussmann's perception of the *Grosstadt* is usually seen either in purely aesthetic terms or (by people with a little more insight than the traditional *Beaux Arts* architect) as an elegant geometric model of traffic flow. But, like all true vision, Haussmann's plan released tremendous human energies in all areas. The two cities which adopted it in full – his own Paris, and Vienna – should, by all the odds, have been decaying cities in the second half of the nineteenth century, as capitals of defeated countries which were rapidly losing ground in the areas that counted most at the time, that is, in economics, science, and technology, as well as military power. Instead, these two cities became almost immediately the intellectual and artistic centres of Europe, and the cities which to contemporaries, right up until World War I, spelled creative energy, vitality, and the joy of living.

Haussmann's vision also created a market for new technologies and, with them, for new industries. Indeed, the *Grosstadt* was the most important of the nineteenth-century growth markets. It provided the impetus for major inventions, and the market for the development of the industries based on them: light – first manufactured gas and then electricity; electric transportation – whether subway, streetcar, or elevated street railway; the telephone; steel-frame construction for the new tall buildings – the first major breakthrough in construction materials since the Romans; the department store; the newspaper; and many more.

The megalopolis of today is as different from the *Grosstadt* as the *Grosstadt* was from the city of 1800. The difference is not only in size and population. A megalopolis is the dominant habitat, whereas in the age of the *Grosstadt* the majority of men still lived in a rural society and produced in an agricultural economy. While the *Grosstadt* was founded on the industrial worker, the megalopolis is founded on, and organized around, the knowledge worker, with information as its foremost output as well as its foremost need. The college campus rather than the factory chimney is likely to be the distinctive feature of the megalopolis, the college student rather than the 'proletarian' its central political fact.

To organize the megalopolis a new perception is needed. We urgently need a new Haussmann. The lack of such a perception makes all efforts at 'city planning' futile – just as they were futile in the early nineteenth century. Until Haussmann accepted the reality of the *Grosstadt* and thought it through, every 'city planner'* of the time tried to make undone the new industrial city. Similarly all our city planners of today are trying to make undone the megalopolis. But every attempt so far to return to yesterday's *Grosstadt* – the 'Green Belt' around London, to give an outstanding example – has failed.

We also need truly new technologies for the megalopolis.

It is, for instance, not enough to say that we need mass transportation. We need something which does not exist today: transportation which can handle large numbers of people in comparatively little space, but which combines, with the volume and space capacities of the railway, the flexibility of the automobile. For unlike the traditional city, and unlike the *Grosstadt*, the megalopolis does not have one centre, or even a very small number of centres. In Haussmann's model the shortest distance from any point in his city to any other point required crossing only one nodal centre (such as the *Place de la Concorde*). Yet all these nodes were on one axis. All the centres, in other words, were in one small 'core city'.

In today's metropolis, there is no one 'core city'. It does not, therefore, solve the transportation problem of the metropolis to make it possible for everyone to have easy access to such a 'core city' – the assumption, however, on which nineteenth-century transportation systems, and especially the streetcar and subway systems, were built. This explains why, despite all attempts to get people out of automobiles and back again on to trains, streetcars, and subways, the citizen stubbornly clings to

* The term, of course, did not exist then.

the automobile. It alone has the flexibility for going from any point to any other point, so to speak, at random; and only a mass-transportation system which provides for these random movements, and yet gives true access, will be acceptable and will solve the crisis that threatens to paralyse the megalopolis.

Another example of the innovations that are needed is the 'vertical street' inside the new 'neighbourhoods' of the metropolis, the high-rise apartment buildings. A populated and frequented street is the axis of community life and the key to a safe neighbourhood. Neighbourhoods are not 'unsafe' because they are overrun by hoodlums; they are overrun by hoodlums because the streets are empty. In few cities of the world are there more rough elements than in Rome; yet it is quite safe (at least for men) to walk almost anywhere in Rome at practically any hour of the day and night because there are always people on the streets.

The apartment building of the megalopolis contains more people than the traditional neighbourhood did. Yet the elevator – that marvellous contrivance of the nineteenth-century *Grosstadt* – is designed to isolate people in the same building from one another. It is designed to take a passenger from his own apartment door to the street outside without bringing him into contact with the rest of the people in the building. As a result, the large apartment blocks are not neighbourhoods, cannot become communities, and above all, are less and less safe. Yet the 'street' of the megalopolis can only be inside these large structures, simply because this is where people live. To design the vertical street is therefore a major challenge. We may have the technical means for it already available, in the escalator, for instance. But to build on this and create inside the tall buildings the community centres, the shopping centres, the 'outdoors' where people meet, spend time, relax, promenade, and mix, will take a tremendous amount of technical innovation and aesthetic ingenuity.

Mass transportation in the megalopolis and the vertical street are not particularly imaginative ideas – though they may well require highly imaginative solutions. They still assume, by and large, that the megalopolis is an extension of the *Grosstadt*, but the meaningful technologies of the megalopolis may grow out of entirely different assumptions. It is conceivable, for instance, that instead of making it easy for people to move, the traffic problems of the megalopolis will be solved by making it less necessary for people to travel; instead information and ideas will travel to people. This would require industries as new and different from anything we have today as the subway, the telephone, and the electric light were from the urban technologies and industries of the eighteenth century.

These are some of the new industries one can already clearly see, the industries that are already on stage though not yet under the spotlight. Any such forecast runs a greater risk than that of being wrong, that is, of predicting things that will not happen; it runs the risk of being irrelevant, that is, of not predicting the important things that are going to happen. Everything the forecaster predicts may come to pass, yet he may not have seen the most meaningful of the emergent realities or, worse still, not have paid attention to them. There is no way to avoid this irrelevancy in forecasting. For the important and the distinctive are always the result of changes in values, perception, and goals, that is, in the things one can divine but not forecast.

The new industries I have tried to sketch may, therefore, not be the main characters. But they are 'in character' in tomorrow's economic drama. They show that the new, the really new, is already here and not merely in prospect. They show that the new is big enough and dynamic enough to supply forward thrust to the economies of the developed countries for many decades to come. The main point they make, however, is that the emerging technologies are different intellectually, socially, and economically. The new industries are not additions. They are innovations.

THE NEW KNOWLEDGE BASE

All of the new industries are based on twentieth-century knowledge. Their foundations are the physics of this century, the physics of radiation and quantum; the new science of matter and of structure; the physical chemistry of molecular and atomic bonds, and so on. But equally important to the new industries are knowledge areas outside what traditionally is called 'science'. The computer is, above all, founded on symbolic logic. It could not have come into being but for Russell and Whitehead's *Principia Mathematica* (1910). It is no accident that the development of the computer received its greatest impetus from a theoretical mathematician, the late John von Neumann, rather than from electrical or electronic engineers or even from the physicists.

Underlying every one of these new industries is a new perception: the perception of 'systems', which is as crucial to the information industry as it is to the oceanic industry, as fundamental to our concept of 'materials' as it will be to the industries for the new metropolis. This is the translation into technology of the 'configuration' perception which entered the modern world in the years before World War I – in the 'ecology' of the biologist and the 'personality' of the psychologist, in the *Gestalt* of the German students of sense perception and the 'culture' of the anthropologist.*

The new technologies are not 'applied science'; neither the modern mathematics of symbolic logic, nor the perception of configuration is what is normally called 'science'. Yet both are central to the new technologies and, as a re-

* For a full discussion, see Chapter One, 'The New World View', in my book *Landmarks of Tomorrow* (William Heinemann Ltd, London, 1959; Harper & Row, New York, 1959).

sult, to the new industries. This is something new, something that sets the new industries sharply apart from those of the first half of this century. The technology of the twentieth century embraces and feeds off the entire array of human knowledges, the physical sciences as well as the humanities. Indeed in these new technologies there is no distinction between the two. In these new technologies the split between the universe of matter and the universe of the mind – the split introduced into Western thought by Descartes 300 years ago – is being overcome.

This has implications way beyond the economic or even the technological sphere. It explains, for instance, why we are concerned today about the split between the 'two cultures', to use C. P. Snow's popular phrase; that is, between the world of the scientifically-trained and the world of the humanistically-trained man. We cannot tolerate such a split any more. We will have to demand of the scientifically-trained man that he should again become a humanist, otherwise he will lack the knowledge and perception needed to make his science effective, or indeed to make it truly scientific. We will have to demand of the humanist that he acquire an understanding of science, or else his humanities will be irrelevant and ineffectual. We will, above all, have to demand of the people concerned with the economy, whether as politicians, as businessmen, or as researchers, that they understand both cultures and move with equal ease in both.

The fact that the new technologies are not based on science alone but on the new knowledge in its entirety also means that technology is no longer separate and outside culture, but an integral part thereof. Civilization has, of course, always been shaped by technology. The notion that technology has become important only during the last 200 years or so is arrant nonsense. Tools and the organization of work – the two elements of what we call technology – have always moulded both what man does and what he can do. They have, very largely, determined what he wants to be. But for several thousand years – in the West ever since the Greeks made slavery into an economic institution and into the foundation of production – work, and with it its tools, methods, and organization, has been considered as outside culture and unworthy of the attention of a cultured person. If our new technology stands, as it clearly does, in the very centre of present-day culture, this legacy of the contempt of the Greek intellectual for the slaves whose toil made possible his life of luxury and leisure has been finally liquidated, and this, in turn, is certain to alter both culture and technology.

Equally important and equally new is the fact that every one of the new emerging industries is squarely based on knowledge. Not a single one is based on experience.

Every single technology and, with it, every industry before 1850, was based on experience. Knowledge, that is, systematic, purposeful, organized information, had almost nothing to do with any of them. Even the so-called 'modern' industries, which came into being in the second half of the nineteenth century, and which still dominate our economic and industrial life today, were largely experience-based rather than knowledge-based. Science had almost no part to play in the birth of the automobile or the aeroplane, not even the auxiliary role of godmother, let alone that of midwife. These technologies were still experience-based. And so was the electrical industry in large part; Edison, for instance, was much more traditional craftsman than modern researcher. Only in the chemical industry were there inventors with university training in their science. Otherwise, in the 'heroic age of inventions', that is, in the sixty or seventy years before World War I, university-trained inventors were conspicuous by their almost total absence.*

* On this, see my chapters 'Technological Trends in the Twentieth Century', and 'Technology and Society in the Twentieth Century' in Volume Two of *Technology and Western Civilization*, edited by Kranzberg and Pursell (Oxford University Press, New York, London, and Toronto, 1967).

The New Industries and their Dynamics

The new emerging industries, therefore, embody a new economic reality: knowledge has become the central economic resource. The systematic acquisition of knowledge, that is, organized formal education, has replaced experience – acquired traditionally through apprenticeship – as the foundation for productive capacity and performance.

Finally, these new industries differ from the traditional 'modern' industry in that they will employ predominantly knowledge workers rather than manual workers. Computer programming, for example, with its enormous employment opportunities, is semi-skilled work. All that is needed to be a programmer is junior high-school arithmetic, three months of training, and six months of practice. But while the skill is not a very elevated one, it is based on knowledge rather than on experience of manual training. The same goes for the other employment opportunities the new industries are likely to create. In a number of jobs, they may be very large. Some of them will certainly be highly skilled – as, for instance, a good many of the jobs developed for the exploitation of the oceans. But in every case, the foundation of the job, whether skilled or unskilled, will be knowledge. The preparation for it will be a course of study rather than apprenticeship. The productivity of the worker will depend on his ability to put to work concepts, ideas, theories – that is, things learned in school – rather than skills acquired through experience.

It is easy to overrate the impact of new industries with their new technologies. The steamship, after all, only began to replace sail on the oceans after 1860, that is, when the new technologies of electricity and the internal combustion engine were beginning to replace the coal-burning steam engine as the 'modern' prime mover. But the new industries ahead represent a qualitative rather than a merely quantitative shift. They are different in their structure, in their knowledge foundations, and in their sociology. They represent, therefore, not just a stepping up of the rate of change. They represent a discontinuity – fully as great as that of the industries which came into being between the 1860s and 1914.

They will not, therefore, be amenable to policies, whether those of business or of government, that are in effect more of the same. They demand basic changes from both businessman and politician. They require both new policies and the sloughing off of deeply entrenched practices of our industrial society today.

3. The New Entrepreneur

THE FIFTY YEARS before the outbreak of World War I have been called the 'Heroic Age of Invention'. They might equally be called the 'Heroic Age of the Entrepreneur'. The inventors of this period had to know how to convert their technical work into economic performance, and their invention into a business.* It was then that the big businesses of today were founded. Even then the ability to manage – that is, to organize people for ongoing work – was important. Without it the greatest inventor lost his business, no matter how keenly he may have wanted to be a tycoon. This, for instance, was the fate of Edison despite his burning ambition to be the owner and head of a big company. But above all entrepreneurship was needed – that is, the ability to create the new and different.

In the fifty years since World War I, the premium has been on management. Not that entrepreneurship has been lacking, or that the opportunities for it have been limited. On the contrary, in the twenty years since the end of World War II, more new businesses have been founded in every developed country than in any previous similar period – both absolutely and in relation to the number of businesses in the economy. More of these new businesses have grown to respectable size, some into worldwide giants such as IBM, Xerox, and some of the pharmaceutical companies. Yet the great need has been for the productive organization of large numbers of people to do what could already be

* The Germans had a word for it. They called this period the *Gruenderjahre* – the years of the founders.

planned, projected, and laid out, that is, for doing something that was already reasonably well known.

Now we are entering again an era in which emphasis will be on entrepreneurship. However, it will not be the entrepreneurship of a century ago, that is, the ability of a single man to organize a business he himself could run, control, and embrace. It will rather be the ability to create and direct an organization for the future. We need men who can build a new structure of entrepreneurship on the managerial foundations laid down during the last fifty years. History, it has often been observed, moves in a spiral; one returns to the preceding position – or to the preceding problem – but on a higher level, and by a corkscrew-like path. In this fashion we are going to return to entrepreneurship on a path that led out from a lower level, that of the single entrepreneur, to the manager, and now back, though upward, to entrepreneurship again.

The businessman will have to acquire a number of new abilities, all of them entrepreneurial in nature, but all of them to be exercised in and through a managerial, and usually a fairly large and complex, organization.

THE DYNAMICS OF TECHNOLOGY

First of all the businessman will have to learn to understand the dynamics of technology and to anticipate the direction and speed of technological change. As long as new technology originated with the lone inventor operating outside the existing economy, there was no need for such understanding. If, however, a going, developed economy is to be capable of rapid innovation and change, its businessman must be able to anticipate technology and to take advantage of the opportunities which technological developments offer.

'Prediction' of technological change – in the strict meaning of the term – would require ability to know both what changes could be expected and when they would occur. I doubt that the timing of major technological changes can ever be known in advance. But what technological changes are likely; which of those are likely to have major economic impact, that is, to bring about new industries; and whether such changes are indeed approaching or imminent, this we can know with high probability. The dynamics of technology are not particularly mysterious.

The first dynamic element in technology, and the one most easily identified, is economic needs and opportunities. Necessity is not the mother of invention; it is, however, its midwife. The first indicator of the need for major innovation is one with which economists have been familiar for well over a century: declining productivity of capital in a major industry. Wherever a major industry requires increasing investment to produce the same quantity, especially if the higher capital requirements are not more than offset by savings in labour, the industry is in a sharp decline. No matter how prosperous and profitable it may look at the moment, it is rushing towards senility unless it can reverse the trend.

New technology is not produced on command. One cannot simply expect technological results because one puts men and money to work. But at the same time, new technology can only result from human effort. A major industry will rarely put its best brains to work on basic changes; it will rather tend to fritter away its energies on desperate efforts to keep yesterday going a little longer. But in such a situation imaginative and knowledgeable people outside the industry often see the opportunity and go to work. Should they produce results, they are likely to have major impact fast.

One example of such an economic opportunity for major new technology has already been mentioned: the steel industry. Twenty years ago, before anyone had even heard of the new oxygen process developed by an obscure Austrian steel mill during World War II, some people, especially economists outside the steel industry, already saw clearly the need for major technological change that would convert steel-making into a chemical flow process. In fact, they saw this much more clearly than anyone within the industry. (The outsider sees such a basic economic vulnerability almost always much more clearly than the insider, who tends to become a prisoner of the familiar.) Without being able to be specific as to the 'how' of the new process, one could say twenty years ago: 'If anything happens to convert steel-making into a temperature-conserving flow process – or even to bring steel-making a little closer to such a process – it will create a new steel technology fairly fast.'

Similarly one could even before World War II, anticipate major technological changes in ship-building on the basis of a rapid decline of the productivity of capital in ocean-shipping. Again this indicated a fundamental vulnerability in the process – the economic waste of a system of loading and unloading in port which had remained virtually unchanged since the Phoenicians. Perhaps no one in the late 1930s or early 1940s could have predicted the container-ship or the floating military base which the US Defence Department wants to build under the name of 'Fast Deployment Logistics Ship' (and which would, in effect, eliminate the port with its installations altogether). Yet it was possible to say thirty years ago that any process that leads to merchandise freight being handled at the dockside the way we already handle petroleum or iron ore or grain, should have an immediate major economic impact. It would create a new technology rapidly.

One can say the same about the paper industry – again because a steady decline in the productivity of capital indicates that new technology, if developed where the process is economically vulnerable, should have immediate and major impact.

Similar analysis brings out the opportunities created by gaps in a technology.

A good example is the kind of thinking that has made the Swedes leaders in power transmission. The Swedes apparently saw twenty years ago that atomic energy would become competitive, and indeed the most economical form of power generation, provided that very large generating stations were built. They also saw, however, that this meant that the ability to transmit high voltages without loss would become crucial – rather than the ability to generate them. Once this had been seen, it took comparatively little work and little money to develop the required new technology; all the knowledge necessary for it had actually been produced seventy years before.

Such analysis of the dynamics of technology has made Sweden, a small country with limited resources of men and money, the undisputed leader in today's high-power technology, even though other countries with much bigger resources, the United States, Russia, Great Britain, France, Germany, and Japan, all spent much larger sums – but spent them in the wrong place.

The next place to look to anticipate technology, is to knowledge of all kinds. One asks: 'What is going on in knowledge areas and what technological opportunities might this create?'

It is fashionable today to assert that knowledge is being converted into technology much faster than in the past. The evidence, however, fails to support this assertion. On the contrary, the time-lapse for the conversion of knowledge into technology seems to have lengthened. There is nothing today that is comparable to the speed with which, for instance, Heinrich Hertz's scientific discoveries in wave physics were translated into Marconi's new 'wire-less' telegraphy in less than two decades. The time-lapse between new knowledge and new technology today is much more likely to be thirty to forty years. In addition, the time it takes to develop new technology into marketable products and processes seems to have lengthened too.

What has shortened, and appreciably, is the time-lag between the introduction of a new product or process into the market and its general adoption. Fifty or seventy-five years ago there was a good deal of time in which to adapt to the appearance of a new product or a new process. It took five or even ten years for it to cross national boundaries, let alone the Atlantic Ocean (though this did not apply to major new innovations such as the electric light bulb, the telephone, or the streetcar, all of which spread across the whole world with a speed since unmatched). Today the period of diffusion is a few weeks or a few months.

One can therefore anticipate technology by systematically looking for new knowledge – and by being alert to the first sign that it is being transformed into technology. However, the new no longer derives purely from 'science', as the earlier analysis of the new industries should have made clear. It comes from all areas in which there is systematic work on knowledge, whether 'sciences' in the traditional sense or not.

It has always been the rule that the major new changes in one area are more likely to originate in a field or discipline outside that area than from within.

The modern psychologist's configuration concepts such as 'personality' or *Gestalt* originated in the 'field theory' of nineteenth-century physics. In turn, the modern electronics engineer got his idea of 'systems engineering' from the psychologists (with assistance from the biologists). The great contemporary advances in genetics grew in part out of physical chemistry with its discovery of the primacy of spatial relationships, and in part out of electronic engineering which discovered 'information theory' as a general property of electronic circuits.

All through history, human knowledge, no matter how much the 'experts' might departmentalize it, has been like fluid in a set of communicating vessels: an advance in one of them will result in a higher level in other areas.

To understand the dynamics of technology, therefore, one always starts out with areas of knowledge other than one's own. Not only is one likely to be blinded in one's own field where one knows, as a rule, far too much, and especially all the things that cannot be done – most of them untested, of course. A truly major advance is more likely to result from a development in another field than from within a field.

Finally, new major technological opportunities are prefigured in new intellectual attitudes, and even in intellectual slogans. We began to talk, for instance, of 'materials' a good ten or twenty years before we could actually design and make them. Vision, as a rule, comes before action – and understanding comes even later. Thomas Watson, Sr, the man who founded and built IBM, did not live to see the triumph of the computer, but he had begun to talk forty years earlier about 'data processing', even though no one at that time would have been able to say what the term might mean. Everybody today talks of the 'megalopolis', the 'super-city', though no one can define it yet.

Not only do such slogans indicate new needs; they indicate new insight. And a great deal of new technology is not new knowledge; it is new perception. It is putting together things that no one had thought of putting together before; things that, by themselves, had been around a long time.

It is often said, and with considerable justice, that Henry Ford innovated nothing. Indeed, there is no machine, no tool, no new product, no process that bears his name, that was invented by him or could have been patented by him. Everything he used was known. There were plenty of automobiles on the market before he brought out his first one. And yet Henry Ford was a true innovator. What he contributed were mass production, the mass market, the profitability of the very cheap, and so on. Perceptions have greater impact, as a rule, economically, socially, and culturally, than have many 'new' things or even 'new' ideas.

Analysing technology and its dynamics is not a 'scientific' process, but it is not 'intuition' either. It is true analysis. It is not in itself 'technology', and as a rule it is not done well by the technologist himself. It is done best by someone who thinks as an entrepreneur and who asks: 'Where are the opportunities for a new industry, or at least for a new major process?' 'What new technical developments are likely to be of major economic impact because they fit a major need of an existing industry or an existing market?' 'What major new knowledge has come into being that has not yet had an economic impact, has not yet resulted in new industries, new processes, new economic capabilities, or new productivity?' 'What new insights are there, what new perceptions that are likely to make effective new technology – and what kinds of new technology?'

It is not possible from such an analysis to deduce that such-and-such a development, looking this or that way, will come in in a given year and lead to sales of x million dollars within five years. But something much more important can be said, namely, that any development of a certain kind, if and when it appears or is made to appear, will have a major impact, will have the potential for becoming a new industry rather than just a new product, a new technology rather than just a new tool or a new method.

In an age of rapid change, a technological strategy is essential for the success and indeed for the survival of a business and perhaps even of an industrial nation. It is necessary to have thought through in advance where to put one's own technological efforts. Should they focus on modification and improvement – as do practically all the efforts now known in industry under the name of 'research and development'? Should they aim at producing new technology? Or perhaps even new knowledge? Or should they, as the Swedes did in respect to power-transmission, be used to exploit a gap between technological and economic potential? Such strategy would also think through whether a given business should aim to develop fundamental technology for its own use, or whether it should develop technology to license to others. And at what stage should the company, in turn, import technology, and what should it look out for and stand ready to pick up whenever it appears on the horizon?

No one in an age of rapid change can possibly hope to produce all the technology that is needed, not even in one's own area. Not even the biggest company – and not even the most powerful country – can any longer do what the research establishments founded between 1890 and 1930 were meant to do: produce all the new technology and innovation (or even all the new knowledge) in a given field.

This idea of technological self-sufficiency underlay the creation of the first research laboratory in the German chemical industry almost a century ago. It still underlay a generation later the creation of the great government-sponsored scientific research organization of Germany, the Kaiser Wilhelm Institutes (now Max Planck Institutes). It underlay the foundation of the first great research laboratories in the United States; that of the General Electric Company in Schenectady around 1900, and, ten years or so later, the foundation of the Bell Laboratories of the Telephone Company.

Today, however, everyone, even the most powerful research institutes with all the resources of a government behind them, will have to accept that no one can possibly be self-supporting in technology. Everyone will have to learn what to concentrate on, but also what to bring in from others, and at what stage.

69

The most rapidly growing area in international trade is probably no longer the trade in goods, but the trade in technology, in patents and licences. Everybody will have to learn to develop a strategy for it. What are we going to do ourselves? What are we going to sell to others? And what are we going to buy, and at what stage?

An early example of successful technological strategy is Japan. It was obvious to the founders of modern Japan that the country could not attempt to lead in technological innovation; all its energies had to go into social and cultural innovations. And while one could import neither society nor culture, one could import technology. The Japanese, as a result, have learned how to look for the emergence of new technology; how to acquire new technology from abroad at the right stage; and how to develop the foreign-born idea into a successful, marketable product fast. But so far even the Japanese know only how to buy technology and have had little occasion to learn how to sell it, or how to concentrate one's own resources so as to obtain the greatest possible yield in new knowledge, new technology, and economic results from one's own efforts.

In the West, only the Swedes so far have given thought to such technological strategy.

High-voltage transmission is just one example of the Swedish achievement in thinking through where the technological gaps were and how they could be exploited. The Swedish automobile industry with its emphasis on a car that combines passenger-car styling with the ruggedness needed for poor roads is another. And so is the Swedish aircraft industry – the only aircraft industry in a small country – with its emphasis on aircraft capable of landing and taking off on very short runways; that is, again under the conditions that are typical in countries other than the very big or the very rich.

Yet Swedish technological strategy has not been formulated by technologists. It seems to have come mostly from the industrial development bankers who head the country's three large banks. Not one of them is a scientist or an engineer; all of them, however, apparently understand the need for a technological strategy that is appropriate to a small country where available resources have to be concentrated on filling gaps in a few areas rather than on providing the main advance. When World War II ended, Sweden was still largely a mining and lumbering economy. Now she has become, in terms of *per capita* output, Europe's leading industrial economy and has attained a standard of living second only to that of the United States.

THE DYNAMICS OF THE MARKET

The businessman will increasingly have to understand the dynamics of the market. The market is the most potent source of ideas for innovation. A study done by the US Department of Commerce during the last few years showed, for instance, that even among patented products and processes, that is, among products and processes with a high technology content, the majority had their origin in the needs of the market rather than in technology alone.

Understanding the dynamics of the market is necessary to prevent loss of the fruits of technological achievements. Technologically no country has done a better job during the last twenty-five years than Great Britain. Antibiotics, radar, and the jet engine, to name only a few, are all British in origin. The computer, too, owes a great deal to British technology, and so does the atomic reactor. Yet in none of these have the British reaped where they sowed and cultivated. And while there is no single explanation for this, the failure to understand the market and to be concerned with its dynamics is clearly a central reason.

The importance of marketing for technology has been documented in a study of the 'technology gap' said to exist between the United States and Europe.* This study showed that of those inventions which could be attributed almost entirely to work in one country in the post-war period, nineteen were made in the United States and ten in Western Europe – in Britain, France, and Germany. But the United States led in twenty-two of the major innovations flowing from these twenty-nine inventions whereas all European countries together are leading in only seven of them. The difference is entirely a result of marketing,† that is, of the ability to translate the technically new into the economically productive.

But the role of marketing in making technology economically effective was proven much earlier.

The best technical work on the electric light bulb was done not by Edison but by his British competitor, Sir Joseph Swan. And yet it was Edison's bulb that won out in the market-place – for the simple reason that, unlike Swan, Edison looked at the market. He put himself into the position of the electric power companies and asked: 'What do they need and what can they use?' And he put himself in the position of the home owner and asked the same questions. Technically Swan's solution may have been much more elegant; but it just did not fit the expectations, the behaviour, the values of the two markets which had to accept the new product if it was to be economically possible, let alone successful.

Most businessmen when they speak of 'marketing' mean nothing more sophisticated than the systematic and purposeful organization of all the work that has to be done to

* J. Ben David, *Fundamental Research and Government Policy* (Committee for Science Policy, Organization for Economic Co-operation and Development, Paris, 1966).

† The fundamental work in this area is the book by the American economist, J. Schmookler, *Invention and Economic Growth* (Harvard University Press, Cambridge, Massachusetts, 1966).

sell a product, to deliver it to the customer, and to get paid for it. What is needed to be an entrepreneur in an era of rapid technological change is 'marketing' in two other senses.

First, we need 'marketing' which looks upon the entire business from the point of view of its ultimate purpose and justification, that is, from the point of view of the customer (or rather the 'customers' since every business and every product has at least two, and usually many more, quite different kinds of customer to satisfy). This means, above all, that one does not try to look at the customer for 'our product'. As long as one thinks of 'our product', one is still thinking in terms of selling rather than in terms of marketing. What matters is the customer's behaviour, his values, and his expectations. And under this aspect, one's own business, let alone one's own product, hardly exists at all. In a true marketing point of view no product and no company is assumed to have the slightest importance to the customer or indeed to be even noticed by him. It is axiomatic that the customer is only interested in the satisfaction he seeks and in his needs and expectations. The customer's question is always, 'What will this product or this business do for me tomorrow?'

Secondly, businessmen will have to learn to practise 'marketing' as an innovating force in itself. They have to learn that the truly new does not, as a rule, satisfy demands that already exist. It creates new expectations, sets new standards, makes possible new satisfactions. 'Innovative marketing' therefore creates markets. New technology always needs new markets which were not even conceivable until the new technology created new demands.

The chemical industry has known this all along.

Before the chemical industry acquired a substantial number of the carpet mills in the United States, the carpet industry was in a decline. It advertised its products; it sold 'hard'. But its share in the total consumer expenditures on housing and home furnishings steadily diminished. Then, in the early 1950s, the chemical industry came into the carpet business – largely to save an important customer for their synthetic fibres. It immediately began innovative marketing.

It first asked: 'What is the biggest unfulfilled expectation of the typical home buyer?' The answer – and like all right answers, it sounds obvious once it has been given – was: to bring the level of the home which typical young families buy a little closer to their aspirations and tastes; that is, to bridge the gap between the house they read about in the home magazines and the house they can afford. This immediately showed a new role for carpeting. Floor covering is one of the few ways in which the basic taste and comfort level of a home can be raised with comparatively little outlay.

The next question was then: 'What can young people afford?' And the answer – equally obvious – was that they can afford a few pennies more in monthly hire-purchase payments but cannot afford to pay a larger lump sum when they buy the home and are inundated already by demands on their slender resources. The moment this answer had been given, it became clear that the one kind of floor covering that could be bought by a young couple was the most expensive kind, namely, wall-to-wall carpeting. For that, being fixed to the structure, can be included in the home-owner's mortgage.

The final question was: 'Who decides what is being bought?' In other words: 'Who is really the customer?' The answer to this was the mass-builder rather than the young couple. If, in other words, floor covering is offered in such a way that it is attractive to the mass-builder because it enables him to save on flooring – which means wall-to-wall carpeting; because it makes it easier for him to sell a house by making it look better; and because it enables him to sell the carpeted home without any increase in the down-payment and with only a slight increase in the monthly carrying charge – then floor covering becomes immediately a major satisfaction of the home owner. As a result of such innovative marketing, the declining, if not dying, carpet industry in the United States, has again become healthy, growing, and profitable.

Meanwhile electric lighting fixtures – an even better way to upgrade the taste and comfort level of a home – have continued to be a declining industry. All that industry is trying to do is to design 'better' products and to 'sell hard'.

There is a common belief abroad that it is new technology that creates sales and with them jobs and industries. But new technology is only a potential. It is marketing, and especially innovative marketing, that converts the potential into actuality. Only under acute shortage conditions do goods sell themselves. A cancer drug does not require much marketing; here we have an acute shortage in which not even 'selling' would be needed, did we only have the right knowledge and an effective product. But even a cancer drug would have to be in a form in which the medical profession could effectively use it.

Wherever conditions do not resemble the extreme scarcity that prevails in cancer therapy, new technology needs, above all, effective marketing. It needs an understanding of the market and its dynamics. This is necessary to direct the technological efforts – as the examples above of the successful new products of Swedish technology show. It takes innovative marketing to create the new perception for the customer so that he can use the new to expand his horizon, to raise his expectations, and his aspirations, and to derive new satisfactions.

Economic advance is not greater satisfaction of old needs and wants. It is above all new choice. It is the widening of the horizon of expectations and aspirations. This is largely a function of marketing which, therefore, is needed to make technological change economically productive, that is, to result in the satisfaction of human needs and wants.

THE INNOVATIVE ORGANIZATION

Businessmen will have to learn to build and manage an innovative organization. They will have to learn to build and manage a human group which is capable of anticipating the new, capable of converting its vision into technology, products, and processes, and willing and able to accept the new.

During the last half-century, we have learned, by and large, how to organize human energies for joint performance. We have learned how to use organization to do efficiently what we already know how to do. This is a tremendous step forward, and one on which our present society rests. We now need to make possible organization that can innovate.

There are large innovative organizations around.

A good example are the Bell Laboratories of the American Telephone and Telegraph Company which, for almost fifty years, have been a productive source of new technology in a wide variety of areas. Yet they are an integral part of a big, highly structured, managerial organization which is, of necessity, primarily focused on doing efficiently what it already knows how to do.

But Bell Laboratories are an exception so far. Now such accomplishment will have to become common. The ability to innovate is needed. We need to build this into an economy in which we have, as the nineteenth century did not have, large, permanent, managerial organizations.

This will require major organization changes. In the first place, as the success of Bell Laboratories makes clear, innovative organizations must be kept distinct from managerial organizations, which are responsible for exploiting what is already in existence. Such managerial organizations can modify, can extend, can improve; but they cannot truly innovate.

More and more companies have, for instance, learned that it is futile to expect the truly new to come out of the existing product divisions within the company. The new needs a separate 'development' division which is responsible for it until it is no longer 'new' but an established going, successful business. This is also the lesson taught by the chemical company which has been most successful as an innovator, the DuPont Company in Wilmington, Delaware. Forty years ago it set up a separate 'development department'.

But perhaps even more important is that an innovative organization requires a different structure of the relationship between people. It requires a team organization rather than a command organization, and it requires flexibility in relationships. Yet there has to be discipline, there has to be authority, and there has to be someone who can make decisions. Team structure is largely unknown to classical organization theory – though a jazz combo or, for that matter, a surgical team in the operating theatre exemplifies it.

The innovative organization needs a new attitude on the part of the people at the top. In the managerial organization, the top people sit in judgement; in the innovative organization it is their job to encourage ideas, no matter how unripe or crude. It is the job of the top people in the innovative organization to try to convert the largest possible number of ideas into serious proposals for effective, purposeful work. It is their job to say: 'What would this idea have to be for it to be taken seriously?' It is not their job, as it is in the managerial organization, to say: 'This is not a serious proposal.'

No idea for the really new ever starts out as a realistic, serious, thought-through, worked-out proposal. It always starts out as a groping, a divining, a search. To be sure, nine out of ten of these 'bright ideas' turn out to be nothing but epigrams. Of the small proportion that are left, the great majority also never get anywhere. The mortality of 'bright ideas' is as great as the mortality of frogs' eggs; ideas are a part of nature – and nature is prodigal. But then there is never a shortage of ideas, just as there is no shortage of frogs' eggs in the pond. One has to have a thousand to hatch one viable end result. One does not know in advance which one of the thousand will survive and grow to maturity.

The innovative attitude requires willingness on the part of the people at the top to listen, to encourage, and to go to work themselves at converting crude guesses into understanding, the first glimpse into vision, and excitement into results. This is not, as so many people believe, 'creativity'. Nor is it 'disorganized'. It is a highly organized, disciplined, and systematic process. But it requires a different approach and different procedures from those of the well-managed organization.

'Professional' management today sees itself often in the role of a judge who says 'yes' or 'no' to ideas as they come up. This leads, inevitably, to the situation described in the famous jingle which, legend has it, was found one day pinned to the organization chart on the bulletin board of the Unilever Company in London:

> *Across this Tree*
> *From Root to Crown*
> *Ideas flow up*
> *And Vetoes down.*

A top management that believes that its job is to sit in judgement will inevitably veto the new idea. It is always 'impracticable'. Only a top management that sees its central function in trying to convert into purposeful action the half-baked idea for something new will actually make its organization – whether company, university, laboratory, or hospital – capable of genuine innovation and self-renewal.

One risk an innovative organization cannot afford is the risk of aiming too low. It takes as much ingenuity and work to do a little better what we already do as it takes to do something entirely different. It takes as much work and effort to create one addition to the product line as it does to create a new business. In genuine innovation one cannot afford to come out with just another product. The work needed for it is too great for the possible results – and the risk is exactly the same as that of aiming for a new business or perhaps even for a new industry. What distinguishes the truly productive scientist from the merely competent one is rarely knowledge or effort, let alone talent. The men who are truly productive – leaving out the few towering geniuses such as the Newtons or the Faradays – are men who focus their knowledge, their intelligence, and their efforts on a big, a truly worthwhile goal; men who set out to create something new.

I have been reading for years the acceptance speeches of Nobel prize winners. Again and again one hears them say, 'What started me on the work that led to this achievement was a chance remark by a teacher who said: "Why don't you try something where the results would really make a difference?"' The first question to ask in an innovative organization is: 'Is this big enough so that we will have at least a new business, if not a new industry or a new technology, if we succeed? If not, we cannot afford the risks.' This is a very different question from the ones asked in the managerial organization when it does 'long-range planning' or allocates resources. There one tries to minimize the possible loss. In innovation one has to maximize the possible results.

4. The New Economic Policies

AN ERA OF INNOVATION and technological change makes great demands on government policies. The demands may be even more difficult to satisfy than those on the entrepreneur.

In a period of rapid change in which new industries emerge as the new dynamic forces, government policy must, above all, not prevent or inhibit the mobility of productive resources. Men and capital, the two mobile resources of any economy, must be able to move into the most productive allocation and out of employment in yesterday's work.

Such mobility is essential for the welfare of the individual. Less productive employments pay less, of necessity. To impede movement into more productive ones therefore imposes a lower income on the individual who is supposedly 'protected'. In fact, it threatens the individual with loss of job – or at the least, with insecurity, fear, and worry. The more productive the employment, the more enjoyable it also is as a rule, and the more satisfaction does it offer to the individual. This is particularly true today where the employment of greatest productivity in the developed countries increasingly is not manual work but knowledge work which offers the individual greater opportunity to make his living by doing what he enjoys and what he feels pride in.

Capital too must be able to move towards the productive investments. The more advanced an economy, the more important is optimum utilization of capital. For 'advanced' means in effect an economy in which capital steadily increases its productivity, an economy in which capital steadily moves from employments of lower productivity to employments of higher productivity. This is the one and only way in which a country can enjoy a high or a rising standard of living, *and* full employment. This is also the one way in which a developed country can stay competitive as other, less developed, countries begin to grow and expand their economic capacities and performance.

As a result of fifty years of economic continuity, however, the developed countries today are organized to prevent mobility of people as well as to penalize mobility of capital. This tendency is particularly pronounced in the United States and Great Britain – it may indeed be one of the major reasons why Great Britain has become a declining rather than a growing economy. But the other developed countries, whether in Western Europe, the Soviet Bloc, or Japan, are not too different, even though some of them have found means to inject some mobility into their economic structure.

The greatest obstacle to economic growth in the United States and Great Britain is the craft organization of work and especially the craft union, which puts a tremendous premium on doing things the way they used to be done. The craft union with its 'jurisdictions' and 'demarcations' (the former, the American – the latter, the British, term for union restrictions) prohibits, by definition, the learning of new skills by its members, and at the same time forbids access to skilled jobs by outsiders.

The craft is obsolete. It is the wrong way to acquire skill. We can no longer afford apprenticeship, neither economically nor educationally. Skill, to be productive today – in fact, to be 'skill' today – has to be based on systematic knowledge. But even if craft skills were still the right skills, craft organization of work would be the wrong organization.

Craft skill is the enemy of the craftsman himself. By asserting that skills are unchanged and that skilled workers are immovable, craft unions increasingly deny their members jobs and condemn them to sterility. The example of the

81

newspapers in New York City and of the American shipping and ship-building industries should be grim warning of the growing threat of the craft unionism to the craftsman himself.

The aim of the craft union, namely, security of income and employment, can be attained much better and more easily by promoting mobility.

Sweden has demonstrated this in the policy worked out twenty years ago by one of its trade-union leaders, Gösta Rehn. Under this policy an autonomous agency working with the government, with industry, and with the labour unions, is systematically promoting mobility of workers. It anticipates the job opportunities of tomorrow as well as the job redundancies likely to occur within the next year or two. It systematically prepares men to move from one kind of employment into another – and it has done so with singular success. It organizes, if necessary, the physical move of a man and his family out of a decaying into a growing community. Withall, this policy has been infinitely less expensive than paying for unemployment would have been.

As a result, Sweden, which has undergone a more drastic industrial transformation during the last twenty years than any other Western country, has developed the work force for the new industries, while, at the same time, the Swedish worker, his skill, his standard of living, and his job satisfaction have constantly been upgraded.

There is no reason why the Rehn policy could not be adopted in any other industrial country. It would accomplish everything the trade union wants – and do it much better than today's trade-union policies. It would, as it did in Sweden, bring out clearly that economy and society are committed both to mobility of labour and to making mobility a source of strength, of job security, of prosperity, and of satisfaction for the individual.

But in the United States and even more in Great Britain, craft unionism is deeply embedded. This is not a 'law of nature'. It is not even a 'law of industrialization'. No other industrial country has craft unionism. In the countries that have grown the most in the last twenty years, Japan, Germany, and the Soviet Union, it is conspicuously absent.

In Germany, labour was organized on a craft basis before Hitler. When the labour unions were restored after Hitler, however, they were based on industries rather than on crafts. As a result, the constant fights in American and English industry as to who is entitled to do which job are unknown in Germany today, despite union strength and power.

It will be exceedingly difficult to liquidate craft unionism in the Anglo-American countries – and yet it will be increasingly urgent to do so. Predictably this is going to be a central political problem for the United States and Great Britain. If it cannot be solved, economic decay in these two countries will be almost impossible to prevent.

In every developed country there is a similar need to do what the Swedes have done: to make mobility a goal of national policy. It must be accomplished in such a manner, however, that it strengthens job and income security for the worker and becomes something he wants and desires rather than something he dreads.

THE WRONG TAX INCENTIVES

Equally important and equally difficult will be the shift from a policy that penalizes the mobility of capital to one that encourages it.

Folk wisdom has long held that new technology does not come out of the old, and especially the big, old company. Although there is no inherent reason why this should be true, there have so far been few exceptions to this rule.

(One, Bell Laboratories, has already been mentioned.) It is not RCA or GE that have the computer, but IBM, which on the eve of World War II had no scientists or engineers and was a very small company despite the ambitious 'International' in its name. It is not the printing-press makers with their seemingly impregnable monopoly who have the new duplication and reproduction technology; it is Xerox, which as late as 1950 was a tiny, local job-shop. It is not the major chemical companies that are the leaders in the new pharmaceutical industry. And General Motors or Ford are not leaders in the aircraft or space industries, despite their tremendous resources of capital and engineering talent.

An apparent exception might be the nuclear power plant, where General Electric and Westinghouse have worldwide leadership. But economically the nuclear reactor is not much of an innovation. All it does is to produce by new techniques the steam that has been producing electric power all along. However great the scientific and engineering achievement, the nuclear reactor is just another 'boiler' as far as the economy, the power user, and even the electric utilities are concerned. Actually, going into nuclear reactors was defensive rather than innovative for GE and Westinghouse who, for almost a century, have had a dominant position in the generation and distribution of electric energy.

In general, though with some important exceptions, the little fellow, whether a small company or the lone 'garage inventor', has been more innovative than the large company.* To cite one example: despite all the money that the aluminium companies are spending on research, only one

* This, at least, was the conclusion of a study made by sixteen of America's leading research administrators, all of them from such large companies as Union Carbide and Xerox, who in the spring of 1967 reported to President Johnson and the Congress on technological innovation.

of seven major changes in aluminium processing has come from a major company. The remaining six have largely been the work of individuals or small companies.

By and large, then, the big and established company has not been a good environment for the new, small, and growing. The least productive environment has clearly been government-sponsored research which almost by definition is 'big research'. While four-fifths or so of all scientists and engineers in research in America today are supported by government money, either in large universities or in big companies, the total output is probably less than one-fifth of the total of new ideas, new knowledge, and new products.

In an age in which technological innovation is likely to be active, rapid, and important, it will therefore be crucially important that small business can come into being and can grow. This, however, means access to capital. Not only is innovation expensive; for every dollar spent on achieving an innovation, ten dollars have to be spent to develop it into a product, process, or service. Even more money – up to a hundred dollars for each dollar originally spent on research – may be needed to make and market the product before it produces a penny of profit.

Yet today's American tax laws put a tremendous premium on capital retention in the existing big and old business. In fact, our tax laws are the greatest engine for monopoly ever devised. No matter how actively the anti-trusters try to prevent concentration of economic power and to stop the big ones from getting even bigger, the tax laws inevitably frustrate their efforts. The double taxation of corporate income paid out as dividends – first as tax on the profits of the corporation and then as tax on the income of the individual who receives a dividend – subsidizes and encourages retention of capital in the existing business, and especially in the existing big businesses. Unless a shareholder's total income is below $8,000 a year, he is better off getting the returns on his investment in the form of capital gains rather than as dividends. The great majority of shareholders therefore want the company in which they invest to keep the money and to invest it for them. This means that more and more of the economy's capital is inaccessible to the newcomer, that is, to the small and growing business and the independent innovator.

What is amazing is not that the old, big companies have been able to maintain themselves. It is that despite our tax laws so many new companies have been able to develop and grow to the point where a great many of the 'giants' of 1930 either do not exist at all today or have become minor and relatively unimportant businesses compared to newcomers nobody had ever heard of forty – or even twenty-five – years ago. But we cannot rely on Providence for ever to bail us out of our stupidity.

The right policy is known. It would not even cost government revenues – in fact, it might increase them. All we have to do is to remove the inducement to retain earnings and to restore the normal desire of a shareholder to receive dividends. If, for instance, our tax laws allowed the recipient of dividends to offset the corporate income tax already paid on his earnings against his personal income tax, we would at once make dividends attractive again to the shareholders. The government revenue this would lose would easily be recovered by raising the individual income tax by a few percentage points, especially in the upper brackets (and, in the United States, by abolishing the innumerable tax privileges on a variety of investments such as municipal bonds, which enable the very rich to pay no income tax at all). Lest this be considered a subsidy to the rich, we might limit the tax-offset to the effective rate of the corporation income tax, that is, to the rate the individual now pays on the kind of middle-class income enjoyed by a judge, a congressman, or a reasonably successful physician.

Another obvious way out of our monopolistic tax policy in the United States would be to substitute the European value-added tax for the tax on corporation profits. There are other reasons for such a shift – it would greatly strengthen the competitive position of United States and British goods in the world markets.

Yet, while technically simple, such changes in the tax laws – and in the basic attitude underlying them – will be, politically, extremely difficult. The real reason behind our tax laws is not hostility to bigness. It is a deep desire to protect the *status quo* and to make life easy and comfortable for the fat and lazy – among businesses as well as among labour unions. Rapid change, with new industries and new business emerging fast, is neither easy nor comfortable, whether for managers, for union leaders, or for government administrators.

There is deep vested interest in double taxation. The labour unions everywhere are committed to high taxation of profits (rather than to high taxation of high incomes, though this would make a great deal more sense from the union point of view). The universities and colleges in the United States – and charities altogether – have a major interest in maintaining the present tax philosophy; corporate contributions to higher education, for instance, would hardly survive a reform under which the individual shareholder again looked upon the corporation as 'his' asset rather than the property of the managers. The managers of the large existing companies too are unlikely to view such a change with great enthusiasm, no matter how much they now complain about the 'burden of taxation' and oppose any increase in corporation income tax. These resistances are actually additional reasons for going through with such a reform anyhow, but they will not make it easier or politically more palatable.

Instead we are almost certain to see attempts to evade the problem. One such attempt was made by the British Labour government in the autumn of 1967. That the failure of capital to go into the new and more productive industries is one of the major reasons for the stagnation of the British economy is generally accepted. It is also generally accepted, even by socialist economists, that British taxation and government policies on investments are a main reason for this weakness. Instead of changing these policies, however, the Labour government in the autumn of 1967 proposed to use government money to subsidize new technology through the purchase of shares in *unprofitable* new ventures. This proposal, if followed, could only lead to a large-scale waste of public funds. In earlier forays along this line, especially in the aircraft industry, the British government invariably backed the wrong innovations and the wrong investments. Moreover, the funds available would be much too small to have any impact and are no substitute for the funds a capital market would provide, if only allowed by the tax structure to move capital where results are likely to be had. Instead the proposed measure would aggravate capital-immobility; for the unprofitable, ie, misallocated, investments in the wrong innovations would require – as did the earlier ones – ever-growing new subsidies.

Government has a duty to protect. In a period of rapid economic change, there will be great and legitimate pressure for protection. It is unrealistic to expect modern government in a developed economy to return to the *laissez-faire* position of the late-nineteenth century, no matter how desirable and socially advantageous this might be. However, the traditional and fundamentally dishonest way to protect, the hidden way, does infinitely more harm than good, and is not even the right way for those in need of protection.

The right way was shown by the measures proposed by President Kennedy and adopted by Congress to shield American industries against sudden impacts of freer trade. These measures provided for general but short-lived subsidies to the companies and the workers who were affected. This open and direct protection is in sharp contrast to tariffs or quotas, which are hidden and do not appear as expenditures of government – though of course they are expenditures of the community.

What we need, therefore, is a commitment of the developed countries to a policy of direct subsidy as against a policy of indirect protection. Protection deforms. Subsidies are at least in the open. More important, protection creates dependence which it is increasingly difficult to abolish. A subsidy, on the other hand, can be directed towards remedying the weakness. It can be directed, as is the Swedish subsidy for mobility of labour, towards making the affected party capable of standing on its feet again. And it can be limited in time – is indeed always limited in time, since public opinion and the legislature will eventually become impatient with any permanent subsidy.

Politicians as well as bureaucrats dislike subsidies precisely because they are in the open. This, however, is their greatest virtue. The developed countries will need the self-discipline and the political honesty to use subsidies to replace indirect, protectionist policies. For these are always restrictive and always end up making the recipient weaker and less capable of survival than he was before.

FOCUS ON WORLD ECONOMY

Finally – and this may be the greatest shock – the large developed country will increasingly have to take its cues from the world economy and its trends and developments.

No large developed economy today has reliable domestic measurements and indicators concerning its markets at home. Every market is so grossly manipulated by government policies of all kinds – price policies, wage policies, tax policies, subsidy policies, budgetary policies, credit policies – that all gauges are 'rigged'. Economic policy, however, needs reliable measurements above all. In particular, it needs reliable measurements as to where the leading edges of technology and economy are. It needs to be able to anticipate what the new industries will be, and where resources, whether of men or of capital, are most productively employed. This, the domestic market no longer signals with any reliability.

There is, however, one area in the economy where manipulation is not – and not likely to become – dominant. This is the international arena. Even in the Soviet Bloc, transactions between the various countries have proved to be incapable of manipulation, and have escaped the most careful 'planning'. Even there, true values have established themselves – the main reason why the attempt to create a unified controlled economy for the entire Communist world collapsed so ingloriously, in China as well as in the European satellites. International trade is not capable of being manipulated beyond a certain point. International transactions altogether – capital transactions, the movement of people, whether tourists or migrants, and the 'balance of technology' – cannot be rigged very far. They can be stopped temporarily; but the moment there is any freedom of movement, whether of capital, of people, of technology, or of goods, a true balance re-establishes itself.

For this reason, governments in the developed economies will have to learn to look outside and to develop their domestic policies on the basis of the indicators of the international economy. This is not making the international economy dominant. It is something much subtler: using the international economy as the yardstick.

The smaller countries, Holland, Switzerland, and Sweden, have had to do this all along. International trade and international markets dominate their economies anyhow, whether they like it or not. But of the large countries only Japan has since 1950 steered by the international economy. This is undoubtedly one of the central reasons for the phenomenal performance of the Japanese economy.

If anyone in the late 1940s had made a bet whether Japan or Great Britain would do better in the post-war economy, he would without the slightest hesitation have bet on Britain. Of the two island economies, the British was not only the greatly more developed, but British industry had come out of the war a good deal stronger than it had entered it, with new factories, new technologies, and a host of new products in which it had achieved leadership. Japan's industry, by contrast, was destroyed. The British were on a much higher level of skill, of education, and of performance. They were admired everywhere and they had maintained a pre-war trading and financial network that covered the world. Whatever the Japanese had had – and it was not much – was gone.

Yet twenty years later, it is Japan that has forged ahead while Britain has fallen behind. One of the main reasons for this is that Japan made the world economy determine her economic policies, whereas Britain made her economic policy serve principally to maintain her traditional, domestic economy. It is fashionable today to blame the 'Welfare State' in Britain. It is true that Japan has not anywhere near the social provisions that Britain – or for that matter, Germany, or the United States – has for her workers and farmers. But compared to Japanese productivity and *per capita* income, Japanese welfare provisions, though organized in very different fashion (largely as customary rather than contractual employee benefits), are at least as high as those of the British Welfare State. Japan has welfare rigidities, such as her 'lifetime employment', which go far beyond any welfare burden the British economy might carry. The real difference is one of fundamental attitude, outlook, and policy.

Everyone (including most Japanese) will say: 'What choice did the Japanese have? Their economy is, after all, dependent on international trade.' But this is not true, no matter how widely it is believed. Of all the major industrial nations, only one, the United States, is less dependent on foreign trade than Japan. All the others, France, Britain, Germany – let alone small countries like Sweden, Holland, and Switzerland – are infinitely more dependent. Barely 10 per cent of Japan's national product is exported, and conversely barely 10 per cent of her national needs are imported. The figure of foreign dependence of the economy is 15 per cent for Britain and Germany – but well above 25 per cent for Holland and Sweden. (It is 5 per cent for the United States.)

What the Japanese realized twenty years ago was that they had to make sure that their productive resources would go into tomorrow's rather than into yesterday's work. They further realized that it is the world economy that indicates where tomorrow is likely to be. For the past twenty years the Japanese have therefore systematically projected the trends of the world economy on to their economic policy, both domestic and international.

Thus in international trade negotiations the Japanese have never bought time for an old industry by concessions in respect to a new one. They have never offered to limit their electronic exports, for instance, to gain greater access to a market for their cotton textiles, their bicycles, or their sneakers. The British, by contrast, have always offered to sacrifice the new industries to get a concession, no matter how small, for yesterday's decaying industries. Modern industry in Britain is the equal of any industry anywhere. Yet Britain's exports are still dependent on the old industries. Japan, on the other hand, has cut the share of yesterday's industries in export from almost three-quarters in 1950 to about one-third in 1967, while at the same time expanding the share of the new, modern industries from one-third of the total to almost two-thirds.

Although Japan is not a 'planned' economy, it is as bureaucratically controlled as Britain. But while the Japanese have used these controls to favour the future, the British have used them largely to defend the past. This is what nationalizing an old industry amounts to. The British have maintained the coal mines, the railways, the steel industry, and (even though without nationalization) most of the cotton-textile industry. The Japanese, on the other hand, have used their bureaucratic controls to push capital into the new industries and to deny it to the old ones. They have used their bureaucratic controls to enable the new industries to obtain the bulk of the educated manpower. And they have used the control of the relationships between Japanese and foreign companies to push aggressively the importation of new technology – in electronics, in optics, in the pharmaceutical industry, and so on – while restricting importation of technology in the old industries.

The difference is best seen in the costumes which don the two economies when they show themselves abroad. At any world's fair or trade exhibition of the last twenty years, the British have featured their good old stand-bys – whisky, woollens, china – all of exceptional quality and all of yesterday. The Japanese have featured the new – eg, the electron microscope (which dominated the Japanese exhibit at the New York World's Fair of 1959–60 to the point where most visitors thought that the Japanese had invented this instrument); modern assembly-line ship-building methods; synthetic fibres; and of course cameras, tape-recorders, and transistor radios.

In Japan itself, the old industries are still tremendously important. No Japanese government would last long unless it supported cotton textiles and coal mines at home. But in economic policy, the Japanese have forced themselves to take their cue from the growing edge of the world economy.

What the Japanese have done for the last twenty years, the rest of us will have to learn to do for the remainder of this century. Even if, as in the United States, the world economy appears to be quite unimportant for the domestic economy, it is the bellwether. It signals where tomorrow will be and where the domestic economy should move to be competitive, to be capable of growth, and to stay abreast, let alone to lead.

Both business and government, in other words, will have to learn to put the future ahead of yesterday – in their policies, in their attitudes, and in their organization and structure. In a period of continuity, yesterday could be expected to stay around for the morrow. To strengthen yesterday was therefore likely to strengthen tomorrow. In a period of change, and especially of rapid technological change in which new industries will appear as the economic leaders, to strengthen yesterday weakens tomorrow.

A good many people may well ask: 'Why do we need all this upsetting new technology anyhow? Isn't it time to call a halt to technological change? Aren't we affluent enough to concern ourselves with distributing better what we have rather than with adding to it?' But the alternative to technological change and economic growth, especially in a period of rapid innovation, is not maintenance of the old; it is decay. This is particularly true for the countries that are today developed, that is, for the countries that have reached economic affluence.

We do indeed face basic questions as to the direction we want science and technology to go. But these are not questions whether we want scientific and technological change but where we should employ what are very scarce human resources to get the best results from knowledge efforts. The debate will be over priorities rather than over the desirability of scientific and technological advance. What is at issue is where the greatest results will be, rather than whether we want results.

The urgent need in the world today is for more production. Indeed distribution cannot get us anywhere, whether we are concerned with the problem of poverty at home or with the problem of poverty throughout the world. The only way to tackle this problem is to enable the poor to be more productive. This in turn demands economic growth in both developed and developing countries.

It does not even matter greatly whether we in the developed countries would prefer to call a halt to technological change and economic growth. There is no sign that man-

94

kind is ready to forswear economic growth and with it technological change. There is no sign that the majority of mankind is willing to take vows of poverty while the minority in the developed countries live in great wealth. Not only are the developing nations desperate for economic advancement; other developed nations, especially Western Europe and Japan (not to mention Russia), are eager to catch up with the United States and to push economic growth as fast as it can be pushed.

Whether we in the United States like it or not, to maintain technological leadership and to encourage technological innovation in important industries will become increasingly important in the next decades. The penalties for failure will be even greater than they have been in the last twenty years – and the example of Great Britain shows how dangerous it is to fall behind, even slightly, in the development and economic exploitation of new technology. We will have to learn that that one as yet barely used economist's term, the 'international balance of technology', is as important as the old stand-bys, 'the balance of trade' or the 'balance of payments' – and maybe more so. Every country will have to be able to import technology. There is so much new technology being produced that no one country, no one industry, and no one company can possibly hope to generate all it needs. But the only way one can, in the long run, pay for other people's technology is by technology of one's own. The only coin that pays for patents and licences is patents and licences.

There is no better and more effective way to create a market for one's own goods, and with them for one's own labour force, than through the sale of technology. Every penny of patent or licence income from a foreign country creates a market for at least a dollar's worth of goods from the country in which the new technology originated. Foreign investment in manufacturing companies abroad has a similar impact on creating export markets, but it requires prior capital outlay, that is, it first puts a burden on

95

the balance of payments. Export of technology, however, requires the foreign buyer to put in capital, while it yields an immediate income in the balance of payments.

The new technologies with the industries based on them are the only means for today's developed countries – and above all for the United States – to maintain their present standards of living and economic health. These new industries use productively the resources in which developed countries have an advantage, that is, educated people. They are one and all 'knowledge industries', using large numbers of 'knowledge workers' and producing goods and services with a high knowledge content. The developing poor countries can become wealthier and economically strong, however, only by developing the industries which have been the 'modern' industries in the developed world for the last fifty years: a modern and productive agriculture, the automobile industry, fertilizer and organic chemistry, steel and machinery, and so on.

In the Thirties the developed nations of the West found out that they could no longer compete with Japan in labour-intensive industries in which wages for unskilled work are the major cost – cotton textiles, footwear, toys, or sewing machines. In a developed economy, unskilled labour is a gross misallocation of the most productive and most expensive of all economic resources, the human resource. Today, only thirty years later, the Japanese in turn are finding out that they are no longer competitive in these industries. Such newcomers as Hong Kong, Singapore, and Pakistan are the truly competitive producers of labour-intensive goods today.

Similarly the West – as well as Japan – is approaching the time when today's 'modern' industries, especially the assembly-line mass-production industries, are no longer going to be competitive with newcomers. For as a country's investment in knowledge and education goes up, employment in mass-production industries becomes increasingly a misallocation of the human resource.

96

The New Economic Policies

The cost level of an economy is determined by the cost of the most productive resource. Any resource which therefore produces a good deal less than the most productive one will inevitably be too expensive to be used widely. Or, to put it simply, the developed economies already pay the cost of knowledge and now will have to obtain the full benefits from the productivity of new knowledge. Unless they do this they cannot expect to remain competitive for very long, especially as it is in the 'modern' industries that the knowledge content is comparatively small and they have been carrying the load in the developed economies during the last fifty years.

The United States, which pays the most for knowledge and produces the most educated people, will therefore be less and less capable of maintaining its competitive position in the world and thus its own standard of economic performance and standard of living, unless it takes and maintains leadership in the development of the new, the knowledge-based industries.

Whether we want technological change and new industries is therefore not particularly relevant. The question before us is how to make a period of high technological change – that is, a period in which new industries are likely to emerge as fast and as frequently as they did a hundred years ago – into a period of economic growth, of social justice, and of individual well-being and achievement.

PART TWO

From International to World Economy

5. The Global Shopping Centre

ONE THING EVERY economist regardless of persuasion knew at the end of World War II: should France (or any of the other Western European countries) ever recover economically and become prosperous again, her economy would be quite different from that of the United States. She would undoubtedly develop markets and consumer habits in keeping with her distinct culture and tradition. This would be true, everyone was sure, even more for Japan with her 'non-Western culture', and certainly for the tropical areas of Asia and Africa.

Even ten years later, Mr Khrushchev, during his visit to the United States, repeatedly stressed that the wants of an 'affluent' Russian consumer would be quite different from those of the 'capitalist' and 'decadent' Americans. There would, for instance, be no demand for private automobiles in large numbers.

There were a few dissenters. But no one listened to them.

When Dr Heinz Nordhoff took over the bombed-out Volkswagen factory in the late Forties, he apparently dreamed of producing a European successor to Henry Ford's Model T. But he could not convince anyone in Germany. He was backed instead by the British Occupation Authorities in Germany – but only because their experts were quite sure that his venture could never succeed, let alone become a competitor to the British motor-car manufacturers.

101

The British were certain, until well in the Sixties, that the European Common Market had to fail. Mass markets, they argued – and most experts concurred – simply were not compatible with the European temperament and its nationalism. Their refusal in 1957 to join with the Continent in signing the Common Market Treaty is one of the major reasons for Britain's trouble since.

Now, of course, the Volkswagen's success is history. The British sue urgently for membership in the Common Market; and Russia has undertaken a crash programme to become a major passenger-car producer by importing entire automobile plants from the West.

We know by now also that the total disproof of what everybody was so sure of twenty years ago was not brought on by 'Americanization' or 'Coca-Colonization', let alone by de Gaulle's 'sinister conspiracy of the Anglo-Saxons'. America had simply reached the mass-consumption economy ahead of the others. Our economy only demonstrated a little earlier the values, the demands, appetites, and economic preferences of peoples everywhere today. As soon as the masses glimpse, even from afar, the promise of economic growth and development, they want to shift from work as a way of life to a job as a means to a comfortable living. As a result, areas of satisfaction which the economist traditionally did not see at all are becoming central everywhere: mobility; access to information and education; and health care.

If people cannot yet afford an automobile, they will at least get a motor-scooter; and if they cannot afford a motor-scooter, they will try for a bicycle. For the masses of the world, radio and TV are not 'entertainment' – as they are for the wealthy who have other means to learn about the world. They are the first access to a bigger world than that of peasant village or small-town slum.

Just before TV got going in Japan, a leading Japan-

ese electronics manufacturer prophesied that it would
never become established on the farm; Japanese farmers
did not have enough money to buy anything as expensive
as a TV set. Three years later, almost every Japanese
farmhouse sported a TV antenna above the rice-straw
thatch of the roof.

Twenty-five years ago, the Andean Indians still sabotaged what few schools the Peruvian government had
built in their remote highlands. They tried hard to keep
themselves and their villages isolated from, and inacces-
sible to, the outside world. Today the lack of schools is
their greatest grievance – and next to it is the lack of
roads to enable them and their produce to get to the outside world.

India may be an underdeveloped country for almost
all industries – but not for the pharmaceutical industry.
It has become, in two short decades, a highly developed
market for advanced and sophisticated drugs, as have
many other developing nations.

A universal appetite for small luxuries has emerged.
They signify a little economic independence, a little control
over economic destiny. They are a badge of freedom.
Where the means are very limited – among the poor or
among teenagers without much income of their own – the
small luxury may be a soft drink, a lipstick, a movie magazine, or a candy bar. For the emerging middle class it may
be the appliance in the kitchen. For the truly affluent it
may be an advanced academic degree. That one can do
without it makes the small luxury into a psychological
necessity.

Underlying these new demands and preferences is an
even newer conviction: that modern man need not tolerate
poverty but can produce economic development and affluence for all. Such a thesis would have been inconceivable
even thirty years ago. But at the very moment when half of
the industrial world lay in rubble and ruin after the most

destructive war ever fought, man decided that poverty in an age of technology and professional management is unnecessary and an engineering defect, rather than ordained and man's natural condition.

Perhaps the best – and also the most pathetic – illustration of this new economic world view is the 'cargo cults' that have sprung up in the most remote and primitive South Sea islands since World War II. These religious sects believe in a magic 'cargo ship' sent by the President of the United States that will land one day and bring to everyone the wealth of the advanced economies – phonographs, smoked meats, transistor radios, motor-cycles, and drugs.

An economy is, above all, defined by demand. Today the whole world, whatever its actual economic condition – and whatever the political system in force in a given area – has one common demand-schedule, one common set of economic values and preferences. The whole world, in other words, has become one economy in its expectations, in its responses, and in its behaviour. This is new in human history.

Underlying this common economic behaviour is a community of information. The whole world today knows how everybody lives. The world economy is the new perception created by the new media – the movies first, followed by radio and TV. Now the communication satellites are lofted overhead everywhere in the Free World – they have been launched over Latin America, for instance. They bring the smallest hamlet in the high Andes or in the steaming jungles of Malaya as close to New York or London or the traffic jams on the Los Angeles Freeway as the people in these communities are themselves. Everyone then will have direct immediate experience of how everybody else lives, what he wears, what he eats, what his house looks like, and what are his standards of living. Everyone will know as much about everybody else as villagers used to know about their next-door neighbours. In fact, everybody will have become everybody else's next-door neighbour. The whole world, in Marshall McLuhan's words, will have become one 'global village'. In terms of information, there is a closer community across continents today than existed between the slums and the mansions of the same eighteenth- or nineteenth-century city.

These electronic media communicate things rather than what people are or think. They communicate, in other words, economics – they create a global shopping centre. This is as great – and as new – an event as the emergence of a common demand-schedule, a common set of values and preferences. It too establishes a new community.

Traditionally a community has always been defined as the area over which information could travel in one day. Up until one hundred years ago, this meant an area within a radius of ten to twenty-five miles. It is no accident that traditional boundaries of local government all over the world conform to this community – the English shire, the American town, the German Kreis, the Japanese ken (established as late as 1870). But today information travels all over the world in a few seconds. It still took fifty hours, before World War II, for a person to travel from one coast of the United States to the other. There is no place on the earth today that cannot be reached from any other place in less than a full day's flying time. One look at the crowds at the airports shows the impact on man's imagination. Deep in Africa or in Asunción in Paraguay, they listen to the loudspeaker announcing the arrival of planes from the world's great cities, and their departure for them. The remotest country is no farther away than a suburban streetcar terminus was to the people who grew up only forty or fifty years ago.

If an economy is defined as a common demand pattern, it

is also a pool of shared information. As soon as we share information, priority decisions on goals and on resource allocation to efforts are made for the entire area concerned. The moment we share information, there is a market. The world 'information explosion' contributes to making the whole world one economy.

This world economy differs in essentials from the 'international economy' that first emerged in the eighteenth century and had, by 1900, become dominant almost everywhere. In an international economy there are no common appetites, no common demands, and only a minimum of common information. Each country in an international economy is a separate unit with its own economic values and preferences, its own markets, and its own largely self-contained information. It exchanges its surpluses against what other nations can produce. The international economy itself differs in its own structure and behaviour from the economies of the individual countries. Traditionally, even between neighbouring countries on the European continent, people differed greatly in what they wore, how they built their houses, and what they ate – so much so that the travel books right up to World War II devoted many chapters to information about these foreign and strange economies. Today this is 'folklore'; the differences no longer lie in what people have or want, but in how much of the same things they have and can afford to buy. The difference lies in whether they are rich or poor; but they all belong to the same economic community.

In many ways the change from international to world economy can be compared to the shift from the economies of the American colonies to the integrated continental United States economy.

Each of the thirteen colonies was deeply immersed in the international economy. Indeed each was far more dependent on international trade, both as to exports and as to imports, than it ever was again after the establishment of the United States. Each was much closer to Europe than to its own neighbours on the American continent. Going to London from Boston or Philadelphia was, until the middle of the eighteenth century, easier than going from either to New York. Each colony had both its own distinct products for export overseas – whether timber in Maine or indigo in South Carolina – and its own distinct import needs.

The United States became the first 'continental economy'. This, however, did not simply mean that it was a large trading area. It meant that it had throughout the whole area the same demands, the same preferences, the same economic values – and common information. The individual acted as a producer and consumer within a continental American market rather than as a 'cosmopolitan' New Yorker or Virginian (indeed he became 'provincial' where formerly he had been 'colonial'). The transformation did not come all at once. It was not really accomplished until after the Civil War, eighty years after political union (and perhaps not fully until 1914 when the Federal Reserve Act had created a continental economy and credit system). But in the end it had become immaterial economically whether a given producer or a given consumer was in the East, West, South, or North of the country. All that mattered was his productive capacity or his purchasing power.

In the United States political unification preceded the unified economy. First came a legal fact and only much later its economic consequences. And the common trading territory came decades before there was a common economic perception, and a common demand-schedule. The 'American economy', as has been said so many times, was an act of political imagination rather than the creation of economic forces.

Today's world economy, however, owes almost nothing to political imagination. It is coming into being despite political fragmentation. The demands, the appetites, the values, are preceding, by a good margin, even the creation of trading units. The European Common Market was a belated institutional acknowledgement of what had become the reality of economic perception and consumer behaviour a good many years earlier.

Altogether the present world economy is one of perceptions rather than of institutions. Historically, eg, in the development of the United States, producers – with the help of governments as a rule – created economic units. Consumers played no role, were indeed (as in the early years of the United States) opposed, or at best lukewarm. The new world economy is, by contrast, an achievement of the consumer. *He* lives in a unified, worldwide economy. Producers – not to mention governments – lag way behind.

This, then, is a world economy in its demands. But there are so far no world economic institutions. There are, therefore, no instruments for a world economic policy, no tools to prevent or fight world economic crises.

GLOBAL MONEY AND CREDIT

The great theme of modern economics is the autonomy of money and credit. The classical economists, including Marx, saw in money and credit a shorthand for events in the 'real' economy of goods. The modern economist – and Keynes in this area was not a pioneer but rather the summation of seventy-five years of work – sees money and credit as an autonomous economic system which largely controls, or at least directs, the 'real' economy. The classic economist wanted his monetary system to be passively responsive. The modern economist calls for initiative in monetary and credit policies and for an organ of purposeful monetary action.

Both, however, agree that an economy must have a monetary system to be viable. Both agree that an economy can expand only if its money and credit supply can expand in step with trade and investment. Both agree that the poor in particular need a strong monetary system. Otherwise the smallest downturn in prosperity must lead to calling in the loans to them and squeezing them in a deflationary vice.

Both classic and modern economists agree that an adequate monetary system is needed to prevent economic fluctuation from turning into severe crisis. Otherwise the slightest economic upset, a mere scratch, so to speak, or an attack of the sniffles, turns into a deadly worldwide economic collapse, into worldwide economic sepsis, or galloping pneumonia.

Both classic and modern economists agree that the major depressions of the century – especially the Great Depression of 1929–39 – were caused, above all, by the inadequacy of the monetary system to handle the needs and cope with the problems of the international economy.

Finally, both agree that the world economy of today does not have a viable monetary and credit system.

Gold has been demonetized, though it is still fashionable to try to conceal this fact from the layman. It matters little in this connexion whether we raise the price of gold to maintain the gold fiction a little longer, whether we stop using gold as a monetary reserve right away, or whether, by great sleight of hand, we manage to maintain the gold price of the last thirty-odd years, that is, $35 an ounce, while moving to another monetary base for the world economy. The very fact that we are now concerned with saving gold as a monetary metal makes it clear that gold is finished as a monetary metal.

Gold has ceased to be capable of serving as the monetary foundation for the world economy, and the United States balance-of-payments troubles have little to do with its demise. Two other factors are much more pertinent: one grounded in the realities of the world economy, the other grounded in a change in the function of gold.

World trade has been growing much too fast to be financed adequately on the gold foundation. The need for money increases faster than trade, whether the trade be domestic or international. Credit always grows faster than physical transactions. The 'symbol' economy of monetary media therefore has to grow at a significantly faster rate than the 'real' economy of goods and their exchange. That we can speed up the growth of the 'real' economy by creating monetary media – the fundamental axiom from which modern economics derives – is not proven. But that lack of adequate monetary supplies strangles the 'real economy' – that, in other words, expanding the production and distribution of goods depends on a continuous and steady growth in money supply – is clear.

What made gold an excellent monetary base, namely its comparative scarcity, therefore renders it unusable as a monetary metal when trade grows faster than gold is being mined. Gold is possible as a monetary metal only in an economy in which trade is limited and static.

Within the domestic economies, we found this out in the early nineteenth century. Today's discussions about world-money are remarkably similar to the great debate of 1820, out of which modern central banking first emerged in England. In this debate which is identified with the name of David Ricardo, the father of economic analysis, and out of which modern central banking first emerged in England, we learned then that a true money economy cannot be based on gold alone – or on any other natural resource – as a foundation for the money supply. The economy needs a central bank that is a specific organ for the creation and management of money and credit. The international economy of the nineteenth century was based on the gold standard; but in every developed country the internal economy, while restrained by gold, was actually controlled and directed by a central-bank mechanism for the management of money and credit.

Now that the world is becoming a genuine economy, we face a repetition of the events of 150 years ago, only on a worldwide scale.

But the second reason why gold is no longer a reliable monetary unit is equally important. It is the increasing usefulness of gold as an industrial material. A monetary metal, every textbook has pointed out for over a hundred years, must not have any other use. It must be totally outside commerce and industry. Otherwise its price, as well as its supply, no longer depends on its monetary function. The money and credit system of an economy becomes subordinate to the vagaries of technology, of industrial fluctuations, and of minor economic events, and this is intolerable.

Silver ceased to be usable as a monetary metal when the photographic film first began to put large quantities of the metal to a non-monetary purpose. By the end of the nineteenth century photography had converted silver into an industrial raw material – and thereby finished its usefulness as a monetary base. The same thing is now happening to gold. Less and less of the newly mined gold is available for monetary purposes. It is being used industrially – and this is the end of it as a monetary metal.

Raising the price of gold is, therefore, at best a temporary expedient. It does not come to grips with the real problem at all. Yet it is far more practical and realistic than the approach which the United States has been taking for twenty-odd years, the policy to which, at this writing, the prestige and power of the United States are still committed. This is the 'key-currency' concept, with the United States dollar as the key currency.

Under such a concept, the currency of a country is at the same time the currency of a world economy.* As we have known since Ricardo pointed it out, however, these two functions are incompatible. Even the cleverest juggling cannot harmonize their conflicting demands.

---

* In Ricardo's days, these discussions were carried on in the context of a national economy – the key currency then was the monetary issue of commercial banks within a nation, and was at one and the same time a medium of exchange, that is, money, and the form in which a bank financed its commercial business.

If the larger economy (in our case the world economy) grows, it requires a steadily growing supply of money and credit. Under the key-currency approach, this means that the supply of the key currency – the United States dollar for the last twenty years – available to the world economy has to increase all the time. The more the world economy grows, the larger the United States balance-of-payments deficit, therefore, has to be – or else the world economy is strangled by a 'liquidity crisis', that is, by a shortage of money and credit to carry on trading transactions.

There is a limit to this process however – and it is never far off. First the other countries in the world economy will not indefinitely accept the currency of one of their members. They will, sooner or later – and rightly – demand that the 'key country' put its own financial house in order and establish a proper balance in its international accounts. This, however, means curtailing the credit supply of the world economy. The more successful an economy is in which the monetary supply is furnished by a key currency, the sooner will it run into a severe and inevitable deflationary crisis. And the more successful the economy has been, the more severe will the crisis have to be.

But the key-currency concept is also an intolerable threat to the key country itself. It can work only if foreigners accept monetary promises, namely, the currency of the key country. This they will do only as long as they are reasonably sure that they can convert these promises at will into their own currency. The more successful the world economy under the key-currency concept, the greater, therefore, is the danger of a 'run on the bank' – that is, on the key country. The greater is the danger that the key country will be paralysed by a self-induced collapse of its own monetary system.

Yet this is the policy to which the United States has been committed ever since the end of World War II. At the Bretton Woods Conference of 1946, where the post-war monetary system was set up, the greatest monetary economist of our times, Lord Keynes, warned against the key-currency approach and proposed instead a truly international currency (he called it 'Bancor'). Keynes knew that the real danger of the key-currency concept is not economic. It is that the key country becomes proud of its prominence, and arrogant. Then it makes, inevitably, the worst mistakes.

Keynes was conscious of this because he had seen it happen in his native Britain after World War I. Then, the pride in the key-currency role of the British Pound led to the re-establishment in 1928 of the old international exchange value of the British currency, a value that was much too high for the economic realities of the post-World War I period. This mistake, which Keynes sharply criticized at the time, undoubtedly was one of the major factors in the collapse of the Pound three years later, and in the worldwide sweep and depth of the Great Depression.

The United States, out of the key country's pride that Keynes had feared, has been wasting years that may never come back. When John Kennedy first became President we could probably have brought about a lasting solution in the form of a genuine world monetary system. We had the economic strength, and we also had unimpaired political leadership. France, which since has been fighting every attempt to establish such a system, had then neither the economic resources nor the political power to play even a negative role. Nor, it should be said, was there any lack of understanding of the problem. Proposals for world currency reform were well formulated and well known in 1960. But instead of pushing them, the United States government until 1966 fought every single one of them.

There are reasons for America's strange behaviour – as for that of Britain and of France. The *economics* of the problem are perfectly clear; but the *politics* are highly problematical. While economically the world (or at least the non-

113

Communist world) is one unit, politically there has been increasing fragmentation. Whereas the largest integrated economy of earlier days, the United States economy, was the result of political action which preceded and created economic unity, the world economy of today has emerged without political foundation.

Yet to 'coin money' has for many centuries been considered a prerogative of the political sovereign and indeed an essential attribute of sovereignty. The world monetary system we need would not require any political power. It would not be 'super-national', but it would have to be 'non-national'. It would have to take control of the world money and credit supply largely out of the hands of political powers and make it into a technical function to be decided by technical, that is, by purely economic, considerations. We did this to some considerable extent with respect to the domestic money supply when we created the modern central bank. But the perennial conflict in every country between the demand that the central bank follow governmental policy and the demand that money and credit be 'non-political' and determined by economic reasoning alone, shows that the 'non-national' money and credit function we need for the world economy would be a difficult political innovation.

The idea that any one country has full monetary sovereignty is, of course, absurd. If such a state ever existed, it disappeared the moment there was an international economy. Every country has always had to adjust its internal money and credit policies to the realities of its international economic position. The last British Labour government was not the first to find this out – but it was also not the first to resent it and to look for a scapegoat (though few earlier resentments found as ridiculous a scapegoat as the one the British picked in 1967, the 'Gnomes of Zürich'). While the authority needed to manage a world economic monetary and credit system would be both limited and under strict supervision and control of the member governments, it would still be an 'authority'. To have such an authority is, of course, the entire purpose. For what is needed is an agency that makes decisions for the best for the world economy and in contemplation of the total economic picture. These decisions will not always coincide with what this or that individual country at the moment thinks best for itself, nor can they be decisions by majority vote. They have to be the result of the best expert judgement by the people in charge of the monetary system of the world economy. Small wonder, then, that the major opposition to any movement towards such a system has been led by President de Gaulle, that is, by the most outspoken and uncompromising representative of traditional national sovereignty in the present world.

EMBRYO INSTITUTIONS

The history of the United States monetary system in the closing years of the nineteenth century and the opening years of the twentieth century is a close parallel to our present difficulties. And the Federal Reserve System as it emerged at the end of this period, in 1914, is a good illustration of how the politically seemingly impossible can be accomplished.

We know today that Bryan and his Silver Bloc were both right and wrong in the 1890s. They were right in their belief that the growth of the United States economy, and especially the economic survival of the poor and the debtors, were strangled by what today we call a 'liquidity crisis'. They were wrong in believing that monetizing silver, ie, inflation at home, could resolve the crisis.

But the 'Gold Bugs', the conservative Eastern bankers, were also both right and wrong. They were right in their opposition to Bryan. They were wrong, however, in denying that there was a crisis and a problem other than that created by the improvidence of farmer and manufacturer.

There was no problem for the 'Gold Bugs' because their superior economic strength enabled them to monopolize the available money and credit supply. But there was a problem all right – for the rest of the country.

The sudden influx of gold in the late Nineties from the newly discovered gold fields of South Africa and Alaska postponed the crisis. It did exactly what raising the price of gold would do now. But by 1905 the crisis was back. It was not resolved until the Federal Reserve System was created in 1914. This system gave the country a financial mechanism which allowed local autonomy and yet provided for central management of money and credit. It, in effect, enabled the same amount of credit to do almost twice, if not three times, as much economic work as before.

The historical parallel could be extended even further. What delayed creation of the Federal Reserve System until it was almost too late was rivalry among the major New York bankers, especially the Morgans, the Rockefellers, and the Stillman groups. Similarly today rivalry among the rich countries – especially the United States, Great Britain, and the Western Europeans – is delaying, already past the critical point, adoption of the needed world-credit mechanism.

In one important respect the United States is much better off than it was seventy years ago. There were then no institutions around that could possibly have done the job. The only thing known were systems that could not work: the anarchy and strangulation of the existing arrangements under which the larger New York banks each managed a monetary system in competition with its New York neighbours – each, to use present monetary terms, claiming to furnish the key currency for the whole country; and the central banks of the small, compact, and homogeneous European countries which would have been quite inappropriate to a country as large and diverse as the United

States. The Federal Reserve System had to be accepted on faith when Frederick Warburg invented it in despair over our monetary chaos.

Today we have, however, an available institution that has proved itself during well over twenty years of service – the International Monetary Fund created in 1946 and blessed since then by a succession of singularly able directors such as the Swede, Per Jacobsson, and the present director, the Frenchman, Pierre-Paul Schweizer – an institution that is universally respected.

Today we could, in other words, move fast, without much legislation, without a great deal of political debate, and without much furore in public. The most essential things for such a move have already been accomplished. We have, to repeat, demonetized gold to all intents and purposes as far as central banks, economists, and ministries of finance are concerned. When the public finds out, it will be a nasty shock; but by that time, the actual event is likely to be well in the past.

Indeed, the decisive step may have been made during 1967 in a highly technical and obscure arrangement between the central banks and the International Monetary Fund. Officially this concerns only the so-called 'drawing rights', that is, the rights of the central banks to borrow from the Fund. Yet, in fact, this agreement may have created the first genuine monetary mechanism of the world economy.

But it is possible still that we will kill off the world economy – and damage ourselves badly in the process – for want of a monetary and credit system appropriate to the economic achievement of the last twenty years. We may bring down on our heads the worst economic crisis the world has ever seen – and largely for lack of political courage, for vanity and pride in the dollar's role as a key currency, and because we preferred for twenty long years to be clever rather than right.

There is a second institution which the world economy

117

needs: a producing and distributing institution which is not purely national in its economic operations and point of view. The world economy needs someone who represents its interests against all the partial and particular interests of the various members. It needs an institution which has a genuine self-interest in the welfare of the world economy; an institution which, in pursuing its own goals, serves the world economy rather than any one of the individual national economies.

Traditionally such an institution has always been political, that is, a government. Since world economy is strictly an economic community, the institution which represents it will have to be an economic rather than a political institution. It cannot possibly function unless it respects the political institutions of the nation-state. The individual sovereign states, especially the big, strong, developed countries of the West, will not accept a super-government of any kind.

Such an institution, too, we already have at hand. Its development during the last twenty years may well be the most significant event in the world economy, and the one that, in the long run, will bring the greatest benefits. This institution is the 'multi-national' corporation.

For a long time businesses have been operating all over the globe. There were the great trading companies like the East India Company and, in the nineteenth century, the merchant bankers, especially those of London. Manufacturing industry too has long ventured abroad. International Harvester, Singer Sewing Machines, Standard Oil, and the Ford Motor Company all started to manufacture and sell in many countries almost the moment they got going in the United States. The chemical and machinery companies of Switzerland and the electronic and chemical firms of Holland started early to branch out internationally. Their home markets were too small to permit efficient operations.

Even in the case of the Swiss and the Dutch companies, yesterday's international operations were, however, different from today's. The operations outside the mother country were 'subsidiaries'. They were started primarily because tariffs created barriers to exports from the parent company. They were managed from the home office and, as a rule, by nationals of the home country. They were run in strict subordination to the needs and interests of the parent company at home. They were, in effect, sales agencies that manufactured abroad because they had little choice. They were not members of a multinational business but subsidiaries of a national one.

The difference shows, above all, in management structure. In the international company of yesterday, top management was typically also the management of the domestic operations, that is, of the parent company. Its main concern was with the original, the home market. The foreign or international operations were managerially quite subordinate. They had to be content with whatever time top management could spare them after the needs and demands of the parent company had been taken care of.

The famous organization structure which Alfred Sloan built for General Motors in the 1920's, and which, in most management textbooks, is still presented as the 'last word', shows this focus clearly. The domestic business of the company in the United States was organized in several big groups, each headed by a group executive who was a member of top management. The entire international business was in one separate group – but the head of this group was not a member of corporate top management and did not have a seat on the major committees that governed the company.

By contrast, the organization General Motors adopted in 1967 separates corporate top management from operations in any one geographic area, whether the United States, Europe, Asia, or Africa. And while the United

States still dominates in the managerial structure – in which respect the General Motors organization is well behind the economic realities of General Motors' business – it is at least now headed by a group executive with equal status in top management.

Increasingly the multi-national corporation structures itself so as to have only one top management which does not concern itself at all with the operations of the business in any one area. The operating units are not set up by area but rather by stages of development. The developed countries may be one major managerial responsibility, with the United States, Canada, Europe, and Japan in one organizational component. The developing areas – South America, India, the Middle East – might be the second managerial unit. And the undeveloped areas might be the rest.

The multi-national corporation of the period since World War II is largely the result of a deliberate planning effort which sees the economy of the entire Free World as one, and then tries to find the places where economic resources produce the greatest results and bring the highest returns. The rationale is increasingly not the inability to export over tariff barriers, but the need to plan, organize, and manage on a scale appropriate to the magnitude of technical and managerial resources required for modern technology, economical operations, low-cost production, and mass distribution.

The multi-national corporation tends increasingly to operate in terms of a world economy. This applies to the American companies that have been going into Europe, into joint ventures in Japan, or into fertilizer plants in India. It also applies to the Swiss pharmaceutical companies. After World War II the Swiss, rather than use their capital for expansion in Europe, deliberately poured it into the expansion of their United States subsidiaries until these became larger than the parent companies.

The multi-national corporation is multi-national in its

management personnel and increasingly in its scientific and technological foundations.

Up until and during World War II, it was almost unheard of to have nationals in senior management positions of foreign subsidiaries in developing countries. The first Indian in a senior management position of a Western-owned company – a director of Hindustani Lever, a subsidiary of Unilever – was appointed only after the start of World War II. For many years the New York industrial and trading firm of W. R. Grace & Co was almost alone in putting Latin Americans into the management of its subsidiaries in Peru, Chile, and Colombia – but then W. R. Grace was originally founded in Peru, albeit by an Irishman who soon moved to New York City.

It is still comparatively rare to find foreigners at the very top of the parent company in a multi-national corporation (though this is the case now in such major companies as IBM, Corn Products, and Standard Oil of New Jersey among the Americans, and in the Anglo-Dutch Shell Oil Company), but it is increasingly common to find foreign nationals just below the top.

The Swiss pharmaceutical companies, with their headquarters in Basle – perhaps the last remaining 'city-state' in Europe – were notorious for not admitting anybody but Basle natives into their management. In one of them a Frenchman is now in charge of scientific research, and an American is now the worldwide marketing coordinator who decides which of the company's plants – in Switzerland, in other Continental European countries, in Great Britain, in Japan, in Berlin, and in the United States – should supply which drug to which of the company's many markets the world over.

Increasingly, research and development are becoming

multi-national if only because they have to go where qualified people can be found.

An American pharmaceutical company has built a major research centre in England and another one in France; it is a partner with a Japanese company in a research centre near Tokyo. IBM has major technical centres in at least five countries – the United States, Britain, Germany, France, and Japan (and one in Latin America is probably not far off in the future). The list could be continued indefinitely.

The impact of this development has been great, even though few policy-makers in government have yet taken cognizance of it.

That there is a European Common Market in reality and not just on paper, one of the leading economists in Europe commented at a recent meeting, is the achievement of the American multi-national companies. This is also a main theme of Jean-Jacques Servan-Schreiber's *Le Défi Americain* (*The American Challenge*) which has been a European bestseller since it first appeared in 1967. American companies started out with the assumption that a Common Market makes sense. They were used to large markets and knew their economic impact and importance. They therefore began to plan, as soon as the Treaty of Rome was signed in 1957, in terms of a unified European market with free movement of goods, of people, and of capital from one end to another.

Few European businesses have so far acted as 'Europeans'. The Dutch, the Swiss, and the Swedes are the exceptions – they had already been 'multi-national' for some time. The Germans, by and large, did not see or understand the opportunity. The British, with few exceptions, still look 'overseas' rather than to the European continent. The French have been forced by their own government to resist European unification actively.

De Gaulle in particular had forced French industry to follow a course guaranteed to be least beneficial to French business, to the French nation, and to Europe. He had forced those French companies that were too small and too weak to compete successfully in the big integrated European Market to merge with one another. This has created companies that are still much too small – and too parochial – to compete successfully in the European Market, and yet so big as to endanger the French economy should they get into trouble. The one thing de Gaulle had achieved this way – it is a most dubious accomplishment – was to make almost certain that the French government will eventually have to take over the purely national dinosaurs he had foisted on France. For every business, sooner or later, gets into trouble.

But for the American company, in other words, the European Common Market would have been effectively sabotaged, whatever the provisions of the Treaty of Rome or the decisions of the Council of Ministers, by the narrow parochialism of most European business aided and abetted by European governments. Because of the American company, however, there is a functioning European Common Market today. As Servan-Schreiber points out, American business in Europe is the world's third-largest industrial complex, producing more overall than either Germany or Japan; and (as Servan-Schreiber does not seem to know) it is primarily the European investor who has financed the American expansion in Europe.

Similarly today in Latin America multi-national corporations – mostly American, of course, but also Dutch, Swiss, and to some extent British – are planning in terms of Latin America and of a Latin American Common Market. Most Latin American businesses, and even more their governments, worry how to protect themselves against economic integration. The multi-national outsiders take it for granted that Latin American economic integration is beneficial and ask: 'How can we speed it up?'

Most Latin Americans accept that economic integration is essential to the economic growth of their continent. Yet at a conference of Latin American businessmen which I attended in the spring of 1967 the major topic was: 'How can we escape getting hurt by a Latin American Common Market?' At the same time, an American multi-national company, Singer Sewing Machines, held a meeting of all its Latin American managers in the same hotel to discuss how to take fullest advantage of the economic integration of the South American continent. And a few weeks later a leading Dutch company in South America held a similar meeting.

Equally important is the contribution of the multi-national corporation as the engine of human development.

The most encouraging development in the poor nations today is the emergence, everywhere, of small clusters of men who are taking initiative and responsibility for the development of their own community. They are the men I call the 'entrepreneurs'. Though most of them come out of business, they do not confine themselves to business. They also take responsibility for the local hospital and the local university, for housing, public health, and local government. They were behind the revolution that prevented collapse into anarchy or Communist takeover in Brazil a few years back. They are the force behind whatever development there has been in India (for the Indian government, it is clear, has shown more capacity to retard development than to advance it). They are responsible for the remarkable achievement of the Chinese in Formosa, and so on. The leaders of these groups started, as a rule, as managers in the local subsidiary of a multi-national corporation, particularly in South America, or, as in Formosa, as local partners in joint ventures with a multi-national corporation.

The multi-national corporation is thus proving itself the most effective tool for the most important job to be done if there is to be economic and social development: the development of leaders.

Finally, the multi-national corporation is the only institution so far – and the only one visible on the horizon – that creates a genuine economic community transcending national lines and yet respectful of national sovereignties and local cultures.

The management meeting of one of the multi-national corporations is the only truly supra-national occasion in the world today. Here men of different nationalities, each a member of his own culture and proud of it, come together in a common purpose. The purpose is an economic one and therefore fairly easy to define, to measure, and to control.

The multi-national corporation is still a most imperfect institution. It abounds in problems – of organization, of personnel, and of communications. But its most serious problem is simply that 'multi-national' today in most parts of the world means 'American'. Even though there are a good many non-American multi-national corporations around, the Americans greatly outnumber all the others. Indeed the Americans are so visible that the others are rarely seen.

The Swedish multi-national companies may have grown much faster than the Americans. The Swiss or the Dutch company may very well dominate a certain industry in a small country, as for instance Philips of Holland dominates consumer electronics in a good many Latin American countries. But when people in Latin America talk of the 'octopus', they do not mean Philips. They rarely realize that the largest Inter-American company (other than the petroleum companies) is not a United States business, but an Argentinian one, Bunge & Born, whose plants for edible oils, cosmetics, paint, and soaps blanket the continent. Even those who know of the existence of Bunge & Born – and not many do – think rather of much smaller American businesses (eg, W. R. Grace & Co), when they discuss the 'multi-national' company.

The reason is, of course, that in the American company the economic power of a giant business is conjoined to the economic and political power of the world's richest and most powerful nation. No one is afraid of Swedish or Swiss 'imperialism', but the American multi-national company represents America. It represents managerial competence; but it also represents power. It, therefore, casts a much bigger shadow than its economic resources alone would justify.

This is greatly aggravated by the traditional insensitivity of the American government both in the executive branch and in Congress, which is a greater enemy of the multi-national corporation than General de Gaulle was or ever could be. He opposed it, of course, because it is multi-national. But the American government, unwittingly, wants it to be American first and last.

Our politicians in Congress, as well as our bureaucrats in the government offices, insist on treating the foreign affiliate of an American-based company as an extension of America. This is not only revealed in their subjection of the foreign affiliates to laws – anti-trust laws are one example – that are incompatible with the legal ethics of the countries in which they operate; it appears even more in regulations which impose on subsidiaries, that legally are citizens of a foreign and sovereign country, American policies in direct violation of the policies of the country of domicile.

A good example of this attitude – and of the harm it can do – is the imposition of our peculiar regulations for doing business with Communist countries (which, anyhow, are in violation of international law as we ourselves have always understood it) on companies domiciled in Canada but owned by an American parent. Nothing perhaps has created as much resentment against 'American domination' of Canada as this assertion of economic might over legal right.

The multi-national company is exceedingly profitable for the United States. For every dollar of investment in a subsidiary abroad creates many dollars of American exports within a very short time, not to mention a copious flow of dividends. In fact, investment abroad during the last twenty years has fuelled full employment in the United States, quite apart from making possible the maintenance of an American foreign policy based on lavish expenditures of money, largely earned by the multi-national companies through the exports and dividends they generate. Altogether the foreign-exchange earnings of the American-based multi-national corporation have become the largest source of income in the American balance of payments.

But, above all, the multi-national corporation is the one instrument, so far, which has effectively stimulated economic development way beyond anything governmental aid programmes have achieved. It is, therefore, in the best interests of the United States, as well as in the best interests of a developing, peaceful, prosperous world, to strengthen this instrument. To forget that it can only be effective if it acts as a 'multi-national' institution is extremely short-sighted.

Our politicians and our bureaucrats are still living in a world in which America was isolated. Their belief that the laws of international comity bind the foreigner but not the American government was gross stupidity even when we could afford it, that is, when America was the only healthy and strong economy around just after World War II. But that period came to an end with the Suez Crisis in the mid-Fifties. Now the United States needs the outside world as much as it needs us. American economic strength will count for naught unless we succeed in getting economic development going in a few important areas in the poor world. This, in turn, requires that we enable the multi-national corporation to do its job. Nobody else has done anything remotely as effective to date. It means self-restraint and respect for others in the treatment of what is a most important but also a fragile instrument and one that deserves a great deal more attention and care than the American government has so far given it.

If 'multi-national' remains a euphemism for 'American', the multi-national corporation will not long survive. The rapid development of new additional multi-national corporations with a non-American base is also essential to the survival of a valuable institution. It is important to the world economy, for instance, that the Japanese, rapidly growing into the second-strongest industrial nation of the Free World, develop their own multi-national corporations. This is also in the urgent interest of Japan, for the Japanese cannot hope to increase their exports much further unless they create manufacturing subsidiaries abroad, above all in the developed nations. As Japan's industry becomes increasingly highly developed and technological, it will need the export markets which only the subsidiaries of a multi-national corporation can adequately produce.

Europe, too, to remain competitive and viable in the world economy will have to develop new multi-national corporations, European in their scope, but also, like their American counterparts, capable of operating anywhere in the world. The great European economic revival of the last fifteen years is unlikely to maintain itself if it remains European alone. Not only is every single European country too small to be an adequate base for modern large-scale industry; any single area in the world is too small. A world economy requires businesses that can operate all over the world. It requires businesses that can think in terms of the world economy, can plan in terms of the world economy, can make and sell throughout the world economy.

At the same time, we will need to develop laws and policies for the multi-national corporation. It must be a genuine 'citizen' of the countries in which it operates. Yet it must be encouraged to be truly multi-national in its economic policies, in the opportunities, rewards, and incentives it offers its managers, its scientists, and its technical people, and, above all, in economic viewpoint. It must be encouraged – or at least not be discouraged from trying – to represent the unity of the world economy. This means that we need to alter American public law and policy to encourage this development.

I have said earlier that the traditional industries which have carried economic growth and development in the last twenty years are likely to have their greatest potential from now on in the poor, the developing, countries. In those countries the steel industry, the pharmaceutical industry, the electronics industry, the food-processing industry – and other old industries – are still growth industries. In those countries they are likely to be the major growth industries, since they can be built by importing technology, marketing knowledge, and management. For this reason alone the multi-national corporation needs to be developed and fostered. It is the best instrument we have so far for generating entrepreneurial, managerial, and technical competence in the developing nations, and also for calling forth and training genuine patriots willing and able to give leadership to their own countries and their own communities. But unless we make it an ever better instrument it is not going to survive. It will have to become truly multi-national in its mission, in the way it goes about its job, in the way it represents itself in the countries in which it operates, and in the way in which its home government treats it.

The world economy is not yet a community – not even an economic community. Yet the existence of the global shopping centre is a fact that cannot be undone. The vision of an economy for all will not be forgotten again. On the contrary, the worldwide communication of goods, services, standards of living, and ways of life will become ever more pervasive.

To develop into a genuine community the world economy needs to mature the institutions which it has today only in embryonic form. It needs a mony and credit system to provide circulation of purchasing power and investment. The very rich can, perhaps, prosper without it, for it is to them that money and credit flow in the absence of an adequate system. But the poor are deprived even of the little they have unless there is a functioning and well-managed monetary system.

The world economy needs the multi-national business – an institution based on global rather than on parochial economy, on finding and developing the opportunities for common growth, and equipped, in its own interest, to find and develop talents for responsible leadership.

The world economy is a great achievement – and one of business rather than of governments. It is the one positive achievement of the period since World War II. It is also a great opportunity – for economic growth as well as for creating a focus of unity in a fragmented and strife-torn world.

6. Making the Poor Productive

THE WORLD ECONOMY, this great opportunity for peace and growth, also generates a new threat of world revolution; the threat of a war of the poor and largely coloured peoples of the world, against the rich and largely white. There is greater disparity between the rich and the poor today than there has ever been before. It is increasingly a disparity within one and the same community of information. It is, at the same time, a disparity between races rather than a cleavage between classes.

This is new. China was much richer in the sixteenth century than England. But the Chinese gentlemen of Elizabethan times lived by and large on a very similar standard to that of the English gentlemen of the time, and so did the poor in the two countries. Today, however, the English working man (not to mention the American) lives much better than any but the exceedingly rich in most countries of the world can even dream about. Today it is the working man in the developed countries – indeed the poor on relief in these countries – who are the 'rich' in the world. The world has become divided into nations that know how to manage technology to create wealth, and nations who do not know how to do this. Within the rich nations technology has succeeded to an amazing extent in overcoming the cleavage between the rich and the poor, not by making the rich poorer, but by making the poor richer. It has thereby overcome to a very large extent that haunting spectre of the nineteenth century: class war within industrial society. But this has been replaced by a gap in income and opportunities between nations and cultures which never existed before.

Even if such a gap had existed in earlier times, it would not have mattered much. If, 400 years ago, the poorest Chinese had lived as well as the English duke, no one in England would have known about it. It would have been a traveller's tale on a par with stories about mermaids, unicorns, and other fables. Today, however, we see how other people live every day on the TV screen in our living-room, as direct, personal, immediate experience. This is a gap within one and the same community therefore.

The gap is primarily a gap between *races*. It has lately become fashionable to talk about the 'North-South gap', which implies that climate is responsible for the inability of two-thirds of mankind to break out of pre-industrial poverty.* This is a dangerous, self-deluding euphemism. The Chinese, the largest single group among the pre-industrial peoples, are Northerners to a man. All India lies north of the Equator; and the great bulk of the Indian population lives well north of the tropics. Every single population centre of Latin America – Mexico City, Buenos Aires, Bogota, Lima, Santiago, São Paulo, even Rio – lies climatically in the temperate zone. The fact is that all the world's rich nations, excepting only the Japanese, are white – and this includes the Russians of course – and all the world's poor nations, excluding only part of Latin America, are coloured.†

That the cleavage is above all racial shows clearly in the United States where the poor are predominantly Negro. The American Negro is indeed the representative of the

---

* This is, eg, the thesis of Gunnar Myrdal's recent book *Asian Drama* (Pantheon, New York, 1968).

† Even in Latin America the cleavages are largely racial, eg, between the fast-developing and largely white industrial triangle of Brazil – Rio, São Paulo, Bello Horizonte, and the wretchedly poor and entirely black North-east, or between growing, primarily Spanish Lima and the misery of the Andean Indians.

poor races within the richest nation. The American Negro problem is, therefore, the most important, the most acute, and perhaps the most dangerous instance of the worldwide problem. If the United States, the world's richest, technologically most advanced, and managerially most accomplished country, cannot bring about economic and social development of a non-white minority in its midst, then it will be taken as proven, by white and coloured alike, that there is an unbridgeable race conflict. By the same token, however, our ability in this country to resolve the problem of Negro destitution and to bring about rapid Negro development may also be the greatest possible contribution to the world race problem. The American Negro represents the world's pre-industrial rural people in industrial society. He represents also the most acute problem of 'colonialism': that is, of a growing inequality between the white and the coloured peoples of the world.

Yet race is not the explanation. Clearly non-white races are capable of development – as witness the Japanese with nothing in their background, let alone in their genetics, to make them part of the 'Judaeo-Christian Tradition'. The three non-Communist Chinese communities – Hong Kong, Formosa, and Singapore – have shown tremendous capacity for rapid economic and social growth in the last twenty years. At the same time, there are people of European stock, for instance up until recently the South Americans, who apparently do not have this easy capacity. And few areas in Latin America are as 'underdeveloped' or as 'colonial' as most of Spain or Sicily.

Whatever the reasons for it (and we know a good deal about them by now) it is clear that this cleavage will be overcome. Either the poor will become richer, or the rich will not long remain rich.

In the developed countries of North America, Western Europe, and Japan, we are being told today that we will work only half an hour a week by the year 2000 and enjoy a standard of living many times what it is today. This, put bluntly, cannot happen. One-third of a community cannot live in idle luxury while two-thirds toil eighty hours a week to gain the merest subsistence. It cannot happen when everybody knows how his neighbour lives. It cannot happen in the Global Shopping Centre the world economy has become. In one way or another the rich will be stopped from becoming ever richer while the poor at best remain where they are. One obvious way to prevent this is war – however much we may dislike hearing it. Mankind has always found it easier to destroy wealth than to create it. A succession of Vietnams would not, perhaps, prevent increases in the standard of living of the industrial world. But it would guarantee that they would not be accompanied by ever-increasing leisure. That the 'New Left', parroting the Mao line, looks forward to a 'succession of Vietnams' to 'bring down the white Imperialists', is criminal folly. But it is not insanity.

That no country has developed and become an advanced industrial country since World War I, more than fifty years ago, is therefore, a central social and political problem of the world economy. It is also (as said earlier) the greatest contrast between the fifty years before, and the years since, World War I. Between 1860 and 1910 a new major industrial nation emerged every twenty years or so. This created confidence throughout the world that economic development would indeed happen – to the point where nobody thought it necessary to have a *theory of economic development* or even to think much about it. It could be taken for granted.

But for fifty years now it has not happened. Unless we make it happen – and in enough places to show that development is not a matter of race but of the right policies and efforts – we face a spectre much grimmer than that of the class war which haunted the nineteenth century and the opening years of the twentieth century. We face the spectre of international race war.

This, needless to say, is above all a threat to the rich. The poor, coloured nations have little to lose. The United States and Russia have the most to lose. The Japanese would, in such a race war, be caught in a hopeless dilemma between allegiance to a white world to which they belong by reason of their economic and social stature, and allegiance to a non-white world to which they belong by reason of their culture, tradition, and skin colour – without being able to feel at home in either.

That such a race war need not happen, our own history proves. The international scene today greatly resembles the domestic situation in the advanced industrial societies of the North Atlantic in 1870 or 1880. Then, large economic communities had suddenly been created out of what had been scattered, isolated, largely self-contained units. Then, too, one group – large enough to be very visible but still only a minority – was getting rich fast while the majority seemed to be getting poorer and poorer. There were few intelligent or thoughtful people in the United States, England, or Germany in those days who did not know that the tension was becoming unbearable between the tremendous wealth, which the application of technology gave to a few, and the destitution of the many poor.

The class war haunted not only the Marxists, it haunted Henry James (who, in 1886, wrote a first-rate 'proletarian' novel, *The Princess Casamassima*, which is almost apocalyptic in its vision of the inevitable social catastrophe). It haunted J. P. Morgan the banker, and Henry Adams the historian, E. M. Forster, Ibsen, Gerhart Hauptmann, and Zola. To believe in 1880 that there could be a way out short of social cataclysm took either great courage or sublime smugness. What this way might be, even the optimists could not have foretold.

Yet when Marx died in 1883, the leadership of the working class in the Western world had already been lost by the revolutionaries – to the Fabians in England, to Gompers in America, and to the Revisionists in Germany. A decade later Friedrich Engels (in writing a new foreword to Marx's little classic, *The Conditions of the Working Classes in England*) had to admit that the poor were at least no longer getting poorer and that the Marxist 'inevitable revolution' had been delayed indefinitely.

Another twenty years later, by the time of World War I, Marxism in the developed countries had lost its dynamism. It had become an opposition within the system rather than the 'wave of the future'. That no developed country underwent a Communist revolution despite economic collapse after two world wars – and despite an unprecedented worldwide depression – few people in Marx's own lifetime would have considered possible.

But while Marxism has been overcome by our success in making the poor within the developed communities steadily richer, Mao has taken the place of Marx on the world stage. That Mao is 'unscientific' matters as little as that Marx could easily be confuted by any economist of the nineteenth century. What matters in Mao, as it mattered in Marx, is the vision. What matters, above all, is the hatred.

Almost twenty years ago President Truman proclaimed the goal of economic development for the poor nations in his Point Four Programme.

There have been rather impressive results. Measured quantitatively, economic growth has been a good deal greater than even the optimists of 1950 would have dared predict. Industrial production has been growing very fast indeed in a good many parts of the underdeveloped world, South America above all. The urban areas of Latin America – together a larger market in population as well as in purchasing power than Italy – are no longer underdeveloped. They are still poor but they are growing vigorously. Major economies in Latin America – not only Central Brazil but Mexico and the main regions of Colombia – may be close to, if not at, the 'take-off' point and ready for rapid, self-propelled growth. The Latins themselves now say: 'Latin America is no longer underdeveloped. It is simply badly managed.' The three non-Communist Chinese countries also, as said before, have shown amazing capacity to grow.

Similarly, there is within the vast mass of poverty that is India a sizeable modern economy, comprising 10 per cent or more of the Indian population, that is 50 million people. Pakistan too has been growing fast, and so has Iran.

Most encouraging is perhaps that agricultural production and productivity are suddenly jumping ahead – just when everyone had given up hope that world hunger could be averted. Food production in the underdeveloped nations has been growing faster than was planned in 1950 everywhere except on the West Coast of Latin America and in Argentina. But as everyone knows, population growth has been so fast that food output *per capita* throughout the early Sixties barely stayed even – and in drought years in India, for instance, it dipped dangerously below the subsistence level. In the late Sixties, however, there has been a change – the combined result of new seeds and varieties, more fertilizer, and of better farm marketing resulting from modest incentives to the farmer.

A 4 per cent rise in food production and an even faster rise in yields per acre such as has been reported for the decade of the Sixties is actually unprecedentedly high in human history. If maintained, it could double food output by 1985 in large parts of the world. The advances – especially the rapid spread of new and greatly more productive varieties of rice and wheat in South-East Asia and India – have made some conservative and even sceptical observers optimistic for the first time.

Lester R. Brown, the international expert of the United States Department of Agriculture and the man most responsible for the earlier forecasts of worldwide famine by 1970 – to the point where his pessimism all but discredited him among farming experts – said at the Second International Conference on the War on Hunger held in Washington in the winter of 1968:

We may be on the threshold of an agricultural revolution in many of the hungry, densely populated countries of the less developed world, particularly in Asia. Further, we are witnessing some advances in food technology which, if commercially feasible, can make quality diets available to millions at much lower costs.

Brown went on to hold out the prospect that by 1975 the poor nations in the Free World – and this would, of course, include India – would have an adequate diet for everybody (with the West Coast of South America the one remaining deficit area).

One could go on citing statistics to prove that the last twenty years have validated our development policies, and that the popular disappointment that is so much in evidence reflects ignorance of what has been achieved. *Per capita* income, it could be argued, would have gone up even faster than we expected twenty years ago but for the 'population explosion'. Latin America, it could further be said, has undergone, since 1956, the most severe depression in its entire history, and has yet shown continued capacity to develop and to grow. One might say that popular expectations both in the developed and in the developing countries were simply not realistic. It was foolish to expect a transformation of the entire world in a decade or two, though this is what President Truman's Point Four Programme and later President Kennedy's slogan of the 'Decade of Development' meant to a good many people. There has been, one might argue, no failure of development. There has been only a failure of the nerve to continue to work at development at the required level and with the required effort – just when our development efforts are really paying off.

All these arguments would be true. Yet the public would remain unconvinced. And the public would be right. Development as President Truman conceived it and as we envisaged it during the last twenty years, has been a failure. It has failed to produce the one essential result: the example of a new major growth economy. Development aid has resulted in the production of a lot of goods and a lot of jobs. But it has, so far, failed to generate the new vision. The economic results are considerable. The political and moral results, so far, are insufficient.

The demands of economic development are more exacting than we believed when President Truman announced his Point Four Programme twenty years ago. Above all, we need intelligence much more than money – and intelligence is a great deal scarcer.

WHAT WILL NOT WORK

We now understand that development can no longer be financed by agriculture, as it was in the nineteenth century. We understand that it can therefore no longer be 'automatic'. We understand that to provide investment capital from abroad, even on a planned and directed basis, will not, as it did in the nineteenth century, automatically produce development. And we understand the severe limitations on the effectiveness of foreign aid, and of government action altogether.

(1) In the nineteenth century agriculture in the settled countries was touched by technology only marginally. A new industrial civilization came into being next to the old community and economy of agriculture, but largely outside and separate from them.

The people of the countrysides I knew when I grew up – the English counties and the villages of Austria, Switzerland, and Northern Italy – still lived in their traditional culture and civilization, and altogether in their traditional world, as late as the nineteen-twenties. To be sure, they had a good many new tools such as the railways or electricity, but these had little impact on their way of life, on their view of themselves, and on their

139

social, political, or intellectual vision. They had had only limited impact on their economy. The smoky city was just over the horizon. But it had not yet impinged on what was essentially a pre-industrial world. And this was even more true of France and of Scandinavia.

At the same time, the food needs of the nineteenth century 'population explosion' in the countries that were 'developing' then, were satisfied by crops from new virgin lands, crops from soil that had never before been put to the plough.

Eastern Germany, Hungary, Western Russia, the Ukraine, and Rumania became overnight major grain producers and exporters where they had earlier been wastes or at best grazing lands. Above all, there were America, Argentina, Canada, and Australia, the new 'bread baskets', without which the exploding populations of the new industrial cities of Europe and of America's Eastern Seaboard would have starved. Agriculture in these countries was not 'advanced' technologically. Nor did it need to be. It took into cultivation new lands, where anything produced was so much increment, so much surplus.

As a result the population explosion of the nineteenth century was economic opportunity rather than threat. Population in the industrializing countries, that is, in Europe, in North America, and finally in Japan, grew almost as rapidly as it is growing now in the developing countries. But instead of putting pressure on the food base of the economy, it created markets for the agriculture of the new 'bread baskets'.

Because agriculture in the developed countries of the nineteenth century was itself undeveloped, the new countries, whether in Central and Eastern Europe or overseas in the Americas and in the Pacific, could finance their development by farm exports from their new soils. They financed themselves largely by exchanging the products of a technologically pre-industrial agriculture on new land against the manufactured products of the new industries in the old countries. In this way they not only obtained the manufactured goods for their own population, they also financed their capital imports.

The United States obtained more capital between 1870 and 1890 to build transcontinental railways than all the money (adjusted for changes in purchasing power) we have spent in aid to the developing countries in the last twenty years. Not a penny of it was ever paid back. The American railways defaulted on their bonds and wrote off their shares. The money was, however, given against ample security: the new fertile soil the railways were opening to settlement. Europe was repaid by the cheap food it received to feed her urban masses. And the loans to Russia until 1900 (after which they became political and military subsidies) equally reaped ample returns in the form of abundant, cheap, export crops for the urban masses of industrial Europe.

The Japanese pattern of development was only slightly different.* Though Japan had no new land to place under the plough, her development was financed by the exports of silk. While a very old crop, silk had always been an unattainable luxury except for the very rich. Japanese exports made silk for the first time available to the middle class in the industrial countries of the West. Silk exports, in turn, gave Japan the foreign exchange to import machinery and manufactured products from the West. But while the Japanese farmer thus paid for the modernization of his country, he remained largely untouched by it himself. Until

* As has been shown by James L. Nakamura: *Agricultural Production and Economic Development of Japan 1873–1922* (Princeton, 1966).

141

World War II, the Japanese village was pre-industrial in its economy as well as in its culture, and largely in its standard of living.

It is no longer possible, however, to finance development out of agriculture. It is equally impossible any longer to keep the village out of modern society and insulated from modern technology.

Today, agriculture in the developed countries (excepting only Russia) has become the most technologically advanced and the most industrialized of basic industries. Productivity differentials in agriculture between developed and underdeveloped economies far outrun the differentials in manufacturing. We expect a new steel mill in an under-developed country to be one-third to one-half as productive as a steel mill in the old industrial areas of Europe – whether productivity is measured per hour of labour, or per dollar of capital. But we are not surprised to see productivity differentials of 10 to 1 or even 25 to 1 between the agricultures of the developed, highly industrial countries and the agricultures of the underdeveloped countries.

Fifty years or so ago, rice yields per acre in China – and even in India – were higher than those in the West. Today the yield per acre of irrigated rice in California is ten times (or more) that of similar land in China. China, in turn, produces three times as much rice on the same irrigated acre as does Indonesia – and at least twice as much rice as well-managed and well-watered farms in India. No matter how low the incomes of the farmers in Indonesia or India, they cannot possibly be low enough to enable them to compete with the Californians. They can barely compete with the Japanese, despite the high costs of growing rice on the steep hillsides of the narrow Japanese valleys.

Equally important: agriculture can no longer be insulated socially or technologically. In the nineteenth century it was possible, so to speak, to make 'one revolution at a time'. The cities changed drastically, but the rural areas remained largely unchanged. Indeed Marx considered them incapable of change. Today the countryside is the sector most violently affected by technological change and least capable of absorbing it. This is, of course, the underlying fact in the radical revision of Marx by Mao and Castro, with their scorn for the urban masses and their reliance on the 'revolutionary *élite*' on the farm.

Modern technology, the automobile and the truck, the transistor radio and the loudspeaker, as well as electric power, integrate rural society into city society. They abolish rural society as such, dissolve it into a poor and underprivileged component of an urban world. A hundred years ago the city was the exception and society was essentially the countryside. Today rural society rarely exists any more and can only be defined by whatever city-blessings it does not enjoy.

Raul Prebisch, the brilliant Argentinian economist who has become the spokesman for the poor countries at international economic conferences, is right in his constant demand that the rich countries should grant the agricultural products of the underdeveloped countries free access to their markets. The agricultural protectionism of the developed countries (with the United States one of the worst actors) is a scandal.

But abolishing the barriers to the entry of farm products from the poor countries to the markets of the developed Western nations would probably not make enough difference. In the nineteenth century the then developed areas of the West could not have survived without steadily increasing food imports. The agitation against the English Corn Laws and in favour of free trade in food was not meant to help foreign growers. Its purpose was to save the English industrial masses from starvation. Today most of the industrial countries have become food-surplus producers.

Even Great Britain might well become tomorrow a

143

large food producer, raising all the meat, butter, eggs, and cheese her own population could possibly consume, and still have enough left over to convert the deficit in the English balance of trade into a sizeable surplus. If she were to join the Common Market and stop the near-monopoly on access to the British consumer which she has granted to the farmers of the 'White Dominions' (especially those of Australia and New Zealand), a rapid upswing in British farm production – above all in meat and dairy products – could ensue. This was, of course, one reason why General de Gaulle, beset by unsaleable farm surpluses in France, was not eager for Britain to enter the Common Market.

Under these conditions, agriculture in the poor countries simply cannot compete, no matter how low the income of their farmers. Where agriculture provided the investment capital for industry in the nineteenth century – and still did in Stalin's Russia – it requires today very large capital investments of its own. 'Forty acres and a mule' no longer make a productive farmer. They make a rural pauper. The fundamental agricultural equation on which nineteenth-century development was based no longer balances out.

(2) Capital investment from abroad is therefore no longer the answer to development. In fact, heavy capital investment from abroad may become a barrier to development rather than the spur many still consider it to be.

The nineteenth century, as the example of the American railways illustrates, invested a great deal more capital abroad, and especially in development areas, than has been invested in aid since World War II. While international trade has been growing fast and is at a higher level than it was in the nineteenth century – both absolutely and in relation to total production – capital investment lags far behind. The American investments in multi-national corporations, large though they have been, represent a much smaller fraction of United States national income than did the European investments in American railways a century ago.

But the nineteenth-century capital investment was investment 'abroad' only in a geographic sense. Most of it went into productive facilities that were an extension of the lender's domestic economy. Most of it, whether put into harbours or railways or mines, served to produce food and raw materials for the lender's industrial centres in the developed areas.

In financial terms this meant that the foreign investor was being repaid out of what his own countrymen paid for the grain, the cotton, or the copper whose supply his investment had made possible. There was no 'transfer problem'. The investment liquidated itself. To service it financially, whether in the form of interest payments, through dividends, or through amortization of the capital, did not entail withdrawal of currency from the debtor country.

Such investment is by no means unknown today.

Most of the billions invested in petroleum production around the world are being serviced out of the monies paid by the users who, of course, are the developed industrial countries. This applies also to capital invested in copper mines in Chile or in Rhodesia or to the very large amounts now being invested in iron ore or in bauxite in Australia.

But the bulk of development investment today is of a different kind. It aims at creating capacity to produce for the domestic markets of the country in which the investment is made. It does not, in other words, generate the exports out of which the investment can be repaid. This is, above all, a consequence of the change in the position of agriculture, which makes it impossible for the farmers of the poor countries to compete in the markets of the developed countries, and unnecessary for the developed countries to buy from the underdeveloped ones. In fact, the food

needs of the underdeveloped countries are so great that any
increase in production would have to go first towards feeding their own masses, even if the developed countries could
still use large food imports.

Investment of capital in the developing countries, other
than in extractive industries, therefore, tends to create a
foreign exchange liability that is not offset, as it was a
hundred years ago, by foreign exchange earnings created by
the investment. In short order the investment thus begins to
create a demand for foreign exchange to service it and
begins to exert pressure on an already feeble balance of
payment. The investment may generate wealth in the
debtor country and create jobs. But it also threatens to
drain away capital and to create 'disinvestment'. At the
least, it requires a steady new inflow of capital from abroad
to prevent a shrinkage of the capital base of the economy.

This has been painfully demonstrated in Latin
America. It explains in large measure why the last ten
years have been years of trouble there. Latin America,
throughout the mid-Fifties, attracted almost as much
capital as her development economists wanted. As a result, she grew very fast during that period. But when the
inflow diminished a little, crisis immediately set in. Payments on the loans and dividends remitted abroad began
to use up whatever foreign exchange was available. If a
country suspended payments abroad to counteract this,
its credit promptly disappeared and with it foreign capital altogether. If, on the other hand, a country maintained its foreign payments to maintain its credit, its
growth came to an end as its capital base shrank, thus
creating a deflationary crisis. This too brought to an end
the influx of foreign capital.

It has been argued many times in the last twenty years
that the developed countries should organize systematic
capital investment in the underdeveloped countries, in such

a way as to replace the automatic flow of investments of the nineteenth century. But this, while plausible, cannot work. They could, of course, provide investment for a while. But even if heavily subsidized – through artificially low interest rates guaranteed by the rich countries for instance – serving large foreign investment, whether given as loans or in the form of equity, would not be possible. Of course, the underdeveloped countries need capital badly. But they cannot depend on getting it abroad. Nor can the investor abroad be expected to invest heavily in underdeveloped areas. Again the nineteenth-century equations no longer balance out.

Development in the nineteenth century was possible because agriculture, even in the most highly developed country, remained underdeveloped. The moment agriculture became a leading industry itself, the system ceased working. To most nineteenth-century economists – and to many economists today – the mechanism of 'complementary trade' – a kind of economic perpetual motion machine – appeared 'natural' and permanent. Economic development, it seemed, would follow automatically if only trade were allowed to take its natural and inevitable course.

We need all the trade we can get – in that respect Raul Prebisch is right and deserves to be listened to for the sake of the developed countries as well as for that of the underdeveloped world. Capital investment is also needed, and more than we have had in the last ten years. But we can no longer depend on either as the motive power of economic development. All it can be is the catalyst.

(3) But if 'trade not aid', however beguiling, is an unrealistic slogan, 'aid' alone will also not do the job of economic development.

Whenever the developed countries face a problem of poverty, whether domestic or international, their first impulse is to solve it through distributing wealth. Unfortunately, there is not enough wealth around to get them anywhere except to disillusionment.

147

John Pincus of the Rand Corporation has recently*
computed how much it would take to tackle the world's
poverty problems through distributing the wealth of the
rich nations. To raise *per capita* income everywhere to
$1,000 a year – still less than one-third of the United
States figure – would require 1·4 thousand billion dollars
a year, that is, more than the total annual income of all
the developed countries and more than 200 times as
much as we have ever spent on aid in any one year. Even
to raise the income of the poor nations to that of the
richest among them – eg, Northern Spain, Formosa, or
Chile – we would have to distribute each year more than
the total United States national income. Distributing
wealth may be good social justice, but it has always been
absurd economics.

Aid, in other words, can only be a stimulant. The main
growth has to come out of the resources of the poor countries themselves. Effective aid acts as a catalyst releasing
local energies. But aid, unless carefully planned and ruthlessly administered, may also tend to inhibit the energies of
the recipient rather than release them. This has become
apparent in America's surplus-food aid, which, while so
very well-intentioned, is actually causing development
failure.

The United States by giving away its own food surpluses to feed the poor of the developing countries has
often aggravated their agricultural stagnation. It has encouraged politics that cut back rather than improve food
production at home (such as nationalizing the grain trade
in India). It has led to gross misallocation of resources,
as recipient countries (and India is only one example) felt
free to invest in politically palatable but economically

* In the Fall 1967 issue of Columbia University's *Journal of World Business*.

dubious prestige projects – steel mills typically, or jet planes – rather than in agriculture.

The rich countries need to maintain famine relief of starving people; they need to create a 'World Food Bank' for this purpose. But beyond relief for people actually threatened with starvation, food relief should be given only sparingly. It destroys the incentive of the local farmer to increase his output; and there is no incentive to which farmers respond as fast and as reliably as a higher cash income. The 'aid programmes' that have worked give the farmer new hybrid seed which greatly increases his yields and his income. Such aid will generate development.

The United States has had good results with aid programmes in such countries as South Korea and Formosa. In both places there was a 'temporary emergency'. In Korea, a poor but industrious population was overcome by the disaster of the invasion from North Korea and of the ensuing war. Here aid restored a capacity that had been there before. Similarly in Formosa, highly skilled, highly industrious and proud Chinese refugees needed a helping hand to get going again. The Chinese who crossed over to Formosa from the mainland were, by and large, the best trained and the most successful Chinese of their generation – as were the ones who fled from Shanghai to Hong Kong. These two groups contained some two-thirds perhaps of all modern knowledge, technical, economic, and social, China had been able to amass in the first fifty years of the century. No wonder that aid succeeded in sparking rapid development in Formosa.

But where aid is used to substitute for local energies, it never works.

The 'depressed areas' of England and Scotland have soaked up as much aid as was ever put into any 'under-

developed country' overseas. Yet, thirty years of subsidies later they are still as 'depressed' as ever. And so is
Appalachia in America's mid-continent, or Italy's 'Mez-
zogiorno' in the south. The revival of New England did
not occur in the old textile towns on which aid had been
lavished. It came out of the universities which, without
any 'aid', spawned the new 'science industries'.

Aid, by its very nature, will flow towards problems
rather than towards opportunities. It will go where the
needs are greatest rather than where the results are. It will,
therefore, tend to create – or, at least, to perpetuate – dependence.
This is as true of aid at home as much as of aid abroad.

It has dawned on us lately that the social worker in the
big cities often causes the very misery she works so hard
to relieve. She causes dependence. Her clients are treated
as 'relief cases' and – unintentionally – prevented from
even attempting to get back on their own feet, indeed
often penalized if they try (by termination of relief payments, for instance).

'Philanthropy', the early nineteenth century learned,
harms the 'self-respecting poor'.* But reliance on aid also
encourages diversion of scarce resources to the wrong projects whose development impact is minimal.
In any aid programme, the economist, especially the development economist employed by government, tends to

---

* The basic work on this is Karl Polanyi's *The Great Transformation* (New York and London, 1944) which deals with the failure of
the charity programmes of the early Industrial Revolution to aid the
uprooted poor of England's pre-industrial rural society. A good deal
of the aid programmes we have tried in the pre-industrial rural
society of the poor nations – including the pre-industrial rural
Negro society in America's twentieth-century cities – is quite similar
to England's abortive Speenhamland system of 'development aid' in
the early 1800s.

impose his own values on the choice of priorities and projects. Understandably he likes things that look big, impressive, and 'advanced': a petrochemical plant, for instance. He likes the things he knows the poor 'ought' to have. He has nothing but contempt for the 'frivolous', eg, small luxuries. In this respect there is amazingly little difference between the Russian planners and the economists in the governments of the most 'capitalist' nation.

The factory girl or the salesgirl in Lima or Bombay (or the Harlem ghetto) wants a lipstick. She lives in a horrible slum and knows perfectly well that she cannot, in her lifetime, afford the kind of house she would like to live in – the kind of house her counterpart in the rich countries (or the white suburbs) can afford. She knows perfectly well that neither she nor her brothers can get the kind of education they would like to have. She probably knows also that – if lucky – she will marry some boy as poor as herself and as little educated who, within a few years, will start beating her out of sheer despair. But at least she can, for a few short years, try to look like the kind of human being she wants to be, respects, and knows she ought to be. There is no purchase that gives her as much true value for a few cents or annas as cheap cosmetics.

A cosmetics plant gives more employment per dollar of investment than a petrochemical plant. It trains more people capable of developing and running a modern economy. It generates managers, technicians, and salesmen. Yet the economist despises it; and the reliance on aid makes it possible for his moralism to prevail over economics and for his desire for control to prevent development.

Aid is necessary. It is needed not only for the relief of the victims of catastrophe such as famine, earthquake, or pestilence. It is needed to prevent collapse in areas such as the Brazilian North-East or the Black Ghetto of the American city, where centuries of injustice have created frustration, hate, and the habit of defeat. And because the world is one community, aid is needed from the rich to the poor and suffering wherever either may be.

But philanthropy is, so to speak, only 'first-aid' to be administered 'until the doctor comes'. Only for those completely bereft and for those bound to die anyhow is first-aid as good as what the doctor can do. To believe that aid can, or should be, the carrier of development means, in effect, condemning the poor countries to no development at all.

The class war was not overcome during the late nineteenth and early twentieth centuries by philanthropy. The liberals then were as ineffectual in solving the nineteenth-century problem of poverty as the liberals now have been ineffectual in solving the problems of the black ghettoes of America's cities. The settlement houses, whether Toynbee's in London or Jane Addams' in Chicago, gave a new conscience to a whole generation of the rich, but they had practically no impact on the poor. What overcame class war was, firstly, new technology – electric power, above all. This technology created new, more productive, and therefore better-paid jobs. Secondly, the class war was overcome by education, which gave an increasing number of the children of the poor the opportunity to break out of the 'class' to which Marxist ideology had condemned them. But above all, what overcame the class war was Frederick Taylor's *Scientific Management*, which first applied knowledge to work and thereby made the labourer productive for the first time.

The rich countries achieved whatever success they had through making the poor productive. The test for aid to poor nations is therefore whether it makes them capable of being productive. If it fails to do so, it is likely to make them even poorer in the – not so very – long run.

To be sure, development requires substantial amounts of money both in aid and in investment. But to succeed, these must come as support to effective and going efforts of the local community. Aid, for instance, might be in the form of matching grants conditional upon the organization of local efforts by the recipient. Investment might be geared to a country's rate of development.

The developed countries must favour nations that have proved their ability to build if times are propitious. Examples would be Brazil, Colombia, Iran, and Pakistan. At the same time, we need to be able to say to other areas: 'Prove your willingness to develop and then we will help you. So far, you have wasted opportunity.' An example is Argentina which, for the last fifty years, has wasted substance as if by malice aforethought and turned herself from a highly developed and rich country into an underdeveloped and poor one. Another example might be Indonesia. No matter how serious a 'problem' such countries are, we cannot afford to waste exceedingly scarce resources on them. Help in such a situation only makes things worse. But we also need to be able to go to work where the projections of the economists did not predict development, but where, none the less, it is happening. The non-Communist Chinese communities are examples.

This may sound very hard-boiled – and it is. But the choice before us is between wasting aid (and investment) and obtaining real development from it. All aid can do is to encourage and stimulate. We, therefore, had better use it to give us what we need the most: highly visible examples of rapid, self-generated growth.

(4) The United States now knows further that 'intergovernmental programmes' do not produce development. An economy cannot be developed from the outside anyhow – but least of all by 'government-to-government' efforts, whether the foreign government be 'democratic' or 'Communist'.

Foreign governments cannot impose priorities on other countries. They cannot, therefore, resist local pressure to divert scarce development resources, both of money and of men, into the unproductive, the non-development projects.

The example is United States 'military aid' to South America. It has served mainly to feed the ego of generals and colonels. Yet military aid not only uses up scarce funds. An aeroplane or a destroyer is not much use unless fuel for it, lubricants, and spare parts are supplied year-in and year-out. Thus, every dollar spent on military aid for Latin America has not only taken away a dollar that should have gone into development; it has created a demand for an additional five or ten dollars to be diverted out of slender foreign exchange resources to maintain the generals' toys.

The Russians have been just as unable to resist the blackmail of the military.

But development needs, above all, concentration on a few major priorities.

Concentration is fundamental to any successful effort; yet no principle has been so consistently violated in the development efforts of the last twenty years. The developed countries have spent a fair amount of money. We have invested very substantial human energies of good, able, dedicated people. But we have wasted resources by spreading them out so thin that they could not have impact. We have taken, so to speak, the flood waters of the Nile to irrigate the whole of the Sahara. As a result, the soil gets moist all over – but just when the first green shoots come up, the soil is parched again.

This is elementary; but it will not be heeded if inter-governmental efforts are central to development policies. Altogether an inter-governmental programme lacks the multiplier effect needed to produce development. It tends to favour immediate problems over results. Problems are political pressures; problems are visible; problems, above all, are clearly defined. Results, however, are tomorrow; they are risky. And no one has a vested interest yet in results.

Governments must be problem-oriented. For governments are, of necessity, protective institutions. But there is no development potential in problems. All one can do in taking care of a problem is to prevent collapse. One cannot build the new this way.

Governments have to act as governments. They cannot subordinate other goals to the priorities of economic development. They must put other considerations – military or political – first. They must, therefore, misallocate development resources.

This is a fancy way of saying that there are always non-economic strings to a relationship between governments. The Russians who see this quite clearly and make no bones about it, may actually be more realistic than we in the West have been when we insist that all we are interested in is the rapid economic development of our foreign partners. Their realism has enabled the Russians to be highly selective and to give aid only to a few countries with a clear and open political rationale behind their programme. Why Russia's aid has been concentrated on India, Egypt under Nasser, Cuba, and the Congo needs little explanation. None of it was meant to produce 'development'.

Government is needed in a worldwide development policy. The governments of the developed countries must give direction to such a policy. Even more needed is effective, purposeful government in the poor countries. The ineffectiveness of government is indeed a central problem in most developing countries. Conversely, that Mexico has had effective government for thirty years has surely been a major factor in her rapid economic expansion.

But there is one thing government cannot provide: the individual's sense of achievement.

Yet this is the essential element of development. What is needed in this world today is not primarily wealth. It is a vision. It is the individual's conviction that there is opportunity, energy, purpose to his society, rather than problems, inertia, and hopelessness.

If wealth were the one prerequisite America's black

155

ghettoes would be no problem at all. Black Harlem is one of the world's wealthiest communities – fifth or so in *per capita* income of all communities outside North America and Europe, and easily the richest of all Negro communities in the world. Altogether three-fifths of all American Negro families are above the 'poverty line'. And what is considered 'poverty' in the United States – ie, a family income below $3,500 a year – is considered great wealth almost everywhere else. What makes Harlem – and our other black ghettoes – a slough of despond and a cesspool of hatred is the feeling of hopeless stagnation and impotence that pervades it.

Development is thus largely a matter of the dynamics of individuals and of local communities. These can be supplied only by our succeeding in generating local, responsible initiative and in multiplying human energies. Government can stimulate these – or stifle them. But it cannot provide the energies.

– AND WHAT MIGHT WORK

Earlier in this chapter I said that everyone in the nineteenth century took economic development for granted. An exception is Japan. In Japan there was a famous debate, lasting two decades, over the conditions of economic development and the forces making for it. But the debate was not between economists. It was between practical entrepreneurs who founded and built businesses rather than textbook models of a development economy.

The very names of Yatarŏ Iwasaki (1834–85) and Eiichi Shibusawa (1840–1931) are known outside Japan to only a few specialists. Yet their achievements were a good deal more spectacular than those of Rothschild, Morgan, Krupp, or Rockefeller. Iwasaki founded and built the Mitsubishi group of industries – to this day the largest manufacturing complex in Japan and one of the world's largest

and most successful business groups. Shibusawa founded
and built more than 600 industrial companies during his
ninety years of life, which extended well into the twentieth
century. Between them, these two men founded something
like two-thirds of Japan's enterprises in manufacturing and
transportation. No other two men in any economy have had
a similar impact.

And for twenty years, till Iwasaki's early death aged 51,
these two men engaged in a public and often acrimonious
debate. 'Maximize profits,' said Iwasaki. 'Maximize
talents,' said Shibusawa.

Today we know that both were right. For development
we have to multiply the productivity of capital. We have to
attract the available capital of an economy into growth
opportunities. But for development we also have to multiply human resources. We have to attract the human energies of a society into growth opportunities. Wherever we
have disregarded these lessons – as in most of our own
governmental programmes in the United States of the last
twenty years – we have failed to generate development.

Both Iwasaki and Shibusawa worked for a strong and
achieving, rather than for a rich, Japan. Both men knew
that the essence of development is not to make the poor
wealthy; it is to make the poor productive. For this, one
needs to make productive the fundamental resources. One
needs to multiply talent and capital.

Japan was exceptional in the nineteenth century for more
reasons than that she was the one non-white, non-Western
country to become a modern economy. She was poorer than
any of the white countries – probably poorer than any of
the developing countries of today (except perhaps Bolivia
or Tibet). She was an old country and densely populated.
She had silk to export and this paid for imports of manufactured goods and industrial raw materials. But she did
not have new land to put under cultivation. She could not
therefore, as did the new countries outside Western Europe,
rely on imported capital. She could not have serviced such

capital through exports of food or industrial raw materials.

But what made Japan atypical for the nineteenth century makes her typical for today. For today the rich countries not only have to learn how to develop non-white, non-Western countries. Above all, we have to learn how to develop densely populated countries which cannot depend on expanding commodity exports to the developed world. We have to learn how to develop countries which cannot depend on a large inflow of capital from abroad and would be unable to service it. We have to develop countries where the available capital must go into facilities that produce for the domestic – or at best, for a regional – market.

All this Japan accomplished a hundred years ago. The model of development today has to be Japan rather than the United States or Russia or, indeed, any of the white countries.

Japan accomplished development Iwasaki's way, that is, by attracting and mobilizing every penny of capital within the country. As a result, shortage of capital never impeded Japan's development though she did not borrow abroad or depend on foreign investors.

Japan also walked Shibusawa's way and attracted, trained, and mobilized every ounce of human energy. She put to work on growth opportunities all the talent a gifted people could muster.

A well-known story about Shibusawa reports that he refused a loan for a badly needed sugar refinery because the company's promoter was not an educated man. The story is usually told to illustrate Shibusawa's prejudices; and, indeed, the sugar refinery, financed by somebody else, became eminently successful. But the story also illustrates the priority Shibusawa's Japan throughout the entire period gave to the formation of human capital.

If Iwasaki's entrepreneurship gave Japan the highest rate of monetary capital formation ever recorded, Shibusawa's stress on human energy gave Japan, within thirty years, the highest rates of human-capital formation and of literacy ever recorded. Shibusawa himself, for almost fifty years, acted as an unofficial and unpaid 'management development centre'. He counselled and guided hundreds of young civil servants, businessmen, and executives. He was untiring in organizing training programmes and management clubs, setting up all kinds of courses, seminars, and discussion groups. Where Iwasaki left behind a large and highly profitable business concern, Shibusawa's monument is Hitotsubashi, Tokyo's famous economic university.

Yet, the two men differed in their emphasis only. Iwasaki could not have succeeded had he not known how to find and develop large numbers of brilliant young men whom he formed into a worldwide management team of the highest *esprit de corps* and competence. And Shibusawa's command post was the Dai-Ichi Bank which he built into one of the major financial institutions of the country.

The economics of development rests on the twin pillars of developing people and multiplying capital. To get development, both have to be organized. And there must be concentration on both.

In brief, we need to organize the 'contract-growing' of money and the 'contract-growing' of people.

(1) Of the two tasks, 'contract-growing' of money is actually old and familiar. To do the job the nineteenth century invented the venture banker. First conceived around 1820 by the French social philosopher, Saint-Simon, the venture banker's task is to mobilize and multiply the financial resources of society and to switch them from less to more productive investments, that is, from yesterday to tomorrow. Where the Rothschilds were originally money-lenders, Saint-Simon's banker was to become the developer of his economy. Instead of making his profits out of scarcity and need as the money-lender does, the venture banker was to make profits out of growth and newly created productive capacity.

It was this venture bank, as first embodied around 1850 in the famous 'Credit Mobilier' of the Brothers Pereire in Paris, that industrialized Continental Europe. The great banks of Europe, such as the Deutsche Bank which was founded in 1870 with the express purpose of converting Germany from a poor agricultural nation into the leading industrial power of Europe, were all set up as venture banks and created to multiply the productivity of capital. They were all founded to make possible development without large-scale import of capital from abroad. This was also the task J. P. Morgan set himself when he returned from London to his native America in the years after the Civil War.

At the same time, in far-off Japan, and without benefit of European theory, Iwasaki, the former soldier, started similarly to 'contract-grow' capital. Typically, the Mitsubishi empire he built was organized around a major venture bank.

The one difference between those days and today is that we know much better how to organize development banks. In fact, great contributions to development have already been made by such banks. The World Bank, and its affiliate, the International Finance Corporation, started to encourage such banks all over the world in the mid-Fifties.

These banks multiply the capital resources of the community. For every dollar of imported capital from abroad they attract five additional dollars of domestic capital. Their own capital thus represents a multiplication by five of the imported dollars from abroad. Then, for every dollar they themselves invest in a venture out of their own capital they raise another five dollars of investment capital from other sources in the community. By the time they have finished financing a venture, every dollar of imported capital should have triggered the investment of another twenty-five dollars of local capital. And then

160

each of these twenty-five dollars should trigger an additional very large amount of indirect investment from local sources – the way every dollar invested in automobile manufacturing leads to the investment of many more dollars in tyre plants, roads, motels, service stations, and so on.

The success and profitability of a venture banker depend on his ability to mobilize other people's capital, and especially local capital. The venture banker's profit comes essentially from finding investment opportunities for other people's money. It is a commission, a brokerage fee, an underwriting fee, or a participation. The greater the multiplier impact of his own dollar, the greater his profit. Maximizing profits is, therefore, the right motto for the venture banker. It is a direct index of his social and economic contribution and usefulness. Iwasaki in Japan a hundred years ago considered himself as good a patriot and indeed as great an idealist as Shibusawa.

The test of foreign aid or foreign investment in development, therefore, is not how much money has been invested. Rather it is how much of other people's money the money from abroad has mobilized, and especially how much *local* money it has mobilized. The less money the development banker needs from abroad the better he does his job. Ideally, he knows 'how to make bricks without straw', that is, how to find and attract local capital in large quantities without putting in any money of his own, let alone any money from abroad. He gets paid – and paid handsomely – for creating the opportunity and the demand. He gets paid for knowledge and imagination. He gets paid for creating wealth rather than for possessing it.

The development banks that the World Bank has started in the last ten or fifteen years have produced more development than all the aid programmes together, even though the amount of money invested in them from foreign sources is negligible.

But perhaps the best example of development banking is a totally private 'contract-grower', ADELA, an international investment company started in 1964 by some 150 leading banks and manufacturing companies of the developed countries as their vehicle for venture banking in, and the development of, Latin America. Within three short years ADELA had succeeded in getting some sixty enterprises, large and small, going in Latin America. By investing less than 30 million dollars of its own money, it had mobilized almost half a billion dollars of investment, most of it local. It had created at least 25,000 jobs. And it had mobilized for growth opportunities a very large number of entrepreneurs, managers, and technical people. There is now talk of an 'Asian ADELA'.

To speak of a 'lack' of capital is euphemism for mismanagement of capital. The capital is there. But it is kept where it should not be – often locked up in economically marginal land ownership as it was in eighteenth-century France and on today's West Coast of Latin America. Or, it is not invested at all – the treasure of the Indians, from peasant to Maharajah, is an example. Or, it is employed productively but without any 'multiplier' impact. One dollar does the work of one where it should do the work of one hundred.

There is no society in the world that does not have enough capital. What is lacking is effective demand for capital, demand that would really utilize capital. What is needed is the systematic, organized multiplication of capital resources and their employment on opportunities. What is needed is the development banker.

(2) Capital without people is sterile, whereas people can move mountains without capital. Development, therefore, requires rapid growth of human talents and their employment on opportunities. It requires leadership of a high order and also followers who can convert into reality the leader's vision.

162

There is no Shibusawa anywhere today. But what he did by himself a century ago can be done through organized efforts, through organized 'contract-growing' of people.

In the Fifties the American aid programme invested a small sum, barely one million dollars, to form management associations and institutes throughout Latin America. This programme was at first not very popular with the American government. It seemed so insignificant and needed so little money. And the Latin American governments pointed out, with good reason, that associations were one of the few things in abundant supply throughout the continent.

Admittedly, management associations are unromantic. Nor did these do anything unusual. They held meetings, gave speeches and listened to them, ran courses, distributed literature and so on. Surely nothing more prosaic can be imagined than yet another foreman's course or yet another lecture on quality control. But the impact can hardly be exaggerated. Coming at a time when a young generation in Latin America became conscious of the need to manage, it created competence, demands, and self-respect.

This, and similar programmes, are perhaps the only part of the 'Alliance for Progress' that has been both 'Alliance' and 'Progress'. That Latin America has managed to move forward during the last ten years, despite almost crushing deflationary pressures, is owed largely to these programmes for the development of human energies and vision.

Out of this apparently insignificant support for management associations came, for instance, the upsurge of development in the Cauca Valley of Colombia, in and around the city of Cali. The young men who met in the courses of the new Colombian management association rapidly organized themselves to take responsibility for the local university, the Universidad del Valle. There they started a public health programme which, for the first time in the whole region, is systematically training and organizing villagers for public health. They started a series of management courses – above all, courses for the top management people in which the most successful citizens of the area went to school (something almost unimaginable to an older generation of Latin Americans), and in which each of their businesses was examined, diagnosed, and prescribed for by the whole group. Then they began to supply young and well-trained people to local governments, both in state and city.

Cali is still poor; and unemployment is still too high. But out of the work at the Universidad del Valle have come at least 30,000 jobs in the last ten years. More important, out of it has come an entirely different leadership – for the entire community and for all major community activities.

Quite different is the approach taken by a small semi-private group, called the Development Advisory Service. Located at Harvard University and staffed mainly with Harvard economists, this small group – no more than seventy-five – works in small teams as senior advisers and civil servants to developing nations from Pakistan to Indonesia, and from Liberia to Colombia. It decides itself what countries and projects it will work on so that it will get the most results from its small staff. It insists that the host country put its own best people on these projects. And it aims in all its projects at creating human competence and vision throughout a whole area.

There were never more than two dozen men from the Development Advisory Service in Pakistan, for instance. But largely through them, Pakistan industrial output during the last fifteen years has grown at the rate of 15 per cent a year or more, and farm output at better than 5 per cent a year.

The most effective agent of rapid human development in

the economy has been the multi-national corporation as has been said in the last chapter. In fact we should base the activities of the multi-national business in the developing countries less on capital investment and ownership control than on management. The multi-national company should get paid – and paid exceedingly well – for developing both local business and local people. It might not be a bad idea to make a stake in ownership a reward for successfully developing human resources in the local community – thus both giving an incentive to the foreign company to speed the development of local nationals for leadership and making sure that they are truly prepared for responsibility in the business.

And when the multi-national corporation has been primarily in manufacturing we need to focus its skills on agriculture.

Farmers everywhere are highly receptive to monetary incentives. The popular idea of the 'conservative' farmer wedded to his traditional ways is not even caricature. No one is more willing to do something new than the farmer – provided he sees a clear gain. But the farmer in the poor countries cannot take much risk. He knows how close to starvation he lives. He knows that one crop failure or price drop for his harvest may mean total destruction for himself and his family: famine, forced selling of his daughters into prostitution, loss of what little land he has.

What farmers have needed therefore – and what has proved successful wherever tried – is the 'contract-growing' of the new crops, the improved seeds, the better breeds. This, however, requires the skills and resources of a major corporation.

A food processer or food marketer works out the best way to grow the new crop or the new animal, provides the farmer with the necessary supplies – seeds, day-old chicks, feed, implements, fertilizer, and so on – and with the instructions how to use them. He then guarantees the

farmer a definite income at the end of the growing season
– regardless of drought, of animal diseases, of market
price. For these are the risks the farmer in the poor
countries cannot himself take. Most of the crops for can-
ning in the United States – most of our tomatoes, for
instance, or our cherries – are now 'contract-grown'.

In the developing countries where farmers lack the
necessary skills, the risks of 'agribusiness' – a term that is
now becoming popular for the systematic application of
management and entrepreneurship to agricultural development – have to be re-insured – obviously by government –
at least for a few early years. But the risks are capable of
being identified and defined. And except for weather in a
few places – such as areas in India dependent on erratic
monsoon rains – they are not particularly great (though
greater than a private business, no matter how big, or a
farm cooperative could carry by itself at the start).

Such 'contract-growing' in which the cultivation of crops
is being used to change the capacities, aspirations, competence, self-confidence, and performance of the farmer –
that is, of the majority in the poor nations – is perhaps the
only way in which real progress can be made in the most
dangerous areas of human erosion.

Such an area is the Brazilian North-East. There a
black proletariat – the descendants of the slaves on the
sugar plantations – does not dare tackle a new crop or a
new method of cultivation. Starvation is too close to take
any risk. It has no skills, no knowledge, no training. It is,
therefore, forced to continue to live in total dependence
on the plantation owner who, however, is impoverished
himself today, ignorant, without capital, without equipment, without skill, without hope. Land reform, that old
panacea of the liberals, is meaningless in such a situation. It is a threat rather than an incentive where the new
owners of the land are not capable of venturing.

But altogether the idea underlying 'contract-growing' needs to be extended from growing crops to growing skills, self-confidence, and the capacity to achieve. It needs to be extended to 'contract-grow people'.

One promising approach is being worked out in one of our worst black ghettoes in Oakland, California. There, a small local group first obtains definite jobs. It obtains a contract to service the electric typewriters at the university or the car of the telephone company. Then it goes out and trains unemployable and unemployed young Negroes for those already existing jobs. This way it can both guarantee a job and demand high performance standards. A similar approach is taken by *MIND, Inc*, the learning subsidiary of a major food processer, Corn Products Company, with decades of experience in 'contract-growing' crops.

There is much more to development than economics. There are social institutions and culture, for instance.

It is still fashionable, especially among academicians, to believe that development requires the destruction of traditional society. If so, development cannot happen – or only through bloody and disastrous convulsions. To be sure, development will change a society and its traditions. But it must at the same time be based on existing social and cultural institutions and on existing values.

Again Japan offers an instructive example. Japan's Westernization, a hundred years ago, overturned within a few short years the rigid class structure under which for almost three hundred years no commoner could become a soldier (ie, a Samurai), and no Samurai (with rare exceptions) a noble. Japan became a country of great upward mobility. Iwasaki, for instance, had been a Samurai, a soldier. But Shibusawa came from the peasantry.

167

And yet it was Shibusawa who, when still quite young, was given one of the top positions in the new ruling groups, the Ministry of Finance, only to leave of his own free will to become an entrepreneur.

Yet Japan at the same time built her new institution on the basis of the old tribal concepts of mutual loyalty and of 'belonging'. All modern institutions of Japan – the government agency, the university, the business enterprise – no matter how modern and 'Western' their methods and how efficient their output – were *hans*, ie, extended tribal families based on lifelong indissoluble, mutual loyalty. And the Confucian ethic with its demand for service governed both Iwasaki and Shibusawa.

Similarly, in India today, economic development is dissolving age-old customs, eg, the role of women or the physical separation of castes at work. But it is an old merchant caste that is forging ahead as the new entrepreneurs, as is also that traditional business group, the Parsees of Bombay.

Hispanic America is replacing the 'oligarchs' with a new middle class of humble origins. Yet the centre of social change is the oldest institution of Spanish America, the University. University reform leads to social and political reform and to the emergence of new values.

The problem of the traditional culture and values is, in other words, much subtler than most of us think. Gunnar Myrdal, the Swedish economist and sociologist, in his recent study of South-East Asia, *Asian Drama*, referred to earlier, asserts that development cannot occur unless there are first massive social and cultural reforms. But in the ten years during which Myrdal worked on his survey, major development did occur in Pakistan without prior social change. Rather, development initiated social changes while at the same time reaffirming traditional social values and using them as an engine of development. There seems to be no way to decide in advance which cultural traditions are 'remnants of feudalism' and have to go, and which are 'cultural values' and have to be used.

Even the most fundamental disagreement about development, that between the Marxists and the Capitalists, is probably misunderstanding – in so far at least as it concerns economics at all. Our experience would indicate that government control may be a transitory phase in development rather than either its essence or its denial. In the early stages of development, government ownership may be essential. Only government commands the high-grade human resources needed. The Army, in particular, is often the only educational institution in the nation. As development proceeds, however, government becomes less and less necessary. Moreover, it becomes less and less effective as other institutions – businesses, hospitals, universities, and so on – become more complex. Who owns these institutions is much less important than who manages them and how. As they become more highly developed and more complex, the institutions increasingly require managerial autonomy as well as control by non-governmental forces such as the market. (This is what underlies the much-publicized new 'New Economics' of the Communist countries of Europe.)

Japan demonstrated this a century ago. Large-scale industry in Japan was started by the government and as government enterprises. Within a few years, however, these enterprises outgrew the competence of the government bureaucracy. After 1880, that is only a dozen years after the beginning of Westernization, they were sold off to private enterprise, primarily because the government lost too much money running them. And then they – and Japan – really started to grow.

Whatever the political, social, and cultural problems and uncertainties, development still remains above all an economic process. Economic success does not by itself solve all problems. It creates many new ones. But it makes it much

169

easier to live with problems and even to assuage them –
perhaps ultimately even to solve them.

Development is no panacea. Indeed it is very dangerous.
It is growth; and growth is never orderly. It is also change.
And change in society and culture is dislocation. The
period during which a society takes off in sustained development is a most dangerous time. Economically speaking, development has become a success and an accomplished fact. But the leaders still act in terms of the traditional society rather than respond to the new reality. At this
moment there is grave danger of social and political catastrophe.

No country that has gone through the development process has been able so far to avoid this transition period and
its dangers. England, the first country to develop, went
through a period of near-revolution and social crisis in the
generation after the Napoleonic Wars. The collapse into the
First World War – above all, a total collapse of leadership
in the major Continental countries, France, Germany, Austria, and Russia – resulted in large measure from the inability of traditional ruling groups to understand the new
social and economic reality, which development had
brought about. They could see the material, the technical
achievements. But they failed to see that society had
changed and that the new technology had changed the
character of warfare and had destroyed for ever the easy,
short, riskless 'limited war' of the eighteenth century. Something similar happened in Japan after World War I, leading
to a relapse into military dictatorship which throughout
Japan's earlier history had been the way out of major
crises.

In the United States too there was a time of danger. The
moral and political *malaise* of the generation after the Civil
War, the paralysis of the political will during that period,
and the absence of leadership, represented a much more
serious crisis than our historians have acknowledged. The
racial crisis that threatens the nation today is in large

measure the result of the abdication of political leadership during that *post-bellum* period. It permitted, even encouraged, the South to establish 'white supremacy' over the liberated Negro. In America, we had during the Eighties the same violence and unrest in the industrial cities that England had undergone half a century earlier. We had, above all, the withdrawal of the traditional ruling groups of the country from political responsibility, of which Henry Adams was such a visible symbol. We had, in other words, a long period of steady decay, culminating in the election of 1896 in which collapse was just barely averted. Recovery did not begin until Theodore Roosevelt reasserted political and moral leadership and led a new generation back to contact with reality.

We can see the making of such crises today wherever there has been development. In Brazil, for instance, the tremendous growth of the central region has made the non-development of the North-East increasingly unbearable and increasingly a threat to the country's social fabric. In India it is clear that economic development, limited though it has been, has made language into a problem that threatens the cohesion of the whole sub-continent. Even in France, as the events of the spring of 1968 showed, development into an economy of mass affluence created a severe crisis of the still largely Napoleonic, institutional structure.

Development, in other words, is risky. But the alternative is infinitely riskier. At least we can direct, lead, control, and inspire development. The alternative we can barely even hope to survive.

President Truman had true vision twenty years ago in his call for economic development. It is the central economic task of this age. But so far we have misunderstood it. We have believed that the task is to make the poor wealthy. We have to learn that the task is to make the poor productive. This requires the realization that development of the

171

poor world is a self-interest of the rich nations. It is not philanthropy. It is self-interest in the narrowest sense: the creation of profitable markets for the products of the rich industrial countries. It is also self-preservation. There is no greater threat to the prosperity and to the survival of the rich than the threat of a race war of the poor two-thirds of mankind against the one-third that is productive, affluent – and largely white.

7. Beyond the 'New Economics'

THERE ARE FEW areas where right action depends as much on right theory as it does in economics. Yet in few areas is accepted theory as inadequate to the demands of practice and policy or to what we actually know.

The 'new economics' is being advertised with a great fanfare in every developed country. Americans, Englishmen, Germans, Frenchmen, and Japanese are being told that the economists have finally learned how to manage the economy. They can, we are being assured, prevent or at least cure depressions and can guarantee continuous growth and prosperity. As proof of this assertion the economists point to the record of the twenty years since the end of World War II – indeed a period of full employment, economic growth, and prosperity.

There is only one thing wrong with this wonderful news: no two of the bottles labelled 'new economics' have the same contents. The practices in each major country may be similar; but the theories underlying them are quite different and indeed incompatible. What is touted as a panacea in one country is considered deadly poison next door.

The United States has practised since World War II a Keynesian eclecticism, with full employment as the announced goal and with budget deficits as the main tool. Great Britain has been all-out Keynesian with banking and credit policies, especially the discount rate, as the mainstay. But the Germans, who apparently never

173

heard of Keynes, have been preaching the sound 'liberal' economics of 1910, in which *laissez-faire* is imposed on cartel-minded businessmen by an enlightened bureaucracy. The French have not even been that 'modern'. Their economic policies since World War II have been the purest mercantilism as laid down by Colbert, the great Minister of Finance of Louis XIV, well before 1700; a century before the Anglo-Saxons discovered 'economics'. In France the bureaucracy is imposing tight cartels on business. The Japanese do not seem to have any economic theory at all. They swing back and forth from being ultra-conservative to ultra-radical, all the time using whatever seems to work whenever the situation seems to call for it.

Our experience with these various brands of 'new economics' permits only one conclusion: a healthy and growing economy can stand a lot of economics, just as a healthy and growing boy can survive a lot of physic.

There is actually not much evidence that the 'new economics' really manages the economy. To be sure, there has not been a major worldwide depression during this period; but major depressions have always been quite rare, occurring no more often than every fifty years. Minor depressions, however, we have not, the record shows, been capable of preventing or of curing. Whether called 'recessions', 'rolling readjustments', 'periods of consolidation' ('depression' having become a dirty word), these moderate fluctuations have been only a little less frequent during the last twenty years than since we first began to keep records a century and a half ago.

While none of these recessions has degenerated into worldwide depression, not one – whether in the United States, in Japan, in France, or in any other of the developed countries – has lasted much less than the 12 to 24 months reported in any economics textbook of 1910 as the normal duration of short-term swings. Of course, various remedies

– for instance, the 'Kennedy tax cut' – were given the credit for recovery just as quite different remedies were given similar credit a hundred years ago. The record indicates, however, that the recession had in every case run its course anyhow before the remedy began to take effect. One is reminded of the old saying that the common cold takes fifteen days if you do nothing about it and a fortnight if you take medicine.

To be sure, we know how to cure pneumonia even though we do not know what to do about the common cold. It is, therefore, not impossible that we can, as the 'new economics' claims, prevent or assuage a major depression. However, wherever major economic problems have cropped up, they have not yielded to the 'new economics'. We have had no success treating British economic stagnation, the American balance-of-payments problem, or even the purely local, though severe, problem of the Continental European coal-mining industry and its long-term decline and depression.

A cynic may well come to the conclusion that economic performance in the Western countries has been inversely proportionate to the number and prominence of economists in government service. The more economists and the more attention paid to them, he may conclude, the worse the economy performs. Certainly Britain and the United States, where economists are riding high, have grown the least in the post-war period. And Japan, which has done by far the best, has no economists in the government; the decisions are made by civil servants, and, in the oldest Japanese tradition, on what at any given moment is the balance of power between competing bureaucracies – the Bank of Japan, the Ministry of Finance, the Ministry of International Trade and Industry, and so on.

Economic theory is in even worse shape on the other side of the Iron Curtain. There, the crisis of the 'new economics' has become overt and admitted. Unemployment has proved to be endemic and unmanageable in the European satellite

175

countries (and, one gathers, in substantial areas in Russia as well). Planning became a near-fiasco as soon as extreme shortages disappeared, that is, as soon as the economy moved from the 'temporary emergency' of a wartime, forced draft, to the long-term 'normal' of economic development. Then it became clear, almost at once, that Communist theory offers no economic criteria for the priorities in investment and disinvestment, that is, for the key economic decisions. The appropriate economic criterion – now increasingly applied by Communist economists – is quite incompatible with Marx and indeed with any genuine socialism. It is the productivity of capital.

To accept this, means accepting that profit fulfils a vital and irreplaceable economic function and that profitability is the one reliable *economic* yardstick of investment decisions. It means also that the Labour Theory of Value, which claims labour as the source of all economic contribution and which underlies the whole of Marxism, has become untenable. This is gross heresy but perhaps less important than the acceptance of genuine uncertainty which it implies. Risk rather than cost becomes crucial. The market test rather than efficiency determines success. The more nearly, therefore, an industry behaves like a 'capitalist' business, and optimizes profit, the more will it contribute to national income and economic growth.

The Chinese, faced with these unpalatable conclusions, threw out economics and perhaps even the goal of economic growth. The sharp attack of Mao's 'cultural revolution' on 'economism', that is, on the expectation of economic betterment under Communism, makes a great deal of bureaucratic sense. Otherwise, the political system of Communist control could not be maintained. That this is pure Confucius rather than Marx or Lenin need bother only Marxist theologians. But, of course, there is still need for economic policy and, therefore, for economic theory.

When the Chinese recover the capacity for effective government, whether of the whole of their territory or of parts thereof, they will have to tackle again what they now spurn, namely, economic policy. Then they will have to admit that Communist economics is in insoluble crisis. Then they too will have to become 'revisionists' one way or another.

But the Chinese (and Castro) are certainly right in accusing the 'revisionists' in the European Communist countries – in Moscow, Prague, Warsaw, Budapest, and, above all, in Belgrade – both of deserting Marx and of endangering the political basis of Communist society. That the European Communists nevertheless are all frantically engaged in economic reform is a measure of their economic desperation and of the depth of the crisis. The belief among Westerners that Communist economies are becoming 'free-enterprise' is naïve. But the Communists are certainly finding their economic theories even less appropriate to the economic tasks than are those of the West.

Paradoxically it is the advance of economics that is producing the crisis of economic theory. The modern economist is infinitely more knowledgeable and infinitely better prepared for his profession than his predecessors were only a short generation ago. There has been a tremendous advance in his information and in his analytical tools.

The modern economist in the developed countries has at his disposal a wealth of data such as his predecessor could not have dreamed of. Where the economist, as late as World War II, had to guess, the economist today can say, 'I know.' Even more impressive is the advance in the capacity to analyse events, and modern economics quite rightly calls itself 'economic analysis'. Most of this advance has come within the last generation. It is hard for us today to realize that everyday terms such as 'gross national product', or 'balance of payments', were only coined thirty or forty years ago. The greatest economists of the past, down to and

177

including Keynes, had to do their work without these concepts – not to mention the figures that quantify them.

The computer with its twin capacity for storing data and for manipulating large numbers of variables now makes it possible to use the figures and to put the tools to work. It makes it possible to test and verify hypotheses regarding the relationship between economic phenomena, where in the past we always had to rely on opinions and anecdotes. 'Input-output analysis', for instance, shows the effects which a change in output in one sector, eg, agriculture, will set off throughout the whole system. Economic analysis, thus supplied with information and equipped with a computer, is becoming a genuine 'economic mechanics' – just as the introduction of the first usable tool for data recording and data manipulation, the Arabic numeral with its decimal point, led to the 'celestial mechanics' of Kepler, Galileo, and Newton, and to modern physics.

But as every book on the history of science stresses, Tycho de Brahe, in about the year 1600, was the first modern astronomer rather than Kepler or Galileo, and the first systematically to observe the stars and to 'record the facts'. While Tycho amassed the facts, however, he was totally wrong about their meaning. Though perhaps the greatest astronomical observer in history and a 'stellar analyst' of great acumen and prodigious industry, Tycho clung stoutly to the very theories his own observations showed increasingly to be inappropriate and inadequate. It took thirty years of hard work until Kepler – himself trained as Tycho's assistant, as a 'stellar analyst' – could perceive the new theory. Meanwhile, as long as the new facts were being interpreted by the old, wrong theory, their predictions regarding the behaviour of stellar bodies were much less reliable and wider of the mark than those of Tycho's uninformed and unequipped – and therefore much more modest – predecessors. For no ignorance is as great or nearly as dangerous as is precision imposed on misunderstanding or misapprehension.

Economics is today in the position of astronomy in Tycho's time. The new analytical concepts and tools are giving us a tremendous volume of observations and facts. They make it impossible for us to be economic innocents any longer. They force us to have economic policies based on rational argument rather than on 'feel'. Yet our information and tools also make it daily more apparent that we lack adequate economic theory for effective policy. In crucial areas such as economic development, the world economy, or the 'micro-economy' of business, markets, producers, and consumers, we hardly have anything yet that deserves to be called folklore, let alone theory.

There is no question of our going back to classical economics (whether of the capitalist or the Marxist variety). The reasons that made us revise the economics of the nineteenth century are no less compelling today than they were in the early decades of this century, when today's new economics was fashioned. We need instead to go beyond the 'new economics'. And indeed just at the moment when the new economics seems triumphant in public print and public policy, the young and rising generation of economic scholars is beginning to leave it behind.

THE ASSUMPTIONS OF THE ECONOMIST

We have to advance well beyond the 'new economics' in respect to

- the basic assumptions of economic theory;
- the scope of economic theory;
- the concerns of economic theory.

There are several assumptions underlying economics today that are no longer tenable. The fact that most modern economists make them subconsciously – where the founding-fathers of economics in the last two centuries were acutely conscious of them – makes it all the more troublesome that these assumptions are no longer valid.

(1) The first of the obsolete assumptions of economic theory is that of *economic equilibrium*.

Economic theory assumes that the goal of economic policy is a balance. Full employment to which the United States committed itself at the end of World War II is such an equilibrium. It sees growth as needed only in so far as the labour force increases with the growing population. We have since learned that a stable equilibrium is not possible in economics. The only thing that can give full employment is dynamic disequilibrium. An economy is like a bicycle: it only has balance when it is moving. Growth is always unbalanced. Yet only a growing economy can be in equilibrium.

But economic growth is hardly known to economic theory, least of all to the new economics.* If growth is admitted at all, it is treated as a disturbance outside the system. Prevailing economic theory is based on the assumption that an economy oscillates around the same perfect balance – a balance in which there is neither inflation nor deflation, neither unemployment nor labour shortage, neither idle capital nor boom. The assumption is an economy that is briskly standing still. Qualitative structural change, such as growth and its dynamics, are as much beyond the ken of economics today as motion was beyond the capacity of mathematics before the differential calculus.

Economic analysis during the last forty years has, for instance, done a great deal to clarify what is meant by 'productivity' and to give us information on the growth of productivity. But our economic theories still assume

* Some of the new 'new economists', Walter Heller or Joseph Pechman, for instance, or Edward Denison, are conscious of this, it should be said in all fairness.

everywhere that productivity is in fact given. Yet the crucial fact of modern economic life – indeed the great economic change of the two centuries since the Industrial Revolution – is that productivity is the central variable and its increase the test of economic theory and economic policy.

Our most sophisticated economic model today, the input-output model of a whole national economy, cannot embrace any change in productivity at all. All it can do is to work out the consequences of an increase or decrease in production provided that technology and productivity remain unchanged. It cannot predict how a productivity change in a given industry or in a given economic sector will affect the rest of the economy or any other sector. It cannot show what would have to happen for such productivity changes to occur or at least to become possible. This is not because we lack data. It is the result of basic assumptions underlying the model itself.

But growth is a necessary goal of a modern economy. Its absence in the poor countries is our greatest economic danger. The economists know this as well as anyone else, and the best among them spend a great deal of their time working on growth problems. Since, however, their own model excludes growth, they grope in the dark in everything that pertains to growth, try this and try that, and go by fads rather than by knowledge.

This is as true of Communist as of Free World economics. Twenty years ago the Communists did believe that they had a theory of economic growth. The results since have demonstrated to every economist, including those in the Communist countries, that they were wrong. Marx was no more a growth economist than are the anti-Marxists among the equilibrium theoreticians. All one can say about Marx – and it is high and deserved praise – is that he was way ahead of his time and understood that growth would become a central problem when the other economists of the nineteenth century were taking it for granted.

The 'non-Marxist alternative', which Professor Walt Rostow developed in his book, *The Stages of Economic Growth* (1960), is, unfortunately, not the answer either. It is an important book: the first recognition by a prominent economist that we need a systematic theory of economic growth and the first attempt to apply to growth the tools of economic analysis. But the underlying assumption that a high rate of savings by itself both explains and produces growth has not been found valid. Absence of adequate savings makes growth impossible. But even abundant capital investment may produce no growth at all. Capital formation and capital investment may well be the result of growth rather than, as Rostow postulated, its prerequisite.

One twentieth-century economist, the late Joseph Schumpeter (first of Austria and then of Harvard), pointed all this out sixty years ago, before World War I. He also developed the first approach to a theory of economic growth. He identified innovation as the cause of economic growth, and the entrepreneur as its agent. But since then almost no work has been done in the field.

World War I ushered in the long period of economic continuity extending through World War II. During this period, maintenance rather than growth was the central concern. This is, of course, the theme of Keynesian economics, which in turn was a reformulation of equilibrium economics – and a badly needed one. But Keynes' formulation was not the growth theory we need, nor was it intended as such. In Keynesian economics there is a conflict between maintaining what we have and growth beyond it.

If economic theory cannot overcome this conflict, it cannot overcome economic crisis. It is quite clear, to repeat, that we can only maintain equilibrium through a policy of growth. An economy that stands still, however 'briskly', is an economy in decline, as the British example of the last twenty years has shown.

A theory of growth will be both more radical and more conservative than the Keynesian revision of equilibrium theory. It would first require that economics become teleological, that is, that it start out with the goal in the future and work back therefrom to the present. Historically, economic theory has started out with the present arrangement of forces and projected from it. This assumes that the structure of the future is identical with the structure of the present. There is no room in such a projection for true change such as genuine innovation brings about. It can only admit a better allocation of already existing resources of all kinds, including the resource of knowledge.

The theory we need will have to start out with the postulate that the theme of economic policy is genuine change in the wealth-producing capacity of the economic resources rather than their rearrangement. It will have to start out, in other words, with the postulate of innovation.

This must shift the focus of economic theory from cost, where it has always been, to risk. This, in turn, leads to a re-evaluation of the nature, role, and function of profit.

In traditional economics, profit serves at best a marginal economic function. It is a measurement of the allocation of capital resources. If we assume no growth, profit is not even particularly important in this role. We then arrive, as the classic economists did, at a pseudo-psychological explanation for the existence of profits (though no psychologist has ever been able to find the so-called 'profit motive' in nature). Profit, in all traditional economics, is, in other words, a moral rather than an economic category, and the attitude towards profit is ideological rather than economic.

In traditional economies the only risk is lack of information about the past and present; and the aim of economic policy is to minimize risk. But the moment we assume growth, we assume uncertainty; that is, we assume that present resources are committed to genuine risk because

183

they are committed to making a different and unknowable future. Thus the purpose of economic policy in a growth economy must be to enable the economy to take bigger but better risks.

In growth economics, therefore, profit becomes the cost of uncertainty. It is no longer 'surplus'. It can be formulated as a law of development-economics that there is no profit at all (excepting only such profit as results from politically imposed monopoly – which, of course, is 'tribute' rather than profit). All there is are *costs of the future*. They cannot yet be measured but they are as real, as tangible, and as certain as the costs of the past which our accounts record. Just as we ask with respect to the costs of the past whether there is enough revenue to cover them, we must ask with respect to the costs of the future whether there is enough revenue to cover them. The central question in respect to profits is whether they are high enough to allow the economy to take the risks it needs to take in order to grow. This holds true whether we stress capital accumulation or consumption in our theories of economic equilibrium, that is, regardless of the position we take in respect to the economics of today and yesterday.

This view eliminates the 'profit motive'. It also eliminates profit as a 'capitalist rake-off'. The Communist economists today are quite right when they deny that their restoration of profit is a restoration of capitalism. What they have done – and rightly so – is to realize that profit is needed for an expanding economy regardless of political beliefs or economic structure. This is surely not Marx; but it is also not Adam Smith.

To say that profits do not exist but that what we call 'profits' are simply costs of the future which we cannot yet allocate, does not say anything about the way in which we distribute profits. It is clear that we need revenue to cover the risks of investing in growth. These revenues can only come out of current production just as the revenues to cover the costs of doing business today – the accountant's costs – can only come out of current production. Current production is the only thing in the economy we can dispose of. It is the only 'present'. The rest is either memory or expectation.

But it is also reasonably clear that we somehow must get these revenues into the right risks. They must be used to make the future rather than to defend the past. This argues for a capital market and against retention of profits in existing businesses (the arguments already made in Chapters 3 and 4 above). But it does not follow therefrom that the owners of capital necessarily should make the reinvestment decision, that is, that they should control profits.

Both in the Communist and in the Free World economies, there is considerable debate as to who should make these decisions. In the Communist economies the owner of capital is, of course, the State. Yet today's economic debate among Communist economists is largely over the extent to which the managers of a business rather than the political organs – that is the owners – should make the decisions in respect to investment of profit in future risks.

In the Free World economies there is similarly an open debate. In the traditional view, the owner is entitled to maximum earnings, that is, to the full decision-making power. The other view holds that the owner is entitled only to the 'cost of capital'. This latter view underlies the policies of the so-called 'growth companies' of the last few years.

The old concept of 'ownership' may no longer be very relevant. One reason is that knowledge rather than traditional 'property' is the controlling resource today. But we can also today imagine an economy with autonomous markets for goods, labour, and capital in which businesses strive to optimize profits – but in which there is no 'ownership of the means of production'.

The American economy, in which fiduciaries such as mutual trusts or pension funds are the majority owners of the big businesses, knows, in effect, no 'private owner-ship'. Ownership is socialized – even though it has not been nationalized. Similarly Yugoslav business is in the process of becoming 'non-national'. Legal ownership is still vested in the government. But goods, labour, and capital are in a near-market economy. Profit-optimiza-tion is an objective; profitability – as in the 'capitalist' West – decides whether the enterprise can get capital or not. The differences are, of course, still very great. But profit and profitability play the same role, and ownership as such plays no role at all.

While these are vitally important and emotionally highly charged issues, they are quite different from the old battle cries of 'down with profit' and 'down with the exploiter'.

Growth is not the one and only goal of an economy; but neither is equilibrium. We certainly can no longer leave growth out of the model of the economy. It is at least one important goal. It is most assuredly a reality whether present or absent. The moment, however, that we put growth into such a model, profit and its meaning change entirely. The answer to the cry of exploitation is then no longer to get rid of the exploiters, but to create growth and productivity. The answer is to make the poor productive – and this requires risk, uncertainty, and profit.

(2) Closely related to the assumption of equilibrium as the goal of the economy is the neglect of technology in our theory. Economists consider technological change as some-thing outside the economy and an event they cannot deal with – a sort of uncontrollable and unpredictable catas-trophe like earthquake or pestilence. Technological change may explain why the forecasts of economists go awry with such disconcerting frequency. But the economists do not know how to anticipate it or how to explain it and are silent regarding its possible course or consequences.

But unlike pestilence or earthquake, even unlike major war, technological change and innovation are primarily economic events. Their purpose is economic to begin with. They consist in a change in the deployment of economic resources and result in shifts in the allocation of resources. Their purpose as well as their test is economical performance. They are major economic events determining the productivity of land, labour, and capital. For the economist to brush off such a central phenomenon as not truly part of his subject is like the mathematician's saying: 'Number is outside mathematics.'

We may never arrive at a theory of innovation in the sense that we can explain innovation in economic terms and anticipate it by economic analysis. For non-economic factors, intellectual and perceptual, are crucial to innovation. But we should be able to understand how innovation affects an economy and what its economic consequences are likely to be. We should be able to judge with a high degree of probability whether a certain innovation is likely to produce major economic changes or whether it is 'purely technical'.

We need, for instance, to be able to say how a certain innovation, eg, instalment buying, or the introduction by Xerox of a machine for office reproduction and copying on a large scale, has affected the economy or indeed whether it has affected the economy at all. To use the modern economist's terms, we need an 'input-output model' that is sensitive to innovation and at least reports to us when and how innovation changes the relationship between sectors of the economy, between industries and between factors of production.

Without this information we are incapable of rational economic policy. Without it, we cannot know whether a given policy advances economic welfare or undermines it.

Should the United States, for instance, defend its steel industry against foreign imports? That the United States steel industry needs to change its technology fast is reasonably clear. That innovation in the form of new processes is rapidly becoming available is also clear. But would protection of the domestic producers at a time of worldwide overcapacity speed socially and economically desirable innovation? Would it actually strengthen the steel industry, let alone the American economy? Or would it weaken both, even in the short run, by retarding the spread of needed innovation?

No one today can answer this practical question. We do not have enough understanding of innovation as an economic process nor enough information about its economic impacts. Yet we need to make such policy decisions all the time, to make them fast, and to make them with a reasonable chance of being right. For this, we need a change in the traditional assumptions of economic theory that brings technology and innovation into the economist's field of vision so that he can go to work and study them.

(3) Economic theory needs to be restructured on a brand new postulate: knowledge creates productivity.

Economic theory in its early days was much concerned with the question: 'What creates economic value?' The traditional answer from Ricardo (in about 1810) to Marx, was 'labour'. It is still the answer given in Marxist economics.

In so far as the traditional answer implies that the economy is the work of man rather than of nature, it is undoubtedly correct. But it is also irrelevant. In so far as it implies that one attribute of man is more important than any other, it is misdirection. That Marxist economists are stuck with this particular piece of theology is their bad luck. (One way or another, of course, practitioners in Communist countries manage to disregard their theory of value in their daily work, much as Catholic biologists are unhampered in their research in genetics by the fact that the Dogma of the Virgin Birth is an article of their faith.)

During the second half of the nineteenth century it became increasingly apparent that this question was metaphysical rather than economic, and that any 'theory of value' based on it, regardless of the answer, inhibited economic understanding. It is therefore hardly even mentioned in modern textbooks. Instead we began to discuss the 'factors of production' – land, labour, and capital, to which later generations added management.

But little can be done with these 'factors' either. Today they are treated in actual economic work as elements of cost rather than as 'factors of production'. In other words, one has to pay for natural resources, for human work, and for capital (the last being the power to control today's resources and to apply them to future expectations). Within limits one can substitute one of these resources for another. But the working economist today sees in these 'factors' little more than limitations and restraints on production in order to overcome which one has to pay a price. And all factors are always available at a price.

Since Simon Kuznets began his pioneering work on the productivity of the American economy thirty years ago, we increasingly have been focusing on the 'factors of productivity' as the key to economic performance. As development, growth, and change are becoming the phenomena which economic theory has to explain and economic policy has to manage, the 'factors of productivity' are becoming increasingly central. For an economic theory that tries to explain and understand change and growth needs a postulate as to what causes productivity.

Kuznets' work indicates strongly that new knowledge rather than capital (let alone labour) produces productivity. Kuznets' statistics thus bear out empirically what Schumpeter postulated almost sixty years ago, shortly before World War I. Capital flows in response to greater

189

opportunities created by the greater productivity of new knowledge, both of workers and of managers.

This may seem obvious, but it is far from obvious to traditional economics. In fact, it is incompatible with most of it.

Popular economics, that is, the economics that customarily underlies discussions in the newspapers, in parliaments, and in Congress, still assumes, by and large, that advance occurs because labour somehow becomes more productive by working harder. Actually all economic advance in the last hundred years has meant working shorter hours and with less physical effort. There has been no increase in the 'productivity' of labour. We have been able to pay much more for labour of lesser productivity because knowledge has made the economy a good deal more productive. But there is not much more substance to the axiom of most employers' associations that capital is productive by itself.

The old debate as to who is entitled to the fruits of increased productivity, capital, or labour, can be answered simply: neither is 'entitled' to anything. Neither can take credit for producing the fruits. The end result of increased productivity is to have available more for both – but not because they 'earned' it.

The new industries, and the technologies on which they are based, are all founded on knowledge – and on knowledge altogether rather than on 'science and technology'. At the same time, knowledge has become the central expenditure and investment of a modern economy. Knowledge has become the economy's central resource. But knowledge as a factor of production or productivity is still unknown to the economist.

We need an economic theory that can relate economic results to knowledge input, and economic input to knowledge results. We need a theory that can measure the effectiveness of knowledge but also the efficiency of 'knowledge industries' and especially the efficiency of education, that is, of the systematic production and distribution of knowledge. We need to be able to relate the knowledge capital needed to produce development, and perhaps also the form in which this knowledge capital is needed – eg, whether the money available should be spent on making large numbers of children literate or on producing a small number of highly educated men in the universities. And we need measurements of the economic return on knowledge investment and knowledge resources.

We need such an economic theory for the policy decisions with respect to knowledge that confronts us. These decisions will not be made, and should not be made, on economic rationale alone. In fact, one might well argue that the decisions themselves should always be made on non-economic grounds – that is, in contemplation of moral, social, aesthetic, or ethical objectives and values. But each decision then entails an economic cost – and economic decisions made in ignorance of the cost are almost certain to turn out wrong decisions, that is, decisions the results of which are totally different from the expectation with which they were made.

A good economist today knows that equilibrium economics are not enough. He may know that innovation is a recurrent qualitative change within the economic system. He may know that knowledge creates productivity and that the old 'factors of production' are limitations on an economy rather than its driving forces. But as long as he does not have a theory based on these new assumptions, he is either going to disregard his knowledge and rely on the old theory, with its old assumptions leading to wrong conclusions, or he will discard his knowledge and depend upon hunch, experience, and 'feel' – which is, of course, what the gifted practitioners always do when their knowledge base proves treacherous. For effective economic policy, the economist needs new theory based on assumptions appropriate to the economic reality we live in, and to the economic tasks that face us.

WORLD ECONOMICS, INTERNATIONAL ECONOMICS, AND THE MACRO-ECONOMY

The economic theory we have today centres in the domestic economy of a national state – the economist calls it the 'macro-economy'. There is no theory of the world economy, nor is there enough knowledge as to how world economy and domestic economy interact. Modern economic theory still assumes, in effect, a closed economy controlled from within by national, monetary, credit, and tax policies.

In this respect the ultra-conservatives in France differ not a whit from their arch-enemies, the ultra-Keynesians in Cambridge, England, and in Cambridge, Massachusetts. Both see only the domestic economy and analyse only the domestic economy. The economy outside enters into their calculations only as a restraint, a qualification, an environment.

An example of this narrowness is the debate over the 'American domination' of European industry. President de Gaulle complained bitterly that America uses the dollars that its balance-of-payments deficit foists on the credulous Europeans to expropriate Europe and take over European industry. American policy-makers, for their part, complain about the 'outflow of dollars' to finance these acquisitions.

But, in effect, both America and Europe have exchanged investment in local industry for multi-national industry. There has been neither 'take over' nor 'outflow'. The dollars paid to Europeans for their share in European businesses have been used, almost entirely, by Europeans to invest in the American companies which, in turn, invest in Europe. What is happening is the creation of multi-national companies with shareholders on both continents, production and sales on both continents, and, increasingly, managers on both continents who are nationals of Europe as well as of the United States.

Had such a phenomenon occurred within a national economy (as indeed it did occur earlier in this century within the United States when the large companies with their access to the New York capital market expanded from regional into national businesses) everyone would at once have recognized the circular nature of the flow of capital. Inflow and outflow are actually one stream. But when the flow crosses national boundaries, it moves beyond the model with which the economist works and which for him is 'reality'.

This then explains why the measures taken to correct the American balance-of-payments deficit have had different results from those expected by both Americans and Europeans. The 'voluntary' restrictions on American investment abroad that were imposed in 1965 were meant to stop American acquisitions in Europe. Instead they speeded them up. The flow of dollars from Europe to Europe via the American company was simply short-circuited. Instead of dollars flowing from Paris to New York and back to Paris, they were placed by the Europeans directly into the securities of newly-created European subsidiaries of American companies, founded for the express purpose of buying up European businesses and thus bringing them under multi-national management. In other words, the European to go multi-national invests in American companies, and American business to go multi-national uses European acquisition.

The exclusively domestic scope of the model means that economic policies with respect to the outside world are not capable of being formulated or of being carried through effectively. We simply do not know enough.

Shortly before the American government imposed the

first restraint on American investments abroad to reduce the deficit in our balance of payments, that is, in 1965, the US Department of Commerce made a study (published in summary in the Fall, 1966, issue of the *Journal of World Business*, edited by Columbia University) which indicated that it is the American investment dollar abroad that creates the export markets for American goods abroad. Every dollar invested by a United States business generates within a very short period, perhaps two to five years, at least five dollars of American export abroad (plus, of course, a good many dollars of dividends). These figures implied that curtailing American investments abroad would result in a disproportionate drop in American exports and would, therefore, actually worsen our balance-of-payments problem. The development of the American exports and of the American balance of trade since the 1965 restriction lived up to this prediction. Two years later, American exports to Europe began to go down sharply, even though American prices in those two years had not risen nearly as fast as European prices.

But are the United States investment restrictions actually to blame? Investment restrictions are, of course, a traditional prescription to 'cure' a balance-of-payments deficit. Has the cure now become a cause of the disease? No one knows. All we do know is that the American government based its policy on folklore rather than on knowledge.

The same thing obviously applies also to the restrictions on American travel abroad which the US government asked for early in 1968. No one knows the economic effect of this travel on the balance of payments. Most of the money is, of course, spent by businessmen rather than by tourists. Is business travel then the means by which the United States produces its exports and the dividend income on its foreign investments? In other words, is a dollar spent on travel a net expense and an outflow of dollars? Or is it the means by which we earn ten dollars of foreign exchange – and within what period of time? Would travel restrictions mean cutting off our nose to spite our face? Would they stop a dollar drain or create one? To what extent also are a few hundred million dollars spent by business travellers abroad the foundation for the several billion dollars of purchases of American aircraft by foreign airlines? No one has any answer or any means of finding an answer. Yet, these are elementary questions.

As these examples show, such ignorance is bound to lead to wrong action. Being ignorant of the connexion between outflow of dollars to buy European businesses and inflow of dollars to buy United States securities – or of the relationship between investment abroad and exports – the economists, European as well as American, are bound to react so as to inflict harm on their own countries as well as on the world economy.

It is the world economy today that defines the opportunities, the world economy from which effective economic policy has to take its cue. This is the lesson of the growth economies of the last twenty years – Japan, Sweden, and the non-Communist Chinese countries. The United States and Western Europe, however, are kept from profiting by this lesson by the blinkers imposed on our vision by the macro-economic scope of economic theory.

The major economic threat to every nation is a crisis originating in the world economy. This has been true for the last hundred years, that is, since the panic of 1873. The depression of 1929, to be sure, started in large measure with the collapse of a domestic stock market boom in the United States. But it was the collapse of the international monetary system, jerry-built after World War I – and especially the devaluation of the British Pound, caused in turn largely by a bank collapse in Austria – that converted

195

a 'normal' depression into the nightmare of total economy and monetary paralysis. If 1929 had been primarily domestic, President Hoover would have been right: the United States would have been well on its way to recovery by 1932.

Similarly the crises of 1877, of 1896, of 1907, and of 1921 were largely, if not primarily, crises of the international rather than of any domestic economy.

But the economist sees only crises originating in domestic prices, domestic over-consumption or under-consumption, domestic over-investment or under-investment. He promises to fight and overcome any crisis entirely within the domestic economy and by domestic policies. This is a most unconvincing promise. A crisis originating in the world economy, eg, in a lack of world liquidity, can only be made worse by domestic measures. Such measures are inevitably protectionist. They attempt to isolate the domestic economy. Any such attempt – comparable to the way the wealthy in earlier times fled to the countryside to escape the plague – can have only one result: the epidemic spreads twice as fast and twice as far, lasts twice as long and does many times as much damage.

Yet the economist and the economic policy-maker are probably better off to have no economic theory for the world economy than to depend on what theory we do have, under the name of 'international economics' – that old museum piece, Adam Smith's theory of international trade. It is elegant theory; but it was valid only for pre-industrial economics.

This theory sees international trade as based on 'differential advantage' in the 'factors of production'. Its famous example (used first by David Ricardo in the early 1800s) is the exchange of Portuguese wine against English wool where the climate of the one country favours wine while that of the other favours sheep-raising. It concludes that the greatest opportunities are for 'complementary' trade and exist between countries of different technological levels and of different economics in their 'factors of production'.

India and the United States, in terms of the theory of international trade, are 'complementary'; Germany or Switzerland and the United States are 'competitive'. International trade should be greatest, therefore, between the United States and India. And between two technologically equal countries, such as the United States and Switzerland or Germany, there should be no trade at all, or only the most limited one.

The exact opposite is true. The more nearly equal two countries are in their economic structure, their technology, and their factorial costs, the greater and the more intensive is the trade between them. The more complementary they are, the less trade there is between them. This has now been known for well over a century. When the continent of Europe first started to industrialize and thus to become 'competitive' to Great Britain, its trade with Great Britain, until then quite small, started to expand rapidly.

The economist's standard excuse for the failure of reality to behave according to the predictions of international trade theory has been that India is too poor to buy the advanced goods America produces. But the lack of purchasing power in India does not explain the high level of trade between the United States and Switzerland, which is the truly important phenomenon. It does not explain why Swiss–American trade is increasing faster the closer Swiss productivity, Swiss technology, and Swiss standards of living come to those of the United States.

The theory of international trade assumes that goods move, but that the 'factors of production' are fixed in place. But even if the 'factors of production' were defined as 'land, labour, and capital', this is not valid. 'Land', of course, does not move. But labour has at times been very mobile, in the settlement of North America for instance, and also within the last twenty years in the migration of rural proletarians from Southern Europe (where they were an economic drag) into the industrial areas of Central and Northern Europe (where they became productive) – a migration, in other words, that raised both the productivity of the areas the migrants left and the productivity of the areas to which they moved. And capital has high mobility unless restricted by government.

Much more important, however, is that knowledge, the true 'factor of productivity' enjoys almost unlimited mobility. It is not the investment of American companies in Europe that creates productivity. It is the fact that this investment is predicated on the movement of knowledge from America to Europe, both technological and managerial, which underlies the capital investment. Knowledge is a very peculiar economic resource. When moved from the United States to Europe, it is a net import to Europe and a net addition to the European stock of capital. But there is no corresponding decrease in the American stock of capital. We have conveyed knowledge, and we get paid for it. But we have not 'exported' it. Indeed, we have probably enriched our own knowledge resources and made them more productive. This is not possible with any other resource. No other resource can be conveyed from one man to another in such a way that the process of transfer enriches both. To the extent to which knowledge can be transferred, trade is created. Obviously it is much easier to transfer knowledge between areas of comparable knowledge level, that is, between countries on the same level of development, than it is to transfer knowledge where there are not many people ready to receive it.

This does not deny the importance of comparative costs. But it makes comparative costs a restraint on international transactions rather than the basis thereof, at least between countries capable of putting knowledge to work. It also does not invalidate Adam Smith's theory that the largest possible amount of trade between nations is the greatest benefit to all of them. But his rather simple conclusions on how the system works which nineteenth-century free-trade doctrine put into practice, may need considerable revision. Free trade in goods, on which Smith put the stress, is important. But free movement of capital and free movement of knowledge may be more important still.

Adam Smith's complementary trade has not disappeared. To be sure there is little English raw wool today, though there is still Portuguese wine. But petroleum is still being produced where it can be found. Being 'land', in Adam Smith's terms, a petroleum field cannot be moved. Its product must be brought to the market for energy. With atomic energy, however, this 'complementary' trade is likely to become a good deal less important, though not necessarily smaller. Similarly, wheat grows only in the temperate zone. If people in the tropics want it, it must be brought to them, and so on. But 'complementary' trade is today only one component of trade and only one element in the world economy.

It is 'competitive' trade that provides the thrust to international trade by and large. World trade in manufactured goods has increased much faster than both 'complementary' trade in natural products, and production of manufactured goods. Between 1816 and 1950 such trade tripled *per capita*. Between 1950 and 1966 it more than doubled again – increasing at an annual rate of 7·5 per cent, ie, doubling every ten years. The great bulk of this increase from 1870 on, when our statistics began to be reliable, is trade between highly industrialized countries, that is, 'competitive' rather than 'complementary' trade. Most international trade today is 'competitive' trade, that is, trade in manufactured products in which the 'comparative cost' is the result of the application of knowledge rather than of the exploitation of nature. Yet we have no theory for it. According to our theory this trade – the reality of the economic world we live in – cannot happen.

How dangerous such deficient theory can become is shown by the example of Britain. In international trade negotiations the British still follow the traditional theory. They, therefore, have put all their emphasis on keeping open markets for British 'complementary' trade, ie, for whisky, china, and so on. But they have tended to neglect 'competitive' trade. They have looked for areas where nature (or history) rather than knowledge gives them an advantage. As a result, they have focused on yesterday's opportunities and denied themselves the fruits of their own – very great – knowledge achievements.

Adam Smith explained the *international* economy for his day. There is urgent need now for an economic theory that starts out with the *world* economy and then explains the domestic economy as part of the world economy. We are not going back to the nineteenth-century separation of domestic and international economy. But we must go beyond the traditional limitation of economic analysis to the domestic economy.

MACRO-ECONOMY AND MICRO-ECONOMY

Economists speak of their theory as one of the 'macroeconomy'. This, however, not only fails to take in the true 'macro-economy', that is, the world economy, it also leaves out the economic areas where actual costs are incurred and actual results are achieved, the 'micro-economy' of producer, consumer, and market.

The 'macro-economy' deals with one nation as a whole. It is essentially an economic theory of the national government, of national income and its distribution, of national flows of credit and money, and of overall price levels.

To its macro-economic focus, modern economic theory owes its penetrating power. In fact, 'economic analysis' would not be possible except for this voluntary confinement to macro-economic events. Modern economics really began when the last attempt at an economic theory of individuals and businesses – the theory of the Austrian school of 1880 – was pushed aside in favour of statistical approaches to the behaviour of money, credit, employment, and production within the overall, the national, the 'macro' economy.

The assumption underlying this modern approach is plausible: individual components of an economy – whether private persons, consumers, businesses, local governments, and so on – tend in the aggregate to behave like the particles in the physicists' 'ideal gas'. Each particle may have its own motion brought about by forces that act exclusively on it, or even by forces entirely within it. Yet in the aggregate the whole mass will have one behaviour, governed by probability distribution and conforming to an 'average'. The only true actor, the only force capable of directing and controlling the behaviour of the individual particle is outside force, that is, the government through its fiscal and monetary policies.

This, however, is less and less accurate as a description of what goes on. Even though government sometimes appears to have become all-powerful, the divergence between the behaviour of the aggregate, as predicted on the basis of probability, and actual events, is becoming greater, rather than smaller.

Economists admit this but they tend to explain it away as something that 'ought not to happen'. They attribute it to the effects of monopoly, for instance. But the purpose of a theory is to make possible effective action, that is, to be able to predict what is likely to happen. It is quite immaterial that what has happened should not have happened. If 'what should not happen' is the rule rather than the exception, then we had better get a different theory. Increasingly, what the 'macro-economic' model tells us should happen and what really happens are almost opposites.

Here are some recent examples. In 1966, the Federal

Reserve Board which, by common consent, is a singularly well-informed and effective organ of economic policy and largely independent of political pressures, raised interest rates so as to put the brakes on what threatened to become a runaway boom. But the Federal Reserve Board did not want to disturb home building, if only because the next major economic advance in the American economy was thought to depend on family formation and home building as large masses of young people reached working age and entered the labour force. The actual result was an almost complete collapse of home building, when mortgage money practically disappeared. At the same time, the industrial boom was hardly affected. Rather than slow down, business reacted to the Federal Reserve measures by building up inventories even faster.

In retrospect it is easy to see what went wrong. But then everything is obvious to hindsight. There is absolutely no guarantee, however, that the next time a similar situation arises, a similar Federal Reserve Board Action will have better results – though it is reasonable to assume that it will have different results. And again, hindsight, a year or two later, may then tell us why.

The repeated failures of successive British governments in the post-war period to spur exports is another illustration. Every single measure taken by British governments, whether Labour or Conservative, led to a curtailment of exports rather than to the expansion the measure was intended to bring about. Every single one penalized the efficient and technologically advanced industries on which growth and exports depend. The only difference between various measures by succeeding governments was that the inefficient industries with obsolescent technology were sometimes penalized along with the efficient and modern ones and sometimes escaped unscathed. In other words, sometimes these measures hurt the domestic economy more than they did at other times. But not one of them produced improvement in British international accounts even though this was the sole aim of the policy. Again and again businesses simply did not react the way the economists 'knew' they would and must react.

We have no economic theory regarding the relationship between events in the 'macro-economy' controlled and predicted by economic theory, and events in the 'micro-economy' controlled by businesses, municipal governments, research scientists in industrial laboratories, or plain consumers. As a result, the 99 per cent of economic decisions which deal with policy in respect to businesses, municipal governments, consumers, and so on, have to do without benefit of theory and without much rational guidance.

The daily actions of government agencies in all countries – local-government budgets and taxes; regulation of business; or consumer policies – frustrate the overall economic policies of the same government agencies for the 'macro-economy'. This happens in all areas, anti-trust for instance, or in the way transportation is regulated. Yet we simply do not know enough about the 'micro-economy' to predict this. All we can offer is hindsight. All we can offer before the damage has been done are opinions, based perhaps on experience but without sanction in economic theory or foundation in economic analysis. All one can argue is that 'common sense' makes it appear that this particular 'micro-economic' policy of government is not truly compatible with the government's macro-economic goals. But opinions, needless to say, are cheap, plentiful, and not particularly convincing.

As a result, the modern economy – by definition an economy in which government policy and the economic behaviour of all other groups and persons are intimately intertwined – has little capacity for economic policy. On the one side, there is a beautiful, elegant model of the 'macro-economy'; on the other side there is an ungodly mess of unrelated, improvised, opinionated actions and policies. Monetary and fiscal measures which derive from the neat, clean, elegant model of economic analysis have results in the real economy that have nothing whatever to do with the intent of the policy or the arguments behind it; and events in the micro-economy, which no one foresaw, completely change the behaviour and results of the macro-economy.

The evidence admits of only one conclusion. The postulate that the micro-economy has no power or motion of its own but that it is controlled in a probability distribution by events in the macro-economy – especially fiscal and monetary ones – is not tenable. At the very least, the micro-economy can vary its responses to the same macro-economic events so as to make the same macro-economic policy come out differently under apparently identical circumstances.

It is more intelligent to postulate that the 'particles' are 'organisms' rather than 'atoms'. They are more nearly capable of determining their own behaviour and action, at least at times, rather than being confined to reacting to outside stimuli. Our experience has been that the macro-economy while limiting the organisms in the micro-economy does not control them.

WHAT WE NEED

A theory of the micro-economy will require a good deal of information which we today have at best in fragmentary form. It will also require new concepts.

An enormous amount is known, for instance, about the market. But the information is scattered. It is primarily what the 'practical' people know – the people in business, the marketing people, the advertising people, the merchants. In many cases it is not even known consciously but simply applied in day-to-day work – without much thought as to what proportion of what is considered 'knowledge' is really untested opinion, if not near-anecdote.

To give but one example: no one really knows whether advertising does anything or, if so, what. There is a belief abroad that advertising is omnipotent. But again and again the most lavish advertising campaign fails to produce any demand. The Ford 'Edsel', which was such a complete failure, had, for instance, the biggest advertising appropriation and the best-planned campaign in all automotive history. There is another belief, popular among another school of intellectuals, that advertising has no effect whatever and is sheer waste of money. But no one has any information.

Advertising is mass marketing. If effective at all, it should be the most economical and cheapest method of distribution. For every dollar of advertising spent, countless dollars should be saved that would otherwise have to be spent to bring a product to market. But no one has ever tried to find out whether advertising is in fact economical mass distribution or what its economics are. No one, to my knowledge, even knows how one might frame the hypothesis so that it could be tested.

Traditional economic theory knows only 'commodities'. It does not know 'products'. A commodity is defined entirely by physical characteristics. Competition, therefore, is always between units that are clearly defined and distinguished and differ from each other only by their price. Products are, however, much more complex. They are usually not capable of being defined in physical terms alone. They are usually differentiated in the value they offer the buyer – a house built in one style differs from another, even though its physical characteristics, such as the number and size of the rooms, may be identical. And there the traditional commodity concept is simply not adequate.

Nor do we have any adequate understanding of 'price',

even in the economist's traditional definition of 'price' as being what the supplier receives. It is, for instance, absolutely impossible under prevailing theory for a price to be too low from the point of view of the buyer. It is impossible, in other words, for an increase in price to result in an increase in demand. Yet this happens every day in the actual economy. The economist, when confronted with such a phenomenon, is liable to talk of the 'irrational customer'. But this is about as sensible as for the doctor to talk of an 'irrational infection' when a certain strain of bacteria refuses to yield to an antibiotic. The fact is that something is happening that is not in accord with what the theory has predicted. The theory needs to be changed.

We probably need to shift from a theory that focuses on cost to the producer to one that defines 'price' as what the buyer pays to obtain whatever he bought an article for. Instead of the maker's costs being central, the buyer's value should be. This may seem easy. But the US Department of Defence has for a decade been working on 'life-cycle costing' under which weapons and supplies are to be bought on the basis of what they will cost the government over their entire estimated service life, including the cost of maintenance and repairs and the cost of training people in their use. The more deeply we go into this, the more complex 'price' becomes.

The reality of the market will have to be understood in terms of what it is, rather than in terms of what it is not. We take the market for granted in the West. But we need to realize why the Communists had to rediscover the market, even though this not only denied Marx but threatens the central control of the economy by their governments. The market is not determined by macro-economic forces as the macro-economist maintains (and in this respect the 'capitalist' economists are no different from their Communist brethren). It was this belief that led the Communist planners into all their mistakes. They have now learned that the market determines. It is the mechanism for allocating resources to results.

The market is an autonomous force with its own values, its own dynamics, and its own decisions. It can, of course, be influenced by macro-economic events. But even if the macro-economy controls completely what is produced and how it is distributed – as it attempted to do in the Russian Five-Year Plans – the market is not subdued. It can be distorted. But it cannot be thwarted. The moment the consumer has any choice, the market, rather than the planner, is back in control.

The new economics is therefore only a beginning. It is a magnificent beginning in many ways – in its penetrating power, its analytical definitions and concepts, and in its rigour. But to give us the economic understanding and policy we need requires a great deal more.

We need a theory of economic dynamics in addition to the theory of equilibrium which is all we have now. We need a theoretical understanding of technological innovation as an economic event and its integration into economic theory and economic policy. We need a model of the world economy and an understanding of the complex relationships between the world economy and the domestic economy. Finally, we need a theory of micro-economic behaviour; that is, of the behaviour of the actors – the 'organisms' – of the economy. For it is the micro-economy, in the end, that produces economic results, goods and services, jobs and incomes.

Ideally, all these new understandings should be one unified theory. We should be able to integrate micro-economy, macro-economy, and world economy into one 'economic field'. Certainly the same basic concepts will run through all of them, eg, the concept of knowledge as the central factor in productivity. But it is conceivable that we will have to be content with a number of theories which, while constructed on the same general plan, will differ and be separate. After all, physics throughout the entire nineteenth century was a series of separate fields; optics, thermodynamics, electricity, and mechanics were but loosely connected. It was not until quantum mechanics in this century that physics became unified again as it had been at the time of Newton – and today, only half a century after Planck, Bohr, and Rutherford, physics is again split into a number of discrete fields. Yet there is physics as a discipline, unified by a common approach and by a general plan and method. No one would carp if economics had a similar development.

The 'new economics', whatever the brand, is not a theory of the economy. It is, at best, an anatomy; a static, rather lifeless and mechanistic description of an important but limited segment: the governmental economy of the nation-state *sans* world but also *sans* entrepreneur, business, and consumer. It is, to continue the medical metaphor, the skeleton. Without it, one cannot understand or treat the body. But by itself it does not explain the body nor permit diagnosis or treatment. It is the necessary starting point. But nothing could be more dangerous than to pretend, as the new economics does in every country, that this is *the* answer and truly *the* economic theory, which – as a kind of economic philosopher's stone – enables us to prevent, or at least to cure, serious economic ailments such as depressions or stagnation.

Fortunately this is beginning to be realized – none too soon. While all these grandiose claims are being made on behalf of the new economics, serious economists are beginning the work that is so badly needed. The textbooks for the student are, to be sure, still those of the new economics, and the broad public is still being encouraged in the belief that the real battles of economics today are over what Keynes said and whether he was right. But the 'hot' economics in the United States are quite different from those that dominate the President's Council of Economic Advisers and the Press.

For the last few years, the hero of the young American

economists has been Milton Friedman of the University of Chicago. And he has nothing but contempt for the new economics.

Friedman's theory focuses on growth instead of equilibrium. He brushes off all fiscal policies as irrelevant – if not harmful. Instead he demands a commitment to a systematic, planned, and continuing expansion of money and credit at a fixed rate, such as 3 per cent a year. This would then do away, according to him, with the need to manage the national economy through fiscal measures, tax policies, budgetary deficits or surpluses, discount rates, and so on. This may well be the most radical proposal in economics since Adam Smith startled the eighteenth-century world with his conclusion that tariffs and subsidies only weaken national economies. Despite this, Friedman has been President of the American Economic Association. Ironically, this iconoclast is considered an arch-conservative and was Senator Goldwater's economic adviser during the 1964 campaign. Friedman is indeed an arch-conservative. Yet once he had put growth, rather than equilibrium, in the centre of his monetary theory, his radical conclusions were inevitable.

No American economist surpasses Milton Friedman in gathering monetary data. No one can outdo Friedman as a virtuoso economic analyst. Friedman, despite his reputation as the great conservative, is not, in other words, going back to the time before the new economics. He is going beyond it.

In Great Britain today the rising star in economics is not one of the Keynesians in the public eye, whether Labour or Conservative. He is G. L. S. Shackle, Professor of Economic Science at the University of Liverpool rather than at one of the prestige universities such as Oxford, Cambridge, or London, whence government advisers are usually drawn. Shackle is the only English economist to have been brought out in a paperback, and by the Cambridge University Press at that. By no means an easy author to read – the paperback title, *Economics for Pleasure*, is a gross misnomer – he is increasingly being read, especially by the younger British economists.

Shackle himself is thoroughly modern, in fact he first made a name as a guide to the Keynesians and post-Keynesians. He attracts the young precisely because he starts off – as did the classical economists a century ago – with the behaviour of the individual in the economy and indeed with the axiom of man, the individual, as the 'moving part' of the economy. His most original contribution is an attempt to base a comprehensive theory of economics on the expectations of businessmen and entrepreneurs. Here he starts with the goal, the future and our ideas thereof, and works back therefrom to present actions. His is the first true economics of a moving goal, the first economics based on teleological dynamics.

It makes little sense to ask whether these new economics 'beyond the new economics' are going to be 'conservative' or 'liberal'. Actually both are needed. Moreover, the coming economics will not repudiate the new economics. On the contrary, they will take from it the analysis, the rigour, the emphasis on quantification and the insistence on copious information rather than on opinion. But the coming economics will differ greatly from the new economics in its subject matter, in its concerns, and in its approach to economic activity.

A Society of Organizations

PART THREE

A Society of Organizations

8. The New Pluralism

HISTORIANS TWO HUNDRED years hence may see as central to the twentieth century what we ourselves have been paying almost no attention to: the emergence of a society of organizations in which every single social task of importance is being entrusted to a large institution. To us, the contemporaries, one of these institutions – government, big business, the university, or the labour union – often looks like *the* institution. To the future historian, however, the most impressive fact may be the emergence of a new and distinct pluralism, that is, of a society of institutional diversity and diffusion of power. He may report for the closing decades of the twentieth century an upsurge of creative thought in the social and political sphere as great as that of the seventeenth century when Bodin, Locke, and Hobbes gave us what we still call 'modern social theory'.

To most of us today, the power of central government seems to be unchallenged – whether we applaud or deplore it. Tomorrow's historian may come to call our era 'the twilight of central government'. Impotence rather than omnipotence may well appear to him the most remarkable feature of government in the closing decades of the twentieth century. And new political theory regarding the structure, organization, and limitations of power and government, both domestically and internationally, may play a prominent part in his narrative.

Sixty years ago, before World War I, the social scene everywhere looked much like the Kansas prairie: the largest thing on the horizon was the individual. Most social tasks were accomplished in and through family-sized units.

213

Even government, no matter how formidable it looked, was really small and cosy. The government of Imperial Germany looked like a colossus to its contemporaries; but an official in the middle ranks could still know personally everyone of importance in every single ministry and department.

The scaling up in size since then is striking. There is no country in the world today where the entire government establishment of 1910 could not comfortably be housed in the smallest of the new government buildings now going up, with room to spare for a grand-opera house and a skating rink.

This is true of the United States, where all the government agencies of Teddy Roosevelt's time – federal, state, and local – would find ample office space in a single one of the regional buildings of the Federal service that are now going up in Denver or Boise. It is just as true of Japan. Even the smallest Japanese prefecture has a brand-new office building that rivals the Tokyo ministry buildings that sufficed Imperial Japan when it challenged the West for world leadership twenty-five years ago.

Shortly before World War I, the citizens of Zürich in Switzerland built a new City Hall. At the time it was strongly criticized as an extravaganza grandiose beyond anything that would ever be needed. Zürich has grown little in the half-century since. And the Swiss rightly pride themselves on the simplicity and modesty of their local governments. Yet Zürich has long outgrown the City Hall of 1910; most of the local government is now in office skyscrapers all over the town.

The army of little Israel that clobbered the Arabs in June 1967 had less than one-tenth of the manpower of the army that Imperial Germany launched against France and Russia in 1914. But each Israeli soldier had at his disposal about two hundred times the firepower of

214

his 1914 Prussian counterpart. Indeed the Vietcong soldiers in Vietnam, for all that they were 'guerrillas' and 'lived off the land', had many times the firepower per soldier as the most highly powered army prior to the closing years of World War I.

The hospital of 1914 was a place for the poor to die. Fewer than three out of every hundred babies born in America (or anywhere else in the West) were born in hospitals at that time. Today all but one or two out of every hundred babies are born in hospitals – and most of the exceptions are born in the ambulance on the way there. For every hundred patients the hospital fifty years ago had thirty employees, most of them washerwomen and cooks. Now for every hundred patients it has three hundred employees, most of them highly trained 'health-care professionals' (such as medical and X-ray technicians, dietitians, psychiatric and social case workers, physiotherapists, and so on). The doctor of 1900 could easily practise medicine without access to a hospital. If he spent any time there, he did so out of the kindness of his heart to tend charity patients. Today the doctor is increasingly dependent on the hospital. Twenty years hence, doctors may well have their offices in the hospital. The hospital rather than the doctor's office is rapidly becoming the centre of modern health care.

No university in the Western world had more than 5,000 students before 1914. Even so the largest of them – Berlin – had become too big to be manageable; the Germans, in the years before World War I, had to split out research in the sciences and set it up in separate institutes. Today, universities of 20,000 students are 'medium-sized', and the research laboratory has grown just as fast. The first of the early German institutes for pure research, which numbered such giants as Planck and Einstein among its members, had a total employment of twenty or thirty scientists. Today, the Menninger Foundation in Topeka, Kansas – a specialized centre for research in psychiatry and mental health and by no means a very large one – has nine hundred employees of whom two hundred are professionals: psychiatrists, psychologists, neurologists, and so on.

In the days before World War I, the one 'large' organization around was business. But the 'big business' of 1910 would strike us today as a veritable 'minnow'. The 'octopus' that gave our grandparents nightmares, John D. Rockefeller's Standard Oil Trust, was cut into fourteen pieces by the Supreme Court in 1911. Less than thirty years later, by 1940, every one of these successor companies was larger than Rockefeller's Standard Oil Trust had been – by every measurement: employees, sales, capital invested, and so on. Yet only three of these fourteen Standard Oil daughter companies (Jersey Standard, Secony Mobil, and Standard of California) were 'major' international oil companies. The rest ranked from 'small' to 'middling' by 1940 yardsticks and would be 'small business' today, another thirty years later.

In America, we cannot hope to understand this society of ours unless we accept that *all* institutions have become giants. Businesses today are a good deal bigger than the biggest company was in John D. Rockefeller's time. But universities are relatively a good deal bigger than Rockefeller's other creation: the University of Chicago, which he founded, at about the turn of the century, as perhaps the first modern university in America. Hospitals are relatively bigger still, and a great deal more complex than any of the other institutions.

Even voluntary or charitable associations have become giants. The Young Men's Christian Association (YMCA) of the United States now has a budget in excess of 200 million dollars – more than even large states in this country spent before World War II. The YMCA employs thousands of people, and has its own internal staff concerned with management and organization.

The Carnegie Foundation – America's oldest – was a veritable giant of philanthropy only a generation ago. But the new giant, the Ford Foundation, in one recent year (1966) outspent Carnegie twenty-five times. Instead the Ford Foundation's disbursements that year – 350 million dollars – were larger than Carnegie's total assets. And the Ford Foundation staff is so huge that it has its own big office building not only in New York City but also in many capitals throughout the world where Ford has a larger mission than any but the Great Powers.

The problem of the 'concentration' of power is no longer peculiar to the American economy. Business concentration has not increased in the last sixty years or so, and 'small' business (which is also a good deal bigger than it used to be) is holding its own, apparently without difficulty. But the three or four largest labour unions hold relatively much more industrial power than the ten or twenty or thirty largest businesses. And we have a 'concentration of brain power' in a few large universities such as was never seen in any other area of social life – and such as would not have been tolerated earlier. The great majority of all doctors' degrees in the United States are given by some twenty universities – one-tenth of 1 per cent of all institutions of higher learning in the country. And nothing resembling the concentration of military might in the arsenals of the 'superpowers', the United States and Russia, has been known in international society since the Roman Empire at the peak of its power in the first century AD.

But the scaling up in size and budget is not the most important change. What makes the real difference is that all our major social functions are today being discharged in and through these large, organized institutions. Every single social task of major impact – defence and education, government and the production and distribution of goods, health care and the search for knowledge – are increasingly

217

entrusted to institutions which are organized for perpetuity and which are managed by professionals, whether they are called 'managers', 'administrators', or 'executives'.

Government looks like the most powerful of these institutions – it is certainly the one that spends the most. But each of the others discharges a function that is essential to society and has to be discharged in its own right. Each has its own autonomous management. Each has its own job to do, and therefore its own objectives, its own values, and its own rationale. If government is still the 'lord', it can no longer be the 'master'. Increasingly, whatever the theory of a government or its constitutional law, government functions as a 'coordinator', a 'chairman', or at most a 'leader'. Yet, paradoxically, government suffers from doing too much and too many things. For government, to be effective and strong, may have to learn to 'decentralize' to the other institutions, to *do* less in order to *achieve* more.

What has emerged in this half-century is a *new pluralism*. There is little left of the structure that our seventeenth-century political theory still preaches, a structure in which government is the only organized power centre. It is totally inadequate, however, to see just one of these new institutions – business, for instance, or the labour union, or the university – and proclaim it *the* new institution.* Social theory, to be meaningful at all, must start out with the reality of a pluralism of institutions – a galaxy of suns rather than one big centre surrounded by moons that shine only by reflected light.

---

* I must plead guilty to having done this myself – twenty-odd years ago. In *Concept of the Corporation* (published in the UK under the title of *Big Business*, William Heinemann Ltd, 1946), I called big business the 'determining' institution of our time. However, the other institutions were then barely visible; the crystalline structure of our society had not yet become apparent. There is little excuse today, however, for such oversimplification as that in John Kenneth Galbraith's latest book, *The New Industrial State* (Hamish Hamilton, London, 1967; Houghton Mifflin, New York and Boston, 1967).

Pluralist power centres of yesterday – the duke, the count, the abbot, even the yeoman – differed from each other only in titles and revenues. One was the superior and overlord of the other. Each centre was limited in territory but each was a total community and embraced whatever organized social activity and political life there was. Each and every one of them was concerned with the same basic activity, above all wresting a livelihood from the land. The Federalism of the American system still assumes this traditional pluralism. Federal government, state and municipalities all have their own distinct geographic limitation and stand to each other in a position of higher and lower. But each has essentially the same function. Each is a territorial government with police powers and tax powers, charged with traditional governmental tasks, whether defence, justice, or public order.

This is simply not true of the new institutions. Each of them is a special-purpose institution. The hospital exists for the sake of health care; the business to produce economic goods and services; the university for the advancement and teaching of knowledge; each government agency for its own specific purpose; the Armed Services for defence, and so on. Not one of them can be considered 'superior' or 'inferior' to the other – for only a fool would consider the advancement of knowledge superior to health care or to the provision of economic goods and services. But, at the same time, not one of them can be defined territorially. Each, in other words, is 'universal' in a way that none of the old institutions (excepting only the medieval Church) ever claimed to be. And yet each of them is limited to a small fragment of human existence, to a single facet of human community.

The problems of this new pluralism are quite different from the problems of both the pluralisms of our past and the unitary society of our political theory and constitutional law. In earlier pluralisms every member of the system, from the yeoman up to the most powerful king, understood exactly the positions of the other members of the hierarchy, their concerns, and their problems. Everyone had exactly the same concerns and the same problems – only the scale varied. In the new pluralism each institution has different concerns. It takes different things for granted. It considers different things to be important. While the vice-president of a big business, the division chief in the government agency, and the department chairman in the university may operate on a very similar scale and have managerial problems of comparable magnitude, they do not easily understand each other's roles, tasks, and decisions. The members of earlier pluralisms were for ever worried about their 'precedence' and their place in the hierarchy relative to each other. This is not a major concern in today's pluralism. The hospital administrator is not particularly concerned as to whether he equals in rank the corporation president or the union leader or the Air Force general. But they all worry about 'communications'. It takes a great deal of experience – or at the least, a great deal of imagination – for one of the executives in today's pluralism to have any idea what the other ones are up to and why.

These organizations have to live together and to work together. They are interdependent. Not one of them could exist by itself. Not one of them is by itself viable, let alone a total community, as were the components of earlier pluralist society.

A theory of the society of organizations would have to be built on organizational interdependence. The modern Armed Services depend fully on the civilian apparatus of government. They depend equally on the economic institutions. Most of all, perhaps, do they depend on the universities. Dwight D. Eisenhower in his Farewell Message as President in 1961 warned of the 'military-industrial complex', formed by the symbiosis of a powerful and permanent military establishment and a powerful and permanent defence industry. But actually, even at the height of the Vietnam War, the United States economy was not particularly dependent on defence business. If all the defence business had been eliminated with one stroke, there would have been no great crisis except in a few spots such as Southern California. The large universities of the country are, however, increasingly dependent on the military – and the military, in turn, on them. To speak of the 'military-university complex' makes a good deal of sense. And government depends on the economic fruits of business and the taxes they generate. The labour union is dependent on management; it is equally dependent on government. Of all our major institutions, the union is the most nearly derivative. It requires both business management to produce the economic results which sustain the union and satisfy its demands, and government to provide the political support without which no union movement would last long.

Never having known anything remotely like the society of organizations we now have, we have yet to learn to understand our pluralist society and to formulate a policy for it. What is required is acceptance of its structure, realization that every single major task has become institutionalized, and that we will have to deal with the problems this creates as generic problems of our society and as its norm.

This is a big change in perception. The first to make it were the 'hippies'. Where the 'liberal' and the 'conservative' alike still singled out this or that institution as either the 'villain' or the 'hero' of society, the 'hippies' during the last ten years have seen clearly that all society is one of organizations. While not all the young people are 'hippies', the perception of our society as one of organizations is shared by the entire generation that is now reaching adulthood. It is the most visible characteristic of the 'generation gap'. The young are as alienated from the university as they are from the Armed Services or the government agency.

We will not be granted the luxury of the hippies' rejection of all organization. This is a luxury only the very young can afford, a luxury that presumes that the adults are taking care of things. But the adults will have to concern themselves with the reality that the hippies would like to make go away – the reality of a society of organizations.

THE SYMBIOSIS OF ORGANIZATIONS

The interdependence of organizations is different from anything that was ever meant before by this term. It is not new, of course, that no man in society is an island. It is not new that all of us, including the hermit, can only live in our own way because it can be taken for granted that a host of other people will do their jobs for us.

This physical interdependence is what people usually have in mind when they think about 'interdependence' at all. And, of course, this traditional kind of interdependence has become much more pronounced. The megalopolis, above all, is a universe of interacting, interdependent services, each absolutely essential for the functioning of the whole and for the very existence of each member of the community.

But the new interdependence among organizations is not primarily physical. Increasingly major organizations farm out to each other the very performance of their own functions. Increasingly each organization is using the others as agents for the accomplishment of its own tasks. There is an intertwining of functions such as has never been known before. The roles are subject to rapid change; what one organization was expected to do today, another one may take on tomorrow.

In the United States defence production was, prior to World War II, conducted in and by government-owned arsenals and dockyards, excepting only during major wars. It was almost an axiom in American government that defence production had to be a government monopoly, with outside buying confined to rare and short periods of emergency. But since World War II, defence has primarily been supplied through buying from private contractors outside. We are closing the government's own shipyards and are concentrating Naval ship-building in private yards. What was considered rare emergency procedure has become the rule.

Even more amazing, work on military technology is also being contracted out. Increasingly business and the university have taken on defence research. To be sure, the Federal government has become the main source of research funds in the United States, in the defence and space fields, in medicine, and the social sciences as well. But, at the same time, the government itself conducts proportionately a good deal less defence research than it did a generation ago when it was axiomatic that research relating to the defence of the nation is conducted in government establishments.

Defence may be considered a poor example. We do not live in 'peacetime' but in a permanent twilight between war and peace. Everything related to defence, including production, procurement, and research, it might be said, is therefore certain to be a new kind of hybrid.

But the same 'hybrid' can be found in areas where defence considerations do not enter. Politicians who are by no means noted for being conservatives (such as the late Robert Kennedy) have been proposing that metropolitan housing be handed over to private business. The only part of the War on Poverty that is not hopelessly bogged down in confusion and splintering, the Job Corps, is largely run by private companies such as Litton, ITT, and Westinghouse. In the state of California, private business has been used, with conspicuous success it seems, to study major policy problems facing the state – the rise in crime, for instance.

For the first time in United States history, a major benefit programme for soldiers, the insurance programme for the men in Vietnam, has been farmed out entirely to private insurance companies (with the Prudential as prime contractor). Blue Cross and private insurance carriers are running Medicare for the government. And with Medicare and Medicaid it is reasonably certain that the Veterans' Hospitals – the oldest 'socialized' medicine in America – will disappear, with the job taken over by the voluntary and non-governmental community hospital as agent of the government.

Large universities such as Massachusetts Institute of Technology and California Institute of Technology, as well as Harvard and Columbia University, have become the most prolific breeders of new private businesses. The 'science industry' of the last decades largely grew out of specialized university laboratories. Theoretical physicists in particular have proved extraordinarily capable as entrepreneurs and promoters of new companies.

A good example – only one of many – is ITEK in Boston, a leader in space optics and one of the 'glamour' stocks of the last years, which started as a physics laboratory of Boston University in World War II.

Another example of this trend towards the blurring of the lines that only a generation ago separated 'public' from 'private', is the growth of business into education.

One big company after the other – IBM and General Electric, Time Inc, Westinghouse, Litton, RCA, and Raytheon, to name only a few – has decided that education is the most promising field for business expansion. Litton, for instance, under a contract with Oakland County, Michigan (just outside Detroit), has designed and is largely running a big new community college which experiments with all kinds of new learning techniques and tools. Westinghouse and IBM are busy in the

Palo Alto, California, school system. Even a small company like Revell, a manufacturer of hobby kits, is running an educational experiment in a high school in Colorado.

It no longer shocks anyone to hear that the hospital of tomorrow or the school of tomorrow may be designed, built, and largely run by businesses – for the trustees or the board, of course. It no longer shocks anyone to hear the Mayor of New York City propose that the city hospitals be turned over to the private hospitals – just at the time when the private hospitals increasingly talk about turning over their administration to large companies with 'systems' experience. And what many hail as the first promising attacks on the horrible mess of urban housing are the proposals of a few large companies, eg, General Electric, to develop whole planned cities within reasonable commuting distance of the major metropolitan areas. Another large company, US Gypsum, has been developing new approaches to housing for the poor which, by using new materials and methods, convert slum dwellings into decent housing at fairly low cost and without 'bulldozing off' the poor in the name of 'slum clearance'.

The United States government has moved massively into research in the industrial fields and in medicine, but it has moved out of the one area of research where it used to have a monopoly: agriculture. Our textbooks still teach that governments, federal and state, do most of the agricultural research work. But it is no longer true. Most of today's research in agriculture is done by private enterprise such as the seed companies, the farm-implement makers and the fertilizer manufacturers. Thirty years ago the governmental extension service was the prime agent in moving new technology – seeds, feeds, fertilizers, methods of cultivation and implements – from the test plot to the farm. Today this work is done largely by the sales and service organizations of private companies. The government confines itself increasingly to testing claims made by private developers of the new agricultural technology.

What used to be simple relationships in which major institutions rarely met each other, and even more rarely had much to do with each other, is becoming an increasingly complex, confused, diffuse, and crowded living together. It is a chaotic, a developing, and by no means a clear, let alone a clean, relationship. Political scientists are wont to talk of the 'web' of government. But what we now have could only be described as a 'felt' of government in which strands of the most diverse kind are tangled together in no order at all.

The head of one American corporation – a sizeable one, though not one of the giants – had five emissaries from government calling on him separately during one day not so long ago. The first one brought an invitation from President Johnson to serve on a commission to study trademark laws. The next one served an indictment from the Anti-Trust Division of the Department of Justice, charging the company with conspiracy to restrain competition in the use of a trademark. Then came the Department of Defence, urgently requesting the company to take on a research contract – in the same area in which Anti-Trust had just charged the company with criminal conspiracy. The mayor of the city followed with a request that the company should take on a training programme for the underprivileged designed to give them craft skills rapidly. A European government wanted to discuss a proposal that the company should take over and manage an ailing government-owned plant. 'I was interrupted by these government people so often,' said the president, 'that I could not finish what was on my agenda for the day – we are thinking about contracting out a good bit of the applied research we are today doing in our own laboratories to a major new research centre, founded cooperatively by a number of universities in the Upper South.'

Small wonder that our traditional rules, regulations, and customs cannot handle these almost incestuous love–hate relationships. The laws for defence procurement in the United States, for instance, are all based on the assumption that outside buying is 'temporary emergency'. They are further based on the assumption that what the government buys are normal civilian supplies, such as uniforms. Specific defence material, it is assumed, will be made essentially by the government itself. That these laws cannot easily be applied to the design and production of a missile system by private industry is not astonishing. What is astonishing is that we get anything designed and produced at all under the existing defence procurement regulations.

I served several years ago on a panel on patent law. My colleagues on the panel were all patent lawyers. They were concerned with technical reforms. As I listened to their talk, however, it became clear to me, the outsider, that technicalities were not the reason why the patent law had become a matter for discussion. The underlying assumptions were changing – and the law had not changed with them. It simply had been taken for granted by the authors of our present patent law that research and invention in mechanical and industrial areas are done by private individuals either working for themselves or for private entrepreneurs. The law does not yet know that 75 per cent of the money spent today on research and invention is federal money. The patent law is saved, at least for the time being, by the fact that the government so far only knows how to spend money on research but not how to produce inventions. Much more than 75 per cent – closer to 90 per cent – of all patentable inventions are still the result of private innovative activities. Government-financed research so far has been remarkably sterile. Even so, however, the patent law no longer fits reality. This is the reason why there are difficulties with it. Tinkering with

227

technicalities will not fix them. Yet no one so far understands sufficiently what the new reality is, will be, or should be, to write a patent law appropriate to it.

These are truly *liaisons dangereuses* and difficult relationships. The more results they produce, the more friction they also entail. If government, for instance in the defence programme, insists that its private contractors adapt to the logic and rationale of a government service, they smother the contractor in red tape, in regulations, and in bureaucratic restrictions. And in the end, government is greatly irked because the contractor does not produce. But if government accepts the contractor's rationale and way of operating, that is, a business logic, the hard-won principles of accountability for public money all go by the board. In public accounts it is assumed that results, as a rule, cannot be clearly measured. What matters, therefore, is that costs be scrupulously recorded. Costs exist – results are hypothetical. But in business logic, costs exist only in contemplation of results. As long as the results are there, the less spent on controlling costs the better. The government servant simply does not understand this. But the businessman equally does not understand the government man's logic. Both rub each other raw trying to work together, both resent the attitude of the other and are deeply suspicious of it – and yet both are dependent on one another.

The same is true of yoking together government and the medical profession. Medical men see individuals. None of us would want to be treated by a physician who treats 'averages'. But no government can handle anything but large numbers or go by anything but 'averages'. The relationships between university and business, between university and government, between university and the Armed Forces is similarly one of mutual failure to understand, of mutual suspicion, and constant friction. And yet we will continue to see more of these relationships. They are necessary to produce the results which society wants.

Bureaucracies, whether of government, of big business,

of the large hospital, or of the large university, share at least common patterns. But legislative bodies are baffled and deeply disturbed by the symbiotic relationships of the society of organizations. These relationships defy any control by the purse. They elude control by the legislature, whether the legislature be a parliament, a congress, or even the rubber-stamp of a Communist assembly. As a result legislatures feel that they no longer understand, let alone control. The more intimately the various large organizations work together, the more irked and perturbed will legislatures become.

I have taken my examples from the United States. But the phenomenon is universal – both in respect to the growing interdependence of the various organizations and to the friction it creates. One of the best examples of both would be the Ferranti affair which, a few years ago, made headlines in Great Britain. The problem there was apparently that Ferranti – a large electronics company – had taken on a design contract for British defence which it performed so well that it made a large profit on it – to everybody's shocked surprise. But the problem is just as acute in the relationship between the British National Health Service and the British teaching hospitals. Each needs the other. Increasingly the hospitals act as agents and sub-contractors to the Health Service – but increasingly the two rub each other up the wrong way.

The problem exists in the Communist world as well. There is mutual dependence, for instance, between 'politicians' and 'managers' – and deep rivalry and mutual suspicion between them as well.

THE NEED FOR THEORY

The pluralist structure of modern society is independent, by and large, of political constitution and control, of social theory, or of economics. It has, therefore, to be tackled as such. It requires a political and social theory of its own.

This is true of each individual organization as well. It, too, is new. We have, of course, had large organizations for centuries. The pyramids were built by highly organized masses of people. Armies have often been large and highly organized. But these organizations of yesterday – Lewis Mumford calls them the 'Megamachines'* – were fundamentally different from the institutions of today.

Great architects designed the pyramids – their names are recorded, and they were worshipped as gods. But other than those few artist-geometers, there were only unskilled manual labourers, peasants from the villages, who pulled the ropes to move the big stones. Henry Ford's River Rouge plant making the Model T was an organization of the same kind – a handful of bosses who knew whatever was known, gave whatever orders were given, and made whatever decision was made. The rest were unskilled manual labourers doing repetitive work. The basic difference between the pyramid builders and Henry Ford's men on the assembly line was that 'Scientific Management' of the task made possible very high pay for the automobile worker. But the work and its organization was the same – and Henry Ford was conscious of this in his insistence that he be the only 'manager' in the Ford Motor Company.

Today's organization (including today's Ford Motor Company) is, however, principally a knowledge organization. It exists to make productive hundreds, sometimes thousands, of specialized kinds of knowledge. This is true of the hospital where there are now some thirty-odd or more health-care professions – each with its own course of study, its own diploma, and its own professional code and standards. It is true of today's business, of today's government agency, and increasingly of today's Army. In every

* In his book *The Myth of the Machine* (Secker & Warburg, London, 1967; Houghton Mifflin, New York and Boston, 1967).

one of them the bulk of the workers are hired not to do manual work but to do knowledge work. The Egyptian *Fellahin* who pulled at the ropes when Cheops' supervisors barked out the order did not have to do any thinking and were not expected to have any initiative. The typical employee in today's large organization is expected to use his head to make decisions and to put knowledge responsibly to work.

But perhaps even more important: today's knowledge organization is designed as a permanent organization. All the large organizations of the past were shortlived. They were called into being for one specific task and disbanded when the task had been accomplished. They were temporary.

They were clearly the exception as well. The great majority of people in earlier society were unaffected by them. Today the great majority of people depend on organization for their livelihood, their opportunities, and their work. The large organization is the environment of man in modern society.

It is the source also of the opportunities of today's society. It is only because we have these institutions that there are jobs for educated people. Without them we would be confined, as always in the past, to jobs for people without education; people who, whether skilled or unskilled, work with their hands. Knowledge jobs exist only because permanent knowledge organization has become the rule.

At the same time, modern organization creates new problems as well – above all, problems of authority over people. For authority is needed to get the job done. What should it be? What is legitimate? What are the limitations? There are also problems of the purpose, task, and effectiveness of each organization. There are problems of management. For the organization itself, like every collective, is a legal fiction. It is individuals in the organization who make the decisions and take the actions which are then ascribed to the institution, whether it be the 'United

States', the 'General Electric Company', or 'Misericordia Hospital'. There are problems of order and problems of morality. There are problems of efficiency and problems of relationships. And for none of them does tradition offer us much guidance.

The permanent organization in which varieties of knowledge are brought together to achieve results is new. The organization as the rule rather than as the expection is new. And a society of organization is the newest thing of them all.

What is therefore urgently needed, is a theory of organizations.

9. Towards a Theory of Organizations

IN THE SPRING of 1968, a witty book made headlines for a few weeks. Entitled *Management and Machiavelli** it asserted that every business is a political organization and that, therefore, Machiavelli's rules for princes and rulers are fully applicable to the conduct of corporation executives.

Of course, this is not a particularly new insight. More than a century ago Anthony Trollope used the theme of Machiavellian politics in a British diocese to write one of the great Victorian classics, *Barchester Towers*. C. P. Snow, especially in *The Masters* (1951), has presented the university as an interplay of power. And the point that the corporation is a polity and a community fully as much as it is an economic organ has been made many times by now.†

The suburban ladies, at whom the reviews of *Management and Machiavelli* were largely aimed, are probably fully aware that the Bridge Club and the PTA have nothing to learn about politicking from big business, or indeed from Machiavelli. That every organization must organize power and must therefore have politics is neither new nor startling.

---

* By Anthony Jay (Hodder & Stoughton, London, 1967; Holt, Rinehart & Winston, New York, 1968).

† For instance, in my two books, *Concept of the Corporation* (published in the UK under the title of *Big Business*, William Heinemann Ltd, 1946) and *The New Society* (William Heinemann Ltd, London, 1951; Harper & Row, New York, 1950).

But during the last twenty years, non-business – government, the Armed Services, the universities, the hospitals – have begun to apply to themselves the concepts and methods of business management. And this is indeed new. This is startling.

When the Canadian Armed Services were unified in the spring of 1968, the first meeting of general officers from all the Services had as its theme, 'managing by objectives'. Government after government has organized 'administrative staff colleges' for its senior civil servants in which it tries to teach them 'principles of management'. And when 9,000 secondary school principals of the United States met in the crisis year of 1968, with its racial troubles and its challenges to established curricula, they chose for their keynote speech, 'The Effective Executive', and invited an expert on business management to deliver it.

The British Civil Service, that citadel of the 'arts degree' in the classics, now has a management division, a management institute, and management courses of all kinds. Demand from non-business organizations for the services of 'management consultants' is rising a great deal faster than the demand from businesses.

What is new is the realization that all our institutions are 'organizations' and have as a result a common dimension of management. These organizations are complex and multi-dimensional. They require thinking and understanding in at least three areas – the functional or operational; the moral; and the political. The new general theory of a society of organizations will look very different from the social theories we are accustomed to. Neither Locke nor Rousseau have much relevance. Neither have John Stuart Mill nor Karl Marx.

MAKING ORGANIZATION PERFORM

How do organizations function and operate? How do they do their job? There is not much point in concerning ourselves with any other question about organizations unless we first know what they exist for.

The functional or operational area by itself has three major parts, each a large and diverse discipline in its own right. They have to do with goals, with management, and with individual performance.

(1) Organizations do not exist for their own sake. They are means, each society's organ for the discharge of one social task. Survival is not an adequate goal for an organization as it is for a biological species. The organization's goal is a specific contribution to individual and society. The test of its performance, unlike that of a biological organism, therefore always lies outside it.

The first area in which we need a theory of organizations is, therefore, that of the organization's goals. How does it decide what its objectives should be? How does it mobilize its energies for performance? How does it measure whether it performs?

It is not possible to be effective unless one first decides what one wants to accomplish. It is not possible to manage, in other words, unless one first has a goal. It is not even possible to design the structure of an organization unless one knows what it is supposed to be doing and how to measure whether it is doing it.

Anyone who has ever tried to answer the question, 'What is our business?' has found it a difficult, controversial, and elusive task. 'We make shoes' may seem obvious and simple. But it is a useless answer. It does not tell anyone what to do. Nor, equally important, does it tell anyone what not to do. Are we primarily concerned with the conversion of leather into goods that consumers will want to pay for? Or are we primarily concerned with mass distribution? Or are we in the fashion business? 'Shoes' are simply a vehicle. What we actually do depends much less on the vehicle than on the specific economic satisfaction it is meant to carry and the specific contribution for which the business expects to get paid.

Is a company that makes and sells kitchen appliances, such as electric ranges, in the food business? Or is it in the home-making business? Or is its main business really consumer finance? Each answer might be the right one at a given time for a given company. But each would lead to very different conclusions as to where the company should put its efforts and seek its rewards.

If the answer given is 'the food business', the company might go into preparing and marketing ready-cooked meals that require only heating to be served and eaten. But, if the answer is 'consumer finance', the company might go out of manufacturing altogether and instead distribute a wide variety of high-cost consumer goods from wedding rings to trailer homes. These, however, would be the vehicle to carry the real 'product' of the company, which would be consumer credit.

In each of these definitions, different economic factors are seen as dynamic and as determining results. Each, in turn, requires different abilities and defines both 'market' and 'success' differently.

Similarly, 'patient care' might seem an obvious and simple answer for the hospital. Hospital administrators, however, have found it impossible to define 'what is patient care' or 'what is health care'.

One reason why these questions are so difficult is that people differ in their judgements regarding the needs of the community. They set different priorities. There is also always a conflict between those who want to do better what is already being done, and those who want to do different things.

In fact, it is never possible to give a 'final' answer to the question, 'What is our business?' Any answer becomes obsolete within a short period. The question has to be thought through again and again. But if no answer at all is forthcoming, if objectives are not clearly set, resources will be splintered and wasted. There will be no way to measure the results. If the organization has not determined what its objectives are, it cannot determine what effectiveness it has and whether it is obtaining results or not.

The cost/effectiveness concept which Robert McNamara introduced into the management of the American military forces while Secretary of Defence under President Kennedy was, above all, an attempt to force the military to think through objectives. Starting out from the truism that everything requires scarce resources and therefore incurs a cost, McNamara demanded that costs are related to results. This process disclosed at once that the military had not thought through what results it expected because it had not thought through the objectives of strategy of a command (eg, the Tactical Air Force) or of a weapon. Is the objective to win a war? Or is it to prevent one? What kind of a war and where? These were the questions the cost/effectiveness formula forced the generals and admirals to think through and to work out among themselves and with their civilian superiors. Cost/effectiveness could not make policy decisions. But it did bring the confusion of policy and objectives into the open. It did show both how vital the decision on objectives is, and how difficult and risky it is.

There is no 'scientific' way to set objectives for an organization. They are rightly value judgements, that is, true political questions. One reason for this is that the decisions stand under incurable uncertainty. They are concerned with the future. And we have no 'facts' regarding the future. In this area, therefore, there is always a clash of programme and a conflict of political values.

Yet the twentieth-century political scientist was not entirely irresponsible when he abandoned concern with values, political programmes, and ideologies and focused instead on the process of decision-making. The most difficult and most important decisions in respect to objectives are not what to do. They are, firstly, what to abandon as no longer worth while; and secondly, what to give priority to and what to concentrate on. These are not, as a rule, ideological decisions. They are judgements, of course; they are, and should be, informed judgements, they should be based on a definition of alternatives rather than on opinion and emotion.

The decision what to abandon is by far the most important and the most neglected.

Large organizations cannot be versatile. A large organization is effective through its mass rather than through its agility. Fleas can jump many times their own height, but not elephants. Mass enables the organization to put to work a great many more kinds of knowledge and skill than could possibly be combined in any one person or small group. But mass is also a limitation. An organization, no matter what it would like to do, can only do a small number of tasks at any one time. This is not something that better organizations or 'effective communications' can cure. *The Law of Organization is Concentration.*

Also inherent in organization is the separation of those who decide from those who carry out.

In single combat, as under the walls of Troy, the individual swordsman was also his own strategist. But a military organization does not have to be very large before those who fight must get their commands from somebody else who is far from the scene of combat. This means that there has to be a 'plan', a preparation for carrying it out, and preparation for changing it if necessary. If the plan is changed fast or without preparation, total confusion ensues. Some of the people at the front will still follow the old plan and simply get in the way of those who have switched to whatever the new plan demands. The bigger the organization, the longer it takes to change direction and the more important it is to maintain a course.

Yet modern organization must be capable of change. Indeed it must be capable of initiating change, that is, innovation. It must be able to move scarce and expensive resources of knowledge from areas of low productivity and non-results to opportunities for achievement and contribution. Organization is a maximizing device. And modern organization is our device to maximize that unique human resource, knowledge. This, however, requires the ability to stop doing what wastes resources rather than maximizes them.

An organization, whatever its objectives, must therefore be able to get rid of yesterday's tasks and thus free its energies and resources for new and more productive tasks. If it wants to be able to work on opportunities, it must be able to abandon the unproductive and to slough off the obsolete.

No organization which purposefully and systematically abandons the unproductive and obsolete ever wants for opportunities. Ideas are always around in profusion. This is certainly true for the kind of ideas an organization needs and can use, that is, ideas of sufficient clarity, definition, and acceptability to be applied in performance. These are not 'original' ideas as the artist would define this term. They are, so to speak, ideas that are ready for the popularizer, ideas which have already passed the test of imagination and now only await the test of application.

Lack of 'creativity' is, therefore, not the problem of organization. Rather it is organizational inertia which always pushes for continuing what we are already doing. At least we know – or we think we know – what we are doing. Organization is always in danger of being overwhelmed by yesterday's tasks and being rendered sterile by them.

If a subject has become obsolete, the university faculty makes a required course out of it – and this 'solves the problem' for the time being. Hospital administrators have known for decades now that the open ward is un-economical. Their figures show plainly that the private room for single occupancy is the most economical accommodation (for the simple reason that it permits mixing the sexes on the same floor and thus makes possible having one full floor rather than two half empty ones each of which requires full staffing). They also know that the open ward is undignified, medically undesirable, and an impediment to rapid recovery. Yet they are still building new wards when adding wings to existing hospitals, and even in brand-new hospitals. And while every medical school has added new medical specialities to the curriculum, I know of none that has dropped a single one of the old ones.

The worst offender is government. The inability to stop doing anything is the central degenerative disease of government and a major reason why government today is sick.

Several years ago a Royal Commission on the Government of Canada took an inventory of all Canadian government agencies. It found that there was still a 'Halifax Disaster Commission' in Nova Scotia, busily copying the records of relief payments that had been made forty years earlier, at the end of World War I, to the victims of a 1917 explosion of an ammunitions ship in Halifax Harbour. Yet the Canadian government has been fairly tight-fisted and closely controlled, by and large, if only because each of the ten provinces resents the spending of tax money outside its own borders.

Hospital and university are only a little better than government in getting rid of yesterday. But business does reasonably well in this area. Businessmen are just as sentimental about yesterday as bureaucrats. They are just as reluctant to abandon anything. They are just as likely to respond to the failure of a product or programme by doubling the efforts invested in it. But they are, fortunately, unable to indulge freely in their predilections. They stand under an objective discipline, the discipline of the market. They have an objective outside measurement, profitability. And so they are forced (much to their chagrin) to slough off the unsuccessful and unproductive sooner or later.

Concepts and measurements are needed that give to other organizations what the market test and the profitability yardstick give to business. The tests and yardsticks will undoubtedly be quite different. Economic results, which in a business are determining, are only limitations and restraints for other organizations. For profit measures economic performance, and this is the purpose only of an economic organization, that is, a business. In other organizations – government, hospitals, the military, and so on – economics is only a restraint. These institutions need a noneconomic equivalent to the profitability yardstick. They also need a substitute for the objective force of the market.

All organizations need a discipline that makes them face up to reality. They need to recognize that the probability of any activity or programme failing is always greater than the probability that it will turn out successfully, let alone that it will accomplish what it was designed to do. They need to know that virtually no programme or activity will perform for a long time without modifications and redesign. Eventually every activity becomes obsolete.

Equally crucial to the area of objectives is the decision concerning priorities of concentration.

If there is one dependable finding from a century's study of the political process, it is that action decisons are rarely made on the basis of ideology. The crucial question is:

'What comes first?' rather than 'What should be done?' There is often substantial agreement as to what should be done, but there is always disagreement as to what should be done first.

The normal human reaction is to evade the priority decision by doing a little bit of everything. This, I am afraid, is what President Johnson meant by his famous 'consensus'. The result, predictably, was that nothing got done. In the end there was greater conflict and dissension than any debate over priorities could have engendered.

(2) In their objectives the major organizations are all different. Each of them serves a different purpose of the community. In the managerial area, however, organizations are essentially similar.

Since all organizations require large numbers of people brought together for joint performance and integrated into a common undertaking, they all have the problem of balancing the objectives of the institution against the needs and desires of the individual. Each organization has the task of balancing the need for order against the need for flexibility and individual scope. Each requires a structure determined by the task and its demands. Each also requires a structure determined by generic 'principles of organization', that is, in effect, by constitutional rules. Unless each recognizes the authority inherent in the 'logic of the situation' and the knowledge of individuals there will be no performance. Unless each also has a decision-making authority beyond which there is no appeal, there will be no decision. And the two different structures, each with a logic of its own, have to co-exist in dynamic balance within the same organization.

It is in this field of management that the most work has been done during the last half-century. The task had never before been faced of organizing and leading large knowledge organizations. We had to learn rapidly. No one who knows the field would maintain that we yet know much. If there is any agreement in this hotly contested area, it is that tomorrow's organization structures will look different from any we know today. Yet work in management is by now no longer pioneering. What is taught under this name in our universities may be 90 per cent old wives' tales – and the rest may be procedures rather than management. Still the main challenges in the area are sufficiently well known.

We know, for instance, that we have to measure results. We also know that, with the exception of business, we do not know how to measure results in most organizations.

It may sound plausible to measure the effectiveness of a mental hospital by how well its beds – a scarce and expensive commodity – are utilized. Yet a study of the mental hospitals of the Veterans Administration brought out that this yardstick leads to mental patients being kept in the hospital – which, therapeutically, is about the worst thing that can be done to them. Clearly, however, lack of utilization, that is, empty beds, would also not be the right yardstick. How does one then measure whether a mental hospital is doing a good job within the wretched limits of our knowledge of mental diseases?

And how does one measure whether a university is doing a good job? By the jobs and salaries its students get twenty years after graduation? By that elusive myth, the 'reputation' of this or that faculty which, only too often, is nothing but self-praise and good academic propaganda? By the number of PhDs or scientific prizes the alumni have earned? Or by the donations they make to their Alma Mater? Each such yardstick bespeaks a value judgement regarding the purpose of the university – and a very narrow one at that. Even if these were the right objectives, such yardsticks measure performance just as dubiously as the count of bed utilization measures performance in the mental hospitals.

There are also unsolved problems in respect to top management which is the crucial organ in any institution. We do not really know how to train, select, and test people before they are entrusted with the top jobs. Yet this is one decision which is usually almost impossible to undo once it has been taken – regardless of the legal structure of the institution. It is also undesirable to have to undo such a decision fast. Instability at the top is as bad as incompetence at the top. General de Gaulle was absolutely right in his insistence that the ability of French parliaments to overthrow any cabinet at any time was a fatal weakness of the French Republic. But he may also have lived long enough to demonstrate that the inability of an institution to get rid of a top man who has outlived his usefulness is just as serious and as dangerous.

No one has been able to find a solution – indeed there is reason to believe that there is no solution. The top position requires an ability to make decisions and to assume command which cannot be tested except in the top job. Whatever we train and test for is also likely to be nullified by events. No chief executive, whether of a Great Power or of a Boy Scout troop, has ever, in his tenure, had to tackle the problems for which he was selected and put in the job. The one thing that is known about the chief executive's job is that the challenges are always different from what was foreseen when he took over.

But there are also some fundamental philosophical issues that have been around for a long time. Should structure, ie, constitution, be absolute and according to principles of organization? Or should it be focused on specific objectives and strategy, that is, tailored to the needs and the logic of the situation? How about the balance between efficiency and effectiveness in management? The two, it is clear, are not the same. But are they even easily compatible?

To be concrete: there is a sharp clash today between stress on the efficiency of administration (as represented, above all, by the governmental administrator and the accountant) and stress on effectiveness (which emphasizes results). The efficiency approach insists that results will come automatically if things are done right, and therefore mistrusts any deviation from proper procedure. The effectiveness approach, however, points out that in any social effort, 80 per cent of the results are achieved by the first 20 per cent of the efforts and that the remaining 80 per cent of efforts only produce 20 per cent of results. The last 5 per cent of results, above all, in any social activity require as much efforts as the first 95 per cent.

In the first approach, efforts are seen as central; in the second, results. In the first, the hallmark of good management is order. In the second, it is vitality. The efficiency approach sees administration as desirable and as the strength of an organization. The effectiveness approach sees it as support, a necessary evil to be confined to the minimum needed to prevent collapse. The efficiency approach wants to make mediocrity capable of producing predictable results again and again. It is based on a realistic view of men, and of men in organization. The effectiveness approach wants to liberate creative energy. This too is a realistic view of man.

In short, whatever one's inclinations – and my own bias is all on the side of effectiveness – both approaches are needed. If we let efficiency predominate, as governments tend to do, procedures will overgrow results. No defence contractor in the United States has ever been criticized either by the General Accounting Office or by Congress for hiring too many clerks or for filling in too many forms. But where we let effectiveness predominate, we are in danger of being tripped up by the slighted routine. Battles are not won because horses are properly shod; but as the old nursery rhyme of the junior accountants reminds us, 'for want of a nail, the kingdom was lost'.

We do not truly understand how one manages knowledge for productive work. We do not yet truly understand how one integrates men of different knowledge and skills, each making a specific contribution, into one joint venture for common results. The knowledge worker makes possible modern organization. In turn, the emergence of organization has created the jobs and opportunities for the knowledge worker. But how to make knowledge productive, we do not yet know. Where it is being done, it is by accident or by intuition.

We have, in other words, a great deal to learn about management. Indeed, the great age of management as a discipline is probably still ahead. But the 'heroic age' in which the discipline was founded is behind us. It lay in the quarter-century before World War II. Then the basic thinking was being done by such men as the Frenchman Fayol, the British Ian Hamilton and L. F. Urwick, and the American, Alfred Sloan at General Motors – to name only a few of the pioneers. They made possible the great organizing feats of World War II in all combatant countries. Since then, in business and government, as well as in the military, we have, by and large, only refined what was first learned in the Twenties and Thirties and first applied in the early Forties.

(3) The last field within the operational area is probably the one in which there is the least difference in organizations. This is the area of personal effectiveness within organizations.

Organizations are legal fictions. By themselves they do nothing, decide nothing, plan nothing. Individuals do, decide, and plan. Above all, organizations only 'act' in so far as the people act whom we commonly call 'executives', that is, the people who are expected to make decisions that affect the results and performance of the organization.

As I pointed out in an earlier book,* in the knowledge

* *The Effective Executive* (William Heinemann Ltd, London, 1967; Harper & Row, New York, 1967).

organization, every knowledge worker is an 'executive'. The number of people who have to be effective for modern organization to perform is therefore very large and rapidly growing. The well-being of our entire society depends increasingly on the ability of these large numbers of knowledge workers to be effective in a true organization. And so, largely, do the achievement and satisfaction of the knowledge worker.

Executive effectiveness is not only something the organization needs. It is not the formula for the 'organization man' of popular myth. It is, above all, something the individual needs. For the organization must be *his* tool, while at the same time it produces the results that are needed by society and community.

Executive effectiveness is not automatic. It is not 'how to be successful without half trying'. It is not even 'how to be successful while trying'. The organization is a new and different environment. It makes new and different demands on the executive. But it also gives him new and different opportunities. It does not require so much new behaviour as it requires new understanding.

Ultimately it requires that the individual be able to make decisions that get the right things done. This demand is not made on people in traditional environments. The peasant is told by tradition what to do and how to do it. The craftsman had his guild practices that laid down the work, its sequences, and its standards. But the executive in organization is not informed by his environment. He has to decide for himself. If he does not decide, he cannot achieve results. He is bound to be both unsuccessful and unfulfilled.

So far, management theory has given little attention to this area. We have stressed the abilities of the executive, his training, and his knowledge, but not his specific attribute, which is effectiveness. This is what the executive is expected to be – yet we do not know, by and large, what it means. All anyone knows is that few executives attain one-tenth of the effectiveness their abilities, their knowledge, and their industry deserve.

Executive effectiveness will eventually occupy, in the theory of institutions, the place that, throughout the history of political theory, has been occupied by the discussion of the education of the ruler (to which tradition Machiavelli fully belongs though his answers are different). The constitutional lawyers, the earlier exponents of what we now call 'management', asked: 'What structure does the polity require?' The thinkers and writers on the 'education of the ruler' (of whom Plato, in the *Republic* and in the *Seventh Letter*, was the first great name) asked: 'What kind of a man does the ruler have to be, and what does he have to do?' It is this question which is now being asked again when we talk of the 'effective executive'. Only we no longer talk of the 'Prince', that is, of one man in a high place. In the knowledge organization one talks about a great many men. For in the knowledge organization, almost everybody occupies a 'high place' in the traditional meaning of the term.

These three areas: policy objectives and the measurement of performance against targets, management, and executive effectiveness are quite different. Yet they all belong to the same field and the same dimension of organization. They all deal with the functioning of organization.

ORGANIZATION AND THE QUALITY OF LIFE

The 'social responsibility of business' has become a favourite topic of journalists, of business leaders, of politicians, and of business schools. The ethics of organization is indeed a central concern of our times. But to speak of the 'social responsibility of business' assumes that responsibility and irresponsibility are a problem for business alone. Clearly, however, they are central problems for all organizations. All institutions have power, and all of them exercise power. All of them need to take responsibility for their actions, therefore.

The least responsible of our major institutions today is not business; it is the university. Of all our institutions, it probably has the greatest social impact. It has a monopoly position such as no other organization occupies. Once a young person has finished college, he has a multitude of career choices. But until then education controls him and controls his access to all the choices: the business corporation and the Civil Service, the professions and the hospital, and so on. Yet the university has not even realized that it has power. It has not even realized that it has impact and, therefore, a problem of responsibility. The 'New Left' sees this clearly. It may not be enchanted by business, but it is positively hostile to the university and its authority.

In any case, the approach from 'responsibility' is too limited and is therefore misdirection. There is, as every constitutional lawyer knows, no such word as 'responsibility' in the dictionary of politics. The word is 'responsibility *and* authority'. Whoever assumes 'responsibility' asserts 'authority'. Conversely, one is responsible for whatever one has authority over. To take responsibility where one has no authority is usurpation of power.

The question, therefore, is not what are the 'social responsibilities' of organizations. The question is: what is the proper authority? What impacts do the organizations have because of their function?

(1) Any institution has to have impact on society in order to carry out its mission. Similarly an institution has to be somewhere. This means impacts on the local community and the natural environment. Every institution, moreover, employs people, which implies a good deal of authority over them. These impacts are necessary; we could not otherwise obtain the goods and services from business, the education from the schools, the new know-

ledge from the research laboratories, or the traffic control from local government. But they are not the purpose of the organization. They are incidental to it.

These impacts then are a necessary evil in the fullest meaning of the phrase.

We would most certainly not permit authority over people if we knew how to obtain without it the performance for the sake of which we maintain the institution. Every manager, if he had sense, would be happy to get the job done without people. They are a nuisance. He does not want to be a 'government'. It only gets in the way of his doing his job. For the duke or the baron of yesterday, people were 'subjects' and represented strength and wealth. For the hospital, the government agency, or the business of today, people are 'employees', and represent 'cost'. This is increasingly true of the modern military service as well, where firepower and mobility matter rather than numbers.

The first law of 'social responsibility' is, therefore, to limit impacts on people as much as possible. And the same is true for all other impacts. The impacts on society and community are interferences. They can be tolerated only if narrowly defined and interpreted strictly. In particular, to claim 'loyalty' from employees is impermissible and illegitimate. The relationship is based on the employment contract which should be interpreted more narrowly than any other contract in law. This does not rule out affection, gratitude, friendship, mutual respect, and confidence between the organization and the people in its employ. These are valuable. But they are incidental, and they have to be earned.

The second law, perhaps even more important, is the duty to anticipate impact. It is the job of the organization to look ahead and to think through which of its impacts are likely to become social problems. And then it is the duty of the organization to try to prevent these undesirable side-results.

This is in the self-interest of the organization. Whenever

an undesirable impact is not prevented by the organization itself, it ultimately boomerangs. It leads to regulation, to punitive laws, and to outside interference. In the end, the annoying or damaging impact leads to a 'scandal'; and laws that result from a 'scandal' are invariably bad laws. They punish 99 innocents to foil one miscreant. They penalize good practice, yet rarely prevent malpractice. They express emotion rather than reason.

Conversely, whenever the leaders of an institution anticipate an impact and think through what needs to be done to prevent it or to make it acceptable, they are given a respectful hearing by the public and the politicians. This is particularly true of business. Whenever business leaders have anticipated an impact of business and have thought through its prevention or treatment, their proposals have been accepted. Whenever they have waited until there was a 'scandal', and a public outcry, they have been saddled with punitive regulation which, only too often, has aggravated the problem.

Examples abound. It is for instance not true that the American automobile industry has not been safety-conscious. On the contrary, it pioneered safe-driving instruction and the design of safe highways. It did a great deal to reduce the frequency of accidents – and with considerable success. What it is being penalized for today, however, is its failure to make an accident itself less dangerous. Yet when the manufacturers tried to introduce safety-engineered cars (as Ford did in the early Fifties) the public refused to buy them. The automobile manufacturers bitterly resent as rank ingratitude that they are being blamed for unsafe cars, are being subjected to punitive legislation, and are held up to public scorn.

Similarly, the electric utilities resent that they are being blamed for air pollution today. For many years leading utilities had been trying to convince the regulatory agencies that they should be allowed to use cleaner fuel despite its higher cost, and to install air-purification equipment. The regulatory agencies, however, concerned only with the cost of power, never gave the necessary permission.

Tomorrow the academicians are going to complain that they are being pilloried for the damage the PhD system does to society and education. They will point out that society imposes the system on them, and that, in particular, the public demands that the tax-supported public institutions employ teachers with the PhD degree.

But no one else is going to feel sorry for the automobile industry, the electric power industry, or the academicians. They are not to blame for unsafe cars, polluted air, or the PhD blight in the sense that they caused it. Theirs is a greater blame: they have not lived up to the demands of leadership. It is the task of the leader to anticipate. It is not sufficient for him to claim that the crowd went the wrong way. It is his job to find the right way and to lead the crowd.

When Ford found that the American public did not buy safety-engineered cars but switched to competitive makes without safety features, Ford had no choice but to produce what the public was willing to pay for. Similarly, the individual university cannot, as a rule, drop the PhD requirement without catastrophic harm to its standing and its scholarly reputation. But this is all the more reason to go to work on designing the right public policy and to get it accepted.

Whatever can be done only if everybody does it requires law. 'Voluntary effort' in which everyone has to do something that in the short run is risky and unpopular has never succeeded. There is always, in every group, at least one member who is stupid, greedy, and short-sighted. If one waits for 'voluntary action' on the part of everyone, one never acts. The individual organization that anticipates a problem has, therefore, the duty of doing the unpopular:

to think the problem through, to formulate a solution, and to lobby for the right public policy despite open disapproval by other 'members of the club'. No one who has taken this responsibility has ever failed – or ever suffered. But whenever an institution shrinks back, pleading 'the public won't let us', or 'the industry won't let us', it pays a heavy price in the end. The public will forgive blindness. It will not forgive failure to act on one's own best knowledge. This is rightly considered to be cowardice.

(2) Ideally an organization converts into opportunities for its own performance the satisfaction of social needs and wants, including those created by its own impacts. In pluralist society every organization is expected to be an 'entrepreneur' in the traditional meaning of the term, that is, the agent of society which shifts resources from less productive to more productive employment. Each organization defines 'productive' in terms of its own area of performance. Each, therefore, measures results differently. But all of them have the same task.

This means, in particular, that it is an ethical demand on business to convert into profitable business the satisfaction of social needs and wants.

George Champion, Chairman of the world's second-largest bank, New York's Chase Manhattan, pleaded in the *Harvard Business Review** for creative entrepreneurship in satisfying the needs and wants of the poor in the urban ghetto. These needs – in education or in housing – he argued, should lead to the creation of new and highly profitable businesses which at the same time would overcome the urban ills. George Champion is not exactly known as a 'liberal'. Yet his proposed business solutions were quite a big more 'radical' than those of the advanced civil-rights liberals.

The needs and wants of society should be opportunities to every institution. The rising cost of health care is a major opportunity for the hospital. It demands innovation

* *Creative Competition*, May–June issue, 1967.

and entrepreneurial leadership on the part of hospital administrators; but this is, after all, what they are paid for. The needs of modern society for education for both excellence and competence, offer a major entrepreneurial challenge and opportunity to the schools.

This aspect of the 'social responsibilities of organizations' – the anticipation of social needs and their conversion into opportunities for performance and results – may be particularly important in a period of discontinuity such as we are facing. For the last fifty years or so, these opportunities were not common. The major challenge to all institutions lay in doing better what was already being done. Opportunities for tackling new and different things, whether in business, in health care, or in education were scarce.

But this was not always so. A hundred years ago the great entrepreneurial opportunities lay, like those of today, in the satisfaction of social needs and wants. To make education into a profitable large business, or to make urban housing into such a business, may strike people today – businessmen as well as their critics – as rather outlandish. But these are not too different from the opportunities that led to the development of the modern electrical industry, the telephone, the big-city newspaper and the book publisher, the department store, or to urban transit. All those were community wants a hundred years ago. They all required vision and entrepreneurial courage. They all required a considerable amount of new technology and also a good deal of social innovation. They all were needs of the individual which could only be satisfied on a mass basis.

These needs were not satisfied because they were seen as 'burdens', that is, as 'responsibilities'. They were satisfied because they were seen as opportunities. To seek opportunity, in other words, is the ethics of organization.

Organizations, to sum up, do not act with social responsibility when they concern themselves with 'social problems' outside their own sphere of competence and action. They act with social responsibility when they satisfy society's needs through concentration on their own specific job. They act the most responsibly when they convert public need into their own achievements.

Social awareness is organizational self-interest. The needs of society, if left unfilled, turn into social diseases. No institution, whether business or hospital, university or government agency, is likely to thrive in a diseased society.

Social awareness is also incumbent upon the leaders of modern organizations. To be the leader of one of these institutions means to be one of the leaders in our pluralist society. The individual institution may be 'private', but the people at the head of the university, the hospital, the government agency, the business corporation, are 'public'. Leadership in the society of organizations is not a function of position in society. It is a function of position in society's organs, the diverse pluralist organizations.

Society, in turn, has a right to expect the executives of its major organizations to anticipate major social problems and to work at their solution. Society can expect these men to take leadership responsibility. For the executives of these organizations have taken the place of the *élites* of the past, whether nobility or millionaires. They are not *noblesse* and must not say *noblesse oblige*. They owe their leadership position to proven competence in social affairs. Hence it is only natural for society to look to them to think through solutions to serious social problems and social needs.

The best way for business and its leaders is to make the satisfaction of a social need an opportunity for a profitable new business. The right way for the school is to make the satisfaction of a social need an opportunity for better teaching and better learning. The right way for the hospital is to convert social need into an opportunity for better and more effective health care, and so on. These institutions and their leaders would best discharge their 'social responsibility' if that term never had to be used.

The great new fact is that a society of organizations holds institutions and their executives not only accountable for quantities – whether of goods, or of cures, or of degree recipients. It holds its institutions collectively accountable for the quality of life. This is, above all, a new opportunity for the organization and its executives, a new dimension of performance and results – but also a new and rather frightening challenge.

THE LEGITIMACY OF ORGANIZATIONS

The great majority of people, and especially the overwhelming majority of the educated people in our society, are employees of large organizations. As such, the organization exercises, of necessity, considerable authority over them. It is, in fact, the one immediate authority for most of them. There are also the students of the schools, colleges, and universities, and a great many other publics who are inexorably subject to direction and control by one or more of these institutions. The legitimacy of organizational power and of organization managements – whether of government agency, of hospital, or university, or of business – is, therefore, a problem. It is the political problem of the society of organizations.

However, the organizations of our pluralist society are not and cannot be genuine communities. The aim of true community is always to fulfil itself. But within itself today's organization has no aim, just as within itself it has no results. All it has within itself are costs.*

* At first sight, this may seem not to apply to the university. It proudly calls itself a 'community of scholars' and claims that it is an end in itself. But this is, of course, why today's students rebel against the traditional university. They demand that the university serve an outside need, namely, the students' learning need. In an 'educated society', in which knowledge is becoming the central resource, the traditional self-serving 'community of scholars' is no longer tenable, if indeed it ever existed.

The comparison of management, whether in business, in the university, the government agency, or in the hospital, with a true 'government', which is done so entertainingly in *Management and Machiavelli*, is, therefore, half-truth. The managements of modern social institutions (including the government agency that administers, eg, the Post Office) are not 'governments'. Their job is functional rather than political. Such power and authority as they have, they exercise to satisfy one partial need of society. Unlike earlier pluralist powers, their sphere is not the totality of social and community needs or of social and community resources. Their sphere is one specific social demand and want. Their command is over resources allocated to a specific and limited – though vital – task. Whatever capacity to perform these institutions enjoy, they owe to their specialization, to their confinement to one limited task, and to their investment of their resources in a specific definable and limited purpose.

What this means, above all, is that their leaders, the heads of these organizations, cannot base their position, power and authority on any traditional principle of legitimacy. They cannot, for instance, base their authority on the 'consent of the governed'. For the 'governed', are not and cannot be, as in a true political society, the beneficiaries and the purpose of the 'government'.

The large business corporation does not exist for the sake of the employees. Its results lie outside and are only tangentially affected by employee approval, consent, and employee attitude. Similarly the hospital's 'constituency' are not the people who work in the hospital, but the patients. This holds true for every one of the institutions of pluralist society, including the government agency. Whether the financial policies they administer are in the best interests of the employees of the Treasury Department, is not very relevant.

The members of organizations, whether employees or students, should be expected to take the largest possible responsibility for managing the community life of their institutions. A great deal of what managements are doing today is not related to performance and function. Why management should run the plant cafeteria, for instance – or student discipline – is not very clear. And there are many other areas where community self-government can and should take over.

Altogether a wise management does not speak of 'management prerogatives'. It does not even think of them. It limits itself to the spheres of direct relevance to its central task. Everything else it tries to unload. Wherever even serious malfunction would not endanger the attainment of the organization's objective – student discipline is an example – the wise executive says, 'this is your job'.*

It is also highly desirable to bring these 'members' of organization as far as possible into the decision-making process. Otherwise they cannot acquire any understanding of the realities of their institution. It came, for instance, as quite a shock to the workers who were elected to the boards of German steel companies to find out that profits, at their lushest, are a fraction of wages, that prices are determined by competition rather than by management, and that jobs depend on the company's ability to invest capital. Similarly, it always comes as a shock to students sitting on a curriculum committee with faculty and administrators, to find out how stubborn and complex the apparently simplest question of educational policy always is. Precisely because organization is complex, the outsider rarely understands what really goes on 'upstairs'. Without such understanding, organization is always endangered. And we know that participation in the actual decision-making process is the only way to acquire the rudiments of understanding.

Organization, in its own interest, needs to force the utmost responsibility on its members.

But in the areas that directly affect standards, perform-

* On this, see my *The New Society* (Heinemann, London, 1951; Harper & Row, New York, 1950), especially Part Eight.

ance, and results of the institution, the members cannot take over. There, the standards, the performance, and the results must rule them. What is done, and how, is largely determined by what outsiders want and need. It is largely determined by 'discipline', whether that of a science or of the market-place. The vote of General Motors workers on a new automobile design would be totally irrelevant. What matters is whether the consumer buys it or not.

The old response of the Left to this is, of course, the demand that these institutions be 'legitimized' by being taken over by the 'political sovereign', the State. Their managers would then be appointed by legitimate political authority and derive their power from the true sovereign. Experience has shown this to be naïve sophistry. All that really happens is that the same losses, which formerly were censured as horrible examples of mismanagement, now become highly desirable contributions to social welfare. Government ownership or government appointment of managers does not alter the function of institutions. The moment organizations begin to discharge their function they are outside effective political control by government. Indeed they have to be outside it to perform. They have to be controlled by function and measured by performance.

The most instructive lesson is surely that of the laboratory of post-Marxist Socialism – Yugoslavia. There government, to enable the economy to function, returned control of business to the enterprises themselves and specifically to workers' councils elected by the plant. But the workers soon found out that they had to hand over management to trained, qualified, and autonomous executives if the plant was to produce goods and to produce jobs. Wherever Yugoslav industry is performing adequately, the control is functional and technical rather than by government or by 'consent of the governed' in the plant. Performance is in the saddle and decides.

What applies to the 'consent of the governed' applies to

every other known principle of political legitimacy. Of course, an institution, the members of which reject it altogether, cannot function. The institution must make it possible for its members to achieve their own ends. We have long known that modern organization must give its members status and function.* But the members must also serve and accomplish the institution's purposes, which can never be their own. To satisfy their workers is not and can never be the first task or the test of the pluralist organizations of our society. They must satisfy people outside, must serve a purpose outside, must achieve results outside. At best, they can integrate and harmonize the ends, values, and wants of their members with the demands of their mission. But the mission comes first. It is given. It is objective. It is impersonal. It is, at the same time, specific, limited, and aimed at only one of the many needs and wants of society, community, and individual.

It is this dedication to one limited purpose of larger society that makes our modern organization effective.

Clearly there is only one foundation for the authority which our organizations and their managements must have: performance. It is the only reason that we have them at all. It is the only reason why we can tolerate their exercise of power and their demand for authority.

Specifically this means that we need to know what 'performance' means for this or that institution. We need to be able to measure, or at least to judge, the discharge of its responsibility by an institution and the competence of its management. We need to insist that institutions and their managements confine themselves to the specific tasks whose performance justifies their existence and their power. Everything beyond is usurpation.

Concentration on the specific task emerges as the key to

* For a fuller discussion, see my books, *Concept of the Corporation* (published in the UK under the title of *Big Business*, William Heinemann Ltd, 1946), and *The New Society* (William Heinemann Ltd, London, 1951; Harper & Row, New York, 1950).

strength, performance, and legitimacy of organization in the pluralist society. Opinions can and should differ as to the specific task of a particular organization. The definition will change as circumstances, social needs, community values, and technologies change. Different institutions of the same kind, eg, different universities within a country, might define their objectives quite differently, as should different businesses within an industry, or even different hospitals. But each of them will be stronger the more clearly it defines its objectives. It will be more effective the more specific the yardsticks and measurements against which its performance can be appraised. It will be more legitimate the more strictly it bases its authority on justification by performance.

'By their Performance Ye shall know them—' This may well be the fundamental constitutional principle of the new pluralist society.

10. The Sickness of Government

GOVERNMENT SURELY HAS never been more prominent than today. The most despotic government of 1900 would not have dared probe into the private affairs of its citizens as income tax collectors now do as a matter of routine in the freest society. Even the Tsar's secret police did not go in for the security investigations that are now taken for granted. Nor could any bureaucrat of 1900 have imagined the questionnaires that governments now expect businesses, universities, or citizens to fill in in ever-mounting numbers and ever-increasing detail. At the same time, government has everywhere become the largest employer.

Government is certainly all-pervasive. But is it truly strong? Or is it only big?

There is mounting evidence that government is big rather than strong; that it is fat and flabby rather than powerful; that it costs a great deal but does not achieve much. There is mounting evidence also that the citizen less and less believes in government and is increasingly disenchanted with it. Government is sick – and just at the time when we need a strong, healthy, and vigorous government.

There is certainly little respect for government among the young – and even less love. But, the adults, the taxpayers, are also increasingly disenchanted. They still want more services from government. But they are everywhere approaching the point where they balk at paying for a bigger government, even though they may still want what government promises to give.

The disenchantment with government cuts across national boundaries and ideological lines. It is as prevalent in Communist as in democratic societies, as common in white as in non-white countries. This disenchantment may well be the most profound discontinuity in the world around us. It marks a sharp change in mood and attitude between this generation and its predecessors. In the seventy years or so, from the eighteen-nineties to the nineteen-sixties, mankind, especially in the developed countries, was hypnotized by government. We were in love with it and saw no limits to its abilities, or to its good intentions. Rarely has there been a more torrid political love affair than that between government and the generations that reached manhood between 1918 and 1960. Anything that was felt needed doing during this period was to be turned over to government – and this, everyone seemed to believe, made sure that the job was already done.

The Fabians in Great Britain or the German Social Democrats started their love affair with government before 1900. It became general with World War I when government, using taxation and the printing press, mobilized social resources way beyond what anyone earlier would have thought possible. The German war economy, the War Production Board in the United States, and the United States propaganda machine dazzled contemporaries. It convinced them that government could do anything.

When the Great Depression hit a decade later, everybody immediately turned to government as the saviour. It is pathetic to recall the naïve belief that prevailed in the late Thirties – such, for instance, as was preached in one of the bestsellers of the depression years, *To Plan or Not to Plan* by the British Labour economist Barbara Wootton. The book's author, honoured by the British government with a life peerage as Lady Wootton, is still alive and active. But nothing is more remote from us today, or less appealing, than the messianic innocence of this fervent love letter to government. All it says, and it says it on every page, is: 'Utopia is here – all that's needed is to take everything away from the wicked, selfish interests and to turn it over to government.'

World War II reinforced this belief. Again government proved itself incredibly effective in organizing the energies of society for warfare.

But now our attitudes are in transition. We are rapidly moving towards doubt and distrust of government and, in the case of the young, even to rebellion against it. We still, if only out of habit, turn social tasks over to government. We still revise unsuccessful programmes over and over again, and assert that nothing is wrong with them that a change in procedures or a 'competent administrator' will not cure. But we no longer believe these promises when we reform a bungled programme for the third time. Who, for instance, believes any more that administrative changes in the Foreign Aid programme of the United States (or of the United Nations) will really produce rapid worldwide development? Who really believes that the War on Poverty will vanquish poverty in the cities? Or who, in Russia, really believes that a new programme of incentives will make the collective farms productive?

We still repeat the slogans of yesteryear. Indeed, we still act on them. But we no longer believe in them. We no longer expect results from government. What was torrid romance between the people and government for so very long has now become a tired, middle-aged liaison which we do not quite know how to break off but which only becomes exacerbated by being dragged out.

What explains this disenchantment with government?

We expected miracles – and that always produces disillusionment. Government, it was widely believed (though only subconsciously), would produce a great many things for nothing. Cost was thought a function of who did something rather than of what was being attempted.

There is little doubt, for instance, that the British in

adopting the National Health Service believed that medical care would cost nothing. All the Health Service is and can be is, of course, 'pre-paid' medical care. Nurses, doctors, hospitals, drugs, and so on have to be paid for by somebody. But everybody expected this 'somebody' to be somebody else. At the least, everyone expected that under a 'free' Health Service the taxes of the rich would pay for the health care of the poor.

There are, of course, never enough rich people around to carry the burden of any general service. Both in the British Health Service and in American Social Security (and generally in services of this kind) the rich are subsidized by the working and lower-middle class. In such a service everybody, as a rule, pays the same contribution through his taxes. In proportion to their wealth and income, the rich therefore pay less than lower income groups. Financing nationalized services is a classic example of what the economists call 'regressive taxation', the burden of which declines with rising income.

This is not an argument against such services. A mass basis is the only way to finance what everyone should have. Nor are such services necessarily inefficient. But they are not 'free' – and their cost is inevitably high, since they have to provide for contingencies and benefits for everyone even though only a minority may ever require a particular benefit. It is no accident that the most economical and effective health service today is not the 'free' British service nor American Medicare. It is the much older German Health Insurance under which the individual is compelled to sign up for pre-paid medical care but left free, in large measure, to choose between a great variety of plans, both public and private.

All such plans are, in effect, taxation and compulsory saving that force the individual to pay for something whether he wants it or not. This is their whole rationale. But obvious though this may seem, the illusion that government could somehow make costs go away and produce a great deal for nothing was almost universal during the last half-century. And the distributive fallacy which assumes that government distribution of wealth solves economic problems that are rooted in inadequate productivity is still far from dead (as stated earlier in Chaper 6).

This belief was, in effect, only one facet of a much more general illusion from which the educated and the intellectuals in particular suffered: that by turning tasks over to government, conflict and decision would be made to go away. Once the 'wicked private interests' had been eliminated, the right course of action would emerge from the 'facts', and decision would be rational and automatic. There would be neither selfishness nor political passion. Belief in government was thus largely a romantic escape from politics and responsibility.

One root of this argument was hatred of business, of profit and, above all, of wealth. Another – more dangerous – root was the rejection of responsibility and decision that played such a major role in the rise of Fascism and Nazism and in their attraction for so many otherwise sane people. Erich Fromm, in his first book (1940), called it *Escape from Freedom*.

That motives other than the desire for monetary gain could underlie self-interests and that values other than financial values could underlie conflict, did not occur to the generation of the Thirties. Theirs was a world in which economics seemed to be the one obstacle to the millennium. Power did not appear in their vision – though this blindness in the decade of Hitler and Stalin is hard to imagine, let alone to understand. C. P. Snow's description in *The Masters* (1951), of the conflict for power within the 'self-less' and 'disinterested' small community of a Cambridge or Oxford College profoundly shocked the sensibilities of a generation that had grown up believing that conflicts were always motivated by economic self-interest and could be avoided by eliminating gain, that is, by nationalizing the economy.

One need not be in favour of free enterprise – let alone a friend of wealth – to see the fallacy in this argument. But reason had little to do with the belief in government ownership as the panacea. The argument was simply: 'Private business and profits are bad – *ergo* government ownership must be good.' We may still believe in the premise; but we no longer accept the *ergo* of government ownership.

The Labour government felt committed in 1967 to re-nationalize the British steel industry (just at the time when, ironically, the industry was on the verge of a long-term decline, and when, therefore, takeover by the government meant the highest possible windfall profit for the shareholders). But it immediately declared that the industry would have to be run for profit and put in as chief executive the purest of arch-capitalists, Lord Melchett, heir to one of the world's greatest industrial fortunes (his grandfather and father founded and built Imperial Chemical Industries), a hereditary peer and a top-flight investment banker, in addition to being a life-long Tory! By contrast, less than twenty years earlier, when steel was first nationalized in Britain by an earlier Labour government, an ideologically 'pure' trade-union stalwart had been the chief-executive-designate.

There is still a good deal of resistance to the responsibility of politics and resentment of the burden of decision. The young today want to 'drop out' altogether – in a frightening revival of the hostility to responsibility that made an earlier young generation, forty years ago, so receptive to totalitarian promises and slogans.

But no one, least of all the young, believes any more that the conflicts, the decisions, the problems would be eliminated by turning things over to government. Government.

on the contrary, has itself become one of the wicked 'vested interests' for the young. And few even of the older generation expect any more that the political millennium will result from government control.

The Soviet Press still writes routinely that under 'socialism' there can be no tension between management and labour in industry except as a 'remnant of capitalism'. But no one in Russia or in the satellite countries of Eastern Europe takes this seriously. Labour conflict is routinely reported in the news stories that appear in the column next to the editorial on the 'remnants of capitalism'.

Similarly, in the West no one believes any more that by nationalizing this or that industry or by turning over this or that social task to government, decisions have been eliminated and conflicts have been aborted. No one would be shocked any more by the plot of C. P. Snow's book or, for another instance, by the disclosures of how bitterly the various Nazi factions struggled over each decision behind the propaganda façade of unity.

In fact, most of us today realize that to turn an area over to government creates conflict, creates vested and selfish interests, and complicates decisions. We realize that to turn something over to government makes it political instead of abolishing politics. When the garbage collectors went on strike against the City of New York in the winter of 1968, many good liberals seriously proposed turning garbage collection over to 'free enterprise' to 'ease the tension'. We realize, in other words, that government is no alternative to decision. It does not replace conflict of interests by rational decision-making.

But the greatest factor in the disenchantment with government is that government has not performed. The record during the last thirty or forty years has been dismal. Government has proved itself capable of doing only two things with great effectiveness. It can wage war. And it can inflate the currency. Other things it can promise but only rarely accomplish. Its record as an industrial manager, in the satellite countries of Eastern Europe as well as in the nationalized industries of Great Britain, has been unimpressive. Whether private enterprise would have done worse is not even relevant. For we expected perfection from government as industrial manager. Instead we only rarely obtained even below-average mediocrity.

Government as a planner has hardly done much better (whether in Communist Czechoslovakia or in de Gaulle's capitalist France).

But the greatest disappointment, the great let-down, is the fiasco of the Welfare State. Not many people would want to do without the social services and welfare benefits of an affluent modern industrial society. But the Welfare State promised a great deal more than to provide social services. It promised to create a new and happy society. It promised to release creative energies. It promised to do away with ugliness and envy and strife. No matter how well it is doing its job – and in some areas in some countries, some jobs are being done very well – the Welfare State turns out at best to be just another big insurance company, as exciting, as creative, and as inspiring as insurance companies tend to be. No one has ever laid down his life for an insurance policy.

This explains why President Johnson's spectacular performance in enacting the unfinished welfare tasks of the New Deal failed to make him a hero with the public. It also explains why the equally spectacular failure of his predecessor to get the same measures through Congress did President Kennedy no political harm whatever, not even with the old New Deal faithful in the trade unions.

The best we can get from government in the Welfare State is competent mediocrity. More often we do not even get that; we get incompetence such as we would not tolerate in an insurance company. In every country there are big areas of government administration where there is no performance whatever – only costs. This is true not only of the mess of the big cities, which no government – United States, British, Japanese, or Russian – has been able to handle. It is true in education. It is true in transportation. And the more we expand the Welfare State the less capable even of routine mediocrity does it seem to become.

I do not know whether Americans are particularly inept at public administration – though they are hardly particularly gifted for it. Perhaps we are only more sensitive than other people to the incompetence and arrogance of bureaucracy because we have had, until recently, comparatively so much less of it than other people. But no matter how bad others might be, it is hard to conceive anything more chaotic than the huge, blundering, disorganized establishment of an American embassy even in a small country – both totally unmanaged and totally over-administered.

During the past three decades, federal payments to the big cities have increased almost a hundredfold for all kinds of programmes. But results from the incredible dollar-flood into the cities are singularly unimpressive. What is impressive is the administrative incompetence. We now have ten times as many government agencies in the United States concerned with city problems as we had in 1939. We have increased by a factor of a thousand or so the number of reports and papers that have to be filled in before anything can be done in the city.

Social workers in New York City spend some 70 or 80 per cent of their time filling in papers; for Washington, for the state government in Albany, and for New York City. No more than 20 or 30 per cent of their time, that is about an hour and a half a day, is available for their clients, the poor. As James Reston reported in the *New York Times* (November 23rd, 1966) there were then 170 different federal aid programmes on the books, financed by over 400 separate appropriations and administered by 21 federal departments and agencies aided by 150

Washington bureaux and over 400 regional offices. One Congressional session alone passed 20 new health programmes, 17 new educational programmes, 15 new economic development programmes, 12 new programmes for the cities, 17 new resources development programmes, and 4 new manpower training programmes, each with its own administrative machinery.

This is not perhaps a fair example – even of American administrative incompetence. That we speak of 'urban crisis' when we face a problem of race, that is, of the conscience, explains a lot of our troubles. Even the stoutest advocate of the Welfare State never expected fundamental problems of conscience to yield to social policy and effective administration (though he probably would have argued that there are no 'problems of conscience' and that everything is a 'social problem' and, above all, a matter of spending money).

But in other areas, the Welfare State does not perform much better. Nor is the administrative mess a peculiarly American phenomenon. The daily Press in Great Britain, in Germany, in Japan, in France, in Scandinavia – and increasingly in the Communist countries as well – reports the same confusion, the same lack of performance, the same proliferation of agencies, of programmes, of forms – and the same triumph of accounting rules over results. Everywhere rivalry between various agencies is replacing concern with results and with responsibility.

Modern government has become ungovernable. There is no government today that can still claim control of its bureaucracy and of its various agencies. Government agencies are all becoming autonomous, ends in themselves, and directed by their own desire for power, their own rationale, their own narrow vision rather than by national policy and by their own boss, the national government.

This is a threat to the basic capacity of government to give direction and leadership. Increasingly policy is fragmented, and policy direction becomes divorced from execution. Execution is governed by the inertia of the large bureaucratic empires, rather than by policy. Bureaucrats keep on doing what their procedures prescribe. Their tendency, as is only human, is to identify what is in the best interest of the agency with what is right, and what fits administrative convenience with effectiveness. As a result the Welfare State cannot set priorities. It cannot concentrate its tremendous resources – and therefore does not get anything done.

The great achievement of the modern state, as it emerged in the seventeenth and eighteenth centuries, was unified policy control. The great constitutional struggles of the last three hundred years were over the control powers of the central government in a united and unified nation. But this political organ, no matter how it is selected, no longer exercises such control.

The President of the United States may still be the most powerful ruler – more powerful than either the Prime Ministers of parliamentary régimes dependent upon a majority in parliament, or the dictators who can be overthrown by conspiracies against them among the powerful factions within their totalitarian apparatus. And yet even the President of the United States cannot direct national policy any more. The various bureaucracies do very much what they want to do.

The Anti-Trust Division of the Department of Justice, for instance, has been making its own policies and pursuing its own course during the last twenty years, with little concern for what the incumbent President believes or orders. None of the Presidents we have had since Harry Truman would have agreed with the interpretation the Anti-Trust division has given to the Anti-Trust laws. The Soil Conservation Service and the Bureau of Reclamation, the Forestry Service and the Weather Bureau, the Federal Trade Commission and the Army

Engineers have similarly become 'independent' rather than 'autonomous'.

Nor did Harold Wilson as Prime Minister, or his Conservative predecessor, have more effective policy control. Obviously this is also the situation in Russia, and was in de Gaulle's France.

Not so long ago policy control by the political organs of government could be taken for granted. Of course there were 'strong' and 'weak' Presidents as there were 'strong' and 'weak' Prime Ministers. A Franklin Roosevelt or a Winston Churchill could get things done that weaker men could not have accomplished. But this was not, people generally believed, because they knew how to make the bureaucracy do their bidding. It was because they had the courage of strong convictions, the willingness to lay down bold and effective policies, the ability to mobilize public vision.

Today a 'strong' President or a 'strong' Prime Minister is not a man of strong policies; he is the man who knows how to make the lions of the bureaucracy do his bidding. John Kennedy had all the strength of conviction and all the boldness of a 'strong' President; this is why he captured the imagination, especially of the young. He had, however, no impact whatever on the bureaucracy. He was a 'strong' President in the traditional sense. But he was a singularly ineffectual one.

His contemporary, Mr Khrushchev in Russia, similarly failed to be effective despite his apparent boldness and his popular appeal. By contrast, bureaucratic men who have no policies and no leadership qualities emerge as effective – they somehow know how to make red tape do their bidding. But then, of course, they use it for the one thing red tape is good for, ie, to bundle up yesterday in neat packages.

This growing disparity between apparent power and actual lack of control is perhaps the greatest crisis of government. We are very good at creating administrative agencies. But no sooner are they called into being than they become ends in themselves, acquire a 'vested right' to grants from the Treasury and to continuing support by the taxpayer, and achieve immunity to political direction. No sooner, in other words, are they born than they defy public will and public policy.

The crisis of government domestically is nothing compared to the crisis of government as an effective organ in international life. In the international arena government has all but disintegrated. The 'sovereign state' no longer functions as an effective organ for political tasks. This is not happening as the liberals would like to believe, because a political world community has transcended the narrow, petty boundaries of national states. On the contrary, the national state is everywhere in danger of collapsing into petty, parochial baronies – whether French Canada or an independent Flanders, Biafra in West Africa, or Scottish nationalism.

To our grandparents in 1900 it was clear that the trend ran towards larger government units. It was clear to them that the national state created political organisms capable of effective cooperation in international society. This had been the lesson of nineteenth-century history. Indeed the century closed with the last 'unification', though an imposed one: the taking over of the Boer Republics of South Africa by the British and their incorporation into the British Empire.

Since then, the process has been one of steady fission. It began in the Balkan Wars which, undertaken to create larger unified countries, ended by creating more small ones. It has accelerated ever since. Even Czechoslovakia, the most successful of the new countries created in World War I, proved incapable of becoming the effective agent of unification but was torn apart by the strife of the national minorities – German, Hungarian, and Slovak – which refused to be 'unified'.

Not one of the new countries established since World War II has so far created the unified nation which to the nineteenth century was so obviously the end point of history. Instead we are getting tribal splinters, pretending to be national states, imposing on their citizens all the costs of a national state, driven by all the jealousies, resentments, and pride of a national state – but incapable of being an effective organ either of domestic government or of the international community. Increasingly we are fragmenting the world into governmental pygmies, each endowed with tremendous power *vis-à-vis* its citizens, each perfectly capable of tyranny, but incapable of governing.

In 1900 there were fewer than fifty sovereignties in the whole world – twenty in Europe and twenty in the Americas, with the rest of the world having fewer than a dozen. World War I increased the number to about sixty. Now we have more than 160, with new 'mini-states' joining the ranks almost every month. Only on the American continents has there been no splintering of sovereignties. There the twenty-odd sovereignties of 1900 are still, by and large, the political reality of today (except in the rapidly fragmenting Caribbean area). Some of the new sovereignties are very large countries: India, Pakistan, and Indonesia. But most of them are smaller than the Central-American countries an earlier generation contemptuously dismissed as 'banana republics', and much too small to discharge the minimum responsibilities of sovereignty. Today we have scores of 'independent nations' whose population is well below a million people. We have some whose population is hardly as large as a good-sized village.

At the other end of the scale we have the 'super powers' whose very size and power debar them from having a national policy. They are concerned with everything, engaged everywhere, affected by every single political event no matter how remote or petty. But policy is choice and selection. If one cannot choose not to be engaged, one cannot have a policy – and neither the United States nor Russia can, in effect, say: 'We are not interested.' The 'super-powers' are the international version of the Welfare State – and like the Welfare State incapable of priorities or of accomplishments.

The might of the super-powers is much too great to be used. If all one has at hand to swat flies is a 100-ton drop hammer, one is defenceless. The super-powers, therefore, invariably over-react – as Russia has done in the satellite countries and as the United States has done in the Congo, in Santo Domingo, and perhaps in Vietnam. Yet they under-achieve. Their might, while great enough to annihilate each other – and the rest of us into the bargain – is inappropriate to the political task. They are too powerful to have allies; they can only have dependants. And one is always the prisoner of one's dependants, while being hated by them. Only a government totally bereft of moral authority and self-confidence would act the way the Russian government in August 1968 reacted to the development in Czechoslovakia.

This means that decisions in the international sphere can no longer be made in an orderly and systematic fashion. It is no longer possible for any decision to be arrived at by negotiation, consultation, and agreement. It can only be arrived at by dictation or by exhaustion. While force has, therefore, become infinitely more important in the international system, it has become infinitely less decisive – unless it be the ultimate force of a nuclear war that might destroy mankind.

Decisions are also no longer effective. No longer can they be expected to be carried out. In the international sphere we have the same divorce of policy from execution that characterizes domestic government. We get more and more and more governments. But all this does is to increase costs. For each of these sovereignties has to have its own Foreign Service, its own Armed Forces, and so on. With a multiplication of government agencies and costs has gone a steady decrease in effectiveness.

And no government, whether its territory spans the continents or is smaller than one city block, can any longer discharge the first duty of government: protection from, and defence against, attack from outside. It is perfectly true that most of the new 'mini-states' are political absurdities, defenceless against the threat of instant annihilation. But so are the 'super-powers' in this age of nuclear 'over-kill'. With nuclear weapons being easy to make and, in effect, available to the smallest and weakest country, there is no 'defence'. There is only – questionably – 'deterrence' by the threat of retaliation. But if government cannot defend its people, the first reason for the very existence of government has gone.

This may be regarded as gross exaggeration. It certainly is not the picture the older generation still sees. But it is, increasingly, the reality. It is the situation to which we react. And the young people, who are not, as we older ones are, influenced by the memories of our love affair with government, see the monstrosity of government, its disorganization, its lack of performance, and its impotence rather than the illusions the older generation still cherishes and still teaches in the classroom.

WHAT GOVERNMENT CANNOT DO

Yet never before has strong, effective, truly performing government been needed more than in this dangerous world of ours. Never before has it been needed more than in this pluralist society of organization. Never before has it been needed more than in the world economy.

We need government as the central institution in the society of organizations. We need an organ that expresses the common will and the common vision and enables each organization to make its own best contribution to society and citizen and yet express common beliefs and common

277

values. We need strong, effective governments in the international sphere so that we can make the sacrifices of sovereignty needed to give us working supra-national institutions for world society and world economy.

The answer to diversity is not uniformity. The answer is unity. We cannot hope to suppress the diversity of our society. Each of the pluralist institutions is needed. Each discharges a necessary economic task. We cannot, as I have tried to show, suppress the autonomy of these institutions. Their task makes them autonomous whether this is admitted by political rhetoric or not. We, therefore, have to create a focus of unity. This can only be provided by strong and effective government.

This is even more apparent in the developing, poor countries than it is in the developed countries of Europe, North America, and Asia. Effective government is a prerequisite of social and economic growth.

We cannot wait until we have new political theory or until we fully understand this pluralist society of ours. We will not re-create the beautiful 'Prince Charming' of government, or the all-wise economist-king of Barbara Wootton's *To Plan or Not to Plan*. But we should be able to come up with a competent, middle-aged professional who does his work from nine to five and does it well – and who, at least, is respected as a 'good provider', though the romance has long gone out of him. In the process, government may shed the megalomania that now obsesses it, and learn how to confine itself to realistic goals and to cut its promises to its capacity to deliver.

Certain things are inherently difficult for government. Being by design a protective institution, it is not good at innovation. It cannot really abandon anything. The moment government undertakes anything, it becomes entrenched and permanent. Better administration will not alter this. Its inability to innovate is grounded in government's legitimate and necessary function as society's protective and conserving organ.

A government activity, a government installation, and government employment become immediately built into the political process itself. This holds true whether we talk of a declining industry, such as the nationalized British coal mines, or the government-owned railways of Europe and Japan. It holds equally true in Communist countries. No matter how bankrupt, for instance, the Stalinist economic policies have become in Czechoslovakia, Hungary, or Poland, any attempt to change them immediately runs into concern for the least productive industries which, of course, always have the most, the lowest-paid, and the least-skilled – and, therefore, the most 'deserving' – workers.

The inability of government to abandon anything is not limited to the economic sphere. We have known for well over a decade, for instance, that the military conscription that served the United States well in a total war is immoral and demoralizing in a 'cold war' or 'limited war' period. No one defends our present system – yet we extend it year after year on a 'temporary' basis. The same inability to abandon applies to research projects supported by government. It holds true as soon as government supports the arts. Every beneficiary of a government programme immediately becomes a 'constituent'. He immediately organizes himself for effective political action and for pressure upon the decision-maker.

All institutions, as I said in the last chapter, find it hard to abandon yesterday's tasks and to stop doing the unproductive. All of man's institutions – and for that matter, all men – are committed to what they are used to and are reluctant to accept that it no longer needs doing or that it does not produce results. But government is under far greater pressure to cling to yesterday than any other institution. The typical response of government to failure of an activity is to double its budget and staff.

Nothing in history, for instance, can compare in futility with those prize activities of the American government, its welfare policies and its farm policies. Both policies are largely responsible for the disease they are supposed to cure. We have known this for quite some time – in the case of the farm programme since before World War II, in the case of the welfare programme certainly since 1950.

The problem of the urban poor is undoubtedly vast. No city in history has ever been able to absorb an influx of such magnitude as the American cities have had to absorb since the end of World War II. Wherever it happened in the past, there was the same collapse of family, community, and local government – in the cities of England in the late-eighteenth century, when the Irish came in; in the cities of North America in about 1840, again with the coming of the Irish; in the cities of Continental Europe later on, as for instance when the Czechs started to migrate in large numbers into the Vienna of the Hapsburgs in the closing years of the nineteenth century. The influx of almost two million rural Negroes and Puerto Ricans into New York City alone in less than a fifteen-year period exceeded any of these earlier migrations. It is unprecedented in the history of cities.

But we certainly could not have done worse if we had done nothing at all. In fact, the nineteenth-century cities that did nothing did better. And so, during the last twenty years, has São Paulo in Brazil, which, inundated by similar floods of rural, illiterate Negroes, fresh from serfdom, did nothing – and which is in better shape than New York City.

Our welfare policies in the United States were not designed to meet this problem. They were perfectly rational – and quite effective – as measures for the temporary relief of competent people who were unemployed only because of the catastrophe of the Great Depression. Enacted in the mid-thirties, the relief policies had essentially finished their job by 1940. But being government programmes they could not be abandoned. Far too massive a bureaucracy had been built. The emotional investment in these programmes and in their slogan had become far too great. They had become 'symbols' of the 'New Deal'.

Small wonder, then, that we reached for them when the entirely different problem of the Fifties arose, that is, when the rural Negro moved into the core-city in large numbers. And small wonder that these programmes did not work, that instead they aggravated the problem and increased the helplessness, the dependence, and the despair of the Negro masses. For the rural Negro was not competent to manage if only he had a job; he was not trained; and he was not already settled in the city in a stable family unit.

But all we could do when relief failed to relieve, was to double the budget and to double the number of people engaged in filling in forms. We could not detach ourselves from the programme. We could not ask: 'What is the problem, and what needs to be done?'

The farm programme tells the same story. It was designed – also in the Thirties – to save the family farmer and to restore his economic and social health. Instead it has subsidized his replacement by large, heavily capitalized, and highly productive 'industrial farms'. This may well be a more desirable result than the one the farm programme was meant – and is still meant – to produce. But it was abysmal failure in terms of the programme's announced objectives. Yet again – to everybody's pained surprise – increasing the budget has only speeded up the disappearance of the family farm.

Lest this be read as a criticism of the American government, let me add that this experience knows no distinction of race, creed, or nationality.

The depressed-areas policy in Great Britain dates back to the Twenties. In all that time it has not restored to economic health one single 'depressed area'. But it has effectively penalized the shift of labour to areas of higher productivity, higher wages, and better jobs. It has thereby slowed growth in the healthy regions. Yet wherever it is realized that the 'depressed areas' are still depressed, the budget goes up. That the Swedes, faced with a similar problem, actually got rid of their 'depressed areas' by subsidizing migration of labour out of them rather than, as the British do, migration of inefficient industry into them, is well known in England. But it has made no impression on government or public in Britain.

Similarly, the German *Osthilfe* designed after World War I to reconcile to the Republic the distressed East German landowners, the Junkers, and to help them to become productive farmers, had exactly the opposite effect. It only aggravated their plight while at the same time penalizing the productive farmers in West Germany. It made both willing supporters of Hitler. Yet all that could ever be done politically was to raise the money spent on *Osthilfe*.

This is not to say that all government programmes are wrong, ineffectual, or destructive – far from it. But even the best government programme eventually outlives its usefulness. And then the response of government is likely to be: 'Let's spend more on it and do more of it.'

Government is a poor manager. It is, of necessity, concerned with procedure, for it is also, of necessity, large and cumbersome. Government is also properly conscious of the fact that it administers public funds and must account for every penny. It has no choice but to be 'bureaucratic' – in the common usage of the term.

Whether government is a 'government of laws' or a 'government of men' is debatable. But every government is, by definition, a 'government of forms'. This means inevitably high cost. For 'control' of the last 10 per cent of phenomena always costs more than control of the first 90 per cent. If control tries to account for everything it becomes prohibitively expensive. Yet this is what government is always expected to do.

The reason is not just 'bureaucracy' and red tape; it is a much sounder one. A 'little dishonesty' in government is a corrosive disease. It rapidly spreads to infect the whole body politic. Yet the temptation to dishonesty is always great. People of modest means and dependent on a salary handle very large public sums. People of modest position dispose of power and award contracts and privileges of tremendous importance to other people – construction jobs, radio channels, air routes, zoning laws, building codes, and so on. To fear corruption in government is not irrational.

This means, however, that government 'bureaucracy' – and its consequent high costs – cannot be eliminated. Any government that is not a 'government of forms' degenerates rapidly into a mutual looting society.

The generation that was in love with the State thirty or forty years ago believed fondly that government would be economical. Eliminating the 'profit motive' was thought to reduce costs. This was poor economics, to begin with. If there is competition, profit assures accomplishment of a task at the lowest cost. It is a measure of an index of the most economical allocation of resources, that is, of the optimum in terms of costs as well as of results. This is the reason why the Communist countries are all rushing now to re-introduce profitability into their system.

This was, of course, known to the economists of thirty or forty years ago. But within an economic theory of equilibrium rather than of dynamics and growth, profit (as Chapter 7 explains) could be disregarded. And the inherent wastefulness of government had yet to be demonstrated.

The politician's attention does not go to the 90 per cent of money and effort that is devoted to existing programmes and activities. They are left to their own devices and to the tender mercies of mediocrity. Politics – rightly – is primarily concerned with 'new programmes'. It is concerned with whatever is politically 'hot'. It is focused on crises and problems and issues. It is not focused on doing a job. Politics, whatever the form of government, is not congenial to managerial organization and makes government slight managerial performance.

In government, loyalty is more important than performance – and has to be. Whatever the system – and in this respect there is little difference between Presidential America, Parliamentary England, and Polit-Bureau Russia – the first question is, 'Whose man is he?' After that – and long before performance – come party allegiance and connexions. In fact the man who does well but belongs to the wrong faction, or gives allegiance to the wrong person, is a major threat to the people in power. Nothing is disliked as much – and nothing is feared as much – as the outstanding man whose performance makes him independent of politicians and politics. Nothing is prized as much as the faithful follower.

We have built elaborate safeguards to protect the administrative structure within government against the political process. This is the purpose of every Civil Service. But while this protects the going machinery from the distortions and pressures of politics, it also protects the incumbents in the agencies from the demands of performance. Of course, we maintain officially that Civil Service tenure is compatible with excellence. But, if we had to choose, we would probably say that mediocrity in the Civil Service is a lesser evil than politics. As far as the judiciary is concerned – where we first created 'independence' – this is certainly true. How far it is true in administrative agencies is debatable. A good many people today have come to believe that we need some way of rewarding performance and penalizing non-performance, even within Civil Service.

Still the premium within government will be on not 'rocking the boat' in existing agencies, that is, on no innovation, no initiative, but rather on doing with proper procedures what has been done before. Within the political process attention will certainly not be paid to the on-going, routine work, unless there is the publicized malfunction of a 'scandal'. As a result, management of the daily work of government will remain neglected – or be considered a matter of following 'procedure' and of filling in forms. By excelling as a manager no one in politics will ever get to the top, unless at the same time he builds his own political machine, his own political following, his own faction.

We can – and must – greatly improve the efficiency of government.

There is little reason these days to insist on '100 per cent audit', for instance. Modern sampling methods based on probability mathematics actually give us better control by inspecting a small percentage of the events. We may even, one day, hope to get approval on the part of legislature, and understanding by the public, that no system as large as government can or should work at 100 per cent efficiency. An aim of 92 per cent performance is more realistic and can be attained at much lower cost. We may eventually understand that it does not matter if a government agency or a military service overpays $50,000 in a $50 million budget, even though today this is seized upon as a horrible example of governmental laxity (and leads immediately to the employment of a hundred more book-keepers). We may even get acceptance by government of the principle of management by exception, in which we only audit where results deviate significantly from expectation, although experienced administrators in government may smile at such Utopian *naïveté*.

We need something much more urgently: the clear definition of the results a policy is expected to produce, and the ruthless examination of results against these expectations. We need to be forced to admit at an early stage that the relief policies or the farm policies of the United States government do not produce the intended benefits. This demands that we spell out in considerable detail what results are expected rather than content ourselves with promises and manifestoes.

In the last century, the Auditor General became a central organ of every government. We learned that we needed an independent agency to control the daily process of government and to make sure that money appropriated was spent on what it was intended for, and spent honestly. Now we may have to develop an independent government agency which compares the results of policies against expectations and which, independent of pressures from the executive as well as from the legislature, reports to the public any programme that does not deliver. Robert McNamara's 'cost/effectiveness' for the programmes and policies of the American military forces may have been the first step in the development of such a new organ. And that President Johnson has introduced cost/effectiveness into all United States government agencies may be one of the most significant events in American administrative history.

We may even go further – though only a gross optimist would expect this today. We may build into government an automatic abandonment process. Instead of starting with the assumption that any programme, any agency, and any activity is likely to be eternal, we might start out with the opposite assumption: that each is shortlived and temporary. We might, from the beginning, assume that it will come to an end within five or ten years unless specifically renewed. And we may discipline ourselves not to renew any programme unless it has the results which it promised when first started. We may, let us hope, eventually build into government the capacity to appraise results and systematically to abandon yesterday's tasks.

Yet such measures will still not convert government into a 'doer'. They will not alter the main lesson of the last fifty years: *government is not a 'doer'*.

– AND WHAT IT COULD BE

The purpose of government is to make fundamental decisions, and to make them effectively. The purpose of government is to focus the political energies of society. It is to dramatize issues. It is to present fundamental choices.

The purpose of government, in other words, is to govern.

This, as we have learned in other institutions, is incompatible with 'doing'. Any attempt to combine governing with 'doing' on a large scale, paralyses the decision-making capacity. Any attempt to make decision-making organs actually 'do', also means very poor 'doing'. They are not focused on 'doing'. They are not equipped for it. They are not fundamentally concerned with it.

There is good reason today why soldiers, civil servants, and hospital administrators look to business management for concepts, principles, and practices. For business, during the last thirty years, has had to face, on a much smaller scale, the problem which modern government now faces: the incompatibility between 'governing' and 'doing'. Business management learned that the two have to be separated, and that the top organ, the decision-maker, has to be detached from 'doing'. Otherwise he does not make decisions, and the 'doing' does not get done either.

In business this goes by the name of 'decentralization'. The term is misleading. It implies a weakening of the central organ, the top management of a business. The purpose of decentralization as a principle of structure and constitutional order is, however, to make the centre, the top management of a business, strong and capable of performing the central, the top-management task. The purpose is to make it possible for top management to concentrate on decision-making and direction by sloughing off the 'doing' to operating managements, each with its own mission and goals, and with its own sphere of action and autonomy.

If this lesson were applied to government, the other institutions of society would then rightly become the 'doers'. 'Decentralization' applied to government would not be just another form of 'Federalism' in which local rather than central government discharges the 'doing' tasks. It would rather be a systematic policy of using the other, the non-governmental institutions of the society of organizations, for the actual 'doing', ie, for performance, operations, execution. Such a policy might be called 'reprivatization'. The tasks which flowed to government in the last century because the original private institution of society, the family, could not discharge them, would be turned over to the new, non-governmental institutions that have sprung up and grown during the last sixty to seventy years.

Government would start out by asking the question: 'How do these institutions work and what can they do?' It would then ask: 'How can political and social objectives be formulated and organized in such a manner as to become opportunities for performance for these institutions?' It would also ask: 'And what opportunities for accomplishment of political objectives do the abilities and capacities of these institutions offer to government?'

This would be a very different role for government from that which it plays in traditional political theory. In all our theories government is *the* institution. If 'reprivatization' were to be applied, however, government would become *one* institution albeit the central, the top, institution.

Reprivatization would give us a different society from any our social theories now assume. In these theories government does not exist. It is outside society. Under reprivatization, government would become the central social institution.

Political theory and social theory, for the last two hundred and fifty years, have been separate. If we applied to government and to society what we have learned about organization during the last fifty years, the two would again come together. The non-governmental institutions – university, business, and hospital, for instance – would be seen as organs for the accomplishment of results. Government would be seen as society's resource for the determination of major objectives, and as the 'conductor' of social diversity.

I have deliberately used the term 'conductor'. It might not be too fanciful to compare the situation today with the development of music 200 years ago. The dominant musical figure of the early-eighteenth century was the great organ virtuoso, especially in the Protestant North. In organ music, as a Buxtehude or a Bach practised it, one instrument with one performer expressed the total range of music. But as a result, it required almost superhuman virtuosity to be a musician.

By the end of the century, the organ virtuoso had disappeared. In his place was the modern orchestra. There each instrument played only one part, and a conductor in front pulled together all these diverse and divergent instruments into one score and one performance. As a result, what had seemed to be absolute limits to music suddenly disappeared. Even the small orchestra of Haydn could express a musical range far beyond the reach of the greatest organ virtuoso of a generation earlier.

The conductor himself does not play an instrument. He need not even know how to play an instrument. His job is to know the capacity of each instrument and to evoke the optimal performance from each. Instead of being the 'performer', he has become the 'conductor'. Instead of 'doing', he leads.

The next major development in politics, and the one needed to make this middle-aged failure – our tired, overextended, flabby, and impotent government – effective again, might therefore be reprivatization of the 'doing', the performance of society's tasks. This need not mean 'return to private ownership'. What is going on in the Communist satellite countries of Eastern Europe today – especially in Yugoslavia – is reprivatization in which ownership is not involved at all. Instead, autonomous businesses depend on the market for the sale of goods, the supply of labour and the supply of capital. That their 'ownership' is in the hands of the government is a legal rather than an economic fact – though, of course, important. Yet to the Yugoslavs it does not appear to be incompatible with that *ultra-bourgeois* institution, a stock exchange.

What matters, in other words, is that institutions should not be *run* by government but should be autonomous. Cooperatives, for instance, are not considered 'capitalist' in the Anglo-American countries, although they are 'private' in that they are not run by government. And the same applies to 'private' hospitals and the 'private' universities. On the other hand, the German university has traditionally been almost as autonomous as the American 'private' university, even though it is a State institution.

Reprivatization, therefore, may create social structures that are strikingly similar, though the laws in respect to ownership differ greatly from one country to another and from one institution to another. What they would have in common is a principle of performance rather than a principle of authority. In all of them the autonomous institution created for the performance of a major social task would be the 'doer'. Government would become increasingly the decision-maker, the vision-maker, the political organ. It would try to figure out how to structure a given political objective so as to make it attractive to one of the autonomous institutions. It would, in other words, be the 'conductor' which tries to think through what each instrument is best designed to do. And just as we praise a composer for his ability to write 'playable' music, which best uses the specific performance characteristics of French horn, violin, or flute, we may come to praise the law maker who best structures a particular task so as to make it most congenial for this or that of the autonomous, self-governing, private institutions of pluralist society.

Business is likely to be only one, but a very important, institution in such a structure. Whether it be owned by the capitalist, that is, by the investor, or by a cooperative or a government, might even become a secondary consideration. For even if owned by government, it would have to be independent of government and autonomous – as the Yugoslavs show – not only in its day-to-day management, but, perhaps more important, in its position in the market, and especially in a competitive capital market.

What makes business particularly appropriate for reprivatization is that it is predominantly an organ of innovation; of all social institutions, it is the only one created for the express purpose of making and managing change. All other institutions were originally created to prevent, or at least to slow down, change. They become innovators only by necessity and most reluctantly.

Specifically business has two advantages where government has major weaknesses. Business can abandon an activity; indeed it is forced to do so if it operates a market – and even more, if it depends on a market for its supply of capital. There is a limit beyond which even the most stubborn businessman cannot argue with the market test, no matter how rich he may be himself. Even Henry Ford had to abandon the Model T when it no longer could be sold. Even his grandson had to abandon the Edsel.

What is more: of all our institutions, business is the only one that society will permit to disappear.

It takes a major catastrophe, a war or a great revolution, to allow the disappearance of a university or of a hospital, no matter how superfluous and unproductive they might have become. Again and again, for instance, the Catholic Church in the United States attempts to close down hospitals that have ceased to be useful. In almost every case, a storm of community nostalgia forces the supposedly absolute bishop to retract his decision.

Only a foreigner, a Canadian, sent as a provincial from the outside, could force the English Jesuits to abandon their boarding school even though it had become an anomaly. And this provincial had then to be pulled out of England fast and moved back to Canada. The Russians had the same experience when they tried, in the late Forties, to consolidate a number of provincial universities. Even Stalin had to give in and rescind the order.

But when the best-known aeroplane manufacturer in the United States, the Douglass Company, designer and producer of the DC3 (or Dakota, as the military and the Europeans call it) was in difficulty in 1967, neither the American public nor the American government rushed to its rescue. If a competitor had not bought the company and merged it into his operations, we would have accepted the disappearance of Douglass – with regret, to be sure, and with a good deal of nostalgic rhetoric, but also with the feeling: 'It's their own fault, after all.'

Precisely because business can make a profit, it *must* run the risk of loss.

This risk, in turn, goes back to the second strength of business; alone among all institutions it has a test of performance. No matter how inadequate profitability is, it is a test for all to see. One can argue that this or that obsolete hospital is really needed in the community or that it will one day again be needed. One can argue that even the poorest university is better than none. The alumni or the community always have a 'moral duty' to save 'dear old Siwash'.

The consumer, however, is unsentimental. It leaves him singularly unmoved to be told that he has a duty to buy the products of a company because it has been around a long time. The consumer always asks: 'And what will the product do for me tomorrow?' If the answer is 'nothing', he will see its manufacturer disappear without the slightest regret. And so does the investor.

This is the strength of business as an institution. It is the best reason for keeping it in private ownership. The argument that the capitalist should not be allowed to make profits is a popular one. But the real role of the capitalist is to be expendable. His role is to take risks and to take losses as a result. This role the private investor is much better equipped to discharge than the public one. We want privately owned business precisely because we want institutions that can go bankrupt and can disappear. We want at least one institution that, from the beginning, is adapted to change, one institution that has to prove its right to survival again and again. This is what business is designed for, precisely because it is designed to make and to manage change.

If we want a really strong and effective government, therefore, we should want businesses that are not owned by government. We should want businesses in which private investors, motivated by their own self-interest and deciding on the basis of their own best judgement, take the risk of failure. The strongest argument for 'private enterprise' is not the function of profit. The strongest argument is the function of loss. Because of it business is the most adaptable, and the most flexible of the institutions around. It is the one that has a clear, even though limited, performance test. It is the one that has a yardstick.

Therefore, it is the one best equipped to manage. For if there is a yardstick for results, one can determine the efficiency and adequacy of efforts. One can say in a business: 'Our greatest profits are at a level where we control 95 per cent of the costs rather than where we control 99 per cent. Controlling and auditing the last 4 per cent or 5 per cent costs us much more than the profits from these marginal activities could ever be.' One cannot say this with respect to patient care in a hospital. One cannot say this with respect to instruction in a university. And one cannot say this in any government agency. There one has to guess, to judge, to have opinions. In a business one can measure. Business, therefore, is the most manageable of all these institutions, the one where we are most likely to find the right balance between results and the cost of efforts. It is the only institution where control need not be an emotional or a moral issue, where in talking 'control' we discuss 'value' and not 'values'.

Reprivatization is still heretical doctrine. But it is no longer heretical practice. Reprivatization is hardly a creed of 'fat cat millionaires' when Black Power advocates seriously propose making education in the slums 'competitive' by turning it over to private enterprise competing for the tax dollar on the basis of proven performance in teaching ghetto children. It may be argued that the problems of the black ghetto in the American city are very peculiar problems – and so they are. They are extreme malfunctions of modern government. But, if reprivatization works in the extreme case, it is likely to work even better in less desperate ones.

One instance of reprivatization in the international sphere is the World Bank. Though founded by governments, it is autonomous. It finances itself directly through selling its own securities on the capital markets. The International Monetary Fund, too, is reprivatization. If we develop the money and credit system we need for the world economy, we will have effectively reprivatized creation and management of money and credit which have been considered for millennia attributes of sovereignty.

Again business is well equipped to become the 'doer' in the international sphere. The multi-national corporation, for instance, is our best organ for rapid social and economic development through the 'contract-growing' of people and of capital. In the Communications Satellite Corporation (COMSAT) we are organizing worldwide communications (another traditional prerogative of the sovereign) as a multi-national corporation. A Socialist government, the Labour government in Britain, used reprivatization to bring cheap energy to Britain – in contracts with the multi-national oil companies for the exploration and development of the natural gas fields under the North Sea.

And the multi-national corporation may be the only institution equipped to get performance where the fragmentation into tribal splinter units, such as the 'mini-states' of Equatorial Africa, makes performance by government impossible.

But domestically as well as internationally business is, of course, only one institution and equipped to do only one task, the economic one. It is important (as discussed in the last chapter) to confine business – and every other institution – to its own task. Reprivatization will, therefore, entail using other non-governmental institutions – the hospital, for instance, or the university – for other, non-economic 'doing' tasks. The design of new non-governmental, autonomous institutions as agents of social performance under reprivatization may well become a central job for tomorrow's political architects.

We have the first beginnings of worldwide universities – with their roots probably in the 'extra-mural accreditation' which London University extended gradually to new institutions in the last decades of the British Empire. Today, American universities are building more and more multi-national institutions. There is also a group of aggressive new business schools throughout Latin America – it calls itself the 'Healthy Baby Group' – in which nine separate schools in nine different Latin countries run themselves increasingly as one institution with common goals, a common faculty, and interchanges of programmes and students. In fact, the multi-national university may be our best tool to stop, if not to reverse, the 'brain drain'.

We do not face a 'withering away of the State'. On the contrary, we need a vigorous, strong, and very active government. But we do face a choice between big but impotent government and a government that is strong because it confines itself to decision and direction and leaves the 'doing' to others. We do not face a 'return of *laissez-faire*' in which the economy is left alone. The economic sphere cannot and will not be considered to lie outside the public domain. But the choices for the economy – as well as for all other sectors – are no longer *either* complete governmental indifference or complete governmental control.

In all major areas we have a new choice in this pluralist society of organizations: an organic diversity in which institutions are used to do what they are best equipped to do. This is a society in which all sectors are 'affected with the public interest', while in each sector a specific institution, under its own management and dedicated to its own job, emerges as the organ of action and performance.

This is a difficult and complex structure. Such symbiosis between institutions can work only if each disciplines itself to strict concentration on its own sphere, and to strict respect for the integrity of the other institutions. Each, to use again the analogy of the orchestra, must be content to play its own part. This will come hardest for government, especially after the last fifty years in which it has been encouraged in the belief of the eighteenth-century organ virtuoso that it could – and should – play all parts simultaneously. But every institution will have to learn the same lesson.

Reprivatization will not weaken government. Its main purpose is to restore strength and performance capacity to sick and incapacitated government. We cannot go much farther along the road on which government has been travelling these last fifty years. All we can get this way is more bureaucracy but not more performance. We can impose higher taxes but we cannot get dedication, support, and faith on the part of the public. Government can gain greater girth and more weight, but it cannot gain strength or intelligence. All that can happen, if we keep on going the way we have been going, is worsening sickness of government and growing disenchantment with it. And this is the prescription for tyranny, that is, for a government organized against its own society.

This can happen. It has happened often enough in history. But in a society of pluralist institutions it is not likely to be effective too long. The Communists tried it, and after fifty years have shown – though they have not yet fully learned – that the structure of modern society and its tasks are incompatible with monolithic government. Monolithic government requires absolute dictatorship, which no one has ever been able to prolong much beyond the lifetime of one dictator.

Ultimately we will need new political theory and probably very new constitutional law. We will need new concepts, and new social theory. Whether we will get these and what they will look like, we cannot know today. But we can know that we are disenchanted with government – primarily because it does not perform. We can say that we need, in a pluralist society, a government that can and does govern. This is not a government that 'does'; it is not a government that 'administers'; it is a government that governs.

11. How Can the Individual Survive?

STUDENT UNREST IS nothing new. But the present alienation of the most privileged of today's society, the college youth, is something very new indeed.

All earlier student outbreaks were local, and directed at specific institutions of an individual country or society. This was true in the major previous epoch of student unrest in the West, the rebellion of the students of Continental Europe against absolutist government after the Napoleonic Wars. It ushered in long, bitter struggles in Russia, Germany, and Italy, but it evoked only a faint echo west of the Rhine, and England was not touched by it at all.

Similarly the massive Chinese student unrest in the early years of the century, while eventually leading to the downfall of the Manchu Dynasty and to a half-century of civil war (which may not be over yet), was confined to one country. Even the large Chinese populations outside mainland China were hardly affected by it.

Today, however, there is a true 'student international'. There is, of course, no central command, no common creed; but there is a common enemy. It is organization. Today's student 'activists' are against organization and its authority in any form or shape. Above all, they oppose what used to be considered the 'good guys' among organizations, university, and government. The young priests and religious of the Catholic Church are equally opposed to the authority and organization of the Roman Curia. And that traditional symbol of rebellion, the Communist Party, was one of the main targets of the French students and of the young among the French workers in the uprising against all authority in May 1968.

The war in Vietnam and the racial troubles of the black ghetto may explain the rebellion of the young people of America. But they hardly explain why the Italian students storm their university buildings, or why the students of Poland and Yugoslavia battle with their respective régimes and its police. Nor do they explain the outbreaks of student rebellion in India and Indonesia, let alone the organized anarchism of the Chinese students who enrolled by the hundreds of thousands in Mao's 'Cultural Revolution' against school, government, and Communist Party authority. Clearly the 'causes' only trigger the rebellion. They do not 'cause' it.

The perception of the young that society has become a society of organizations, and that this is in striking contrast to the society of our textbooks, our political rhetoric, and our conventions, is sound and realistic insight. The response, however, is futile. There is no sign that our society has decided to do without the services that only the organization can supply. We are not willing to do without defence or without education, without economic goods and services, or without health care. The organizations will not go away. Repudiating them is not going to make them disappear. It will not even reduce their power.

Scorning power only makes it more oppressive. Power has to be used. It is a reality. If the decent and idealistic toss power in the gutter, the guttersnipes pick it up. If the able and educated refuse to exercise power responsibly, irresponsible and incompetent people take over the seats of the mighty and the levers of power. Power not being used

299

for social purposes passes to people who use it for their own ends. At best, it is taken over by the careerists, who are led by their own timidity into becoming arbitrary, autocratic, and bureaucratic.

Anarchism is a valid philosophical position and perhaps the only 'pure' political theory. The only trouble with it is that it does not work. In practice it inevitably leads to oppression, the first victims of which are the philosophical anarchists themselves.

But there is an even greater danger in the rebellion against organization by the young people of today: their vulnerability to false leaders. It is not true that young people repudiate leadership. They seek leadership. They need leadership. If they cannot find it in the 'establishment' – not even within the 'loyal opposition' – they become easy prey to the demagogues. If one 'cannot trust anyone over thirty', one trusts, in the end, someone who acts the juvenile, for one has to trust someone.

There is a frightening resemblance between the student 'activists' of today, with their slogans of 'idealism' and 'sincerity', and the German youth movement just before and just after World War I. The resemblance even extends to externals, to long hair, to folk songs, and to such slogans as 'make love, not war'. Yet the idealistic, anti-authoritarian *Wandervoegel*, of the German youth movement – who also did not trust 'anyone over thirty'– became in short order fanatical, dedicated, unquestioning Nazis and idolators of Hitler. The young want and need faith. And the demagogue is the specialist in 'sincerity'.

The 'activists' represent a tiny fraction of the youth of today. The 'lunatic fringe', the 'hippies', the 'beats', and so on, are a smaller fraction still. The great majority of today's students will, as their predecessors did, settle speedily into the deep ruts of convention. They will soon enough conform to middle age as they now conform to 'flaming youth'. Maybe they will keep on complaining about the 'organization man'. But the young engineers, scientists and – above all – the young college professors who so desperately want to be 'accepted' by the kids, are the ones who impose conformity on organization. No one is more conformist than the 'conventionally unconventional'.

Students have always tended to be restless. Suddenly the number of students everywhere has tremendously increased. To a large extent, the present student unrest is but a symptom of the 'educational explosion' as a result of which we now keep in school very large numbers of young people who, in earlier days, would have been at work.

That the great bulk of today's college students come from homes without tradition of higher education is in itself a major reason for student unrest. In that respect, today's student rebellion can be compared to the traditional rebellion of the second-generation American against the immigrant background of his parents. And just as these rebels from the Irish, Swedish, Jewish, or Italian homes soon settled down as comfortable members of American middle-class society, the students of today can be expected to settle down soon as middle-class members of educated society.

The generation gap is particularly wide today. Societies are younger in their average age than they have been for a long time. Yet, because life-span – and especially working-life span – has been greatly extended, a far larger number of the older men are living much longer, and holding on much longer to positions of leadership and power. Never before in modern history have there been so many young educated people; yet never before has leadership been so old. Leadership in every institution and in every country is still held largely by a generation that has its roots in the era preceding World War I. Only in the last ten years have leadership positions passed into the hands of people even born in this century.

In few eras was the gap in experience between generations greater than the one that divides those for whom

World War I, the Twenties, and the Great Depression were the formative experiences from those who were still children when World War II came to an end – but who are today in their mid-thirties and well into middle age. For those who were born after World War II, the world of their elders, the world of the Thirties and early Forties, is almost unimaginable. Action and behaviour based on these earlier experiences – that is, the action and behaviour natural to the older generation – must seem to the young irrational, meaningless, and totally irrelevant.

The alienation of the young could therefore be explained away – as confined to a small fraction; as nothing more than a fashionable pose and the current expression of the shortlived *Weltschmerz*, that common, but rarely fatal, disease of adolescence; or as an accident of demography that will rapidly straighten itself out. But as a symptom, the alienation of the young needs to be taken seriously. Underlying it is the realization that the society of organizations poses problems to the individual which social and political theory does not yet see, let alone answer.

The 'student activists' are certainly not going to answer the question of the fate and role of the individual in this pluralist society of organizations. Indeed they do not even address themselves to it. Yet their rebellion establishes that the question is central and will have to be tackled.

THE BURDEN OF DECISION

Erich Fromm's first book, *Escape from Freedom* (1940), was written just before World War II to explain the attraction of totalitarianism – of the Right or of the Left – for the young after World War I. A similar book today, trying to explain the alienation of the young, might well be entitled *Escape from Decision*.

It is, above all, the burden of decision imposed by the society of organizations which the young find frightening and against which they rebel. Suddenly there are career choices; the great majority only yesterday had their careers determined from birth on. Suddenly there are decisions on the direction and purpose of knowledge. Suddenly we have to have new economic policies; we can no longer trust either the automatic operation of Adam Smith's 'complementary trade', nor the 'inevitability of history' of the Marxian *schema*. Suddenly we have acquired enough knowledge in medicine to have to make decisions – on heart transplants or artificial kidneys, for instance – about whom to keep alive and whom to let die.

The rhetoric of the young complains bitterly about being 'manipulated'. But their actions make it clear that it is the burden of decision that frightens them. They want to 'drop out' to where there are no decisions, no choices, no responsibility.

To sidestep decision is also a decision – and as the young will find out, the one least likely to be right. The students, for instance, who stay on in graduate school (or who join the Peace Corps) to avoid having to decide, are likely to find, a few years later, that they have made the wrong decision. They are lucky if all they have lost is time.

But the reaction of the young, while futile, again reflects true insight. The society of organizations demands of the individual decisions regarding himself. At first sight, the decision may appear only to concern career and livelihood. 'What shall I do?' is the form in which the question is usually asked. But actually it reflects a demand that the individual take the responsibility for society and its institutions. 'What cause do I want to serve?' is implied. And underlying this question is the demand that the individual take responsibility for himself. 'What shall I do *with myself*?' rather than 'What shall I do?' is really being asked of the young by the multitude of choices around them. The society of organizations forces the individual to ask of himself: 'Who am I?' 'What do I want to be?' 'What do I want to put into life and what do I want to get out of it?'

These are existential questions for all that they are

couched in secular form and appear as choices between a job in government, in business, or in college teaching. They have not been asked – at least not by Western man – for several centuries. The Protestant Reformation four hundred years ago last posed them as general questions to be answered by everyone. Where medieval Catholicism had given an 'automatic' answer of salvation through observance, the Reformation demanded of the individual that he should ask himself: 'Who do I *want* to be in order to be saved?'

Ever since Descartes in the mid-seventeeth century brushed aside man's spiritual existence as irrelevant, the West has concerned itself with what goes on outside of man – nature and society. Of all the major thinkers of the nineteenth century only Kierkegaard ever asked 'How is human existence possible?' To all the others this was a meaningless and unfashionable question. They all asked: 'How is society possible?' Rousseau asked it, Hegel asked it, the classical economists asked it. Marx answered it in one way, liberal Protestantism in another. The concern all through the last two centuries of Western history was the society, its rights, its functions, its performance.*

Now for the first time, we are again face to face with the age-old question of individual meaning, individual purpose, and individual freedom. Narcotic drugs and avoidance of soap are not particularly relevant answers. But at least the alienation of the young throughout the world today ensures that the questions will have to be considered. For the society of organizations offers choices, and therefore imposes on the individual the burden of decisions. It demands of him the price of freedom: responsibility.

* This paragraph is from my essay, 'The Unfashionable Kierkegaard', which first appeared in the autumn 1949 issue of the *Sewanee Review*.

How Can the Individual Survive?

Totalitarianism differs from all tyrannies of the past in that it aims at total control of society rather than at control of government alone. Therein lies its danger; in a society where every social task is discharged in and through a large organization, total control seems both attractive and possible.

But at the same time, in such a pluralist society the danger of traditional, purely political tyranny is remote. As long as no one organization is permitted to become *the* organization – as a Communist or a Nazi Party strives to be – a pluralist society guarantees freedom from domination by any single group. Pluralist society is an organization of 'countervailing powers', as J. Kenneth Galbraith pointed out almost twenty years ago.* In fact, the danger in pluralism, as history teaches, is not domination by this or that interest group; it is collapse into indecision and into a stalemate of competing 'countervailing powers'.

But the individual may still be oppressed, even though the powerful institutions fight each other to a stalemate. Galbraith held out the promise of freedom in the interstices between powers. But this is precarious living. Little Black Sambo did indeed survive because 'the tigers ate each other up'. But I doubt that Little Black Sambo greatly enjoyed the experience or that he would wish to go through it again, let alone to spend his life between those snapping and snarling jaws.

The sociologist of the 'New Left', the late C. Wright Mills, was on shaky ground in his talk of a new 'power *élite*' based on a conspiracy of the managers – of business, of the military, of the labour unions, of the big universities, and so on. Conspiracies are rare, and successful conspiracies are exceedingly rare. And this particular conspiracy was a figment of Mills' imagina-

* In his book, *American Capitalism* (1952).

tion. Yet the fact that the 'New Left' believes in it should give us pause. Even though these *'élites'* see themselves in sharp and bitter competition with each other, they may well appear to the individual as the tigers appeared to Little Black Sambo. There is no guarantee that they will not, at any one moment, make common cause against the individual. And that, ten minutes later, they will fight each other again is scant comfort to the individual whom they have devoured in the meantime.

There is only one dependable safeguard of freedom in such a pluralist society: to confine each institution to its task and mission. The demand that each institution concentrate on its task is a political demand in addition to being a managerial and a social demand. The slightest attempt on the part of any one institution to claim 'responsibility' beyond its narrow sphere should be considered usurpation. It may be meant well. It may, in the short run, appear to be in the social interest. It may indeed be the only way to get an urgent job done and done well. But it is incompatible with a free society. It is a threat to freedom.

This needs to be stressed for the government agency. The government agency is not part of the sovereign. It is not a necessary part of the decision-making, the governing, the directing intelligence of society. It is an organ of society for the discharge of a specific, a particular, a partial task. That its ownership is public and its management appointed by the political authority is irrelevant. To make the agency a part of the 'sovereign' is, in effect, to usurp power.

The public knows this. It feels the need for a line between 'government agency' and 'government'. When judges go on strike, the public is upset, if not outraged. But when subway works go out, the citizen treats it as just another fight between labour and management, even though it inconveniences and endangers him more than a strike by the judges. To dispense justice is a function of the sovereign. Transportation is an 'industry', albeit a vital one. To inject economic warfare into a sovereign function is inappropriate and outrageous. To use it in an industry, while a nuisance, is appropriate. The first to strike and the last to go back in the French general strike in May 1968 were the men of the government-owned French industries, especially in the automotive and aircraft plants.

We are, in other words, approaching the point where the distinction we make between various kinds of strikes is not a formal and legal one, but one of substance. Whether a government agency is involved or not is no longer relevant. We have come to look upon a number of areas as essential to the functioning and survival of modern society. Disruptions of such services are threats to the public. Whether they should be allowed and under what conditions is a hotly disputed and a difficult question. The solution will be the same, however, whether the service is performed by government or not. And 'nationalizing' a service is no substitute for a solution.

This distinction is, however, quite incompatible with the positions still maintained by political theory and public law. Both still follow John Austin's nineteenth-century doctrine of 'formal sovereignty'. Both still hold that anything is an act or a sphere of the 'sovereign' that can be traced back through formal, logical analysis to a legally valid 'sovereign' act, a law, an ordinance, or a verdict. The most extreme Austinians in their legal doctrine (if not in their political theory) are the orthodox Communists, to whom every institution, including the chess club, is an organ of the government, and every organ of the government an embodiment of the ultimate sovereign, 'the working class', and as such, infallible and absolute.

In the pluralist society of organizations, the rule will have to be the opposite: every organization, no matter what its legal position or ownership, is a special-purpose tool. Only in so far as its actions are necessary for the discharge of its special purpose are they legitimate. Otherwise they are null and void. Function rather than form determines what is lawful for an organization.

This also means, however, that regardless of legal form, institutions doing different tasks must be autonomous. The freedom of the individual in a pluralist society demands autonomy of institutions.

Practice may have moved further in this direction than our theory or our rhetoric might indicate. To convert the Post Office into a 'public corporation' may not bring about the great increases in efficiency promised by advocates of this step. But that we can take such a step – when postal communications have been considered an 'attribute of sovereignty' since Roman times – indicates clearly that we are already considering function rather than form. No one (except the postal workers' union) would be terribly shocked any more by the idea that the postal service might eventually be 'reprivatized'. Few would even be terribly surprised at the suggestion that, twenty years hence, we might abandon the postal service altogether as no longer capable of competing with new and different forms of telecommunications, no matter how deeply entrenched as an 'attribute of sovereignty' it might once have been.

Similar developments are going on in Communist countries; in large measure, they explain the institutional crisis in the developed Communist countries, ie, Russia and her European satellites.

Traditionally European jurisprudence, since the days of Justinian, divided law into 'public' and 'private'. We may have to add a third category: 'organizational law'. It would be 'private' law, even if the organization were government-owned and government-run. But it would be 'public' law even if the organization were totally owned by private investors and run by their representatives. Every institution would be considered as limited to the specific service to the members of society which it is intended to perform, and as such, 'private'. Yet since every institution has power within its sphere, it would be, as such (in the elegant phrase of the American lawyer), 'affected with the public interest'.

Such a new view of all organizations as being autonomous *and* limited is needed both to make organization perform and to safeguard the individual's freedom.

A similar approach might have to be thought through with respect to the internal powers of organization, the power over what have been called its 'members'. The very term 'member' is impermissible. There are only 'employees', as regards the rights and powers of organizations over people. 'Member' implies that the institution controls, that the bond is indissoluble. To cut off a member is to destroy it (or him). An arm is not capable of sustained existence without being a 'member' of the body. Employment, however, is a specific and limited contract in which both parties retain their identity and their freedom. And the employment contract can always be terminated. This may seem like semantic quibbling. But the ultimate safeguard of freedom for the individual, Rousseau taught two hundred years ago, is the right to emigrate.

We need safeguards against arbitrary cancellation of the employment contract by the employer. The law has a duty to protect the weaker in a contractual relationship and to constrain the more powerful from abuse of his advantage. Limitations on the right to terminate employment arbitrarily are therefore legitimate (though not without dangers to the capacity of a society to adapt to change). But restrictions on the mobility of the employee are quite illegitimate and must not be allowed if the pluralist society of organizations is to have a meaningful sphere of individual freedom.

This is going to be particularly important for the central employees of the society: the knowledge workers. Where this freedom does not exist today, we already see them demanding it.

The young educated Japanese, for instance, would be most unhappy were Japanese employers to abandon the tradition of 'lifetime employment'. They strongly resist all attempts to give the employer power to discharge any but top management people. But they increasingly demand for themselves the right to leave and go elsewhere, even though it is contrary to tradition. One Japanese company, SONY, the electronics manufacturer, has been highly successful in attracting unusually able people to its employ. This success is largely traced by SONY managers to their practice of offering senior jobs to able people who work for other companies and of helping employees who want to leave to find better jobs elsewhere – both in violation of Japanese custom. At the same time, every SONY employee has all the 'rights' of 'lifetime employment'. Once he has joined he can stay on the payroll until he retires if he so desires.

The other Japanese employers are still afraid of such mobility. They fear that knowledge workers – engineers, accountants, or computer experts – will become migratory. But, of course, there are never many who 'emigrate' in any society.* What matters is that the escape routes remain open. This requires both that employees can quit and that they can go to work elsewhere. Both must be possible without paying an exorbitant legal or economic price. The fear of losing people is the best incentive to respecting them.

The most dangerous restrictions on mobility are not police stockades. They are restrictions that present themselves as benefits. The greatest obstacles to organizational mobility today are the 'golden fetters', such as pension

---

* The Japanese, as well as the Europeans, grotesquely exaggerate the extent of actual 'job-hopping' in American industry. After the first five years, the great majority of knowledge workers in America become as settled as the Europeans and almost as immobile as the Japanese.

plans, stock option plans, delayed compensation schemes, and so on, with which we tie managers, professionals, and skilled people to a particular employer. These benefits are to be looked at with grave suspicion. They are eagerly sought by the employees themselves. They offer a means to escape the crushing burden of taxation. They are, in turn, favoured, if not subsidized, by government and by the tax authorities. But they are anti-social. It is, of course, the government rather than the employer – whether a business or a university – that is anti-social by offering tax induce-ments that make these benefits all but irresistible, thus in-dicating that they are what public policy desires.

The serfdom of medieval Europe was originally an 'employee benefit' which was sought eagerly by the peasants. It guaranteed to a weak man the protection of a powerful lord, and especially of the holy men of a monastery. It guaranteed a poor man the enjoyment of his meagre holding of land. It shielded against greedy gatherers of tax and tribute. Yet within one generation, it turned into loss of freedom and subjection. The worst fetters are those that make our self-interest enslave us. They are the ones against which we have to be especially on guard.

In addition to legal safeguards against oppressive power, we need administrative safeguards against oppressive rule. In organization small men have a good deal of power. The postal clerk behind the counter of a sub-station is a nobody in the post office and probably in his home as well. But he can, and will unless sharply restrained, 'throw his weight around' and act the *fonctionnaire*, abusing the public, keep-ing it waiting, and so on. If he could be reformed by re-minding him that he is being paid to serve the public, French and Austrian postal clerks would be the most considerate and friendliest servants of the public – instead of being the surliest of petty tyrants. That postal clerks in the United States are, by contrast, normally considerate and helpful is the result of a system of 'postal inspectors' who secretly monitor the clerk's behaviour and take disciplinary action against *fonctionnaire*-like arrogance.

With organization the pervasive reality of society, defence of the individual against administrative sloth, arrogance, and petty tyranny becomes an essential safeguard.

This is the idea behind the Swedish invention of the 'Ombudsman' – now introduced in Britain – whose job it is to protect the citizen against bureaucracy. What the Ombudsman (or the postal inspector) does is not nearly as important as his existence. The knowledge that such a person exists, that he is independent, and that to be found remiss by him is likely to be painful, is a powerful deterrent. He cannot prevent the subversion of freedom by dictatorship. But he can curb the erosion of liberty through thoughtlessness, laziness, carelessness, and arrogance. He forces officialdom to think before it callously treats the individual as a 'case'. He will not make rude men polite. But he may make thoughtless men a little considerate.

One of the rights of the individual the Ombudsman needs to guard the most jealously – and against all organizations – is the right to privacy. To be sure, no such right ever existed. In the communities of yesterday, the tribe, the village, the small town, privacy was unknown. A hermit in his cave was the only man who ever enjoyed privacy. Everybody else was public in all his actions and in all his circumstances – his thoughts, at best, were private. Even the greatest men of earlier times had no privacy. Nothing less private could possibly be imagined than the life of the king of yesterday. Compared to the total lack of privacy Louis XIV had to put up with, even the glare of television cameras in which the modern ruler lives seems private.

Privacy is a boon of the Industrial Revolution and of

a middle-class society. The number of people who really want privacy is probably small. Yet in a world of powerful organizations, it is a necessary safeguard of freedom. Protection of the citizen's privacy is one of the important political innovations we need. The question should always be asked: 'Is the knowledge about the individual necessary?' If the answer is 'No', it should be denied – even if the individual is perfectly willing to grant it. Privacy is not an individual privilege but a social need. There should therefore be a way to stop the gathering of information about individuals unless the social need can be shown to be paramount.

That we can put all the information – and misinformation – about people on computer memories is not the reason for our concern with privacy. The computer memory is only the mechanical expression of the organizational fact: organizations operate on information, and therefore always try to gather as much as they can. The line between the information the organization truly needs, and which therefore is justly 'affected with the public interest', and the citizen's privacy, which is essential to his freedom, needs to be established, and reaffirmed again and again.

In a pluralist society there are neither 'good guys' nor 'bad guys' among organizations. All are needed, yet all are capable of degeneration. All are threatened by the bureaucratic disease that subordinates the true rationale of the institution – the satisfaction of an individual need or want – to the procedure, inertia, and convenience of its bureaucracy. The Ombudsman is therefore needed in and against all organizations. He is needed to champion the individual against management in the business corporation, but also against the labour union, whatever the latter's claim to 'represent the workers'. He is needed in and against the government agency, but also in and against the university. The Ombudsman is, so to speak, the hygiene of organizations – or at least their toothbrush.

313

All this is really implied in the general proposition that each organization, the government agency included, must be held to its own specific task and must be forced to keep its authority, as well as its responsibility, within the narrow and strictly interpreted limits of the task. For a pluralist society strict adherence to specific purpose and narrow boundaries is the first law of liberty.

Businesses, no matter who owns them, should stick to providing economic goods and services in the expectation of economic returns. Universities should stick to advancing and teaching knowledge and to making it effective. The military should stick to the defence of the nation. No doubt it is tempting to have business take on 'social responsibilities' – and gratifying to the businessmen to be invited to do so. It is tempting for the Department of Defense to apply its fantastic purchasing power to the reform of education (as Mr McNamara proposed while Secretary of Defense), and especially tempting for the university to play universal aunt to every community need. But no matter how well meant, it is irresponsibility. It is usurpation. It goes beyond the authority for which the institution exists. It goes beyond the task whose fulfilment is the sole reason for its authority.

Pluralist societies do not degenerate into tyranny because of the power lust of the barons. This is easily curbed by other barons. The Europe of Charlemagne degenerated because abbots and bishops, ie, the good, saintly men in a violent and wicked society, took upon themselves 'social responsibilities' that were none of their business, to wit, the administration of justice. This only meant that the mighty and wicked, the great barons, had no opposition when they took the prerogative of justice by force from the abbots.

The rise of England to greatness, historians have long agreed, rested in large degree on the control of justice by the Crown. Governing England by right of conquest, the Plantagenet kings – otherwise no models of virtue or

314

effectiveness – never allowed anyone else to take over the administration of justice. The difference between England and the European continent did not lie in the assertion of judicial autonomy by archbishops. The difference was that Thomas à Becket's claim to 'social responsibility' for justice was put down – brutally, cravenly, by assassination, but effectively. What the kings of England knew was that one cannot grant authority to one power within pluralist society without granting it to others. One cannot grant it to archbishops in respect to their flock without having barons grab it without any pretence to 'social responsibility'.

We will have to learn again that power we grant to one pluralist body, eg, the government agency, will in the end be demanded by all the others as well. If we do not want this to happen, we had better deny the power to any of them, including the government agency, the university, or any other 'good guy' of political folklore. We will have to learn that all organizations are tools of society, each 'good' for a specific purpose, each a menace beyond it.

ORGANIZATION AS INDIVIDUAL OPPORTUNITY

So far, we have been talking about what the Germans used to call the *Rechtsstaat*: a political society in which the individual is protected against abuse of power on the part of authority. We have been talking of providing for the individual a preserve on which he will not be hunted down by organization, a 'national park' outside organization, so to speak, in which he will be undisturbed in his 'natural habitat'.

But this *freedom from* the abuse of power is not enough for a free society. A free society rests on the *freedom to* make responsible decisions.

Modern organization frees the individual to move out of the narrow and tightly restricted environment of tribe, vil-

315

lage, and small town. It is the modern organization that is creating the opportunities for educated people to put knowledge to work and to get paid for it – and paid very well. But these benefits impose on the individual the burden of decision. They impose on him responsibility for what he wants to be and what he wants to become.

It also imposes on him responsibility for what the organization should be and should become. What then should the individual demand of organization? And what must he do himself to make organization serve his ends? We will have to learn to demand of organization that it provide status and function to the individual.* But of ourselves we will have to demand that we learn how to use organization as opportunity for our own accomplishments and achievements.

The young are right when they protest against the tendency of organization to look upon an individual as a tool. But they are wrong when they blame organization for this. They have never asked themselves: 'How can I make this or that organization serve *my* end and *my* needs?' 'How can I make it enable *me* to perform, to achieve, to contribute?'

That the young rebel against being 'inputs' to the computer is understandable. But the clever demonstrations in which they dress up as punch cards and parade with the slogan: 'Don't fold, don't mutilate, don't spindle', miss the point. That's what cards are for. The question is: 'How can we use the computer and its cards as tools for individual ends?' For this one has to understand a little bit about the computer – though not much more than that one can always pull out the plug and stop it (something the fanciful myths of the computers' taking over the world tend to overlook). Then one sees right away that the computer, for those who understand

* On this see my book, *The New Society* (William Heinemann Ltd, London, 1951; Harper & Row, New York, 1950).

anything about it, is emancipation for the individual. The purpose of the computer is to enable us not to spend time on 'controls', but to use time for tasks that require perception, imagination, human relations, and creativity – the tasks in which the young rebels profess to believe.

This is only one illustration. Modern organization makes demands on the individual to learn something he has never been able to do before: to use organization intelligently, purposefully, deliberately, and responsibly. If he runs away from this task and its decisions, organization will indeed become the master. If the individual accepts this responsibility, he will be free and in control.

Organizations themselves see this only dimly. Yet we talk today increasingly about the 'free-form' organization as alone appropriate to knowledge work – in business, as well as in the military, the university, and government service. This is an organization in which discipline shifts to the individual. What controls is not rank but the task. For people who believe that true love consists of being promiscuous (as the very young have always tended to believe), this is, of course, still 'restraint'. What it really is, however, is responsibility.

To make the society of organizations a free society requires acceptance of responsibility by the individual; above all, acceptance of responsibility for contribution – his own, as well as that of organization. This is frightening, and not only to the young. But it is not particularly new. We have known all along that freedom is responsibility, and not licence.

Young people in the society of organizations need systematic information how to make organization serve their own purposes, values, and aspirations. They will have to learn organization as their forefathers learned farming. It is the mark of a mature person to ask: 'What do I want to get out of life?' – and to know that one gets out only as much as one puts in. Tomorrow it will be the mark of a free person to ask: 'What do I get out of organizations?' – and to know that he gets out only as much as he puts in.

To make our society function requires that we know how to manage, ie, how to obtain organizational performance through the work of the individual. To make our society free will also require that the individual learn how to manage organization – how to make organization and his job in it serve his ends, his values, his desire to achieve.

A society needs to be able to allow the individual to opt out and lead a 'private life'. But this is not freedom. This is indifference. In a free society, the citizen takes responsibility, above all, for his society and its institutions. In the society of organizations, the pluralist society of our time, this is a different task from that of the eighteenth century. The political tradition of the eighteenth century, the tradition of Locke, is clearly at its end. But the society of organizations may offer greater opportunities for meaningful, effective, responsible freedom than earlier society. Whether they will be realized or not depends on what *we* do rather than on what 'they', the institutions, do.

We face a period of hard new thinking on the political structure of society and on the position and role of the individual in it. What we have so far is a new pluralism, a new society of organizations. What we need is a new individualism, a new responsibility.

PART FOUR

The Knowledge Society

12. The Knowledge Economy

THE 'KNOWLEDGE INDUSTRIES'* which produce and distribute ideas and information rather than goods and services, accounted in 1955 for one-quarter of the US Gross National Product. (This was already three times the proportion of the national product that the country had spent on the 'knowledge sector' in 1900.) Yet by 1965, ten years later, the knowledge sector was taking one-third of a much bigger national product. In the late 1970s it will account for one-half of the total national product. Every other dollar earned and spent in the American economy will be earned by producing and distributing ideas and information and will be spent on procuring ideas and information.

From an economy of goods, which America was as recently as World War II, we have changed into a knowledge economy.

The figures are impressive enough. Ninety per cent of all scientists and technologists who ever lived are alive and at work today. In the first 500 years since Gutenberg, from 1450 to 1950, some 30 million printed books were published in the world. In the last twenty-five years alone an equal number has appeared. Thirty years ago, on the eve of World War II, semi-skilled machine operators, the men on the assembly line, were the centre of the American work force. Today the centre is the

* The term was coined by the Princeton economist, Fritz Machlup, in his book *Production and Distribution of Knowledge in the US* (1962).

knowledge worker, the man or woman who applies to productive work ideas, concepts, and information rather than manual skill or brawn. Our largest single occupation is teaching, that is, the systematic supply of knowledge and systematic training in applying it.

In 1900 the largest single group, indeed still the majority, of the American people, was rural and made a living on the farm. By 1940, the largest single group, by far, were industrial workers, especially semi-skilled (in fact, essentially unskilled) machine operators. By 1960, the largest single group were what the census called 'professional, managerial, and technical people', that is, knowledge workers. By 1975 or, at the latest, by 1980, this group will embrace the majority of Americans at work in the civilian labour force.

Since the knowledge worker tends to be a good deal better paid than the manual worker, and also to have much greater job security, knowledge has already become the central cost of the American economy. The productivity of knowledge has already become the key to productivity, competitive strength, and economic achievement.

But the statistics, impressive though they are, do not reveal the important thing. What matters is that knowledge has become the central 'factor of production' in an advanced, developed economy.

Economists still tend to classify the 'knowledge industries' as 'services'. As such, they contrast them with the 'primary' industries – agriculture, mining, forestry, and fishing, which make available to man the products of nature – and with the 'secondary' industries – that is, manufacturing. But knowledge has actually become the 'primary' industry, the industry that supplies to the economy the essential and central resource of production. The economic history of the last hundred years in the advanced and developed countries could be called 'from agriculture to knowledge'. Where the farmer was the backbone of any economy a century or two ago – not only in numbers of people employed, but in importance and value of what he produced – knowledge is now the main cost, the main investment, and the main product of the advanced economy and the livelihood of the largest group in the population.

Increasingly knowledge is the key factor in a country's international economic strength. Increasingly we hear discussions of the 'brain drain', which pulls educated people from countries of relative knowledge backwardness towards countries of advanced knowledge status.

The best-known example is the 'brain drain' from Britain to the United States – which is certainly closely connected with the fact that, of the major industrial countries, Britain today has the lowest educational level for the great bulk of the population, with 80 per cent of her people leaving school at the age of 15. It is also the country in which access to productive livelihoods is still gained primarily through apprenticeship, that is, through experience rather than through knowledge.

But the 'brain drain' may be an even more serious problem for the underdeveloped countries whose educated people tend to go to work in the advanced industrial nations, especially in Britain and the United States (and to a lesser extent in France) rather than stay at home.

Similarly during the last few years there has been more and more talk of the 'technology gap' that is supposed to have opened up between the United States and Western Europe. There has been a good deal of fear, even by European friends of the United States, lest Europe become technologically subservient (a fear, for instance, expressed in the brilliant book of the French writer and journalist, Jean-Jacques Servan-Schreiber, *Le Défi Americain* (*The American Challenge*) which became a European bestseller in 1967).

In 1900 steel was the economic measurement – and the steel industry was based squarely on skill rather than on knowledge. If all the men of knowledge at work in a nation in 1900 had suddenly been taken away, the economy would hardly have noticed the difference. Knowledge was then ornament, economically speaking, rather than functional. Today it is the foundation and measurement of economic potential and economic power.

'Knowledge' rather than 'science' has become the foundation of the modern economy. This has already been mentioned in Part One, but it needs to be said again. To be sure, science and scientists have suddenly moved into the centre of the political, military, and economic stage. But so have practically all the other knowledge people. It is not just the chemists, the physicists, and the engineers who get fat on consulting assignments in universities – to the point where they may have a larger income from consulting outside the university than from teaching and research inside. Geographers and mathematicians, economists and linguists, psychologists, anthropologists, and marketing men, all are busy consulting with government, with industry, with the foreign aid programme, and so on. Few areas of learning are not in demand by the organizations of our pluralist society. There is, I admit, little call for the consulting services of the classics faculty.* But there is more demand for the theologians than most people realize. Altogether it is the exceptional area of knowledge which is not today being brought into play in business and industry, in government and the military, in the hospital and in international relations.

This demand, in return, reflects the basic fact that knowledge has become productive. The systematic and purposeful acquisition of information and its systematic application, rather than 'science' or 'technology', are emerging as

* Though Bible scholars are highly prized by both Israeli and Arab Armies as consultants on topography, hidden water resources, etc.

the new foundation for work, productivity, and effort throughout the world.

This development has gone furthest in the United States. But in this area, as in so many others, the United States only started moving a few years earlier than the others. The trend runs the same way in every one of the advanced industrial countries. There is a close correlation between the ability of an economy to grow and compete in the world today and the rate of increase of its population at school beyond the age of fifteen – with the United States, Japan, Israel, and the Soviet Union at the top, and Great Britain at the bottom among the developed industrial nations. When the Europeans complain about the 'brain drain' and the 'technology gap', they are only asserting that their economies are not sufficiently 'knowledge-based' to perform, to grow, and to compete.

The demand for knowledge workers in the future seems insatiable. In addition to a million computer programmers, the information industry in the United States will need in the next fifteen years another half-million systems engineers, systems designers, and information specialists. We need, perhaps, two million health-care professionals – nurses, dietitians, medical and X-ray technologists, social and psychiatric case workers, physiotherapists, and so on. These people are both highly trained, well above secondary-school level, and highly skilled. They are fully the equivalent of the skilled machinist or the skilled carpenter with his years of apprenticeship. But their skill is founded on knowledge.

Maintenance of the air fleets of tomorrow – the jumbo jets and jet freighters which, between now and 1980, are likely to become the main carriers of people and freight – will require more workers than now keep all the railways running. These men, while highly skilled, will greatly differ from the traditional railway craftsman. First, they will be able to do the entire maintenance operation.

They will not, like their predecessors, have been trained in a specific craft, whether sheet-metal work or electronics, but in a specific function: keeping an aeroplane operating safely. Second, their skill will rest on theoretical knowledge and formal schooling rather than on apprenticeship in a craft. While they work with their hands, they will apply knowledge rather than skill. Manuals, charts, and texts will be at least as important to them as the traditional hand tools are to the artisan.

These examples bring out some fundamentals of the knowledge economy.

(1) Knowledge work does not lead to a 'disappearance of work'. Eminent doctors tell us today that work is on its deathbed in the rich, industrially advanced countries such as the United States, Western Europe, or Japan. The trends are actually running in the opposite direction. The typical 'worker' of the advanced economy, the knowledge worker, is working more and more, and there is a demand for more and more knowledge workers. The manual worker, the typical worker of yesterday, may have more leisure. He may go home at five in the evening. But the knowledge worker everywhere works increasingly longer hours. The young engineer, the accountant, the medical technologist, or the teacher, take work home with them when they leave the office. Knowledge work, like all productive work, creates its own demand. And the demand is apparently unlimited.

(2) Knowledge does not eliminate skills. On the contrary, knowledge is fast becoming the foundation for skill. We are using knowledge increasingly to enable people to acquire skills of a very advanced kind fast and successfully. Knowledge without skill is unproductive. Only when knowledge is used as a foundation for skill does it become productive. Then it enables us to acquire in less time and with less effort what it took years of apprenticeship to learn. It enables us to acquire new skills, ie, computer programming,

which could never be acquired through apprenticeship alone. Knowledge, that is, the systematic organization of information and concepts, is therefore making 'apprenticeship' obsolete. Knowledge substitutes systematic learning for exposure to experience.

We learned in World War II, with respect to manual crafts, that we could compress years of apprenticeship into weeks, or at most months, of organized and systematic learning. Once we had converted the experience of a craft to a systematic 'programme', people without great native talent or intelligence, that is, average people, became highly skilled craftsmen in little time, and enjoyed the learning experience. Britain after Dunkirk demonstrated this first, followed on a large scale by the United States in 1942–4. We demonstrated this in metal work such as welding or riveting, in shipbuilding, in engineering work of all kinds, and in construction. The Armed Forces used systems and programmes as the foundation for a great variety of skills – clerical, supervisory, and medical. With this experience the shift to knowledge work and knowledge industry actually began.

The man or woman who has once acquired skill on a knowledge foundation has learned to learn. He can acquire rapidly new and different skills. Unlike apprenticeship, which prepares for one specific craft and teaches the use of one specific set of tools for one specific purpose, a knowledge foundation enables people to un-learn and to re-learn. It enables them, in other words, to become 'technologists' who can put knowledge, skills, and tools to work, rather than 'craftsmen' who know how to do one specific task in one specific way.

Applying knowledge to work has a long history. The priests who thousands of years ago organized Egypt's agriculture – and indeed her entire political and social life – around the knowledge of the flood tides of the Nile, were 'knowledge workers' and applied knowledge to work.

But these were exceptions. Knowledge and work, until very recent times, were separate and rarely touched each other. Knowledge was desirable for its intrinsic beauty, and at best as conducive to wisdom (though the evidence for this old belief is not overwhelming). Work was based on experience – and this was as true, until a century or two ago, even of the work of the physician. As regards the lawyer, Mr Justice Holmes' dictum: 'The life of the law has not been logic, it has been experience', is as valid today as it was a century ago.

'Knowledge' as normally considered by the 'intellectual' is something very different from 'knowledge' in the context of a 'knowledge economy' or of 'knowledge work'. For the 'intellectual', knowledge is what is in a book. But as long as it is in the book, it is only 'information' if not mere 'data'. Only when a man applies the information to do something does it become knowledge. Knowledge, like electricity or money, is a form of energy that exists only when doing work. The emergence of the knowledge economy is not, in other words, part of 'intellectual history' as it is normally conceived. It is part of the 'history of technology', which recounts how man puts tools to work. When the intellectual says 'knowledge' he usually thinks of something new. But what matters in the 'knowledge economy' is whether knowledge, old or new, is applicable, eg, Newtonian physics to the space programme. What is relevant is the imagination and skill of whoever applies it, rather than the sophistication or newness of the information.

The idea that knowledge, systematically acquired, could be applied systematically to work is no more than 200 to 250 years old. It first occurred to the long line of English tool makers and tool designers of the eighteenth and early nineteenth centuries, which culminated in the towering figure of Joseph Whitworth (1803–87). These men were not only great inventors without whose work modern industry and modern technology would never have come into being.* They also set out to systematize what they knew about mechanical work and to build this knowledge into the tool. This not only led directly to 'engineering', that is, to the codification of the right way to do any particular task; it also changed work and work force – the true beginning of the Industrial Revolution. The deliberate design of tools enabled the merely competent workman to turn out – predictably and effectively time after time – work of pre-established precision and uniformity. The famous 'go/ no-go' gauges† which Whitworth designed almost at the beginning of his career enabled every journeyman to know in a single operation what the work was like, what it should be like, and what was needed to bring it up to standard – and then to measure the results against the standards. They were the first 'programmes' ever designed, and to this day they are the most successful ones. They foreshadowed the 'knowledge economy' in that knowledge, and the work of the English tool designers, became the foundation for skill and the means to acquire easily and fast what had, over the ages, been accessible only to near-genius. What formerly required a 'master' now required the 'skilled worker'.

The next step, and a completely different one, was taken in the United States with the Morrill Act of 1862, which established a land-grant college in every state of the Union. What was new was not the idea of research in agriculture and of developing new methods, new seeds, new breeds, and

* Unfortunately, the historian of ideas treats them with contempt because they were not 'scientists'; and the historian of technology is prone to be dazzled by the prime movers, such as the steam engine, and to overlook the tool makers who made possible the new engines and processes. Watt's steam engine would never have worked but for John Wilkinson's new boring mill, which supplied cylinders and pistons that fitted tightly and thus cured the leakage of steam which had been the fatal defect of the earlier steam engines such as Newcomen's.

† Which standardized the inner, as well as the outer, dimensions of a piece of metal so that it failed the gauges if either too big or too small.

so on, but the idea of converting farming altogether from a practice into a discipline, and of making every farmer an agronomist and systematic technologist. This was a pure act of faith at the time. There was no precedent. Indeed there was little in human experience to make the idea sound plausible. For fifty years there were few results; but at about the time of World War I the land-grant college and the extension service* began to have the hoped-for impact on farm work, farm output, and farm productivity. Since then the productivity of agriculture has been multiplied, and agriculture has changed its character. It used to be the way of life of the great majority of mankind, and a subsistence living. Now it has become a capital-intensive, mechanized, and 'scientific' industry. A small number of highly-trained men, equipped with expensive mechanical and managerial tools, produce something totally new in the world, farm surpluses. This is a greater change in culture, society, and economy than most of the technological innovations we marvel at.

The most important step towards the 'knowledge economy' was, however, Scientific Management – that is, the systematic application of analysis and study to manual work, first pioneered by Frederick W. Taylor (1856–1915) in the last decades of the nineteenth century. Taylor, for the first time in history, looked at work itself as deserving the attention of an educated man. Before, work had always been taken for granted, especially by the educated. If they ever thought of it, they knew that work had been ordained – by God or by nature – and that the only way to produce more was to work more and work harder. Taylor saw that this was false. The key to producing more was to 'work smarter'. The key to productivity was knowledge, not sweat.

Taylor did not start out (as most people believe who have

* Which was not provided for in the original Act, but was established in the early 1900s, largely through the vision and efforts of a non-farmer, the builder of the Sears Roebuck company, Julius Rosenwald.

never read his work) with ideas of efficiency or economy, let alone with the purpose of making a profit for the employer. He started out with a burning social concern and was deeply troubled by what he saw as a suicidal conflict between 'labour' and 'capital'. And his greatest impact has also been social. For Scientific Management (we would today probably call it 'systematic work study', and eliminate thereby a good many misunderstandings the term has caused) has proved to be the most effective idea of this century. It is the only basic American idea that has had worldwide acceptance and impact. Wherever it has been applied, it has raised the productivity and with it the earnings of the manual worker, and especially of the labourer, while greatly reducing his physical efforts and his hours of work. It has probably mutiplied the labourer's productivity by a factor of one hundred.

But above all, Taylor's Scientific Management provided the way out of the impasse of the nineteenth century; opened a 'third way' between nineteenth-century capitalism and nineteenth-century socialism. It proved them both false. For both assumed as a law of nature that the economic pie was given and could not be increased, except by putting in more capital or working more and harder. Taylor showed that the economic pie could be enlarged rapidly by applying knowledge to work. This did not create the harmony Taylor had naïvely hoped for. But it replaced an irreconcilable conflict of principles which could only end by subjugating one to the other – either by a dictatorship of the 'capitalist' or by one of the 'proletariat' – with conflict over the division of the fruits of higher productivity. Fighting for 'more' can be bitter and protracted; but it can always be compromised.

It is not true that Taylor took the skill out of manual work, though this has often been asserted. For he applied Scientific Management only to work that had never been skilled, ie, to work of the labourer. His must famous study, made in 1899, dealt with shovelling sand. And Schmidt, his shovelling labourer, was not skilled, had no pride in his non-existent craft, no control over his work, no fun doing it, and a bare subsistence to show for his ten hours of back-breaking, but largely unproductive, daily toil. Taylor's study thus enabled the unskilled man to be paid handsomely, almost at the level of the skilled man, and to be in high demand. The labourer suddenly became productive. Taylor, in other words repealed the 'iron law of wages' under which the unskilled manual labourer had always lived. He did this by creating a skill that had never existed before – the skill of the 'industrial engineer'. It was the first skill to be firmly based on knowledge rather than on experience. The 'industrial engineer' of Scientific Management is the prototype of all modern 'knowledge workers' – and to this day, one of the most productive ones.

(3) But while knowledge eliminates neither work nor skill, its introduction does constitute a real revolution both in the productivity of work and in the life of the worker.

Perhaps its greatest impact lies in changing society from one of pre-determined occupations into one of choices for the individual. It is now possible to make one's living, and a good living at that, doing almost anything one wants to do and plying almost any knowledge. This is something new under the sun.

Most of mankind through the ages has had no choice at all; son followed father. The Indian caste system only gave religious sanction to what was the norm for most people. Of course, there was always some mobility, upward and downward – even the caste system in India could not entirely prevent this. But these were the exceptions, the few lucky ones, the occasional highly gifted one, the victim of war and catastrophes, or the totally improvident who gambled or gave away whatever they inherited. And in a world in which most people eked out a bare subsistence on the land, being a peasant was for most of mankind the one and only occupation.

The Knowledge Economy

A century ago even the educated man could only make a living through knowledge in a few narrowly circumscribed 'professions': clergyman, physician, lawyer, and teacher, plus – the one newcomer – civil servant (engineers came in only at the end of the last century).

In 1930, a friend of mine, one of the ablest young men ever to graduate from a great Oxford college, was offered a junior fellowship in mathematics at All Souls, the most prestigious academic institution in Great Britain. Thereupon his intelligent and well-to-do middle-class family descended upon him in a body and persuaded him to turn down the offer and go into banking in the City instead. They pointed out that the young man would have to earn his living and that there were only half a dozen jobs in England that paid a mathematician a living wage, primarily the few senior professorships at Oxford, Cambridge, and London. Obtaining one of these was as much a matter of being at the right place at the right time, when one of the incumbents died, as it was a matter of mathematical genius and merit. The man who failed to obtain one of these plums could at best hope to be a wretched schoolmaster drilling Euclid into numbskulls for a pittance. The point is not that the young man's family was timid. The point is that they were more nearly right than wrong. Opportunities for mathematicians were almost non-existent in England thirty-five or forty years ago as they were in most countries of the world.

Today, needless to say, opportunities for a mathematician are unlimited. He need not be a Newton or a Gauss to make a very good living doing what he enjoys doing. And the same holds true for almost every other branch of knowledge. In each there are more opportunities for productive, rewarding, and well-paid work than there are men and women available to fill them.

333

At the same time, access to education is becoming the birthright of people in advanced societies – and its absence the badge of 'class domination'. It is the absence of access to education which is now meant when people in the developing countries speak of 'colonial oppression' or 'neo-colonialism'. Education a hundred years ago was still a privilege. In about 1850 it first became an opportunity which the educational systems in the developed countries increasingly made available to the gifted and ambitious among the poor and 'under-privileged'.

Within the last twenty or thirty years, access to education has however become a right. Nowhere is it yet guaranteed in the American Constitution, but it is clearly as important today as any of the rights written into formal 'Bills of Rights'. When the US Supreme Court outlawed 'separate but equal' education for the American Negro and ordered the integration of the schools in 1954, it clearly assumed that the right of access to education was as solemnly embedded in the American Constitution as any of the rights actually guaranteed therein.

Of course, there are still limits – and not only of ability, but of wealth, of the accident of location, and certainly of race, even in the richer countries. On the whole, we are rapidly moving from a society in which careers and occupations were determined, ie, largely by the accident of birth, into one in which we take freedom of choice for granted.

The problem today is not the lack of choice, but the abundance thereof. There are so many choices, so many opportunities, so many directions that they bewilder and distract the young people. No sooner have they shown a passing interest in this or that area than they are encouraged to make it their life's career. There is simply not enough of anything – whether metallurgists or specialists in Oriental languages, whether statisticians or psychologists, whether systems engineers or botanists; all are in chronically short supply. The educated man or woman is over-

334

whelmed. Sometimes I feel that my mathematician friend in Oxford in 1930 had it easier than his children today.

But even though a surfeit of choice can become burdensome, the human horizon has still been widened immeasurably.

(4) Knowledge opportunities exist primarily in large organizations. While the shift to knowledge work has made possible large modern organizations, it is the emergence of these organizations – business enterprise, government agency, large university, research laboratory, hospital – that in turn has created the job opportunities for the knowledge worker.

The knowledge opportunities of yesterday were largely for independent professionals working on their own. Today's knowledge opportunities are largely for people working within an organization as members of a team, or by themselves. This is true even where the organization itself antedates the knowledge society, as do military and government service, university, and hospital. There is still the *Herr Professor* who looks upon the university as existing for him, and who works and teaches by himself as he pleases and at most with 'assistants'. But this is not how most of the work in the university is done any more. It is done by teams, by 'interdisciplinary groups', and in organized research centres.

There is a charming picture of the British Home Office in Victorian times in Anthony Trollope's novel *John Caldigate*. The novel came out in 1879 – in a period of massive reforms in English local government that the Home Office pioneered. Yet the Home Office which Trollope – himself a civil servant and thoroughly familiar with the British government of his time – portrays, is essentially one man, totally anonymous, but very powerful, serving directly under the Minister and assisted by a few clerks. In the bureaucratic Russia of the Tsars, things were apparently not very different judging by what Tolstoy tells us about the official life of that powerful bureaucrat, Anna Karenina's hapless husband. And even later, before World War I, the government agency was still essentially one or a few trained men, each working by himself

No one has ever accused the Austro-Hungarian monarchy of understaffing its government offices. Yet when my father entered the Austrian government service in 1897, he joined a total of ten other 'gentlemen', each with a separate assignment, each reporting directly to an old and powerful chief of the bureau who, in turn, reported directly to the Cabinet. There were simply not enough educated people available to provide a larger staff. Today's Austria, though only one-tenth of the size of the Austria of 1900, employs about 500 university-trained men in the same department, most of them working in large teams rather than on individual assignments.

The knowledge worker of today, in other words, is not the successor to the 'free professionals' of 1750 or 1900. He is the successor to the employee of yesterday, the manual worker, skilled or unskilled.

This is very substantial upgrading. But it also creates an unresolved conflict between the tradition of the knowledge worker and his position as an employee. Though the knowledge worker is not a 'labourer', and certainly not a 'proletarian', he is still an 'employee'. He is not a 'subordinate' in the sense that he can be told what to do; he is paid, on the contrary, for applying his knowledge, exercising his judgement, and taking responsible leadership. Yet he has a 'boss' – in fact, he needs to have a boss to be productive. And the boss is usually not a member of the same discipline but a 'manager' whose special competence is to plan, organize, integrate, and measure the work of knowledge people regardless of their discipline or area of specialization.

The knowledge worker is both the true 'capitalist' in the knowledge society and dependent on his job. Collectively the knowledge workers, the employed educated middle class of today's society, own the means of production through pension funds, investment trusts, and so on. These funds are the true 'capitalists' of modern society with which no private individual, were he richer than Croesus, Rothschild, and Morgan combined, could compete. But individually the knowledge worker is dependent on his salary, on the pension benefits and health insurance that go with it, and altogether on having a job and getting paid. Individually he is an 'employee', even though there is no other 'employer' in our society.

But the knowledge worker sees himself as just another 'professional', no different from the lawyer, the teacher, the preacher, the doctor, or the government servant of yesterday. He has the same education. He has more income. He has probably greater opportunities as well. He may realize that he depends on the organization for access to income and opportunity, and that without the investment the organization has made – and a high investment at that – there would be no job for him. But he also realizes, and rightly so, that the organization equally depends on him.

This hidden conflict between the knowledge worker's view of himself as a 'professional' and the social reality in which he is the upgraded and well-paid successor to the skilled worker of yesterday, underlies the disenchantment of so many highly educated young people with the jobs available to them. It explains why they protest so loudly against the 'stupidity' of business, of government, of the Armed Services, and of the universities. They expect to be 'intellectuals', and they find that they are just 'staff'. Since this holds true for organizations altogether and not just for this or that organization, there is nowhere to flee to. If they turn their backs on business and go to the university, they soon find out that this, too, is a 'machine'. If they turn from the university to government service, they find the same situation there.

What most of them fail to realize is that the choice is not

between these irksome jobs – which are irksome precisely because they are 'jobs' – and an illusory freedom. The choice is between jobs that have opportunity and are paid well, and working in the potato or cotton patch, hoeing or weeding, sixteen hours a day for a bare subsistence. But it may be too much to expect young people to understand this. Certainly every single one of them would argue that this may be true for all the others, but he is the exception, the one who is qualified to be a true 'professional'.

This clash between the expectations in respect to knowledge jobs and their reality will become sharper and clearer with every passing year. It will make the management of knowledge workers increasingly crucial to the performance and achievement of the knowledge society. We will have to learn to manage the knowledge worker both for productivity and for satisfaction, both for achievement and for status. We will have to learn to give the knowledge worker a job big enough to challenge him, and to permit performance as a 'professional'.

But no matter how good a job we do in the management of the knowledge worker – and so far we have barely begun to work in this area – his status, function, and position in modern society is certain to be a central problem, politically as well as socially. It is likely to be *the* social question of the developed countries for the twentieth and probably for the twenty-first century.

THE EMERGENCE OF KNOWLEDGE WORK

How did this shift to knowledge society and knowledge economy come about?

The popular answer is: 'Because jobs have been getting more complex and more demanding.' But the right answer is: 'Because the working life span of man has increased so greatly.' It is not the demand for labour but the supply that underlies this great transformation of society and economy. And this, in turn, also explains the social and economic problems posed by the emergence of knowledge.

The arrival of the knowledge worker changed the nature of jobs. Because modern society has to employ people who expect and demand knowledge work, knowledge jobs have to be created. As a result, the character of work is being transformed.

The demands of most jobs have changed but little, at least until recent years.

There is nothing, for instance, in the work of an American salesgirl that explains why, thirty years ago, junior high school was considered adequate preparation for the work while today the applicant is expected to have finished high school and preferably a few years of college as well. Nor does today's salesgirl at the age of 18 or 20 produce any more sales than the 15-year-old salesgirl of 1935, or the 12-year-old salesgirl of 1910.

The typical foreman in a mass-production plant in the United States in 1929 had gone to work at the age of 15, with six years of schooling. Ten years later, before the outbreak of World War II, the typical assembly-plant foreman already had a high-school education. Today it is increasingly taken for granted that he is a college graduate. Yet the job is exactly what it was forty years ago. If anything, it has become less demanding as more and more of it has either been reduced to a formula or been taken out of the foreman's hands and shifted to such specialists as personnel people, quality controllers, and production planners.

That the much-vaunted 'complexity of today's job' is a myth is also shown by comparing American practice with that of other advanced industrial countries. For while moving in the same direction, Europe and Japan are still well behind in the educational upgrading of the entire population. Jobs which call for a year or two of college education in the United States are being staffed in Germany, for instance, with men and women who have finished what corresponds roughly to the American junior high school (the German *Ober-Sekunda-Reife*). Yet there is no discernible difference in the demands made on the employee, or in his or her productivity.

The best example is found in Canada where there are two educational standards side by side. Toronto and industrial Ontario are on the same educational standard as the American Midwest on which they border. A few hundred miles to the east, Montreal and industrial Quebec are only now starting the 'educational explosion'. The jobs that, in Ontario, are being filled by high-school graduates, preferably with one or two years of college, are staffed by the same employers – supermarket chains, for instance, or commercial banks or manufacturers – with junior high-school graduates in Quebec. They are paid quite differently; yet there is not much difference in the jobs they do or in their productivity.

The direct cause of the upgrading of the jobs is, in other words, the upgrading of the educational level of the entrant into the labour force. The longer he or she stays at school, the more education will be required for entrance into a given job or occupation.

But the extension of the years at school is itself only an effect rather than a cause. It is the result of a long development which drastically changed working-life expectancy in the industrially advanced countries.

That life expectancy has gone up sharply in the advanced countries is common knowledge. But few people seem to have noticed that the years of working life have gone up even faster. Around the turn of the century, that is, in the lifetime of people still alive and working today, few members of the labour force could expect to work to full capacity past the age of 45 or 50. They were at least likely to be impaired physically by then.

Fifty years ago European middle-class mothers used

340

to tell their children: 'A government job does not pay much. But you won't starve if you become an invalid before your time. And it does provide for your widow and the children you leave behind.' The earlier retirement programme, eg, those of the military and Civil Services of Europe, expected the few survivors to retire after twenty-five to thirty years of working life, that is, before the age of 50. One of the oldest general retirement systems, that of the Japanese, still makes retirement at 55 compulsory for all but the people at the very top, with a lump-sum retirement payment equal to two years of salary. This was adequate as late as 1940. Few Japanese lived that long – and those that reached the age of 55 were unlikely to live a great many more years beyond retirement. Today, when Japanese life expectancies and working-life spans are equal to those of the most advanced countries of the West, these retirement provisions have become absurd.

Working-life span half a century ago was already higher than it had been throughout history. Prior to 1850, there was no country where average life expectancy greatly exceeded 33 or 35 years, which limited average working life to 20 years. By 1914 these figures had risen, in the most advanced countries, to around 30 years of working-life expectancy, from starting work at the age of 15 to disablement or death aged 45 or so. Today, working life extends to 65 for the great majority. If people were still expected to start work at about the age of 14, as was the case everywhere up to World War I, there would be a working-life span of 50 years for the great majority – two and a half times that of a century ago, and two-thirds larger than it was only a generation ago. Even with our later age of entrance into the work force – 18 or 20 – the working-life span in the advanced countries today is twice that of a century ago and 50 per cent larger than it was at about the time of World War I.

This means that we have more than doubled the human capital of the economy in the last century. We have also more than doubled the earnings potential of the individual; for a lifetime's income of an individual is, of course, his annual income multiplied by the number of years he is capable of earning it. This is the biggest increase in what the economists call the 'stock of capital' ever recorded in economic history. It is also the greatest advance ever recorded in economic wealth and well-being – infinitely greater than anything shown in the economist's statistics of the supply of *goods*, which is what the economist usually means when he talks of the 'standard of living'.

Extending the working-life span has altered the ratio between the productive and the dependent members of the population. This may have been an even greater boost to productivity than the increase in the stock of capital. How much there is in a society does not depend solely on how much the individual produces; it depends also on how many people have to be supported by the productivity of one producer. In fact, productivity of an economy might perhaps best be expressed as productivity of the individual divided by the number of dependent people he has to support.*

The extension of working-life span in today's developed countries has, during the last hundred years, altered drastically the traditional balance between producers and dependants. Not only do people who survive remain self-supporting until a much later age but, more important, they stay producers so much longer that, even with a somewhat larger family, the number of dependants per producer has gone down sharply.

* This is the reason why the 'population explosion' is such a threat to the social and economic welfare of the developing nations. It increases the number of dependants, particularly small children below the productive age, so rapidly that even great increases in *per capita* production on the part of the producing population do not result in larger *per capita* income and higher standards of living.

The farmer or artisan of 1800 or 1850 who had a thirty-year working life had to support four or five dependants all through this period. On an average, only two or three of his children reached manhood and became producers themselves. But in order to have two or three grown children, his wife (or wives) had to give birth to seven or eight – so that there were always young ones in the home who had to be supported. In addition, his own parents, if they survived, were likely to become dependent in their mid-forties, when he himself still carried a heavy burden of dependent children.

Today, with a working life of forty years or more, and with a child mortality reduced so sharply that babies can be expected to survive to manhood, the producer in the developed countries only has to support two or three dependants at any time, and only, as a rule, for the first half of his own productive life. In other words, extending working-life span amounts to quadrupling the economic potential of the same source, the individual productive human being.

This tremendous enrichment made possible the general adoption of what had always been the rarest privilege of the exceedingly rich: the wife-and-mother was able to leave the labour force and stay at home. As a result, not having one's wife at work became the badge of respectability and affluence in the developed countries during the nineteenth century. Many English workers still consider it an insult to be asked whether their wives work – a self-respecting working man should keep his woman at home.

Meanwhile, of course, the wives of the truly affluent are again going back into the labour force. The steady rise of married women at work in the developed countries is one of the most significant and must universal economic phenomena of the last two decades. It is the result of the productivity that creates 'affluence' and thus makes it possible for even the working-class woman to have 'mechanical servants' which take physical labour and time out of housework. It is the result also of advances in fertility control and infant and child health care which make it possible for the family in the developed countries to 'plan' both the number and the spacing of their children. The mother is no longer tied to the home beyond the early years of marriage and can go back to work when the children start going to school. This, a complete reversal of the earlier trend, again greatly alters the ratio between producers and dependants and, with it, the 'stock of capital' of the advanced economies.

Contrary to popular belief, the advances in medicine had little to do with the lengthening of working-life span. One main cause was undoubtedly the shift from farming as the occupation of the majority to where it now is, the occupation of a very small minority – fewer than 6 per cent of the United States population for instance. For farm work ages people fast, especially the farm work of sixty years ago, before electricity and modern machinery. Also in traditional agriculture disabling accidents occurred far more frequently than even in the most dangerous industrial pursuits. The farmer, and especially his wife, tended to be old and disabled by the time their children reached their teens.

But the shift from labourer to machine operator was hardly less important. Whether Irish or Chinese, the 'navvies' who built the American railways with pick and shovel rarely lasted more than five years or so before they were disabled by accident, liquor, syphilis, or plain backbreaking toil. As late as 1900 seamstresses in the garment lofts of New York, the London East End, Paris, or Vienna, did not last much longer. Within ten years most of them had fallen victim to blindness or to TB, the twin scourges of their trade.

Scientific Agriculture and Scientific Management are, therefore, the true heroes. They are the two main factors in the extension of working-life span. The drop in infant mortality and the advances in public health might well have lengthened total life span, but working-life span would not have moved upwards much. For this, it was necessary firstly to make possible the feeding of large populations by a small number of truly productive farmers, and, secondly, to raise productivity by eliminating the physically destructive tasks from industrial work.

The rise in working-life span, in turn, has led almost everywhere to a substantial extension of years spent in being educated.

It can be argued that this extension reflects a common faith in education as one of the highest human values. People are eager to spend a substantial part of new wealth such as a longer working-life span represents, on education rather than on getting an immediate money income.

It can also be argued that extending the years at school is an economic rationality in which people can indulge once they no longer have to worry where the next meal is coming from. By postponing earnings for a few years, they acquire higher earning power for the rest of their lives. There is no doubt that lifetime earnings rise disproportionately with education. If, in addition, working-life span also rises, the return on the investment in education, made by postponing the start of income by a few years, rises exponentially. In other words, extending the years of schooling is rational economic behaviour. It 'maximizes profits' far more effectively than anything the shrewdest businessman could ever have worked out.

There is one more explanation of this sharp increase in years of schooling. People cannot stand a working life of fifty years. It is simply too long for them. A part of the gain in working-life span is therefore offset by postponing entrance into the labour force to a later age. School is not seen primarily as desirable in itself nor as a means to a better livelihood. It is seen very largely as a way of keeping the kids off the street while still keeping them out of the labour force for a few years.

There is plenty of evidence for this rather cynical view.

Indeed there is evidence that even a working life of forty-five years – that is, a working life that begins at the age of 20 – may be too long, especially for knowledge workers.

Whichever of these three explanations is preferred – and there are elements of all three in the situation – the results are the same. In the advanced countries, man has chosen to take a substantial part of the increased wealth made possible by Scientific Agriculture and Scientific Management in the form of longer years of schooling.

Extending the years of schooling forces us to create jobs which apply knowledge to work. The person who has sat on a school bench until 18 or 20 may not have learned anything. But he has acquired different expectations.

He (or she) expects in the first place a different kind of job, a job that is 'proper' for a high-school or college graduate. This is firstly a job with higher pay. But also a job with greater opportunity. A job that gives a 'living' is no longer enough. It must offer a 'career'. But the job for the highly schooled is also a job in which one no longer works with one's hands but by applying one's mind. It is a knowledge job. Long years of schooling make a person unfit for anything but knowledge work. If he has learned anything at all, it is concept, system, idea; it is not experience. Finally, he is no longer available for apprenticeship; he is simply too old to start acquiring skill in the traditional way which takes five to eight years. The young man or woman who has sat in school until 18 or 20 cannot become a 'skilled worker' in the old style. Whatever he needs to learn must start from a foundation in knowledge.

The 'education explosion' after World War II radically altered the supply of labour – first in the United States and increasingly in all the advanced industrial countries, including the Soviet Union. It made it impossible to continue the traditional job structure. In the United States, in particular, we were faced with the need to shift rapidly from manual jobs, skilled or unskilled, to knowledge jobs, skilled or unskilled, as the centre of employment. At the very least we had to upgrade the pay of a good many traditional jobs even though the jobs themselves did not change at all; the salesgirl is an example.

The basis problem in the American economy during the twenty years since World War II has never been the supply of manual jobs. This has been a concern only because of the special situation of the American Negro. For the white 90 per cent of the population, the problem has been to have adequate supply of knowledge jobs, or of jobs that paid on the knowledge scale. If we had not been able to justify the expectations of educated people for knowledge jobs, we would have today an unemployed and unemployable intellectual proletariat the like of which the world has never seen. It would present an infinitely more dangerous and more explosive problem than our racial ghettoes.

It is amazing that the American economy could satisfy the expectations of all these people with long years of schooling. Even more amazing is that American business, by and large, could raise productivity enough to maintain the competitive position of American industry in the world and the ability of the American economy to grow. For we did not have – and still do not have – much knowledge of how to manage the knowledge worker and how to make him productive. In addition, in many cases, we had to pay much higher wages for people whose expectations were based on their long years of schooling, even though they did the same work with the same productivity as people with much less schooling – and with many fewer expectations – had done before.

As a result of the change in supply, we now have to create genuine knowledge jobs – whether the work itself demands it or not. For a true knowledge job is the only way to make highly schooled people productive.

By a circuitous and quite unplanned route, we are, therefore, arriving at the point at which Taylor aimed seventy-five years ago; we are beginning to apply knowledge to work itself. That the knowledge worker came first and knowledge work second – that indeed knowledge work is still largely to come – is an historical accident. From now on, we can expect increasing emphasis on work based on knowledge, and especially on skills based on knowledge. The new jobs that open up in the economy will start out with theoretical and conceptual knowledge acquired systematically and on a 'course'. Old jobs will either be changed to knowledge jobs or will be replaced by knowledge jobs. We can expect, in other words, that we will develop a true knowledge economy, as we have already developed a knowledge work force. A good deal of this knowledge work, like computer programming, will be semi-skilled rather than highly skilled. But even then it will require a knowledge foundation acquired at school and college.

The social, political, and economic challenges in and from the work force in industrially advanced countries increasingly arise out of the dynamics of knowledge work and out of the needs of the knowledge worker.

13. Work and Worker in the Knowledge Society

IN THE LAST twenty years the base of the American economy shifted from manual to knowledge work, and the centre of gravity of our social expenditure from goods to knowledge. Yet neither the productivity nor the profitability of the American economy so far show the impact. Clearly we do not as yet know how to obtain economic performance from knowledge. We also do not know how to satisfy the knowledge worker and to enable him to gain the achievement he needs. Nor do we as yet fully understand the social and psychological needs of the knowledge worker.

That we do not yet know how to manage knowledge workers for performance is hardly surprising considering how recent the shift to knowledge work has been. After all, it is less than a hundred years since we first began to concern ourselves with managing the manual worker. Robert Owen, to be sure, managed manual workers in his textile mills in Lanarkshire in Scotland as early as 1820. But while his model factories were a tourist attraction of the first magnitude, nobody paid much attention to his management concepts and methods. Not until after the American Civil War – and really not until Taylor another twenty years later – did we start to look at manual work and manual workers. Prior to 1860 or so no one even knew how to measure output. The term 'productivity' as applied to workers is a fairly recent usage.

We could, therefore, hardly expect to know how to define, let alone to measure the output of knowledge work.

For this task we need definitions – not to speak of measurements – that are quite different from those that we have learned to apply to manual work. The most useless and wasteful effort is that of an engineering team that with great speed, precision, and elegance turns out drawings for the wrong product. Knowledge work is not easily defined in quantitative terms, and may indeed be incapable of quantification altogether. The computer, it is reasonably certain, cannot measure the work of the programmer who runs the computer.

We also do not know how to manage the knowledge worker so that he wants to contribute and perform. But we do know that he must be managed quite differently from the way we manage the manual worker. Motivation for knowledge work must come from within the worker himself. The traditional 'motivators', that is, external rewards – pay for instance – do not motivate him. Dissatisfaction with external rewards such as pay destroys motivation, but satisfaction with them is taken for granted. Their absence, in other words, prevents performance, but their presence is neutral. Frederick Herzberg* of Case-Western Reserve University in Cleveland, who has done pioneering work in this area, calls the external rewards 'hygiene factors'.

What the knowledge worker needs to be positively motivated is achievement. He needs a challenge. He needs to know that he contributes. This is in complete contradiction to what we have come to consider 'good management' of the manual worker. The essence of our experience here is summed up in the popular phrase, 'A fair day's work for a fair day's pay'. Knowledge workers, however, should be expected to do 'an exceptional day's work' – and, they should then also have a chance to earn 'exceptional pay'.

The knowledge worker's demands are much greater than

* See his *The Motivation to Work* (John Wiley, New York, 1959) and *Work and the Nature of Man* (Cleveland, World, 1966). See also my book, *The Effective Executive* (Heinemann, London, 1967; Harper & Row, New York, 1967), especially Chapter One.

those of the manual worker, and are indeed quite different. For the manual worker a job is, above all, a 'livelihood'. That jobs ought also to satisfy people is a brand-new idea. The belief of so many critics of the industrial system (including a good many 'human relations' people) that pre-industrial work was satisfying is naïve nostalgia. This idea simply did not enter the heads of the masses of people in the past. What would have been the point anyhow, when one's occupation was determined, more or less by what one's father did – or by whatever work one could find? The traditional view of work was that of the Old Testament which presents it as a curse laid on man, rather than as a blessing or an opportunity. Only recently, when industrial crisis created enforced idleness while industrial productivity enabled us to maintain unemployed men above the subsistence level, have we come to realize that work is a psychological and social necessity for man and not only the way to earn our daily bread.

Knowledge workers cannot be satisfied with work that is only a livelihood. Their aspirations and their view of themselves are those of the 'professional' or the 'intellectual'. If they respect knowledge at all, they demand that it should become the base for accomplishment.

For this reason, it is crucial that knowledge workers should be challenged to achieve. For this reason, in other words, managing knowledge workers for performance is as essential to the knowledge worker himself as it is to society and economy.

Knowledge workers also require that the demands be made on them by knowledge rather than by bosses, that is, by objectives rather than by people. They require a performance-oriented organization rather than an authority-oriented organization.

Knowledge workers still need a superior. The organization structure must clearly identify where final decisions and ultimate responsibility rest. Organization needs constitutional laws, that is, a definition of authority and responsibility within hierarchical structure. But knowledge work itself knows no hierarchy, for there are no 'higher' and 'lower' knowledges. Knowledge is either relevant to a given task or irrelevant to it. The task decides, not the name, the age, or the budget of the discipline, or the rank of the individual plying it. For a disease of the eye, the ophthalmologist is relevant, for removal of a gall bladder it is the abdominal surgeon.

Knowledge, therefore, has to be organized as a team in which the task decides who is in charge, when, for what, and for how long. Organization structures for knowledge work must therefore be both rigid and flexible, both have clear authority and yet be task-focused, informed both by the logic of the situation and the necessity of command.

Two mediocre knowledge workers working together do not produce twice as much as one first-rate one. They do not even produce as much as one mediocre knowledge worker. In all probability they produce nothing – they just get in each other's way. The difference between competent work and excellence is great in all fields – it is the difference between journeyman and master. But in knowledge work it is particularly pronounced.

This does not mean that every knowledge worker needs to be a great man, but it does mean that he has to strive for excellence to accomplish anything. Knowledge work that 'just gets by' is not productive. This has great implications for the life and career of the knowledge worker himself, quite apart from what it means for his management.

To make knowledge work productive will be the great management task of this century – just as to make manual work productive was the great management task of the last century. The gap between knowledge work that is managed for productivity, and knowledge work that is left unmanaged is probably a great deal wider than was the tremendous difference between manual work before and after the introduction of Scientific Management.

KNOWLEDGE WORKER AND WORKING-LIFE SPAN

Yet no matter how satisfying the individual task, a good many knowledge workers tend to tire of their job in early middle age. Long before they reach retirement age, let alone long before they become physically and mentally disabled, the sparkle, the challenge, the excitement have gone out of their work.

There is ample evidence that despite the extension of schooling, working-life span is still too long for all but a limited number.

For manual workers early retirement seems to offer a solution, as witness the eagerness with which it has been accepted in the American automobile, steel, and rubber industries despite heavy financial penalties. The manual worker, does not, it seems suffer from a 'problem of leisure'. Time does not hang heavy on his hands, even though he shows little desire for the 'cultural pursuits' that are pressed on him by the educated. He can sit in a cottage or trailer in Florida, apparently happy and busy with a small garden, occupied with fishing, hunting, and gossiping, without much desire to go back to the mill.

The knowledge worker, however, cannot easily retire. If he does, he is likely to disintegrate fast. Knowledge work is apparently habit-forming in a way in which manual work is not. People who have been doing knowledge work for twenty-odd years or so, cannot stop. But the great majority of them cannot go on either. They do not have the inner resources.

This is not true, it seems, of the few who reach the top, either in terms of power and position or in terms of eminence and leadership in their chosen discipline. They preserve their zest and tend to immerse themselves completely in their work. But a great many members of the educated middle class are only too susceptible to a modern version of the affliction known to the Middle Ages as *accidie*: the emotional malaise and sub-acute despair that was the typical disease of the cleric who realized, at about the age of 30 or so, that he would be neither saint nor abbot.

Similarly knowledge workers who, while successful, remain within a specific function or specific discipline until about 45 or so, often become tired, dispirited, and bored with themselves and the job. There is, for example, the director of market research in a business or the head of quality control; the controller of a Navy Yard or a training officer in the Army with the rank of Lieutenant-Colonel; the senior economist in a government bureau or the senior social worker in a Veterans' Hospital; even the good 'sound' professor on the university faculty.

In business and in government, in the Armed Services, and in the university there is a lot of talk about 'retreads', about 'recharging a man's batteries', about the need for 'sabbaticals' and for 'going back to school'. But it needs to be recognized that this is not a problem of the individual, but a generic problem grounded in the ambivalence of the knowledge worker's status. It is a result – probably an inevitable one – of the hidden conflict between the knowledge worker's view of himself as a 'professional' and the fact that he is within organization and a successor to yesterday's craftsman rather than to yesterday's 'professional'.

Yet we cannot expect to shorten the working-life span of the knowledge worker through extending his years of schooling even further. Indeed we should go the other way and shorten the years the young man spends at school and university before he starts in knowledge work.

The problem cannot be made to go away. But it can – and must – be converted into an opportunity. We must make it possible for the middle-aged knowledge worker to start a second knowledge career.

It is difficult to exaggerate the extent of this need. In an interview which appeared in the May 1968 issue of *Psychology Today* (a magazine which then had only

354

limited circulation) I touched upon this need for second knowledge careers. This provoked an outpouring of letters and telephone calls from all over the United States – I received at least 700 personal letters and hundreds of telephone calls – from ministers of all faiths, university professors, military officers, school principals, accountants, engineers, middle-managers, civil servants, and so on. Almost all recited a life story of substantial success. Yet all asked: 'Now that I am 47, how can I start doing something new and challenging?'

The accomplished knowledge journeyman, at 45 or 50, is in his physical and mental prime. If he is tired and bored it is because he has reached the limit of contribution and growth in his first career – and he knows it. He is likely to deteriorate rapidly if left doing what no longer truly challenges him. It is of little use to look to 'hobbies' or to 'cultural interests' to keep him alive. Being an amateur does not satisfy a man who has learned to be a professional. He may be willing, as he gets older, to spend a little more time on 'interests' outside the job. But he is not willing, nor emotionally able, to make such 'interests' the centre of his life, even if he has the money to do so. To be a dilettante has to be learned in childhood as all aristocracies have known.

One thing this man usually has is a desire to contribute. The children are grown up by this time, and the house is paid for. The man who no longer really cares for the work he has been doing for twenty-odd years, work which he knows so thoroughly that it provides neither challenge nor thrill, now 'wants to give', as so many of these men express it.

Today there is little organized opportunity to do so.

Yet at the same time, we in America have – and will continue to have – a growing shortage of personnel in a good many areas of knowledge work. We are having increasing difficulty, for instance, in recruiting young men for

355

the ministry, for teaching, and for medicine. In the past, young men and women had to go into these areas if they wanted to be knowledge workers at all. Now, however, with all the choices open to young people, these occupations are much less attractive – even if they pay well (as both teaching and medicine do). They demand of the young far too early a commitment, far too irrevocable a choice. Twenty years later, however, these are precisely the occupations sought by the man who 'wants to give'.

Under our present system in the United States, the preparation for these careers assumes a youngster who has to learn everything. No allowance is made for the experience and knowledge of a mature man. In fact, at present we do everything to discourage him.

I know of a Roman Catholic order of nuns which found, to their surprise, that women they had never considered as possible candidates, such as widows of 50 or so, were greatly interested in entering the order. Many of these women had been schoolteachers in their earlier years – and the order was a teaching order. Yet of a hundred or so applicants, only one actually survived the period of probation and took her vows. When the Mother Superior asked her why the other ninety-nine had withdrawn, she was told : 'Do you realize that you tell each applicant that she has to start out taking a course in sewing? Most of us have sewn our own clothes and often those of our children or of nieces and nephews for years. If we wanted to sew, we could have stayed right where we were.'

Our divinity schools, our schools of social work, of education, of nursing, and of medicine are no different. They also expect the applicant, regardless of his age, to start out 'learning to sew'. There is no reason, however, why we should not teach how to be effective teachers, ministers, social workers, nurses, and doctors to experienced, responsible, serious men and women who have shown their capacity to contribute – and train them in a fraction of the time needed to prepare youngsters without experience. Similarly people of this age need organized opportunities to switch from one institution to another while staying in their technical or functional area – again perhaps with a little training.

We have already seen the need for men in all our organizations who know how the other organizations work. We need men in government service who know how business works, how the university works, how the Armed Services work, how the labour union works, and so on. We need people in business who have personal experience of the other organizations. The work itself may not be very different from one organization to another. The accountant in business may well do precisely what an accountant does in the government agency or in a hospital. The government administrator may spend his day in much the way the manager in a business or the hospital administrator does. Yet the environment, the values, the political realities of each of these organizations are sufficiently different to provide a new stimulus to the man who has become tired and bored.

I have personally observed in the last decade maybe fifty to a hundred military officers, men who reached the rank of Commander in the Navy or of Colonel in the Army or Air Force and who were retired, as not promotable any further, aged 48 to 50. When they first left the Service they were pitiful – scared of life, weighed down by the belief that theirs had been a narrow and circumscribed environment, and aware also of being tired and drained. There was not one 'great man' among them – and not a great many interesting ones either.

They were not always easy to place. But the great majority made a successful transition to a different kind of life: as a teacher in a small college or as its business manager; as an auditor in an accounting firm or in local government; as a personnel manager in a hospital or as a traffic manager in a business, and so on. Without exception each of these men became years younger, came to life and started to grow again and to contribute.

Almost all institutions today have compulsory retirement at the age of 65. We do, indeed, have to retire people from organizations. The main reason is not that people become old; it is that opportunities have to be created for the young, or they will either not come or not stay. And an organization that does not have young knowledge workers is an organization that cannot grow, and can only defend yesterday.* But to deny work to a man at any particular age is also needless cruelty and a waste of human resources. While we need to retire early, we also need organized re-hiring for second careers. We need not do the job as ruthlessly as the military which retires a man who will go no further whether he likes it or not (though this may be more merciful than to let him stay on, vegetate, and destroy himself in frustration and self-pity as business and universities are wont to do), but we need to face up to reality the way the military does.

People do not age chronologically. Some, at 65, are younger than others ever were at 35. Nor do people age uniformly. A man who is well gone in years and no longer capable of working strenuously may be unimpaired in his judgement and a better decision-maker than he was twenty years earlier. And the adviser, especially one who combines knowledge with compassion, usually does his best work when old enough to be detached.

* This has been shown unambiguously in the work of the British psychiatrist and social researcher, Dr Elliott Jaques. See his book *Measurement of Responsibility* (Tavistock Publications, London, 1956; Harvard University Press, Cambridge, Massachusetts, 1956).

automation destroys'; but from 1964 on he talked instead about the 'jobs created by automation'.*

There is plenty of evidence that job turnover and pace of technological progress have been lower during the last twenty years in the United States than at any earlier period on which we have data. Outside the United States there is even less evidence of 'automation unemployment', even though the rate of technological change and of increasing productivity has been much greater in Western Europe and in Japan.

The more sophisticated thesis of a good many economists that there has been 'secular stagnation' in manufacturing employment has also not been borne out by the facts. Employment in manufacturing industries did not go up in the Fifties. But we now realize that in the United States in the years after the Korean War we went through a sizeable recession. When we came out of it in 1960–61, manufacturing employment at once began to rise again, and to rise in the traditional pattern. Manufacturing industries that increased their share of the total national income, that is, growing industries, increased their employment faster than their output (electronics, pharmaceuticals, and computers are examples). Shrinking industries decreased their employment faster than their share in total output – for the simple reason that in shrinking industries the least productive units close down first. And in industries that neither grew nor shrank but stagnated, employment decreased by no more than the 2 to 3 per cent a year by which productivity can be expected to be raised in any business or industry through normal, day-to-day, management engineering, without new technology and without new machinery.

* His subordinates, the exceedingly able economists of the Department of Labour, never shared their chief's fears. While Mr Wirtz talked about 'automation unemployment', they kept their mouths shut but published study after study showing that there was no such thing.

Particularly relevant here is the behaviour of employment in the automobile and steel industries. These are old industries where, however, a good deal of new machinery has been coming in. They were therefore expected to show a significant drop in employment even with a considerable expansion of output. This did not occur. These industries increased employment disproportionately fast once output climbed out of the trough in which it had wallowed through the Fifties.

And yet it is not intelligent to dismiss the worker's fear of automation. He explains his fear the wrong way – automation is a bogyman – but he is afraid of something real and menacing.

For as a result of the shift to knowledge work, the unskilled worker is speedily reverting to a position of social impotence and unimportance.

The unskilled worker was the first beneficiary of the application of knowledge to work. Scientific Management gave the labourer – to give him the title by which he has been known through history – productivity for the first time. It made him 'semi-skilled' – but whatever skill there was, was in the design of his job, he himself needed none. It thereby made it possible to pay this worker, the machine operator, wages such as no unskilled worker in history could ever be paid before, the wages of an economic producer. The wage differential between the unskilled man who, historically, was more of an economic liability than he was an asset, and the skilled man, the producer, almost disappeared. This differential had been of the order of three to one or more throughout history; during the last thirty years, in all industrial countries it shrank to a point where – in World War II in the United States – it was less than 10 per cent for many industries.

But even more important was the social upsurge of labour. No class in history has ever advanced as fast in social status and power as the unskilled worker did in the first fifty years of the twentieth century. He – or she – became the hero of World War II; 'Rosie the Riveter', the assembly-line worker who turned out the ships, tanks, and aeroplanes (the heroine of the popular World War II song in the US), was the symbol of industrial society, its achievement, and its power. And in the mass-production unions, which grew to strength and power after World War I, the unskilled worker acquired political power, social cohesion, pride, and leadership.

Paradoxically the next impact of the application of knowledge to work – which is already in evidence – will return the unskilled worker to his earlier low social status. Economically he will retain his gains. In fact, the application of knowledge is likely to make him even more productive and, therefore, capable of earning an even higher wage. Job security is likely to be great; for as education becomes more general, the supply of people available for unskilled mass-production jobs will probably shrink faster than the demand – possibly the one exception in the developed countries being the American Negro.

Yet the unskilled mass-production worker will be seen as an engineering imperfection. He has a job only because we have not taken the trouble to apply enough knowledge to his work, so as to 'programme' it for the machine. A machine can do any mechanical operation once we really know and understand it – the only question is whether it is economical or not.

In a great many cases it is not economical, either because not enough units are produced or because the job of finding out is exceedingly complex, whereas doing the work is simple and requires little learning or instruction. It is, for instance, quite feasible to 'programme' the job of putting on one's overcoat and design a machine to do it. It would take months of time and motion study to figure out what we do, but it would not be beyond the powers of trained industrial engineers and machine designers. It would, however, be quite absurd.

But no matter what his income or job security, the unskilled worker's social position in the United States is going rapidly. With it goes the thrust of his union. The unions can remain powerful for a long time – by sheer numbers and by their concentration of voting power in major industrial centres such as Detroit or Pittsburgh. But the mass-production unions have ceased to be capable of leadership. They can no longer act as agents of social advance, no matter how hard Walter Reuther tries. Any change is a threat to them. They can only become naysayers, timid obstacles to any change, reactionaries pining back to a 'yesterday' that never was but which once looked as if it could and would be 'tomorrow'.

The pressure on government to preserve the unskilled worker, if not to restore his former position, will, therefore, be great. There is every reason to help him – if only because his lack of skill makes him quite unable to help himself. Retraining in America, for instance, is badly needed and so are placement services. But what we need is not to prevent change, but to organize it. We need to learn from the Swedes and adapt Gösta Rehn's approach to change to our own situations (see page 82 above). We need to make change possible, easy, and as painless as it can be.

There is nothing government can do to cure the deep feeling of insecurity of the unskilled machine operator in the United States. Neither government nor management can eliminate the causes of the psychological malaise that haunts him. Participation of worker and union in management, or in profits, whatever else they might do, are irrelevant as remedies for the real problem. Public policy can make sure, however, that the worker knows that government and management will take action to make him cope with change. If government – or management – try to prevent change, they will only make inevitable great suffering a little later on.

Government policy should speed the transition. This is the only way to control it. Unskilled work otherwise will become a trap. We must be able to encourage the individual who can make the shift – or his son – to become a knowledge worker himself. And we must be able to assure the individual who is an unskilled worker that, when his present job becomes obsolete, society will help him to find another job, to acquire the necessary knowledge and skills for it, and to move to it.

This is not a task the individual employer can tackle alone. It might be done cooperatively by a group of employers in a given neighbourhood – as, under union auspices, is being tried in the Toledo, Ohio, area. Or it might, as in Sweden, be handled by government, with the close cooperation of employers and unions. But whatever the community organization for placing the individual, the employer will have to think and plan ahead. In most cases redundancies that outdate the job of substantial numbers of workers can be identified a long time ahead. It is possible to start early enough to find a new job for a man, and to prepare him for it. Such manpower planning has proved highly beneficial to any enterprise that has tried it.

One promising approach might be the New Careers Programme* developed at New York University. This programme starts out by training 'unemployables' – mainly Negroes from the black ghettoes – for the traditional low-skill service occupations in hospitals, schools, social work, or prisons. It capitalizes on the severe manpower shortage in these areas. But while the student is trained for a simple job – eg, nurses' aide or social-work interviewer – he is encouraged, all along, to aim at becoming eventually a fully-fledged professional, that is to move on from being a

* See *Up from Poverty* by Frank Riersman and Hermine Popper (Harper & Row, New York, 1968).

nurses' aide to being a trained nurse and perhaps, in the end, to becoming a physician. This requires not only new learning methods, but also requires the willingness of the professions and of the hiring institutions to remake their career ladders and to reward performance and achievement.

The programme is still quite new. But its results are encouraging enough to show that once a person has learned, and learned systematically, he can unlearn and relearn with relative ease. Of course, Gösta Rehn's programme in Sweden – or the World War II experiences in Great Britain and the United States – should have taught us that. But the New Careers Programme succeeds both in motivating and in teaching people who had been complete failures in earlier, traditional education, and who had been given up as 'unteachable' in addition to being 'unemployable'.

All employers, not only businesses, need to accept that the shift to knowledge work imposes a responsibility on them to think through the future of today's unskilled jobs. Otherwise government will be forced, by public opinion, to become a defender of yesterday's work structure, a defender of yesterday's good economy, and thus the major obstacle to the success of tomorrow's knowledge economy.

Today's skilled worker presents an infinitely more difficult problem. For skilled work is not becoming obsolete. On the contrary, it is becoming more common and more important – to the point where the great majority will soon be employed in skilled work. Only it will not be the craft-based skilled work of yesterday, but skilled work based on knowledge.

The traditional crafts are obsolete. Their basic assumptions no longer apply. Craft assumes that one learns through apprenticeship; but with the years of education expected of anyone today, apprenticeship is no longer a tenable proposition. Indeed there are few qualified candi-dates available for it any more. The complaint that the craft union in the United States keeps out Negro appren-tices is well founded; it is probably our most reactionary, most racist organization. But at the same time, the craft unions are dying for want of new young members. The average age of the membership of most American craft unions is well up in the 50s. New recruits – in ship-building or in the construction industries, in railway shop work or in the printing unions – are hard to come by. The young-sters are expected to stay on at school and to become knowledge workers – and their own fathers, the prosperous craftsmen, raise the roof if the kids drop out to follow in the fathers' footsteps.

Even less tenable are the fundamental assumptions a craft makes about work and workers. A craft assumes that what one has learned by the time one finishes apprentice-ship will last for the rest of one's working life. It assumes that certain work 'belongs' to it and that it has to be done in a certain way. Crafts are inherently conservative. What they do has been proved by long experience and is likely to become hallowed ritual not to be tampered with by 'green kids'. But knowledge is, by definition, inquisitive, innova-tive. It probes. It assumes that what we already know is obsolescent and unlikely to be what we should or could know. And it is no respecter of 'jurisdictional' lines. Just because a hammer is the tool of the carpenter, and the laser the tool of the physicist, is no reason for knowledge not to apply the laser to the carpenter's work tomorrow. As a result, most knowledge-based skills change often and without regard to traditional demarcations and jurisdic-tions.

Learning a craft makes a man unfit for learning anything new or different. He has been trained that this is the one way of doing this job. But nobody has told him that this might also be the right way to do some other job, let alone that there are other ways of doing *any* job.

We have proved that the most complex skill can be acquired by people with little background if taught by 'programme'.

The US Air Force trained almost illiterate Negroes to be electricians. The Air Force had no choice. Qualified white men do not stay in military service long enough to go through an apprenticeship. But these barely literate men turned out to be good electricians. A few years later the Air Force had to turn them, however, into missile maintainers. This is different work – electronic rather than electrical, and 'systems engineering' rather than craft skill. Moreover, missile maintenance is done far away from any base and by men who work by themselves and yet have to be able to diagnose and to remedy complex malfunctions fast. Once, however, the job had been thoroughly studied and reduced to knowledge and system, even these illiterate men learned with few exceptions to maintain missiles with a high standard of performance and responsibility.

This ability to gain advanced skills through programmed acquisition of knowledge makes traditional craft structures untenable. Whether called 'guild' or 'union' they become a burden to society and a threat to the individual member. Maintenance of craft jurisdiction may, for a few years, preserve the union and the jobs of the union leaders as it is doing in American shipyards or in the newspapers. But it rapidly destroys the job and the job security of the individual member. It deprives him of the ability to relearn, to acquire new skills to do the old job, or to apply his old skills to a new job. For this he not only needs knowledge rather than apprenticeship. He also needs an entirely different approach to job – and job security – than that of the traditional craft organization.

To enable our society and economy to grow, and to protect the individual member of a craft or skill, we will have to liquidate the craft union and the craft concept. We have to do this not to abolish skill, but to liberate it and make it truly productive. This is primarily a task for the English-speaking countries, especially for the United States and Great Britain. For these are the countries where craft unionism flourishes.

We can learn from leading industrial countries of the Free World that do not have craft unions, especially from Japan and Germany.

Craft skill was the organizing principle of Japanese industry before the opening of the country and its modernization after 1867. All 'old' industries, silk-weaving or fan-making or lacquering, were strict craft guilds. But the 'new' industries that were established on imported Western technology never adopted the craft principle. Workers in these industries are trained to do any job in the plant. All workers in Japanese industry – including men high up in management – are expected to continue training till the day they retire. All keep on learning both new ways of doing their job and new skills. This continuous training has been based, from the beginning, on systematic schooling rather than on craft skill and apprenticeship.

This, of course, is possible only because the Japanese worker has a 'lifetime' job and will not be dismissed except in a major catastrophe or for gross misbehaviour. His pay has been principally tied to his seniority rather than to his skill or the work he does (though this is changing fast). Therefore the new is an opportunity to him, if only because it makes his company more competitive and therefore makes him more secure. That he is unlikely to find another job should his company go out of business is of course a powerful incentive as well.

The German example is equally instructive. Before Hitler, Germany was organized in strong craft unions, which jealously guarded their respective jurisdictions.

After World War II, however, these unions were not restored – largely because the labour adviser to the American military government, Victor Reuther, a leader of a United States mass-production union, the automobile workers, advised against it. Instead, all German labour is organized in a small number of large industrial unions. The workers of every enterprise belong to one and only one of these unions. The German worker is still being trained in a long apprenticeship. Yet there is little craft rivalry within a given plant; for the workers, regardless of their work, all belong to the same union. Their jobs are not guaranteed by their craft but by their seniority within the overall enterprise. And while it is not always easy to transfer a man from craft work of one kind to craft work of another, it is increasingly accepted by management as well as by the union that it is to the man's own interest to acquire skills beyond one craft area and to become available for whatever opportunities his seniority within the plant may offer him. Even highly skilled men in a German automobile plant move from one craft job to another better-paid one without running into the jurisdictional barriers that prevent such moves in an American or British plant. Again there is a high degree of job security – it not 'lifetime employment' – in Germany, especially for men who have acquired skills.

'Lifetime employment' is no longer desirable, even in Japan. For while it protects a man as long as his company or industry are doing at least reasonably well, it makes it virtually impossible for him to move elsewhere should his company or industry fail. But the underlying principle is sound; it is the responsibility of the employer to provide job security. In a knowledge economy where skill is based on knowledge, and where technology and economy are likely to change fast, however, the only meaningful job security is the capacity to learn fast. The only real security in an economy and society in a state of flux is to know enough to be able to move.

A combination is needed of the Japanese emphasis on continuous training, the German commitment to industry or plant rather than craft, and the Swedish guarantee of job and income through mobility, to make it possible, politically as well as psychologically, to liquidate the self-defeating monopolies of craft unionism.

This transition may be the toughest industrial problem facing the United States and Great Britain. But unless these two countries tackle the job they will not, I fear, be able to retain for long the capacity for economic growth and international competition, and the social flexibility to build and take advantage of the knowledge economy.

Both the transition problems, that of the unskilled mass-production worker, and that of craft skill and craft organizations, will be most acute in the United States. For it is here that the new knowledge economy is developing the furthest and the fastest. Above all, both are inextricably entwined with our most dangerous, most sensitive, and most urgent problem, the race issue.

The American Negro was the most direct beneficiary of the upsurge in the economic and social position of the unskilled mass-production worker earlier in the century. Urban jobs for the Negro in substantial numbers were first created by mass production. These jobs were far better paid than any ever before open to his race. Moreover, they gave him membership and increasing equality in the industrial unions, that is, in a social organization of growing power. The gains began in World War I, and reached their peak in the decade that began with World War II and ended with the Korean War. During these years mass-production jobs were so plentiful that they exceeded the available supply of white workers. The Negro, therefore, found little resistance when he moved in. Indeed the Supreme Court decisions in the 1950s, which knocked down the legal bars to Negro equality in American society, were largely codifications of the tremendous gains the Negro had made in the quarter-century before as a full member of the mass-production work force.

It is no coincidence that the world capital of mass-production industry, Detroit, is the only major American city in which Negro and white live in the same neighbourhoods, the only American city without a clearly delimited Negro ghetto. It is also no coincidence that Detroit had the worst of the recent riots in America – in the summer of 1967, despite record employment in Detroit at the time. For the Negro is also the worst sufferer from the reversal in the ascendancy of the mass-production worker.

As the latest immigrant into the city, he is the least equipped for an economy in which knowledge acquired in formal schooling is the foundation of skill and opportunity. Every immigrant generation into the city came from a background of rural illiteracy and had to jump an educational gap. But while the unlettered rural Irish who streamed into Manchester and Liverpool in 1780, or into Boston and Philadelphia in 1850, lacked only a few weeks of schooling to be fully equipped for practically all the jobs of their society, the gap is now twelve years or so – much more than can possibly be bridged by one generation.

The shift to the knowledge economy, therefore, deprives the Negro masses of whatever gains they see themselves as having made. This is bad enough economically. But the real damage is to social standing and self-respect, to hope and promise. That the Negro is rebellious because he has advanced so much recently as to become impatient, is, I am afraid, a white delusion. The Negro is rebellious because he sees himself deprived of what little gains he has made – they are being knocked out of his hands just at the moment when he first tastes their fruits. And the shift began just at the time when large masses of young Negroes were being lured from the rural South into the Northern city with its promises of well-paid and respected jobs – a promise the city is suddenly no longer living up to.

It is, therefore, urgent to find immediately mass-production jobs for the unskilled young Negro male. But it is not going to be easy, no matter how hard governments and businesses try. In both areas we must expect growing resistance from the incumbents, white or Negro. (Such resistance from skilled Negro craftsmen played a substantial part in the troubles of Eastman Kodak in Rochester, New York, in 1966–7 with an organization of unskilled young Negroes from the rural South – which also explains why the company did not know how to handle the conflict.) Even though jobs are not shrinking in manual work, the present holders still see themselves as threatened. There is growing reluctance to share what to the incumbents seem like shrinking opportunities, and open resistance by unions and worker alike against any attempt to give the new Negro entrant special treatment, eg, job security or special training ahead of workers, white or black, with greater seniority.

Jobs for the urban Negro in the North may be easier to find in skilled work, despite the racist, lily-white tradition of practically all craft unions. For the young white boy with enough wits and education to qualify for a craft apprenticeship increasingly stays on at school and becomes a knowledge worker. Once the original resistance to the black man has been overcome, there should therefore be jobs for him.

But the number of young urban Negroes who can qualify for jobs of this kind is not large. They require a good deal more background, both in skill and in education, than young people fresh from a pre-literate rural environment are likely to muster. Still, recent attempts have proved that quite a few young Negroes, given intensive training – especially classroom training in knowledge skills such as mathematics or blueprint reading – can reach the required entrance standards. Much greater and more sustained efforts are needed to open craft jobs to Negro apprentices.

And yet to find jobs for the Negro in manual work,

skilled or unskilled, is not going to be the solution in the
long run. It may even do long-term harm. There is a real
danger that unskilled mass-production work will box in the
Negro in a new ghetto a few years hence. As children of
white workers acquire the schooling needed for knowledge
jobs, first mass-production and then skilled work might become the new 'Negro occupations'. This has already happened in the meat-packing industry. It is happening in respect to assembly-line work in the Detroit automobile
plants and in the New York garment trade. As the Negro
would be making good money in this new ghetto the conscience of the whites would be assuaged again, with every
attempt of the Negro to gain real membership in American
society resented as 'ingratitude'.

Even greater is the danger that a policy of emphasizing
manual jobs, skilled or unskilled, for the Negro might put
the welfare of the Negro in conflict with the best interest of
the country as a whole. The best interest of the country
demands that the shift from manual to knowledge work
should be speeded rather than retarded. It demands encouragement of a gradual shrinkage of manual jobs,
whether skilled or unskilled, and their replacement by
skilled jobs based on a knowledge foundation. For one
thing, the knowledge jobs are so much more productive.
For another, they are so much more satisfactory, can be
paid so much better, and offer so many more opportunities.
For economy and individual alike, they are a major jump
ahead, whatever their problems. But if manual jobs become the preserve of the Negro, and his livelihood as well
as his claim to equality and self-respect, a national policy
that is in the interest of the country as a whole – and of its
white majority – will be disastrous for the Negro minority
and a direct attack on them. And this is one danger which
neither the white majority nor the coloured minority can
afford.

However badly immediate mass-production and craft
jobs for the Negro are needed, an even more massive effort

is needed to find, identify, develop, and place the largest possible number of Negro knowledge workers as early as possible. This means going into the elementary schools. It means working with boys and girls at a very early age, helping them to plan careers, encouraging them to stay on at school and to learn, showing them opportunities, examples, and models. It means going to the Negro family to encourage the support for school and learning which has been so singularly lacking until the last few years (though no more than it was lacking among the Irish in our cities in the 1880s, among the Italians in New York, or the Polish in Chicago in the 1920s, or among the Czech immigrants in the industrial Vienna of 1910). It means making learning and teaching relevant and effective. It means also the development of programmes – eg, the New Careers Programme mentioned earlier – to give adolescents and even adults a second chance to put to use their native abilities.

There is less resistance to the Negro in knowledge jobs than in manual jobs. Knowledge jobs are expanding so much more rapidly that the Negro is less of a competitive threat. Moreover, any hope for acceptance of the Negro by the white community rests on his being accepted by the leading social groups. Social acceptance never comes up from the bottom – which explains why the membership of the Negro in the mass-production union had so little effect on his acceptance by American society. Social status is determined at the top of the social ladder. And the knowledge worker, needless to say, is the leading group in the knowledge society.

The race problem in America will not be solved even if the Negro overcomes his handicap as the latest to arrive in urban society at a time of great changes. Social action never solves spiritual problems. And the racial problem is America's historical spiritual agony – and one which only suffering and a contrite heart will, in the end, overcome.

But unless we solve the social problem and help the American Negro to become an effective and productive member of the knowledge society and knowledge economy, there is no hope for any solution at all. White leadership must finance, encourage, sponsor, and spearhead the right social action. But the job of developing displaced rural farm labourers into knowledge workers demands above all commitment by educated Negroes. For though discriminated against, kept out, and kept down, they are already inside the knowledge society. And while jobs and incomes for the Negro in America may be found in manual work, equality – whether in separation from, or in integration with, the white world – can only be established today in the dominant, the knowledge society.

The most hopeful development in America today is, therefore, the rapid growth of the Negro knowledge worker in the last few decades. Though still a comparatively small segment of the total Negro population – maybe a fifth or so – Negro knowledge workers have been increasing at twice the rate of the white knowledge workers. And for the first time the Negro knowledge worker identifies himself with the Negro community rather than attempting to escape it.

The rapid emergence of the Negro knowledge worker, capable of acceptance as a leader by the black community and as a peer by the white leadership groups, has therefore become possible – for the first time in American history. It would be tragic folly and catastrophe were this hope to be destroyed by well-meant but short-sighted over-concentration on opening to the Negro yesterday's employments in skilled and unskilled manual jobs.

The emergence of knowledge as central to our society has converted into dead-end streets the avenues by which earlier Negro leaders had hoped to reach the goals of Negro equality, Negro dignity, and Negro fulfilment: ownership of the small farm and access to manual work as an equal. It has instead opened up knowledge jobs as the greatest opportunity the black man has yet had in America.

This makes new – and very great – demands on both the

white and the black community. Above all, though, it dramatizes the demands which the emergence of knowledge society and knowledge economy makes on the traditional knowledge institution, the school.

14. Has Success Spoilt the Schools?

IN THE LATE 1960s the United States, despite the Vietnam War, spent quite a bit more on education than on defence. Education took annually about 70 to 75 billion dollars, of which 50 billion dollars was spent by the school and university systems (public and private) and perhaps half as much again by industry, governments, and the Armed Forces for all kinds of schooling and training. This was twice what the United States had spent in a year in the mid-Fifties, and four times the amount spent annually in the years after World War II when the 'educational explosion' first started.

Education has become by far the largest community expenditure in the American economy. We spend more on education than on all other non-defence community services together – health care, welfare, farm subsidies, and so on. Teachers of all kinds, now the largest single occupational group in the American labour force, outnumber by a good margin steel workers, teamsters, sales people, and even farmers.

These are but the quantitative symptoms of a major change in values by no means confined to the United States. Education has become the key to opportunity and advancement all over the modern world, replacing birth, wealth, and perhaps even talent. Education has become the first choice of modern man.

This is success such as no schoolmaster through the ages would have dared dream of. But can education live with this success? Or, to paraphrase the title of a popular play of a few years ago: 'Has Success Spoilt the Schools?'

Signs abound that all is far from well with education. While expenditures have been sky-rocketing – and will keep on going up – the taxpayers are getting visibly restless. In community after community across the United States they have voted down, in the last few years, proposals for new school taxes or new school bonds or higher teachers' salaries. These may be futile gestures: in the end the school taxes do go up, the money for new buildings is provided – if not out of school bonds, then out of federal subsidies – and the teachers' salaries are adjusted by competitive pressure. But the growing resistance to the cost of education indicates that the public is beginning to be concerned with what it gets for its money.

The ambivalence between faith in education and resistance to its costs is present everywhere. The last British Labour government, committed to rapid expansion of general education accessible to everyone, resisted teachers' demands for higher salaries and tried to postpone the building of badly needed teacher-training colleges. Japanese students, fully aware that education controls what opportunities they will enjoy, still riot against an increase in fees. De Gaulle was willing to spend scarce francs sending teachers to French Canada. But until the students rose up in May 1968, and all but tore down French society, de Gaulle had been resisting all demands to expand the badly eroded and totally inadequate facilities of Paris' famous old university, the Sorbonne. We all love education and want more of it. But we clearly are not at all convinced that we are getting our money's worth for what we spend on it – and with good reason.

Important, if only as a symptom, is the alienation from the school of today's adolescent rebels, the 'beats' and 'hippies'. Adolescent rebellion, almost without exception, has in the past been organized in and around the school,

379

and especially in and around the university. The left-wing radicals of the Thirties in Britain and the United States, for instance, and their imitators, the left-wing students in Latin America today, had the university for their base and considered it their own institution. The 'beats' and 'hippies', however, rebel today against school even more than against their parents.

To find a parallel, one has to go back a good many centuries to the *Goliards*, the 'beats' and 'drop-outs' from the university of the early Renaissance. That the *Goliards* achieved very little, except a few rowdy songs, does not matter. They bespoke the senility and obsolescence of the traditional university as it had come down from the Middle Ages. They heralded its break-up and replacement by the 'modern' university, a very different school, with different educational goals, different values, and entirely different content and curriculum. A hundred years hence, today's 'beats' and 'hippies' may well come to be seen as the *Goliards* of the twentieth century who, without achieving much of their own, heralded the breakdown of the traditional 'humanist' education, which arose in the seventeenth century as education for the new tiny minority of lay scribes, and which by now has been extended uncritically to education for everyone everywhere.

Education has become too important to be left to the educators. In modern society everybody has a right to consider himself an 'expert' on schools, for everybody during his formative years spends more waking hours at school than in any one other institution. Moreover, education is far too big a cost to be accepted without questioning. To ask whether it is a fruitful investment or simply an expense is a legitimate question. Education has also become too powerful to go unchallenged. For schooling increasingly controls access to careers, opportunities, and advancement. For all these reasons education must become a public issue in all advanced countries – and perhaps even more in the developing countries where the costs of education have become a major barrier to economic and social development.

The schools, their structure, their role, their objectives, and above all, what they teach will, therefore, become increasingly a major concern. What do we get out of all the years we sit in schools?

WHAT IS SCHOOL FOR?

Skilled craftsmen, everyone had known for centuries, were a great economic asset. But until recently going to school was, economically speaking, a luxury. Literacy had long been preached among Protestants and Orthodox Jews as necessary for effective religious performance. From the eighteenth century on it had become a foundation for citizenship. Elementary education had, by 1850 or so, come to be accepted as necessary to the individual's ability to 'better himself'. But only a tiny minority needed more than the bare minimum; only a tiny minority was expected to use knowledge in its work at all.

In the early years of this century there was, for instance, no pressure for education in the colonial areas. On the contrary, British attempts to introduce universal primary education in India were steadily resisted by the incipient anti-colonial movement of the day, the early Indian Congress Party. Schools were a shocking waste of the taxpayer's money, from which the country would not derive any benefit. The need felt in the poor countries was for irrigation works, roads, and lower taxes. And the number of educated people who could be usefully employed was so small that the need was easily satisfied by the sons of the wealthy, who could well afford to pay for school out of their own pockets. Until recently economists were severely critical of the Japanese drive for universal literacy after 1870 as a wasteful diversion of badly needed economic resources to an unproductive 'prestige' project.

The greatest sin of 'colonialism' as seen today is that it did not introduce universal schooling and therefore did not produce an educated society in the colonial countries. And no achievement of the Japanese reforms of the Meiji Period after 1867 was so universally acclaimed during the Meiji Centennial celebrations in 1967–8 as the priority given to education as the foundation of a modern productive economy and society.

That education was not seen as economically productive but rather as a luxury the rich could afford, explains in large measure the manner in which the years of schooling were extended. Responding primarily to the increase of working-life span, the schools put more and more youngsters into 'advanced education' – that is, into what had been designed as vocational training for a small number of scribes. What had been highly specialized training became, by default, everybody's general education.

This was not planned; it happened. The last unit of school that was planned and thought through at all was what is known in the United States as 'junior high school' – that is, school for the pre-adolescent from the age of 12 to 15. Junior high school, however, was designed in Europe well over a century ago when in some countries it first became economically possible to keep substantial numbers of children at school beyond the elementary grades.* Conceived as terminal school for the great majority, it was designed to a large extent to blend in with the first years of apprenticeship in craft. Beyond this, however, the new additional students were simply put into existing schools

---

* The first country to develop this school type on a broad basis was Austria (in about 1820). The name it then received: *Buergerschule*, that is, 'school for citizens', was meant as a political manifesto by the liberal educators who designed it. Educated people are 'citizens' rather than 'subjects'.

that had been created originally to train clergymen, lawyers, or civil servants, such as the English public school, the German gymnasium, the American high school, or the French *Lycée*. We repeated this process once more when going to college became common during the last twenty or thirty years.

This process shows best perhaps in the way the arguments for teaching Latin in secondary schools have changed – while the teaching of Latin itself has not changed one bit. In 1700 or 1750 no one would have urged that teaching Latin taught anything but Latin. No one spoke of it as 'forming the mind', no one praised it as a 'discipline', no one asserted that knowing Latin was the key to learning the other European languages more easily. One learned Latin because Latin was the 'communications medium' of educated people. Until the mid-eighteenth century when French cultural imperialism tried unsuccessfully to put the language of Louis XIV into the place of the language of Augustus, books for the educated and documents of importance were normally written in Latin. Latin was taught as a tool of high utility without which a scribe could not properly function. When this came to an end – in the early nineteenth century – all the other virtues of Latin were suddenly discovered. Now, for the last fifty or hundred years Latin is being defended because it has no usefulness whatever – that is, as an ornament. An 'educated man', it is argued, should not learn subjects of utility but subjects such as Latin which are 'liberal' and 'general education' precisely because no one can do anything with them.

This is not an argument against Latin; it is an illustration of the fundamental character of our higher education, a character grounded in its history and original purpose. As a vocational school for the professions that require

383

ability to write – and this is what 'learned' originally meant – it quite properly stressed the verbal skills. The apprenticeship of the carpenter stressed plane and hammer and saw. The apprenticeship of the clergyman, the lawyer, the teacher, the government servant – that is, higher education as it emerged out of the Renaissance and the Reformation – stressed reading, writing, and enough mathematics to be an accountant, a lawyer administering estates, and a surveyor. The school could therefore leave to the other apprenticeships concern with everything that was not verbal skill. Life taught to most people anyhow free of cost the non-verbal: experience and performance.

For employments other than as a scribe, formal education was considered a handicap rather than an asset.

When I started work as an apprentice clerk in an export firm, only forty years ago, I was considered distinctly 'over-educated'. I had finished secondary school – and no apprentice before me, including the owners of the firm and their sons, had entered work that late. They had all started aged 14, and yet considered themselves fully educated and were considered so by the community.

But today the school has become the universal growing-up process for everybody. For this purpose, however, verbal training is not adequate, let alone productive. We can no longer assume that the great majority will have enough non-verbal experience outside of school; the great majority receives its most important learning exposure during its formative years by sitting in the classroom and receiving there the scribe's education. That is much too one-sided, much too restricted, much too narrowly vocational – and, above all, not 'liberal' or 'general', and not truly 'educational'. The greatest weakness of the schools today, and the one youngsters most suffer from, is this verbal straitjacket. Of course, there are also sports – and they are needed. But man is more than verbal skills and muscle.

Few things are as badly needed in growing up as the sense of achievement, which only performance can give. But the schools do not permit achievement. In the 'academic disciplines' a student cannot perform. He can only show promise. All he can do in schools in the verbal areas is to repeat what somebody has already done or said.

Yesterday's educators had no choice but to extend the only school they had, the only school they knew. Their customers would have resented it had they been offered anything but the school they had come to envy as the mark of privilege. But the result is a school that deforms rather than forms. It is a school of boredom, of lack of stimulation, of lack of achievement, and lack of satisfaction. I am not surprised that the kids riot. I am surprised at their patience, considering how bored most of them are in school most of the time.*

The problem of the school is not a matter of 'standards' as schoolmasters tend to define them. It is not a matter, in other words, of 'working harder' and of 'doing more' of what is being done today. What we have learned in respect to all work applies to the work of the school as well. We need to 'work smarter'. We need to do different things and to do them differently.

History shows a frightening parallel to the way our education is going everywhere in the world today. It is the decline of the world's most creative, most advanced, and most exciting civilization, that of China in the fourteenth and fifteenth centuries. Until then China had led the world in the arts and in the sciences, in medicine and in mathematics, in technology and in Statecraft. The re-

---

* A frightening picture of the frustrating boredom which school tends to be even for bright children from educated white middle- and upper-class homes is given by the moving book *How Children Fail* by John Holt (Pitman, London and New York, 1965).

action against independent thinking and artistic creativity that followed the invasion of the Mongols in the thirteenth century imposed the Confucian system of purely literary and purely imitative 'liberal education' to the exclusion of everything else. Within a century China had become sterile and had lost her capacity to do anything new, to imagine anything new, to perceive anything new. We are, I am afraid, on the same road – and we have travelled very far along it.

This is not a plea for what is known today as 'vocational education' – that is, for teaching traditional craft skills, the traditional way, only in a classroom instead of in the shop. On the contrary, nothing is deader than traditional 'vocational education' – assuming (against all evidence) that it ever was alive.

The skills that 'vocational education' teaches are obsolete. They are the craft skills of yesterday. The one thing that is predictable is that by the time the students graduate into jobs – automobile maintenance or woodworking or even cooking – they will no longer be done the way we are teaching these crafts in our vocational schools. This is not the way to teach skill anyhow. The way to teach a skill today is by putting it on a knowledge foundation and teaching it through a systematic course of studies – that is, through a 'programme'.

The worst part of 'vocational education' is, however, that it is being administered as training of the 'second-rate'. The youngsters who are 'not good enough' to go through the 'academic' course of studies are being pushed into 'vocational education' as a means of keeping them off the streets and out of mischief until they are old enough to leave school.

What we need in modern society are people who can acquire skills by having a knowledge foundation. We need only a fairly small number of people who are purely theoretical. But we need an infinite number of people capable of

386

using theory as the basis of skill for practical application in work. These have to be 'technologists' rather than 'skilled craftsmen'. The ablest of the young, the most gifted intellectually, the most brilliant ones need, even more than the dimwits, the ability of the 'technologist' to apply knowledge to work through a knowledge-based skill. At the same time, the academically slow student needs the knowledge foundation to have any skill worth having.

In other words, we will have to replace today's 'vocational training' by the education of technologists. This will have to be 'general' education, indeed in the true sense a 'liberal' education. It should be a cornerstone of tomorrow's education for everybody.*

Equally important is the training and formation of perception and emotion in school. This is needed however we conceive the ends of education.

The trained perception and the disciplined emotion are as pertinent to the ability to earn a livelihood as they are to the mature human personality. They are man, above all. Indeed it is perception, especially tactile perception through the hand, that largely forms the mind of the child (as the greatest contemporary psychologist, Jean Piaget of Geneva, has proved in countless observations). Perception and emotion are trained, developed, and disciplined only in the experience of performance, that is, only under the challenge of objective standards that exist no matter what the individual's ability, inclinations, or proficiency.

Such standards exist for the beginner only in the arts. There alone applies what my piano teacher used to say to me when I was a child: 'You will never play Mozart like the virtuosi, the real musicians; but there is no

* On this point the recent studies of the Organization for European Economic Cooperation are highly instructive. In analysing the 'technology gap' between the United States and Europe these studies found that Europe has proportionately *more* scientists than the US. What it lacks are educated managers at lower and middle levels.

387

reason why you should not play your scales like them.'
In playing an instrument or in painting – in fact, in all
the arts – there are absolute standards even for the low-
liest beginner. There is direct experience of what performance demands. There is achievement. (Writing poetry
or a short story make performance demands too. But
because the level of abstraction is so much higher in the
verbal area, achievement is harder to attain and performance more difficult to perceive for the beginner than
in the performing or graphic arts with their immediacy
of experience.)

Today, music appreciation is a respected academic discipline (even though it tends to be a deadly bore for the
kids who have to memorize a lot of names when they have
never heard the music). Playing an instrument or com-
posing are considered, however, amateurish or 'trade
school'. This is not very bright, even if school is considered
vocational preparation for the scribe. When school becomes general education for everyone, it is lunacy.

I am talking about a good deal more than new subjects.
I am talking about the approach that is needed to design
education on different assumptions. In the past, every
segment of our school system was looked upon as an entity
in itself, as the last school for the great majority of its pupils
and as the only place where specific subjects or vocational
skills could be acquired during the student's lifetime. Today, the correct assumption is, however, that the great
majority of students will proceed from each level of the
school system to the next higher one – and then come back
as adults more than once. We need variety and diversity to
be sure; but we need no longer start out with the question :
What do the youngsters have to know at the age of 12 – or
15 – or 17 – when they will stop going to school for the rest
of their lives?' We can assume that they will stay anyhow
for at least ten and probably twelve or more years. At the
same time, we now know that the most important thing

they will have to learn is not this or that subject matter. The most important thing they will have to learn is how to learn. The most important things, in other words, are not specific skills, but a universal skill – that of using knowledge and its systematic acquisition as the foundation for performance, skill, and achievement.

Educators have always known that this is the proper purpose of education. In the past they never had a chance to try to accomplish it. Now they have reached what they have hoped for for so many centuries; universal education lasting for many years. Now they can use it for what they wanted to do all along. But the result will be a very different school and a very different education from anything we now have to envisage.

Educators can no longer assume that somebody else will do the educational job for them. With everybody going to school until adulthood, school has become the place for learning whatever one needs in order to be both a human being and effective.

A different challenge to the content and structure of education will be posed by the imminent conflict between extended schooling and continuing education.

As long as work was primarily experience, that is, until the last few decades, 'school' and 'work' were on different planes. One started to 'work' when one stopped 'going to school'. And conversely, what one had learned at school had to last throughout the rest of one's working life. Everything the youngster might have to know in the way of general, theoretical concepts and knowledge had, therefore, to be crammed into the early years of schooling, before he went to work. There was never enough time. The result was unrelenting pressure to extend the years of schooling, that is, to keep the young in school ever longer.

But when knowledge is applied to work, continuing education is needed, that is, the frequent return of the experienced and accomplished adult to formal learning. Then it makes absolutely no sense to attempt to give the youngster everything he will need – indeed it becomes absurd. He does not yet know what knowledge he will need ten or fifteen years hence. What he does know increasingly is that he will need things that are not yet available. It is commonplace today that every engineer is obsolete ten or fifteen years after graduation, and has to go back to college to be 'retrained'. The same applies to the physician and the mathematician, to the accountant and the teacher, in short to anyone who is expected to apply knowledge to work. The very fact that we are using knowledge rather than experience makes change inevitable. For knowledge by definition innovates, searches, questions, and changes.

The more people know the more often will they go back to school throughout their working life. The more people have learned and the more they have come to rely on organized learning, the more they get into the habit of school. But also the more they know, the more conscious they are of their ignorance and the more aware of new capacity to perform, of new knowledge, and of the need to hone their knowledge again and again.

We have, of course, had 'adult education' for a century or more, but formerly it was schooling for the poorly educated. It aimed at giving the bright but poor the education their wealthy contemporaries had received as youngsters. Continuing education of highly educated people was confined to the military until World War II. Today, however, it is the fastest growing part of our educational system, and pretty general throughout the professions. The academic community is still somewhat suspicious of anyone past adolescence who wants to learn. Yet at least there is no longer open resistance to continuing education.

But its implications are not yet fully seen.

One implication is that we can now decide when in a person's life and career a given subject matter is learned best. We can now decide when the student should be exposed to this or that topic, rather than insisting that he should get it while he is under the thumb of the school, that is, in his early years. If a subject is learned to greater advantage after a man has gathered experience, we can postpone its study until he comes back as an accomplished practitioner. For we can now be increasingly certain that the accomplished practitioners will indeed come back.

Many subjects are better learned by experienced older men. Management is one of them; in the law, in medicine, in engineering, in education, in architecture, and in many other fields equally there are areas which the inexperienced youngster can hardly learn and the beginner rarely needs. The most important areas in any practice are, as a rule, accessible most easily to the man of experience, and are most meaningful to him.

Today we try to enable the youngster without experience to understand such areas by 'simulating' real-life experience. This is the essence of a 'case study'. But how much better and easier it would be to use genuine direct experience as the foundation for work in these areas.

These are also the areas where only the advanced practitioner needs much knowledge. To know a great deal about organizational planning is essential to a manager. But it is not particularly helpful or meaningful to the young engineer. By waiting until a man has advanced, we make sure that we direct our efforts where they are likely to do some good. Most of the young, into whose skulls we try to cram these topics with great effort, will either not reach a position where they can use the knowledge, or will have forgotten it anyhow by the time they get far enough along to use it.

Continuing education need not be education in specialized subjects of use only to the high advanced professional. The most general subjects – philosophy perhaps, or history – also make more sense as education for the experienced adult. Specialities are what the young learn best and need most. The specialities needed today – as will be discussed in Chapter 16 below – are however not 'Biology' or 'Modern History', but are fields of application, eg, 'Environmental Control', or 'Far-Eastern Area Studies' in which a good many of the traditional specialized disciplines come together and become effective knowledge.

After all, the natural progression is not from 'generalist' to 'specialist', but the other way round. For what makes a generalist is the ability to hold a speciality against the sum total of experience, that is, to relate it to the general. To be sure, the young need a foundation in the general; and they need the big vision. But the synthesis which is the true generalization is largely meaningless to them. For this reason, continuing education may be where the true generalist will come into being. It may be the stage where we look at the whole, the 'big picture', where we can take the 'philosophical view' or where we can ask: 'What does it all mean?'

If educators give any thought to the question, they assume that we should have both over-extended schooling and continuing education. But the two are actually in opposition. Extended schooling assumes that we will cram more and more into the preparation for life and work. Continuing education assumes that school becomes integrated with life. Extended schooling still assumes that one can only learn before one becomes an adult. Continuing education assumes that one learns certain things best as an adult. Above all, extended schooling believes that the longer we keep the young away from work and life, the more they will have learned. Continuing education assumes, on the contrary, that the more experience in life and work people have, the more eager they will be to learn and the more capable they will be of learning.

To the extent that continuing education becomes the norm, we will actually raise the question whether all these years of sitting in school as a youngster are necessary and useful. We will become impatient at keeping the young in school until they are almost middle-aged as is now the fashion. We will, in other words, rediscover experience – but order it on a knowledge basis.

Experience argues strongly that the assumptions of continuing education are a good deal more valid than those of extended schooling. Any teacher who has worked with students with adult experiences has been surprised by their eagerness, their motivation and, above all, by their superior performance in studying. This has been the common experience in every one of the programmes in which students take ordinary jobs in the community and away from school during part of the year.*

The most impressive evidence of the impact of experience on the capacity and willingness to learn were, of course, the returning veterans after World War II, who flooded the American campuses under the 'GI Bill of Rights'. Every educator then 'knew' that these large masses of students would inevitably 'debase' academic standards. Instead, every teacher found out that the real problem was that these students were so incredibly superior that they made demands the faculty could not satisfy. Similarly, every one of the continuing-education programmes for highly advanced adults has revealed that the learning performance of these people is far above that of even the most brilliant of the younger students. Maybe they need a little time to get used to systematic studying again. But they make up for this in superior drive, in the ability to grasp the meaning of what they are being taught, and in the ability to use a theoretical concept to organize their own experience.

Continuing education is a big step beyond traditional education such as extended schooling still represents. It draws the necessary conclusions from the great shift that is making knowledge the foundation for work. It makes

* Examples are the 'cooperative programme' at Antioch, Yellow Springs, Ohio; the programme for engineering students at the University in Cincinnati; and the 'non-resident' programme at Bennington College, Vermont.

school a continuing part of life and work. For surely if knowledge is to be our foundation for organizing experience, then experience in turn must continuously be projected on knowledge to make us see the meaning of what we know as well as the meaning of what we do. In a knowledge society, school and life can no longer be separate. They have to be linked in an organic process in which the one feeds back on the other. And this continuing education attempts to do.

As continuing education advances, we can therefore expect it to collide with extended schooling. Then we will have to face a policy decision: do we want to continue to have *more* years of schooling for the young? Or would we rather have more years of schooling throughout life, which then would mean fewer years of schooling (or at least no more of them) for the young who have not yet started to work.

This is an issue educators have not yet faced up to – in fact, most of them do not suspect its existence. That it will have to be faced is, however, guaranteed by the social impacts of the 'educational explosion'.

THE SOCIAL IMPACTS OF EDUCATION

Advanced education for everyone is a great achievement. But the greater the achievement, the higher the price to be paid for it. The price for universal advanced education was, therefore, bound to be high. Indeed the social impacts of long years of schooling present us with problems we have never faced before, problems we are not yet equipped to handle.

(1) To keep everyone at school until the age of 18 or 20 greatly extends the years of adolescence. Adolescence is not a natural 'stage'. It is a man-made, a cultural, condition. The adolescent lives simultaneously on two age levels; his 'cultural age' is lower than his chronological age.

Chronological age is determined by the years one has already lived. It is physiological and controls physical and mental maturity; independent, on the whole, of society or culture.

Nutrition, however, is important. Because we in the developed countries are so much better fed, we actually mature *physically* and *mentally* earlier than our ancestors did, even though we live so much longer. The stories of the earlier sexual maturity of our ancestors are myth. Both boys and girls in the West (and in Japan) mature sexually several years earlier these days than they did a century or two ago.

But cultural age is determined by the number of years an individual can expect to live, or at least to be productive. Cultural age, in large measure, determines what behaviour is expected of the individual and what *emotional* maturity he attains. The more we expand life expectancy and life span, therefore, the younger people are culturally. A young man of 25 today, who can expect to be still in good health at the age of 65, is culturally younger than a young man was a hundred years ago at the age of 15, when he could not expect to last much beyond the age of 35. As a result, the young man of 25 is expected to behave younger and to be emotionally less mature than the young man of 15 was a century ago. Yet physically (and perhaps even mentally) the boy of 15 today is more mature than the boy of 15 then was. This gap between the attainment of physical and mental maturity at the age of 15 and of cultural maturity which now does not occur until 25 is adolescence.

Adolescence is a recent invention. It was unknown until Goethe published his first book, *The Sorrows of Young Werther*, when he himself was barely 20. It is no accident that this book appeared in 1770 and is thus a contemporary of Watt's steam engine, of Adam Smith's *The Wealth of Nations*, and of the rise of the first class which had a substantially higher than traditional life expectancy, the urban middle classes of the commercial revolution in the West.

Adolescence is of necessity a time of conflict between one's capabilities and what one is expected and permitted to do. It is a time of ambiguity. The adolescent is for ever being told by the adult world to 'act his age', that is, to behave according to his chronological maturity. But he is also being told to stay out of adult concerns, that is, to behave according to his cultural age. Whatever he does, he is wrong. He does violence either to his chronological or to his cultural age. He is, therefore, inevitably a problem to himself as well as to society.

In traditional society, right up to the eighteenth century, there was no problem of the sort because there was no adolescence. The child became a young adult through an initiation rite – whether the circumcision rite of a primitive tribe, or the rite of knighthood, or being sent away from home to his apprenticeship. From that moment on, he was expected to put childish ways behind him and to be a young adult in an adult world.

Extending the years of schooling inevitably extends adolescence. Schools have become, by design, institutions for the preservation of adolescence. They keep the young person in the most unnatural society, a society composed exclusively of his contemporaries. School, even if it builds performance and experience into its curriculum to the fullest extent possible, is finite, certain, predictable. The student who decides to major in Oriental languages rather than in mathematics knows what this means in the way of courses, studies, examinations, and prerequisites. At school one cannot become an adult.

The best example is the delayed adolescence so common among highly trained young physicians. They have a great deal of knowledge. They have seen death and suffering, human stupidity, greed, and cowardice – and also dedication and courage among patients as well as among colleagues. Yet they remain callow adolescents well into their 30s, that is, until they have been out in practice five years or so. As long as they are in training, the loudspeaker or the telephone wakes them up, the schedule tells them what to do, and the attending physician or 'chief of service' makes the final decisions. They simply are not allowed to become adults. The same delayed adolescence is only too noticeable among graduate students who stay on year after year in an environment in which all the emphasis is on their being 'promising' and almost none on their performing.

Whether it was wise or not to extend adolescence by extending the years of schooling is not relevant. It has been done. But we surely do not want to prolong it unnecessarily. Most people recover (though there are indications that prolonged adolescence can become a chronic disease). Yet it is not a healthy condition for society and even less for the individual. A society in which a large part of the young, the physically healthy, the well educated and the promising live in the limbo of adolescence, neither grown up and productive, nor yet still children, is a society plagued by juvenile delinquency, hasty marriage, and excessive divorce. Adolescents are beset alike by fear of taking responsibility and by bitter frustration at being kept out of power and opportunity. Above all, society is ruled by the old – for all its appearances of being dominated by teenagers. If the young feel that they cannot trust anyone over 30 – as the slogan of today's teenagers has it – they have, in fact, abdicated. They have admitted that they can neither become partners of those in power nor overthrow them.

The adolescents, in other words, have a perfectly legitimate grievance. But nothing much can be done about it. The only remedy is to enable the individual to break out of adolescence as soon as possible rather than be confined to it indefinitely by a rigid, unimaginative, and uniform system of education. What the adolescent needs are opportunities for experience and performance throughout the years of school. What he needs are opportunities to do what the child of yesterday did without special efforts: to work with adults as a young adult.

The student needs to get a little experience in school, a little achievement, a little performance. The problem of adolescence demands that we build exposure to areas of experience and performance (especially in the arts) into the normal process of growing up and going to school. We must make it possible for the young man or woman to test himself in work, to spend a few years as an adult worker, and then, if he so desires, to go back to school.

We badly need, for instance, to reverse the recent tendency of American graduate schools to clamp down on the night student who goes out for an advanced degree while working during the day. Of course, the young man or woman who holds a job and goes to school in the evenings is an adminstrative problem. He is a little more likely to 'drop out' without completing the master's or doctor's degree than is the full-time student who has nothing else to do. The part-time student may also be a less docile pupil – and no teacher, no matter what he may say, really likes people in his class who know more about the subject than he does. But to sacrifice the self-motivated adult student to the administrative convenience of the educators is anti-social and should not be tolerated.

For hundreds of years the educators quite properly pleaded and cajoled for a few more years of schooling. They saw their brightest pupils leaving school just when they were beginning to learn something. They saw even more of the brightest not going to school at all. For centuries the educators fought, with good reason, to make a little education universal and a lot of education accessible.

They have achieved these goals. Only the United States has so far committed herself to higher education as a 'right'. But this will sooner or later become general in the advanced countries. But now that we have, or are going to have, all the years of schooling one can possibly ask for, there is no point in pushing for more years of schooling. Now the goal of the educator has to be to make the years of schooling fully productive, rather than to get more of them. Now, above all, it is his job to decide how one can acquire adequate knowledge in less time rather than how one can justify more time for school. The job today is to prevent an unnecessary extension of adolescence.

(2) Long years of schooling create another new problem: the young man (or less commonly the young woman) who is no longer at school even though below the age when we expect young people to stop their formal education is increasingly 'unemployable'.

American statistics still include in the 'working population' anyone above the age of 14. But no one under 18 or 19 in this country is really considered employable. He should, public opinion believes, be at school. If he works, it cannot be in a 'real job'. It is a 'summer job' or a 'weekend job', but not a job which has anything to do with his future work or indeed with the working world of adults. This was vividly expressed in a recent 'public service advertisement' in the New York subways. It showed a husky teenager with the legend: 'Boy, that's what they'll call you all your life if you drop out of school now.'

In the United States, this development has gone the farthest. But it occurs whenever or wherever the years of schooling are being prolonged. It is, according to all reports, appearing in the Russian cities. It is also appearing in Japan.

The teenage jobs in Japan are still there. The traditional industries of pre-industrial Japan, the small shop, the lacquer-maker, or the silk-weaver, still want boys of 15 who have graduated from middle school. But except in the remote villages in the poor North – an area culturally and economically somewhat akin to America's Deep South – the middle-school graduate is no longer considered employable. The traditional industries of Japan, therefore, are drying up for lack of employable manpower. This explains why the young apprentices who by all Japanese traditions are in honourable and secure work, and who can aspire to becoming independent craftsmen and artisans themselves (if not to being adopted by their master and becoming his successor) feel uprooted, dispossessed, and lost. They tend to join the 'Sokka Gakai', the sect of the alienated and uprooted.

In America it is the urban young Negro who is threatened most by this development. To jump from rural illiteracy to twelve years of schooling in one generation is more of a jump than any group can be expected to make, more of a jump than any other group has ever made in the United States or elsewhere (the same problem and for the same reason exists for the Oriental Jew in Israel).

Yet if the Negro boy in the American city drops out of school before he is 18, he is a 'boy' and not a young adult. The traditional labourer's jobs – handyman, deliveryman, garage attendant, gardener – still exist; their number is probably growing. Their pay is low, to be sure, and job security tenuous. But the pay is a good bit better, both absolutely and relative to other wages, than is traditionally given to unskilled, casual workers. And the young Negro needs the jobs, economically and psychologically. But the jobs go unfilled. For culturally the drop-out is 'not employable'. There is something the matter with him, even in his eyes.

The drop-out is a failure of society. He is a failure of the educator who does not know how to attract and hold young people in school until they have reached the age at which our society is willing to let them go to work. The educator has defaulted on his first duty, the duty to the student. We will indeed come to measure the schools by their ability to attract and hold the potential drop-out – not by compulsion or by lowering standards, but by making school more meaningful, more exciting, and more rewarding.

The drop-out is the quality control of education. Today few schools – and few teachers – would pass this test. The majority of those who do not drop out, stay at school not because they want to but because they are made to – by their parents and by their community. In spirit most of the white, middle-class youngsters are drop-outs, kept at school only by parental and community pressure.

The twin problems of adolescence and drop-outs indicate that we will have to learn to build school curricula that serve the individual, that is, school curricula composed of standard units that can be put together to service individual needs, to satisfy individual aspirations, and to conform to the one fact we really know about growing up: that no two people ever grow up exactly alike.

(3) The most serious impact of the long years of schooling is, however, the 'diploma curtain' between those with degrees and those without. It threatens to cut society in two for the first time in American history. We are in danger of confining access to opportunity to those – still less than half our young people – who have stayed at school beyond high school, and particularly to those who have finished college. Even ordinary jobs are increasingly reserved for those who have at least finished high school. We thus are denying full citizenship in the knowledge society to the large group – 15 or 20 per cent perhaps –

who stopped before they could get a high-school diploma. And we are sharply curtailing access to opportunities for half the population – the ones who don't attend college.

This is not only new in American history. It is singularly stupid. The great strength of American society throughout our history lay in our willingness to use human resources, and in our willingness to put ability, ambition, and dedication to productive use wherever it arose. We have never fully lived up to this principle. We certainly did not live up to it in respect to women. And we disregarded it entirely in the case of the black man. But never before did we deny it explicitly as we are now doing.

By denying opportunity to those without higher education, we are denying access to contribution and performance to a large number of people of superior ability, intelligence, and capacity to achieve. There is not much correlation between ability to do well at school and ability to perform in life and work (except perhaps in purely academic work). There is no reason to believe that the diploma certifies very much more than that the holder has sat in school a long time. Human beings mature much too unevenly to trust in a diploma as a final test of a young man's 'potential' and future performance and capacity. Even if the diploma, or its absence, mismeasures only a fraction of our young people (say, one out of four) we cannot afford to lose those that have been unjustly or wrongly cast out. Actually the percentage must be much higher. For going to school beyond high school is still, even among our white population, in large part a matter of accident, family tradition, wealth, local mores, or the luck of being taught by a good teacher. To be sure, three-quarters or more of our present college graduates each year have parents without a college education. But conversely a large proportion, a good half or so, of the children of parents without college education only go to college if there is special encouragement.

Limiting access to opportunity to those with a diploma

is a crass denial of all fundamental American beliefs – beliefs, by the way, that have been amply validated by experience. Maybe such a diploma curtain can be justified in a country where the diploma only controls access to a minority of opportunities, as it used to do. Maybe in a country with a tradition of rigid classes, 'meritocracy' (to use the particularly ugly word the British have invented for the control of access to life's opportunities by the diploma) can be defended as broadening individual opportunities – though the new rigidities will, I predict, be as stultifying and oppressive as the old class barriers ever were. But in the United States where class never controlled, the substitution of the diploma for performance as the key to opportunity and advancement, restricts, oppresses, and injures individual and society alike.

I expect, within ten years or so, to see a proposal before one of the US state legislatures, or up for referendum, to ban, on applications for employment, all questions related to educational status – just as questions regarding race, religion, sex, or age are now banned in a good many states. I, for one, shall vote for this proposal if I can. 'Academic ability' is also an accident of birth – and not a very meaningful one at that.

Outlawing the question on the application blank will, of course, do as little as outlawing similar questions regarding race did for the employment opportunities of the Negro. We need to punch big holes into the diploma curtain through which the able and ambitious can move even though they have not sat long enough on school benches to satisfy the schoolmasters' requirements. Employers, and especially the large companies, need to look within their work force for the people of proven performance and willingness to achieve, though they lack the formal requirements. To spend on this part of the money now spent on college recruitment would be highly profitable. With everyone trying to get the same college graduates, no one can hope to get anyone particularly outstanding or indeed anything but mediocrity. All one can do is to bid up the entrance salary. Perhaps there are fewer big fish in the pool of those who have not gone to college. But the individual employer's chance of landing one of these 'big fish' is infinitely greater in the pool where nobody else fishes than it is among college graduates where he competes even for the minnows with every other employer in the land.*

Once we have identified those performers who lack the formal credentials issued by the schoolmaster, we can give them access to knowledge easily enough. There are few cities in the United States today where continuing education in almost any area is not easily available.

The schools will also have to develop an 'earned degree' for those who have proved their ability in performance even though they lack the hours on the school bench and the credits for courses that would have entitled them to the normal diploma. The schools have to accept the fact that the diploma has become the passport to outside opportunities and that therefore it behoves them to acknowledge parallel paths of achievement. And the path of the 'loner' who gets there in his own way and without benefit of required courses is at least as good and honourable and worth at least as much as the mapped and charted path of the orthodox school curriculum. The standards for this 'earned degree' would, of course, be high – but so they should be for any distinction, including the diploma one gets for attending school.

If we do not eliminate the diploma curtain, it will turn the opportunity of knowledge into a nightmare. It will make the diploma into a symbol of discrimination – which is what it has already become to the poor Negro in the ghetto. It will impoverish our society and economy, and deprive us of a great reservoir of human energies. It will

* The one programme of this kind of which I know is governmental and operates within a Civil Service. It is the Public Employment Career Development Programme which the State of New Jersey has been running with considerable success since 1966.

corrode our ideals and make a mockery of our professions. Perhaps, worst of all, it will substitute the arrogance of titles for the pride of accomplishment as the ruling passion of the knowledge society.

15. The New Learning and the New Teaching

INSTITUTIONS THAT UNDERGO as rapid an expansion as the schools have, outgrow their base as well as their structure. There is a point where quantitative change alters quality; and while we do not know with precision where this point lies, the schools have gone well beyond it. Such growth deforms and explodes any existing structure, any existing philosophy, and any existing system.

The educators still talk of minor changes, of adjustments and of improvements. Few of them see much reason for radical changes. Yet education will in all likelihood be transformed with the next few decades by giant forces from without.

It will be changed, first, because it is heading straight for a major economic crisis. It is not that we cannot afford the high costs of education; we cannot afford its low productivity. We must get results from the tremendous investment we are making. Concretely we are forced to do so by the fact that we cannot indefinitely increase the number of teachers. And – something few understand – money does not produce people. No matter how much money we allot, if the supply of people is exhausted, more money will not buy more. It will only send up the price. We are at the point where increased expenditure for education can only send up the price without increasing the supply. We have to raise the productivity of education if we want to staff it.

It is only a slight exaggeration to say that by 1999, if

present trends were to continue, half the population of
the United States would be up front teaching with half
the population sitting and learning. And at three in the
afternoon, the bell would ring and the two halves would
exchange places. Of course this is not going to happen.

Teaching today requires far too many people. It ought to
be possible to do the job with far fewer. Teaching is where
agriculture was in about 1750, when it took some twenty
men on the farm to feed one non-farmer in the town. We
have to make the teacher more productive, have to multiply his or her impact, have to increase greatly the harvest
from his or her skill, knowledge, dedication, and effort.
Otherwise we shall run out of teachers – even if we do not
run out of money for education.

The productivity of education is too low even for the
richest country. It imposes an intolerable burden on the
poor ones and constitutes a major obstacle to their growth
and development. They beggar themselves – and get
nothing for it.

India today, for instance, gives more schooling to a
larger proportion of her population than the United
States or Japan did at a comparable stage of development a century ago. She spends a larger proportion of
her total national income on schools than the United
States spent then. The achievement, statistically, is impressive. Four times as many Indian children are actually
at school as there were when the British left twenty years
ago. The Indian community colleges that have sprung up
in the urban centres are fully the equals of the 'aca-
demies' that were founded in such profusion in Ohio or
Iowa a century ago.

And yet all this tremendous educational effort is without discernible effect. A century ago in the United States
and Japan the new thrust of schooling produced enough
educated people for a tremendous economic and social

leap forward. But the comparable effort in India today is simply not adequate, nor is it adequate in other countries such as Turkey, West Africa, Malaya, or Colombia.

The threshold of education needed for effective impact on a country's ability to grow and develop rapidly is clearly much higher today than it was a hundred years ago. Yet the effectiveness and productivity of education is no higher than it was then.

We are also heading straight into a pedagogic crisis. The college students who are in open rebellion against the educational establishment everywhere, no longer consider the classroom 'relevant'! And irrelevance is the worst thing one can say about education. Worse still, today's small children are bored stiff by school. Some children cannot rebel by occupying the school or by building barricades in the street. They have, however, a much more potent weapon: they can stop learning. And this is what the generation now reaching school-entering age is apparently about to do everywhere. It has become accustomed to a standard of effectiveness in communications that makes unendurable the low educational productivity of the typical classroom.

Only a generation ago school opened up the world to children. It gave access to an experience that was infinitely wider, richer, and more colourful than the confined static environment which village and family provided. It was excitement, drama, vision, even in the staid and familiar words of the primer. Teaching was poor, and discipline often harsh and unimaginative. Yet to enter school was an adventure.

This is still true in isolated, primitive areas. In rural Mexico, for instance, or in Indonesia, children still stream into the newly opened schools, primitive and ill-equipped though they may be. They arrive full of zeal for school learning and excited with the new world the spelling primer opens up.

But in the developed areas of the world, school no longer is the access to a new world experience. It no longer is the educator. It is rather a pinched and anaemic substitute. The pre-school child, even in the peasant cottage, is today introduced to the world through radio and television in a much more direct, more effective, and more gripping manner than the most gifted schoolmaster could emulate. Whatever the contents of the electronic messages, in form and style they are expert, masterly, educational, and communicative.

Few messages are as carefully designed and as clearly communicated as the thirty-second television commercial. Every split-second counts; every motion is in balance and rhythm; every word is a spell. Few teachers in their entire teaching careers spend as much time or thought on preparing their classes as is invested in the many months of writing, drawing, acting, filming, and editing one thirty-second commercial. That it sells beer or toothpaste or a lipstick is irrelevant to the small child. What matters is that it conveys accessible information, a clear image, and perfect comprehension. It is just the right length for the attention span of the small child. It is perfect 'learning' in its methodology, and is the prototype of the ideal 'programme' with its three key elements: effective sequence of the material; validation through repetition; and self-motivation of the learner through pleasure.*

Children therefore enter school today with different perceptions and different expectations. A level of teaching that was acceptable to older generations who had no standards of comparison, dissatisfies the children of the television age, bores them, offends them. They are in all

* That television exerts such tremendous fascination on children makes it all the more a matter of concern that its programming is so heavily preoccupied with sex, violence, and material possessions.

probability infinitely more ready to learn than earlier generations were, indeed they may be over-stimulated to learn. Sudden 3- and 4-year-olds are found to be eager and ready to read, especially if visual, tactile, and mental experiences are combined in the presentation of the material (as for instance in the much-publicized, computer-connected 'talking typewriter').

The trouble with the 'deprived' children from the black ghettoes may be in part that they have learned far too much before they enter school. They, all our studies show, spend the most time in front of the TV set – there are few other experiences and stimulations in the slum. They may, therefore, both expect too much when they come to school, and expect it in different perceptual form. They may indeed live in McLuhan's 'post-literate' world.

The children do not know, of course, why they find school boring rather than exciting, and stifling rather than informative. But they react by not learning what is presented to them at so much lower a level of professional competence and pedagogic effectiveness than the level to which TV and radio have accustomed them.

MYTHS AND KNOWLEDGE IN EDUCATION

Equaly important: we now are beginning to have the knowledge to change education. Teaching is the only major occupation of man for which we have not yet developed tools that make an average person capable of competence and performance. In teaching we rely on the 'naturals', the ones who somehow know how to teach. Nobody seems to know, however, what it is the 'naturals' do that the rest of us do not do. No one knows what they do not do that the rest of us do. 'Natural genius' is a very scarce resource. No one has encountered many 'natural teachers' in his own school years. Indeed there are a great many people around who in twelve or sixteen years of school have not experienced a single good teacher. The further along we go in school, the rarer are good teachers and the drearier, as a rule, is the learning experience.

The process seems to be unpredictable. There are no measurements for education. There are statistics on how many people are at school and how many graduate. But no one knows whether the students learn anything, let alone how much. We pour money and efforts into education, but what we get out we have to take on trust and hope.

What we need are not 'better teachers'. We cannot hope to get 'better teachers' in quantity. In no area of human endeavour have we ever been able to upgrade the human race. We get better results by giving the same people the right tools and by organizing their work properly. We need to 'learn smarter'.

It will be argued that we have teacher-training institutes with all kinds of courses in all areas of education. But this is self-delusion. What our teachers' colleges do is something that is badly needed and useful; but it is not to teach anyone how to teach. They are recruiting agencies. They procure potential teachers and give them a seal of approval that guarantees their employment and entitles them to tenure. It also gives them self-confidence, and this is no small thing. But beyond this it is hard to see what the graduate of one of these institutions knows or can do that the 17-year-old high-school girl of yesterday did not know or do when she started to teach at elementary school in the rural Midwest.

It is not the fault of the educators that they do not know what to teach future teachers, just as it was not the fault of the professors of medicine at the University of Paris in 1700 – the doctors whom Molière so ruthlessly (but still not ruthlessly enough) castigated – that they did not teach their students how to diagnose and cure patients. Sick people demand to be treated. People who need knowledge demand to be taught. All one can do is try, even if one knows virtually nothing.

411

We still know very little about learning and teaching. But we do know that what 'everybody knows' about learnings and teaching is largely wrong. And this may well be a greater and more important advance than any of the new science technology of which we are so conscious today.

Three specific findings emerge from the research done in learning and teaching in recent years – and to a lesser extent, from the study of what actually goes on in schools.

(1) We have had, since time immemorial, two basic theories regarding learning. The behaviourists asserted that learning is a mechanical process of drill and repetition, forming a mental habit. The cognitive school, on the other hand, taught that learning is understanding, meaning insight. On one point, however, both schools have always been in agreement – that they were mutually exclusive: learning would have to be either behavioural or cognitive. This we now know to be wrong. The two are complementary. Only they are different, dealing with different things. Man is both behaviour and understanding, both habit and reflection. And the two together form knowledge.

In layman's language what we know now can be expressed by saying that 'what can be learned cannot be taught, and what can be taught cannot be learned'. At the same time, we know that one can only learn if there is also teaching. And one cannot be taught unless there is a good deal of learning.

(2) Teachers have always known that there were 'bright' students and 'dumb' students, and that the difference between them was as the difference between day and night.

Psychologists have proved that children vary but little in their learning and abilities. Differences in school performance should be no greater and no more common than they are in the most important and most difficult learning process, that of the infant. But as we know above all from the pioneering work of Jean Piaget there are tremendous differences in rhythm, attention span, and learning pace, especially among young children. If these are suppressed, as all traditional schooling has had to do, 'dumb' children are created. If these are used, however, learning energies are liberated.

(3) It has always been believed that the teacher spends his time teaching in the classroom – and no one ever looked to test this belief. We have, in other words, done with respect to the teacher's work what, before the advent of Scientific Management, we used to do for all work: we guessed. The first systematic time and motion study of work showed that 'what everybody had always known' was pure nonsense. We found this true again the moment we looked at what actually happens in a classroom. Teachers would like to teach, to be sure, but most of them are not teaching, but baby-sitting. Most of them spend most of their time in custodial activities, aimed at keeping the children quiet. Some of our studies make it appear plausible that the productivity of the teacher may, after all, not be so very low; it is simply that he (or she) spends very little time teaching. Certainly one of the main aims of any change in the schools must be to multiply the time that the pupil spends on learning and the teacher spends on teaching.

A few additional words need to be said about each of these findings.

As to (1): 'learning' is the acquisition of information, and this is largely a repetitive process. The mechanics are unknown, but we know that they are different from the 'mechanics' of any machine, such as, for instance, the computer. We acquire information – what the layman would call 'facts' – by repeating until the response becomes automatic and unthinking, that is, until we have created a 'memory'. This is how all of us learned to speak. This is also how all of us learned the multiplication table – if we learned it at all. Nobody ever learned to multiply by being 'bright' or by being 'mathematically gifted'; he learned it by rote and repetition.

Information, however, will only be learned if it is presented as a 'programme'. This means, firstly, that the material has to be in a sequence in which one piece of information leads to the next piece to be learned. It means, secondly, that the arrangement must show a clear purpose – the sequence must make sense to the student. It means, thirdly, that what has been learned earlier has to be repeated again and again, and applied again and again; it has to be reaffirmed or else it is forgotten.

The reason why even children with little mathematical ability or interest can learn the four fundamental operations of arithmetic – addition, subtraction, multiplication, and division – is not that these operations are simple. On the contrary, they are difficult and abstract parts of mathematics; even advanced mathematicians have difficulty explaining them. But they are repeated again and again and again, are used every day, and are thus reaffirmed constantly. In the case of mathematical topics taught later, this is no longer true. They are learned once and then not used again. As a result, they are forgotten fast.

Repetition is necessary also to make sure that we have really learned. The child who misses addition or multiplication the first time, almost invariably gets a second chance soon, and a third one and fourth one. When he gets to logarithms, however, he normally gets only one exposure. If he does not learn them – or if he should happen to be away from school that day or just daydreaming – he is lost.

The motivation, the incentive, the reward for the acquisition of information must be built into the programme itself. External rewards are not motivators. At every step the learner must receive satisfaction from the act of learning and from doing it correctly.

Learning can only be done by the learner. It cannot be

done by the 'teacher'. The teacher can only be a help or an impediment to learning.

No piano teacher knows which of her pupils will turn into a pianist. But every piano teacher knows, almost immediately, which of the pupils will not even turn into a beginner and will be at best a problem for a few years before his harassed mother finally gives up. It is the pupil whom the teacher has to supervise in doing his scales and finger exercises – that is, in learning. The pupil who needs external pushing and supervision for learning will not learn. Supervision sets up internal resistance and fatigue which make learning all but impossible. All the information, all the affirmation and all the motivations should lie in the process of learning itself.

Teaching, on the other hand, has to do with meaning and insight. It has to do with application of information, with reaching out, with understanding and enjoyment, and with the insight that cannot be learned. Teaching has a lot more to do with perception than it has to do, apparently, with intellect. And teaching is done by example. Teaching requires a 'teacher'. The teacher can be a book, a piece of music, perhaps even the student himself. But it is done best by an older, understanding, guiding, helpful, challenging person. Just as learning is individual, teaching is mutual.

The teacher who supervises learning does not 'teach'; he (or she) polices. A very good teacher doing this will not disturb learning; in fact, this is our present definition of the 'good teacher'. But even for the 'good teacher', it is a waste of time that should be devoted to teaching. And the ordinary teacher who supervises learning does more harm than good.

Teaching may turn out not to be very difficult. It is also very enjoyable. It is simply not being done – because we misuse teachers to supervise learning. We misuse them because we have not created the proper 'programmes' for learning. We have not given the student the tools he needs to do what he wants, namely, to learn. As a result, we do not allow the teacher to do what he should be doing, namely, to teach.

It will not be simple to create the right 'programme'. We can do it fairly well for skills that can be defined, ie, welding or flying a jet plane. To write a 'programme' for learning history is something else again – if only because information in history without understanding of history is as useless as is understanding of history without information. Still we do know some fundamentals.

The perennial discussion whether the student needs to learn 'facts' or 'meaning' is pointless. The human being, in order to be able to understand, has to have a substantial information base. It is only by acquiring the habit of learning, that one becomes capable of understanding. On the other hand, it is only by understanding that one can do anything with learning, including remembering it. Students, whether infants or adults, need drill, that is, organized systematic repetition of information. And they need understanding and meaning. This does not mean that any drill is the right one – whether there is much point in learning the dates of the kings of England or Latin irregular verbs is not at issue here. But to learn irrelevant information and to learn it well is still more educational than to learn no information.

In the United States, our Schools of Education and our Departments of Philosophy or Psychology still contain both behaviourists and cognitionists. And they still talk as if we had to choose between the two approaches, and as if each contained 'the truth, the whole truth, and nothing but the truth'. Actually we should be debating the proper balance, the proper relationship and the integration between the two. We need both learning and teaching. And because we now know that these are different, though interdependent, we can hope to learn more about both.

As to (2): nothing man learns is half as difficult and complicated as what practically all of us learned in the first few years of our lives – talking, walking, seeing a complex world, complex relationships to people, or even toilet training. One child is an early talker – and then is likely to be slow in his motor coordination or late in his toilet habits. Another child starts feeding himself at 8 months, and may not say a word until he is past 3 years. In other words, children develop at their own rate. Yet by the time they are 3 or 4 years old, most children have made it in all areas. Most of them are 'normal' by the time they need to have these skills. Indeed the child that has been pushed by his parents into talking or walking or toilet habits while he was busy learning something else is the child with emotional problems, the child that stutters, wets his bed, or is afraid.

The speed with which any one of these early skills is learned has nothing to do with talent. The late talker may become a great orator. There is no correlation between early ability to walk and being an athlete later on. The correlation is to things that are fundamental to the person rather than to areas of achievement. The correlation is to rhythm of learning, pace, and attention span. These are fundamentals of personality – whether genetic and inborn, or the result of early experiences, we do not know (but it does not greatly matter for our purposes here).

These learning patterns are not confined to infancy, though the younger the person is, the greater the differences in rhythm, attention span, and learning speed. If, however, the school imposes uniformity on all children in a classroom, it makes sure that a large proportion of the students (though we do not know how large) will develop emotional resistance and fatigue. This will make them appear even to themselves to be 'dumb' and backward. If we allow each child to learn whatever has to be learned at his rhythm, his attention span and his learning speed, he will get there just as surely as any other child. He will be just as 'bright', only in his own best way.

No one maintains that there are no differences in ability. But it seems likely that over a wide range of 'normality' his abilities are concentrated in different areas at different stages of growth and development, eg, in music or sports or painting or reading, than that there are no differences in overall ability. There is also increasing evidence that abilities develop unevenly. One adolescent may be 'ahead' in musical ability at the cost of being temporarily 'behind' in something else, just as one baby is ahead in walking and the other one in playing games or in feeding himself.

Differences in ability – as against the differences in pace and rhythm – are above all socially conditioned. The Negro slum child at the age of 2 is as bright as the white child from the professional suburban family. By the time he gets to school, at the age of 6, he has been dulled. A main reason is the lack of recognition for achievement. What creates 'dumb' children is the expectation of failure rather than natural endowment or the lack of it.

We know – though only in the roughest outline so far – under what conditions children – and human beings in general – can learn. They can learn if use is made of their own rhythm, their own pacing, and their own attention span. They can learn, in other words, if there is an 'individual' programme – which is exactly what every baby has when he learns to sit up, to walk, to play games, to feed himself, and so on.

It is startling to watch a group of schoolchildren who each have their own individual programme. One child will sit and work for two hours on one subject and will not vary his speed at all during that period. Another child will start every time at top speed and then slow down or switch subjects every fifteen minutes or so. A third one will start slowly and speed up and will stay on one subject for an hour, but on the next one only a few minutes, coming back, however, again and again. Yet eventually they all learn about the same in all areas and subjects – and in about the same time span.

There is another way we can satisfy individual natures: the rousing emotional experience of the 'massed choir'. We can, especially with young people, create a genuine collective speed, attention span, and rhythm. But this requires the emotional excitement that people, and especially children, get from doing something together, in rhythm with one another – and preferably with great, but organized, noise.

In Japan today, Professor Suzuki has hundreds of tots, aged 3 or so, playing the violin, and playing it rather well, even though they cannot read notation. They play in unison and in one rhythm, and get the same 'charge' men get from marching in step. In some educational experiments with deprived Negro children, results have been achieved by making the alphabet, addition and subtraction, reading and writing a rousing group experience in which the whole class shouts the right answers in a rhythmic chant.

There is some reason to believe that the child needs a balance of these two kinds of 'programmes' – the one that utilizes his own individual and highly personal style, and the one that integrates his personality into a group.

The one way a child does not learn is by himself rather than in the 'massed choir', but chained to a rhythm, pace, and attention span which are alien to him and imposed on him. This is, however, exactly what every school has done traditionally (and has had to do in the absence of individual programmes).

As to (3): we have lately been treated to quite a few 'horror stories' about what goes on in the classrooms of our American city slums. But while the classrooms of our 'good' schools are genteel places, they are not much more productive. The teacher spends no time on teaching, and the students spend little time on learning. While the teacher prods, cajoles, and supervises one child in the class, the remaining twenty-four daydream. The teacher cannot spend much time with any one student. But since the student has no tools of learning himself, he does nothing until the teacher has turned his or her attention to him.

Children do need more time for daydreaming than the curriculum officially allows. Some of it may be highly productive time. But there is little doubt that most of it is waste – or else students of all ages would not be so bored as most of them are most of the time. If only students were permitted to learn, they could acquire the total information concept of modern schooling in a fraction of the time – and could make the experience enjoyable to boot.

What we need to do is to relieve the teacher of all but teaching work. Then the teacher, in contrast to today, would have the time to teach individuals. This is, of course, the essence of the tutorial system such as Oxford and Cambridge have used for a long time. But it is rather late to start being taught at the age of 18 or 20.

Most infants are being 'taught' before they go to school. That the slum family does not do enough teaching is the reason why the slum child is deprived – and we rightly consider this exceptional and a disgrace. But the years between the time the child has acquired the fundamentals at home in his family and the time he goes to Oxford or Cambridge – quite apart from the fact that not many go there anyhow – are important years. These are the years in which there should be the maximum of teaching.

To give the teacher time to teach is the key to multiplying his (or her) effectiveness. We are, today, conducting experiments (eg. in Oakland Community College in Michigan) in which a 'master teacher' handles very large classes which meet only once or twice a week. But in between, the students are hard at work learning, without teachers or supervision, through carefully constructed programmes. The master teacher therefore does nothing but teach. As a result the individual student actually receives more personal attention than he does in the typical 'small' class in which a teacher mostly tries to get the students to do a little learning. In fact, the master teacher has time between his few classes for individual students, time spent on getting to know the student rather than on the student's 'problems'.

We are still at the beginning. Indeed I have been guilty of great over-simplification. But we certainly can already reach *two important conclusions*.

The first one is that the 'dumb' child is the shame of the schools. The maxim ought to be: 'There are no "dumb" children; there are only poor schools.' The reason for there being 'poor schools' is not the stupidity or incompetence of the teachers. It is the absence of the right tools and of the right methods.

Secondly, teaching and learning are bound to undergo tremendous change in the next few decades. They will be transformed. Economic necessity forces us to tackle the job, no matter how great the resistance of citizens and educators. And the new understanding of teaching and learning will enable us to do the job. Whenever we have such a conjunction of needs and knowledge, drastic changes occur, and occur rapidly.

The first teacher ever, that priest in pre-literate Mesopotamia who sat down outside the temple with the children and began to draw figures with a twig in the sand, would be perfectly at home in most classrooms in the world today. Of course, there is a blackboard – but otherwise there has been little change in tools and none in respect of methods. The only new teaching tool in the intervening 8,000 years has been the printed book. And that, few teachers really know how to use – or else they would not keep on lecturing what is already in the book.

The priest in ancient Babylon was also the first doctor.

If he returned today to a modern operating-room in the hospital, he would hardly recognize what he saw there, and he would not conclude that he could do as well. Yet today's doctors are no better men than the first doctors were. They certainly are no better than the 'father of medicine', Hippocrates. They stand on his shoulders. They know more – and above all, they know better. They have a different methodology. They have different tools. As a result, they do entirely different things, and do them differently.

It is a fair bet that the first teacher, that ancient Babylonian priest, would not recognize the schoolroom of 1999 and would not understand what goes on in it. We surely will not have 'all the answers' by then; but at least we should know enough to enable children to learn and teachers to teach.

16. The Politics of Knowledge

THE EMERGENCE OF knowledge as central to our society and as the foundation of economy and social action drastically changes the position, the meaning, and the structure of knowledge. Of all the discontinuities dealt with in this book, this is probably the sharpest and most importance one.

Knowledge areas are in a state of flux. The existing 'faculties', 'departments', and 'disciplines' will not be appropriate for long. Few are ancient to begin with, of course.

There was no biochemistry a hundred years ago, no genetics, and indeed hardly any biology. There was zoology and botany. It should not, therefore, come as a surprise that the distinction between organic and inorganic chemistry is no longer very meaningful. We are designing inorganic polymers in which the knowledge of the organic chemist is applied to inorganic substances such as silicones. Conversely, we are designing 'organic crystals' in which inorganic chemistry as well as physics is being brought to bear on organic substances. The old distinction between organic and inorganic chemistry is therefore rapidly becoming an impediment to knowledge and performance.

Similarly, old dividing-lines between physiology and psychology are increasingly meaningless as well as those between economics and government, between sociology and the behavioural sciences, between logic, mathematics, statistics, and linguistics, and so on.

The most probable assumption is that every single one of the old demarcations, disciplines, and faculties is going to become obsolete and a barrier to learning as well as to understanding. The fact that we are shifting rapidly from a Cartesian view of the universe, in which the accent has been on parts and elements, to a configuration view, with the emphasis on wholes and patterns,* challenges every single dividing-line between areas of study and knowledge.

All institutions, as we have seen, need to be able to slough off yesterday. The university is no exception. At the very least, the university needs freedom to introduce new disciplines and to combine traditional disciplines in new ways.

The American, English, and Japanese university systems with their great flexibity have a decided advantage. Or rather the absence of such flexibility is a weakness of the university systems of Continental Europe, with their established 'chairs', their 'titular' and 'ordinary' professorships, and so on. Above all, the traditional European control of academic organization by a Ministry of Education is a liability. Such control tends to prohibit experimentation and to lay down the rule that no new subject can be taught anywhere, unless all the universities in the country adopt it – the rule applied both in France and Italy. This makes for bureaucratic order – which the university needs least today.

The process of introducing new and phasing out old disciplines is now unfamiliar to the university. But it will have to be done much faster now than before. What is totally new, however, and in contradiction to all the modern university has ever believed, is the shift away from the dis-

* On this, see my *Landmarks of Tomorrow*, Chapter One (Heinemann, London, 1959; Harper & Row, New York, 1959).

ciplines as the centre of teaching and learning. But this was bound to happen as application became central to knowledge.

Until the nineteenth century, knowledge and action had almost no contact with each other. Knowledge served the 'inner man'. Action was based on experience and on the skills derived therefrom. On the European continent, systematic schooling had by 1820 become the prerequisite for access to a number of professions, especially the ministry, law, and medicine; but these were legal monopolies granted to powerful guilds to restrict access and curtail competition. Until the end of the nineteenth century, the majority of lawyers and physicians in England and America came up through an apprenticeship rather than through university training. They did not differ much from their university-trained colleagues on the Continent in their capacity to perform, whether as practitioners or as scholars.

Technology altogether, until the second half of the nineteenth century, was separate from science and was acquired through apprenticeship.

To be sure, the first modern technical university, the *École Polytechnique*, was started in 1794. And from 1800 on it was rapidly copied all over Continental Europe, and soon across the Atlantic in the United States. But until late in the century, the country that continued to rely on apprenticeship, that is, Great Britain, held a vast technological lead. Until the chemical and electrical industries emerged in the last quarter of the century, technical advances were made by skill-trained craftsmen and 'inventors' and owed very little to science. Even in Germany engineering graduates did not become common in industry much before 1910.

The search for knowledge, as well as the teaching thereof, have therefore traditionally been dissociated from application. Both have been organized by subject, that is, according to what appeared to be the logic of knowledge itself. The faculties and departments of the university, its degrees, its specializations, indeed the entire organization of higher learning, have been subject-focused. They have been, to use the language of the experts on organization, based on 'product' rather than on 'market' or 'end-use'.

Now we are increasingly organizing knowledge and the search for it around areas of application rather than around the subject areas of the disciplines. Inter-disciplinary work has rapidly grown everywhere during the last twenty years. The many institutes for area studies, whether of Africa, of Russia, or of the modern metropolis, are examples. They bring together men from all disciplines, ranging from economics to psychiatry and from agronomy to art history. Increasingly such inter-disciplinary work mobilizes the energies of the university and determines its direction.

This is a symptom of the shift in the meaning of knowledge from an end in itself to a resource, that is, a means to some result. What used to be knowledge is becoming information. What used to be technology is becoming knowledge. Knowledge as the central energy of a modern society exists altogether in application and when it is put to work. Work, however, cannot be defined in terms of the disciplines. End results are inter-disciplinary of necessity.

We will, therefore, see more and more of the work of the universities organized towards areas of effectiveness rather than towards a discipline. We will see more and more of it organized as the 'Study of China' rather than the 'Study of Government'. We do need, however, for the study of China, knowledge of government and of the political process. We do, in other words, need the discipline as a tool, a resource, a speciality.

This means that pure research increasingly may derive from the need of some specific application. Research into the application, that is, for instance, into China – or into health (as opposed to research into muscle functions) – will become increasingly 'pure', that is, concerned with fundamental understanding, fundamental methods, and general concepts. Above all, the specialist in government who is part of an inter-disciplinary group working on China will, of necessity, become a Chinese scholar as well.

This will raise questions no one today understands or could even attempt to answer. Will the traditional researcher – the *Forscher* of the nineteenth-century German university – become obsolete? Will we instead base research on the questions that arise out of application? Just as the fundamental questions in government and in history come today out of work with a given geographic area, the impetus to pure theory in the physical sciences comes increasingly from new instruments, such as the accelerator designed for work with nuclear particles. The specialist in a given discipline, ie, today's scholar, may be the tool maker of tomorrow, who serves the tool users where traditionally he has been their master. The department or academic discipline may tomorrow be only an administrative unit rather than an area of work, learning, teaching, and study. It may keep the personnel files of a man who is considered an historian. But his real area of work may be in an 'Institute' in which men from all disciplines work together on a given area in a team.

But will the discipline, no matter how defined, even remain as the guardian of the personnel files? Or are we going to shift to the area study – geographic, cultural, ecological, and so on – as the centre of specialization? The existing disciplines might then become what in organization theory is known as 'staff services', to which a man goes to find out something he does not know or to get advice. We could then anticipate that what is now the knowledge of the disciplines will tomorrow become a data bank, and the memory unit of a computer system. For this we would have to solve a great many problems in the collection, storage, and recovery of information. But we have to tackle these problems anyhow in designing information systems.

Ten years ago no one thought about such developments. Today serious work on them goes on in the universities.

That knowledge has become the central resource of modern society adds a third new function to the traditional tasks of the university. It adds to the functions of teaching and research that of community service, that is, the conversion of knowledge into action and results in the community.

We hear a great deal today about the emphasis on research and its incompatibility with teaching and with the needs of the students. This is probably a misunderstanding. The real dilemma is caused by the growing orientation towards community service in the work of the university. The ablest men in the faculty are the ones most likely to be engaged in inter-disciplinary work. The ablest are also in demand as consultants – to government and to school systems, to business and to hospitals, to the Armed Services, as well as to other faculties and departments of the university itself. The consultant ostensibly practises his speciality; but his concern is with the results of his clients. He is a part-time member of a team that is focused on end results in application rather than on the logic of any one discipline. Twenty years ago, consulting was confined to a few faculties – the engineers mostly, the professors of management and administration, public and private, maybe the law-school professors, and the chemists. But today almost all disciplines are drawn into consulting work.

The very fact that the university is increasingly expected to mobilize its knowledge energies for application and results in the community may move us even further into restructuring teaching according to the major areas of application rather than according to the logic of the discipline.

This is what the rebelling students want. The demand by student radicals for a 'critical university', which is being heard in Berkeley, in Berlin, and in Tokyo, is a demand for learning organized around major relevant result areas. The student sees the professor putting his knowledge to work on the problems of the metropolis; on economic development; on the conservation of the natural environment. And he asks: 'Why should we students be bored stiff with information that has no relevance, no application, and no relationship to the important needs which we, as well as society, have?' The educators have no answer, of course. They say: 'You have to learn to use the tools first before you can apply them.' This sounds plausible. But does it really make sense? If the subjects we teach the students are really tools, then they are best learned in application. In fact, the only way one can learn to use a tool is by applying it to a specific and meaningful task which shows at least some results.

At the December, 1967, meeting of the Council of the American Association for the Advancement of Science a distinguished biologist reported that he had changed the students' boredom with the introductory course in biology to enthusiasm by building the course around the problems – pollution, fish life, and so on – of the lake on which the campus bordered. His experience was that this made them receptive to the most abstract theory.

And yet we will still need specialists, that is, people who have learned to do one fairly small task exceedingly well. The academicians who concentrate on the graduate students in a very narrow field are not wrong; they are just one-sided.

The organization of knowledge, and with it the organization of the university, is of necessity becoming both more complex and more controversial. A simple organization is no longer possible.

We will have to organize for teaching, in contemplation of major areas of application (which are always inter-disciplinary) and for specialization within a narrow area. In the former we will have to make sure that the student acquires respect for the depth of analysis needed, that is, for the contribution of the specialist. In the latter the specialist will have to learn first that he applies only one tool which, by itself, achieves little. He will then have to learn how to relate his speciality to the universe of knowledge and how to relate it in application, that is, in concert with other specialities, to end results. We do not know how to do any of these jobs today – which explains why today's students are so deeply disturbed.

At the same time, we will have to recognize that research produces information rather than knowledge, and to organize for application of information to end results, which is what we increasingly mean by 'knowledge'.

We need not one kind of person in the university, but many. Today's insistence on the PhD for any job, that is, on the man with an advanced degree in a specialized discipline in which he has supposedly done research (that is, has gathered information), is obscurantism. To be sure, we need people of this kind, but only a few of them in any area.

The greatest need is for the man who can develop and teach the application to end results of knowledge and information drawn from diverse disciplines.

We need further the man who can, in his own work, bring together knowledge and skills from a great many disciplines and integrate them into effective application outside the university. He is today not officially recognized – but he is the real 'star' in today's large university.

Finally, we need something which higher education has never known it needs: we need managers. The several different kinds of people in the faculties have to be organized into one institution. Yet they have to be organized for a variety of functions. Each of these men will have to be able to achieve his own purposes and to obtain his own satisfaction from his work.

And then students' needs and students' desires will have to be integrated with the other university functions.

This requires high managerial ability. The university may well offer the most challenging, the most difficult, but also the most needed of all managerial tasks around today.

THE KNOWLEDGE BASE

The change in the meaning and function of knowledge raises fundamental questions regarding the knowledge base of society.

The first time this question came up was when Sputnik appeared in the skies in 1957. This event suddenly made it clear to the American public that building and maintaining the right knowledge base for intellectual, economic, social, and military performance is essential for national survival.

It can be argued that the changes in American education would have come even without Sputnik. Certainly the rapid growth in the number of college students would have forced us to raise academic standards, and to change methods of instruction in those fields where traditional approaches were signally unsuccessful, as in mathematics and the sciences. But Sputnik crystallized these developments all at once. Above all, Sputnik taught America that knowledge is no longer a private but a public concern.

Today the same lesson is being taught the Europeans by the 'brain drain' and the 'technology gap', the first primarily in Great Britain, the second primarily in Continental Europe. A brain drain is a symptom of a serious disease. Even if only a small percentage of a nation's men of high knowledge prefer to work elsewhere, it should be cause for concern.

Men of knowledge do not, as a rule, go elsewhere primarily because of pay. Their main reason for leaving is dissatisfaction with the effectiveness their existing environment permits them, and with the respect for knowledge and its impact on society.

It may not be relevant that the brain drain in England sucks off only a tiny minority of English scientists, technologists, and physicians (the number of men who emigrate each year to the United States is only 5 to 6 per cent of the number who qualify in these fields each year). The men who leave are the men others want, that is, the best qualified, mature, and successful. A leakage of these is a serious matter, even though the job of anyone who quits can immediately be filled by somebody who graduated yesterday.

It is equally a severe indictment of military medicine in the United States that it cannot hold good men – even though quantitatively the military can obtain all the doctors it wants through the draft. The military, like the British, tend to blame this brain drain on money – and, like the British, they are wrong; the same young doctor who leaves the military service because, as he complains, he is not being paid enough, works cheerfully for the same compensation or for less in a teaching hospital or in research. What is wrong with the military machine is that its organization, structure, and climate are not appropriate to what today's doctor considers the best practice of medicine and the best development of a medical man. The career opportunities of military medicine are in administration rather than in the practice of a major speciality or in research. But the modern physician has learned that administration is for laymen who know how to manage, and that the proper career and development of a physician is increased competence in a speciality, leadership in the treatment of patients, or research work on the advancement of medical knowledge and patient care.

The standard explanation for the 'technology gap' is also largely incorrect. It is simply not true that the United States has attained technological leadership because it spends more on research than Europe does. Most of this research lead is in defence and space work where indeed a great deal of money is being spent, but where results are meagre especially in terms of their 'fall-out' benefits for the civilian economy. Only in two important areas can American technological leadership be ascribed to the high level of research spending: computers and aircraft. Here the military has, in effect, subsidized American industry. But otherwise, Europe can easily hold its own in terms of inventions. The 'technology gap' is primarily a result of European failure to convert research results into products and to market the products successfully (a point made with great force by Servan-Schreiber's already quoted book, *Le Défi Americain*). The 'technology gap' is in management failures.

This is actually a more serious weakness than a shortage of research money. Money can be allocated. But the capacity to convert scientific results into economic performance, that is, the marketing and managerial capacity, money cannot buy.

For its knowledge base a modern society needs both scientific and technical people and people in the humanist, political, economic, and behavioural disciplines. Above all, it needs people capable of understanding the technological, even though they themselves are not scientists or engineers. And it needs people capable of understanding the humanities, the economic and the political disciplines, though they themselves are not humanists. It needs people who can put knowledge to work rather than people who are the prisoners of discipline or method.

A modern society needs both the 'great man' who can create new knowledge and the 'journeyman' who can convert new knowledge into everyday action.

Traditionally, we have tended to set an *élite* concept of knowledge and education against a mass concept. We have tended to assume that one can focus on producing either a few leaders or a great many followers. But modern society needs both.

One thing it cannot, therefore, afford in education, is the *élite* institution which has a monopoly on social standing, on prestige, and on the command positions in society and economy. Oxford and Cambridge are important reasons for the British brain drain. A main reason for the technology gap is the *grande école* such as the *École Polytechnique* or the *École Normale*. These *élite* institutions may do a magnificent job of education, but only their graduates normaly get into the command positions. Only their faculties 'matter'. This restricts and impoverishes the whole society.

There are, of course, in knowledge as in any other area, differences of ability and interests between people. And in universities, as in all other institutions, there are differences in quality. But it is incompatible with the nature of knowledge, as well as with the needs of modern society, to deny any knowledge worker the opportunity to become a master. Where he has acquired his knowledge, and where he plys it, should be irrelevant five years after he has graduated. Similarly it is incompatible with the nature of knowledge, as well as with the demands of society, to give any knowledge institution a monopoly position. We simply need too many people of knowledge to narrow the channel to achievement, opportunity, and advancement.

The way to raise masters is to educate the largest possible number of journeymen to high demands. This has been demonstrated in the arts – in the Italian Renaissance, for instance, or in the great creative outburst of the sixteenth-century Momoyama period in Japan, or in the Low countries at the time of Rembrandt and Rubens. There is no one way to identify ahead of time the people who will perform during their working life. The only true test is performance in work. And the least reliable test is performance at school. History is replete with the names of great men of outstanding intellectual accomplishment who did poorly at school. Winston Churchill is just one example – Goethe another. History does not, as a rule, record the brilliant students who failed miserably in life – but they are equally common.

Intellectual ability is distributed like any other ability, namely, on a probability basis. The more people we expose to knowledge, the more intellectual leaders will emerge. There is no conflict between mass education and quality education. We need to educate large masses of people to get the large amount of quality we need. We need to have high standards for the masses not only to get large numbers of competent journeymen and followers for the knowledge work force, but also to find and stimulate the largest number of future masters.

That so much of American education before Sputnik (and still today, I am afraid) was content with mediocrity and rather smug about it, is a real weakness of our knowledge base. By contrast, one strength of American education is the resistance to any *élite* monopoly. To be sure, we have institutions which enjoy (deservedly or not) high standing and prestige. But we do not, fortunately, discriminate against the men who receive their training elsewhere. The engineer whose degree is from North Idaho 'A and M' (Agricultural and Mechanical Institute) does not regard himself as 'inferior' or as 'not really an engineer'. He knows that MIT (Massachusetts Institute of Technology) is the tougher school with the more distinguished faculty. But he and his faculty in North Idaho (as well as the faculty at MIT) know that North Idaho is an engineering school that is trying to do the same things as MIT, offers the same curriculum, and attempts to have graduates with the same knowledge, the same understanding, and the same professional qualifications. And five or ten years later, nobody cares much where the fellow got his degree – what matters then is what he can do with it. While MIT sees itself as the leader in technology, and indeed in a wider range of the physical sciences, it still sees as its first task the development of the competent man who can execute a task and who can make knowledge effective in performance and production.

The Harvard Law School might like to be a *grande école* and to claim for its graduates a preferential position. But American society has never been willing to accept this claim. The Kennedy administration seemed to give Harvard Law School graduates the 'inside track'. But this only made certain the dominance of 'outsiders' in the next administration. If high standing in the Harvard Law School class is considered a 'must' to get a good job in one of the big New York Law firms, it is almost a disadvantage to the young lawyer who plans to start in the Midwest or on the West Coast. 'He is a brilliant fellow,' I was told fifteen years ago of Arthur Wood who, in 1967, became President of Sears Roebuck, the world's largest retail chain. 'He got promoted at Sears even though he went to Harvard Law School.' And this was said without irony.

As a result, no American educational institution sees itself as condemned to second-rank. Each knows that it can aspire to more and that it will be accepted if it achieves excellence. Good examples, within the last generation, are such universities as California, Stanford, and Duke, and such engineering schools as Rice and Carnegie Tech. By the same token, no American graduate feels that he is inferior and not entitled to a top position if he earns it.

It is almost impossible to explain to a European that the strength of American higher education lies in this absence of schools for leaders and schools for followers. It is almost impossible to explain to a European that the engineer with a degree from North Idaho A and M is an 'engineer' and not a 'draughtsman'. Yet this is the flexibility Europe needs in order to overcome the brain drain and to close the technology gap. Otherwise Europe will continue to produce far too few people who can convert the insights of the *élite* into results, and will, therefore, lose its own achievements. The European who knows himself competent but who is not accepted as such – because he is not an 'Oxbridge' man or because he did not graduate from one of the *grandes écoles* and became an *Inspecteur de Finance* in the government service – will continue to emigrate where he will be used according to what he can do rather than according to what he has not done.

Altogether the weakness of Europe is not the shortage of men with a first-rate scientific and technical education. Proportionately Europe, especially England and France, produces more such men than does the United States. The shortage consists of non-technical but educated managers, especially on the lower and middle levels.

What is needed is a knowledge base that encourages everyone to become knowledgeable. We need a knowledge base for a society that contains a tremendous and rapidly shifting diversity of knowledge and puts to work a tremendous diversity of knowledge applications. No one test can possibly identify today who will be leadership material twenty years later. For we do not and cannot know what will be needed twenty years hence.

'Oxbridge' and 'Redbrick' in England, the *grandes écoles* and the provincial universities in France, must be equal in the opportunities for performance and in the recognition open to their graduates. At the very least they might adopt the German system which gives a monopoly position to the 'university' but then makes no distinction between universities in the opportunities and careers open to their graduates.

The American system has yet another strength which Europe needs and does not have.

When large numbers of scientists and scholars were displaced by Hitler's persecution of the Jews, the great majority of them were eagerly absorbed into American colleges and universities. Within ten years, this gave

America the ability to leap into scientific and technological leadership. Most of these men, especially the seasoned and mature ones, would probably have preferred to stay in Europe. They were at home there. Economically, it should have been easier for Europe to absorb them in view of the ravages of the Depression wrought in the United States, and especially in the budgets of the still largely private American system of higher education. But Europe did not have the flexibility. If there was already one professor of biochemistry, another one, even the leading man in the field, simply could not be hired. The American system could, and did, create jobs for good men. And once it had given a man a job, it no longer considered him a foreigner or a newcomer but put him to work. At the same time, it readily accepted whatever he had to bring and adapted itself to his ways, his approaches, his strengths.

In other countries, Great Britain as well as France, hiring one of the German refugee professors was charity and a duty. In the United States it was an opportunity – and this difference largely explains both brain drain and technology gap now, thirty years later.

The knowledge base for the knowledge society has to be capable of accepting the new and different, receptive to innovation. It needs the diversity that is generally lacking in the European university. Indeed in education it is Europe – rather than the United States – that is narrowly, parochially conformist. But the growing insistence on the Ph D threatens to impose an even more stultifying uniformity on the American university.

The United States also will have to remember what Sputnik taught us, that a mass system which does not apply to itself leadership standards does not even produce adequate followers. 'Mass education' must be 'quality education'. We need to emphasize, in other words, that there is no reason whatever why high standards and excellence should not be the aim of all education, even though we extend it to the multitude. The educator has, for centuries, warned that educating more people would inevitably 'downgrade standards'. The opposite has always happened. The more students we have, the most we can demand of them. There is no foundation in our experience for assuming that any restricted educational system – whether the restriction be by inheritance, wealth, political reliability, or scholastic test – produces any different distribution of abilities than is contained in the total population.

Even the most demanding schools exploit only a small fraction of the students' true abilities. What schools mean by 'ability' is, as a rule, the capacity to 'work harder'. The need is for a system of education that accepts it as its duty to enable each student to run as far and as fast as he possibly can.

The knowledge base of modern society is not compatible with institutional uniformity in higher education. Again the problem assumes different forms in the United States and in Europe. In the United States (and in Japan) there is educational diversity which, however, is in danger of disappearing, mainly for financial reasons. In Europe there is educational uniformity as a rule, with government-designed and government-imposed patterns.

The United States (and also Japan) should organize financial support for the diversity of private and public institutions. Otherwise there will soon be only one uniform system of public universities, representing at best a small number of types and prevented by sheer size from pioneering and experimentation. We need acceptance of the principle that higher education for every youngster is paid for out of taxes but that it is up to the young person (and his parents) to decide to which specific institutions the student (and the support) should go. This was first worked out after World War II in the GI Bill of Rights. The institution of learning attended by the returning veteran was paid a fixed sum whether it was private or public, subject only to its satisfying academic standards. We need to return to this principle – if only to relieve the taxpayer. For every single student who goes to a private college or university relieves the cost burden on the state university. But the principle is equally necessary to preserve diversity.

In Europe competition will have to be created. To build its knowledge base, Europe needs educational entrepreneurship. It needs experiments which cannot be undertaken if a Ministry of Education is in tight control. Europe, in other words, requires a drastic break with the pattern of government-controlled public universities that has prevailed at least since Napoleon. One possible compromise is the German system under which the universities of the various *Laender*, while all State universities, compete with one another. The local autonomy which de Gaulle proposed for the French universities – in response to the student rebellion of spring 1968 – may be the beginning of the reforms Europe needs.

The knowledge base of our society requires major new thinking and changes within the university. It also requires sloughing off old habits, old traditions, old pride – and the adoption of new public policies.

THE POLITICS OF KNOWLEDGE

Diversity, flexibility, and competition will become more important in respect to knowledge the more knowledge becomes basic to society. This also will raise major political decisions on knowledge and will make it increasingly necessary to have alternatives of knowledge policy.

In the past, knowledge required little money. Today it requires more and more. In fact, it requires so much that only government can supply it. This immediately raises the question of government dictation and thought control. In the United States, government today supports about two-thirds of all research work. In the rest of the Free World the proportion is not much less – though the total amounts

440

are. And, of course, in the Communist countries, government supports all research. But can we expect government to pay the piper without calling the tune? And is government control of the acquisition of knowledge compatible with a free society? Is it even in the best interest of knowledge?

It is being agreed that there are safeguards available against political controls. We have, for instance, created committees of scholars to administer government grants to universities. But it is doubtful that this can be effective when the need arises to ration the available money and to choose among applicants. Nor, frankly, is it wholly desirable. There has to be political control of public money. The alternative is not freedom. It is bureaucratic control by procedure or by empire-building through patronage – both already to be found in the United States as well as in France or in the University Grants Council of Great Britain.

The money the government contributes today no longer goes exclusively to defence or space research. It supports all kinds of research, in medicine and biology, and increasingly in the social sciences. But does a free society want government management of social science research, or must this inevitably misdirect social science towards political control of individual and society?

The academicians (like other groups before them) have been far too eager to get their hands on government money to worry about these questions. They have been far too sure that their own virtue is beyond question, and that no one will expect *them* to become servants because they are being paid. They have been far too confident that they, and only they, are competent to decide on the uses of public money for science and research. But even if they did a better job than human beings are likely to do when their own interests are at stake, they will not be permitted to make these decisions. Nor are they competent to make them.

We face an unprecedented situation in which we will have to set priorities in the search for new knowledge. We face the need to make decisions regarding the direction of knowledge and its consequences.

This is totally new, not only for the men of knowledge. We had never thought of knowledge, and the search for it, as in need of direction, let alone in need of priorities and limitations.

It is becoming abundantly clear that knowledge is no more an absolute good in itself than is anything else. Knowledge may be neutral, but what we do with it is by no means neutral. Should the search for knowledge that could be used only to control and manipulate minds – as is a great deal of research in the behavioural sciences – be encouraged? Or is this a Pandora's Box out of which only evil can possibly come? What about research in germ warfare? Is the old excuse, that the other fellow will do it if we don't, still valid and acceptable?

Even more inescapable – and yet much thornier – is the question of priorities. We are running into physical limitations in the search for knowledge. We have to ration our resources. It is not money that will be scarce. Money, after all, does not do research; men do. And the supply of men capable of producing new knowledge is being used up fast in all the developed countries. In the natural sciences, in medicine, in the social sciences, and in the humanities, results from research are already diminishing as human resources of marginal utility have to be employed.

During the last twenty years, the research force in the pharmaceutical industry has grown twenty-fold. A company which had fifty professional researchers in 1950 is now likely to have well over a thousand. The results have not gone up twenty times: on the contrary, they have gone down. In part this is the result of overtly rapid growth and poor organization. In part it is the result of unmanageable size. But in large part the cause is that one can hire degrees and bodies, but one cannot easily hire men. Men have to be developed, trained and tested. This takes time – one commodity money cannot buy.

The need for priorities is probably greatest in the behavioural and political sciences, in economics and politics, psychology and sociology. Talent for productive work in these areas is apparently less common and develops more slowly than in the natural sciences. Yet we have today more knowledge in some branches of the natural sciences than we can apply, whereas we have a tremendous need for thought, knowledge, and new ideas in government and society. Nature, which we do not create, has not changed; but our man-made environment, our communities, our societies, and our governments have been changing much faster than our grasp of them.

What are the priorities in the search for knowledge? On what work should we deploy the scarce resources of trained, experienced, and tested people? And who should make the decision? The consequences of such decisions are tremendous. There is more risk to them than we have ever faced in allocating resources to economic expectations. Yet we know much less about them than we know about economic risks and economic decisions.

We have as yet no way to decide rationally between different lines of investigation and research. Even if we could assume a definite relationship between effort and results in this work, there is no rational choice between different results.

What should be given priority: research to cure a comparatively rare disease of infants; or research to improve the life expectancy and health of the elderly? What do we need most: methods for learning foreign languages fast and easily; or better methods to speed up economic and social development? Should we devote scarce resources to an improvement of defence capabilities that might make the difference between defeat or survival; or should we rather put the same resources into work on urban transportation?

Clearly the decision will be made neither on 'scientific' nor on purely 'factual' grounds. It must be made as a choice between values and based on highly subjective appraisals of the future. It is, in other words, not a scientific decision at all but a political decision.

At the same time, we need to think through the consequences of new knowledge.

We may, for instance, be able to control the weather tomorrow and to convert an arid desert into well-watered farmland. This may be highly beneficial. But it may, at the same time, deprive some other region thousands of miles away of rainfall and convert it into desert land. At what stage does this consideration enter the decision to go ahead with weather research or to devote resources to something else? Should such research work even be done by one nation and financed by it, or should it be international from the beginning? Who then controls? Who then pays?

These questions assume that we know enough about research and the search for knowledge to predict the results of our allocation of research resources. But no such assumption can be made so far.

We hear a great deal today about the need for 'pure research' and about the great productivity of such work. But there is no proof for this assertion. Knowledge people prefer 'pure research' for aesthetic reasons; I share this preference. But it should not be confused with facts documenting the utility of pure research – we have none. Indeed what little evidence we have would indicate that while highly successful pure research has great impact, most pure research has no impact or utility at all. It produces a footnote to be deleted when the next edition goes to press. Also, as C. H. Townes, the co-inventor of the laser and Nobel laureate showed in a brilliant study,* even the most experienced research directors cannot foretell which line of pure research will lead to practical applications and which will remain a purely academic curiosity.

Evidence rather indicates that in knowledge work we need a balance between pure research on general theory and development work on applications. These two mutually support each other. But the evidence does not indicate which comes first. At some times, pure research has led, at others development. This holds true apparently for all disciplines: the natural sciences, medicine, the social and political sciences. Nor does the evidence make clear what proportion between the two is needed and when – though obviously we need tons of development for every ounce of pure research. We not only have a problem of allocation between end results, where we have to go largely by opinion and judgement; we have an equal problem of allocation of resources within any given area of work.

We have, especially in the natural sciences, made great strides in formulating new knowledge needs in 'systems' which then enable us to put to work people of the requisite skills and to bring together in one team people of the most diverse knowledge. Work on the atomic bomb during World War II was only the first example; the work that produced the Salk vaccine against infantile paralysis is another. We have yet to prove, however, that the systems approach works in the socio-political areas. Even if it does, we still face uncertainties, choices, and considerations of preference which are not within the economic calculus or within the sphere of the policy-maker alone.

These priority decisions arise not only on the international or national level, but within every university, every university department and faculty, and every research

* *Science* (journal of the American Association for the Advancement of Science), February 16th, 1968.

laboratory. Yet the knowledge people, especially the scholars and scientists in our universities, rarely perceive the need to make them. Most of them still believe that government (or the university) has a duty to support any research proposal submitted by a reputable scholar. They do not understand that this is a physical, let alone a fiscal, impossibility.

I took part some years ago in a study group of experienced scientists, from the natural and the social sciences, who for one year discussed the impact of scientific and technological change on national policy. A good deal of the time the distinguished panellists complained about the failure of the politicians to budget enough money for whatever area they were individually most interested in. More often they complained about the politician's ignorance of science. Only rarely did anyone talk about the responsibility of the scientist to enable the politician to function, that is, to anticipate and understand political decisions that a new scientific or technological development might require. The only men who ever struck this note had themselves moved from being researchers or scholars to being scientific administrators and policy-makers. Their brethren in the group, the pure scientists, looked at these men as lost souls.

The abilities and inclinations of the individual scholar and researcher should be an important factor in any priority decision. In the first place, researchers and scientists do a better job if they work on what they want to do rather than on what they are told to do. But also the uncertainties of the decision are so great that the greatest possible weight should be given to the hunch of an experienced man who has proved his capacity to perform. At the same time, most scholars and researchers work best if they are directed towards a goal and if their efforts are organized. It is the exceptional man who works well without such direction. The productivity of directed research was shown in the development of the atomic bomb, where most of the participants did well even though they did not know what they were working on but only knew the specific task they were told to perform. And the Russians have proved it again and again.

If need be, in other words, we could make the decisions without the scientist's informed and willing participation – though at the certain risk of making many wrong decisions. The scientist, however, cannot possibly make these decisions by himself. They are political decisions, that is, choices between values which are non-scientific and non-factual. Political decisions have to be made by politicians.* The decision requires therefore a new relationship between the men of knowledge and the decision-makers – and, so far, neither of them has given much thought to it.

Altogether the need to think through and set priorities for knowledge, to direct it and to take risks, moves knowledge, its direction, its goals, and its results, increasingly into politics. We can no longer maintain the traditional line between 'dirty politics' and 'pure knowledge'.

The shift from skill to knowledge as the foundation for work and performance thus means that knowledge itself is becoming increasingly 'affected with the public interest'. The central decisions of the knowledge society are decisions on knowledge. The central issues in such a society are knowledge issues.

The need to set priorities for knowledge and for efforts to find new knowledge is likely to force a debate on the purpose, direction, and meaning of knowledge altogether. The question, 'Is this new knowledge necessary or desirable, or

* This is brought out clearly in the one 'inside story' of science-policy decisions that has yet been published, C. P. Snow's 1960 Godkin Lecture, *Science and Government*. Snow, in addition to being a novelist, is a scientist who for many years was Civil Service Commissioner responsible for recruiting scientific personnel for the British government.

is some other knowledge more desirable and more necessary?' is almost bound to lead to the next question: 'Is knowledge altogether necessary or desirable?'

Technology will be considered necessary and desirable for a good long time to come – even if large groups in society (eg, the romantics of the 'New Left') oppose it. We will continue to work at it, whether we like it or not. Competitive pressures in the peacetime economy as well as the need for rapid economic development of the poor nations will force us to continue technological work at high speed. And so will, I am afraid, the competition in defence between nations.

But knowledge? There we might well become doubtful, not only in what we say but in what we do. Once we try to differentiate between different kinds of knowledge as 'good', 'neutral', or 'dangerous', we may begin to wonder whether more knowledge itself is either desirable or necessary. We may become sceptical when we find that knowledge which one group of experts considers absolutely necessary is considered quite useless by another group. This is bound to happen fairly regularly once we are forced to set priorities and to argue which direction of knowledge effort is preferable. (It has already happened with respect to high-energy particle physics which happens to be particularly expensive.)

If we come to question the value of knowledge, it will be the first time since Socrates established knowledge as the fountain-head of Western thought and Western world view 2,400 years ago. Ever since then knowledge has been taken for granted by the Westerner. Theologians of various orthodoxies, from Byzantine Christianity to Marxism, have again and again tried to control what 'true' knowledge is or should be. But few people in the West since the Greeks have denied knowledge as such or have questioned its value and virtue. There was one attack on knowledge, that of the Franciscan mystics in the thirteenth century; but it was turned back by the great knowledge synthesis of St

Thomas Aquinas. And then his contemporary, St Bonaventure, himself a Franciscan, established our present position: *all* knowledge, he taught, leads to the ultimate knowledge of Truth: all knowledge is sanctified and sanctifies. Are we about to abandon this, the foundation on which the modern West has been built?

We are likely to question the value of knowledge precisely because of its success. Knowledge is becoming dubious because it has become the foundation for doing and the fundamental economic resource of modern society. Socrates established knowledge as good by asserting against the Sophists that knowledge is *not* application, that indeed the application of knowledge to doing is a misuse of knowledge. The purpose of knowledge was knowledge, and its test wisdom. Today, however, whatever our words, our actions make clear that we consider application to be the purpose, or at least the test, of knowledge. The Socratic position no longer suffices.

As a result, it is quite possible that the great new 'isms' of tomorrow will be ideologies about knowledge. In tomorrow's intellectual and political philosophies knowledge may well take the central place that property, ie, things, occupied in Capitalism and Marxism.

But these are speculations. All one can say today is that application has become the centre of knowledge, of the knowledge effort, and of the organized search for knowledge. As a result, knowledge has become the very foundation of modern economy and modern society and the very principle of social action. This is so great a change that it must have a major impact on knowledge itself and must make it a central philosophical and political issue in the knowledge society.

17. Does Knowledge have a Future?

THE CENTRAL MORAL problem of the knowledge society will be the responsibility of the learned, the men of knowledge.

Historically the men of knowledge have not held power, at least not in the West. They were ornaments. If they had any role at the seats of the mighty, it was that of court jester. There was so little truth, historically, in the adage that 'the pen is mightier than the sword', that it can only be called the 'opium of the intellectuals'. Knowledge was a solace to the afflicted and a joy to the wealthy who could afford it. But it was not power. Indeed, up until recently, the only position for which knowledge prepared was that of servant of the mighty. Oxford and Cambridge, until the middle of the nineteenth century, trained clergymen; the European universities trained civil servants. The business schools in the United States, set up less than a century ago, have been preparing well-trained clerks rather than entrepreneurs.

But now knowledge has power. It controls access to opportunity and advancement. Scientists and scholars are no longer merely 'on tap', they are 'on top'. They must be listened to by the policy-makers. They largely determine what policies can be considered seriously in such crucial areas as defence or economics. They are largely in charge of the formation of the young. (That the TV set – not to mention books, magazines, and comics – is probably at least as powerful an influence on the young, I consider a blessing no matter how questionable TV programmes or

450

comics may be. It is surely better for the child not to be dependent on one source of stimulus and information. 'Character,' said Goethe, 'is formed in the world's turbulence.')

The learned are no longer poor. On the contrary, they are true 'capitalists' in the knowledge society. Salaries have gone up fast in the schools. It is an educationally 'backward' society today in which teachers, whether in primary schools, secondary schools, or the universities are still badly paid. Such a society suffers from a 'brain drain' or a 'technology gap'. The man of knowledge also increasingly has earnings opportunities outside Academia, through research grants or as consultants.

But power and wealth impose responsibility.

The learned may have more knowledge than the rest of us, but learning rarely confers wisdom. It is, therefore, not too surprising that the men of knowledge do not realize that they have to acquire responsibility fast. They are no different from any other group that ever before entered into power. They, too, believe that they owe their position to their virtue and need no other justification than the 'purity of their intentions'. They, too, believe that anyone who questions their motives must be either fool or villain, either 'anti-intellectual' or 'McCarthyite'. But the men of knowledge, too, will find out that power can be justified only through responsibility.

The men of knowledge find it hard to accept that the basic decisions on knowledge are political decisions rather than knowledge decisions and therefore not in their hands. They find it even harder to swallow that we hold them responsible for these decisions, even though they do not control them. Yet unless they accept this, they will not have much say in these decisions. The decisions have to be made. The only choice open to the men of knowledge is whether responsibly to take part in them or have them imposed by somebody else.

We will also demand of the men of knowledge a high

code of morality. This demand will come as an even ruder surprise to the learned. They have always prided themselves on their objectivity and on the morality of science. They end to consider themselves repositories of virtue. But what may have been perfectly adequate as private morality as long as knowledge had no power, is rather irrelevant for a group in power.

The men of knowledge are today where the businessman was in the late nineteenth century with his assumption that the morality of business was his 'private affair'. For a group in power the facile assumption of moral righteousness – if only the heart be pure and the cause just – is crass immorality.

The best example is the *cause célèbre* that has become known as 'Project Camelot'. Project Camelot was the codeword for a secret but worldwide research project conceived in the early Sixties by a group of American anthropologists. Most of the participants came from the 'liberal left', and 'it was not likely that there was a single supporter of the Vietnam War among them'.* Camelot proposed to produce: (a) the systematic identification of the symptoms of the breakdown of a society; and (b) the identification of actions that might forestall such a breakdown.

The US Army in 1963 accepted the Camelot proposal and provided a budget of six million dollars for it. This is more than ever has been spent, I imagine, on any single social-science research project. It would have been enough to give grants to several thousand researchers – which is a good deal more than there are anthropologists and sociologists of proven competence in the world, let alone in the United States. The work was to be done all over the world, in Latin America, the Middle East, the Far East, Europe, and Africa (indeed everywhere except in the American

* As a distinguished social scientist, Professor Robert A. Nisbit of the University of California, pointed out in 'Project Camelot: An Autopsy' (*The Public Interest*, Fall issue, 1966).

Negro ghettoes where the questions it raised cried out for answers).

Camelot was aborted before it got started. A junior member of the team indiscreetly mentioned it to a fellow social scientist in Chile, who leaked the story to a left-wing Chilean newspaper. As anyone could have foreseen, all hell promptly broke loose. The Chilean Chamber of Deputies conducted a formal investigation. The Chilean government – and apparently a good many other Latin-American governments – protested formally to Washington against such gross intervention in the domestic affairs of sovereign countries.

Finally, in 1965, President Johnson ordered the project to be stopped and issued a directive that henceforth all government-sponsored research projects outside the United States had to be approved by the Secretary of State as compatible with American foreign policy. Two years later, in 1967, as a result of disclosures of CIA support for a variety of academic organizations, all work was stopped which, while ostensibly self-supporting academic research, was paid for secretly by the government. From now on such work will be out in the open, which will certainly stop another Camelot before it gets going.

But Camelot, of course, could never have produced re-sults. It was a pure, unadulterated six-million-dollar fraud. There are no research techniques to answer such questions as, 'What causes the breakdown of a society?', let alone 'How do we prevent it?' The sponsors of this project must have known this perfectly well – every social scientist in the world would have known it. But the sponsors also knew that the objective was broad enough to cover every conceivable social-science research and investigation any-one would want to do anywhere. Anything might, after all, be a possible 'cause of the breakdown of society', from marital infidelity and sex mores to the way teenagers buy soda pop. The sponsors argued that it is, after all, 'good' to know these things. 'If the only way to get the government to support social-science research is to tell lies, what's the harm in it?' The only comment of most social scientists when Camelot was cancelled (as Professor Nisbit reports) was that this was 'yet another chapter in the government's discrimination against the behavioural sciences'.

Is such a double standard still acceptable, still permissible, now that knowledge has power and income?

Even if the money had been obtained in good faith, could the project have been justified? Or would any such research be interference with, and invasion of, communities and private lives? Are there no limits to what is permissible in the search for knowledge?

Finally, is an army the right sponsor for such a project? What use is an army likely to make of such findings? What are the reasons an army supports it? The advocates of Camelot – and they were a substantial majority, apparently, among American social scientists – answered this question by saying: 'But we knew perfectly well that there would have been no results that the Army could have used.' Yet the same social scientist would have gone ahead with the project, even if they had expected results. What mattered to them was the money. That such results, in the hands of an army, might lead to actions that they, as 'liberals', would then deplore, did not, it is safe to say, much concern them. They did not even understand why the Latin-American governments were so upset when the news of Camelot leaked out.

Similarly the New York doctors who, in 1967, were found to have injected untested and dangerous drugs into terminal-cancer patients, without the patients' knowledge or consent, were hurt and shocked when their behaviour was questioned (even though they had violated established and published canons of medical ethics as well as state laws). After all, they pointed out, they did not derive any gain from these experiments. They were only trying to obtain knowledge that might help suffering humanity. To criticize what they had done was the worst of all crimes –

interference by laymen with medical research, where only the researcher's peers are entitled to an opinion, and they only to an opinion on the scientific validity of his findings.

The morality of knowledge should indeed be determined and controlled by peers. It should be self-controlled as it is in any self-respecting profession. But if the knowledge people refuse to tackle the problem, if they refuse to admit that a problem exists (as they still largely do) the community will inevitably tackle it – just as it punished the New York doctors rather than leave the job to the medical profession. For power always causes problems of morality. Fraud is fraud whatever the motives. And Camelot is by no means the only example of gross dishonesty and misrepresentation in application for grants from governments or foundations. Where there are large sums of money floating around, one always has to guard against the smart operator. If the knowledge community will not do this by itself, the safeguards will be imposed on it. Similarly, immorality is not to be excused simply because no one makes a profit out of it.

This is only one example, and only one area, in which we have to think through the morality of knowledge power. What about the morality of the restrictions with which the knowledge community – and especially the educators – hedge and safeguard their monopoly? Can the requirement of the Ph D degree be justified (except perhaps in the physical sciences)? Is there any evidence that the Ph D makes a man a better teacher, or even a better scholar? Or is the main reason for this requirement that it reserves access to appointments and emoluments to people who have paid their fees in time and money at the academic tollgate.

Can even permanent appointment be morally justified? We do need a safeguard against political pressure and administrative tyranny over faculties. But is the safeguard of permanent appointment not perhaps worse than the threat of political and administrative pressures? Could we not design a way to protect the individual against these pressures and yet protect the community, the school, and the student against sloth and incompetence – why not have an advisory committee of visiting scholars who would scrutinize the performance and record of every faculty member every three to five years? We have now, in the United States, well over 2,000 colleges and universities – and some 80,000 local school systems. Surely it is not difficult for a teacher who has any competence at all to find another good job should he be dismissed without adequate cause. Our faculties are chock-full of able-bodied people who stopped working the moment they were made associate or full professor and got tenure. And there are few complaints of undue pressure or persecution in industrial-research laboratories where there is no tenure.

As long as the men of knowledge had no power, problems such as these did not matter. Of course they existed. But they concerned only the members of the group. But with the men of knowledge in the centre of power these are no longer 'private matters'. A group in power either takes responsibility for its morality; or it is corrupt and corrupts.

It is equally urgent that the men of knowledge, the learned, take responsibility for content, standard, quality, performance, and impacts of education.

The 'diploma curtain' is not something to gloat over as so many of them do. It is their job to make it socially productive or to get rid of it. The lower productivity of education is a challenge to their responsibility. It is not enough to ask for more money and to complain when it is not immediately forthcoming.

Above all, the men of knowledge have to take responsibility for the performance of education. To blame the students for their failure to learn is no longer permissible. The student who does not learn is a failure of the school. And the student who does not want to learn is the shame of the school and an indictment of school and teacher alike.

It is naïve to expect that the learned will accept such responsibilities voluntarily. They would be the first group in history to have done so. However, like other groups before them, the learned will soon be challenged to take responsibility. It is highly probable that the next great wave of popular criticism, indignation, and revolt in the United States will be provoked by the arrogance of the learned. The young people are already in full revolt.

But the young, the students, also face a problem of responsibility – and they are even less prepared for it. The college student is highly privileged. He has almost a monopoly on the opportunities of the knowledge society. He is more highly subsidized than any privileged group has ever been before. Students are also a large and rapidly growing group. However much they may dislike it, the students today are very much a part of the 'establishment'.

The student revolts everywhere demand a share in the power of the university, and in its government. Few of them realize though that a share in power is a share in responsibility. Fewer still so far ask: 'What do I owe society?' It is fashionable to call today's students 'idealistic'; the students themselves use that term. But idealism by itself no more justifies power than 'sincerity' makes murder into self-defence. Power can be justified only by responsible use. And if the holder of power does not use it responsibly, then he will be used by the demagogue, and for the demagogue's singularly unidealistic ends.

Today's students – and the 'New Left' more than anyone else – tend to ask only: 'What does society owe me?' There is nothing wrong with this question; indeed it needs to be asked. But the other question – 'What do I owe society?' – should come first. This is particularly true if the holder of privilege, power, and opportunities owes his position to the labour of others – parents, taxpayers, and so on.

If we expect gratitude from students, we deserve to be disappointed. If we expect them to conform and to accept the society and the school their elders furnish them, we deprive ourselves of the specific strength of the young, their vision, energy, courage, and imagination. But responsibility – a keen sense of the moral obligation which their numbers, their privileges, and their power entail – that we can (and will) ask for.

This will come as quite a shock to the students. Few of them expect their protests to be taken quite that seriously. But it will be a wholesome shock – if only because it will put to productive use the very real strength of today's young people.

The greatest of the discontinuities around us is the changed position and power of knowledge.

Seven thousand years ago or more, man discovered skills. There were great artists before this discovery. There have never been painters greater than those of prehistoric men who left behind the cave paintings in France and Spain or the rock paintings in the Sahara. But there were no skilled craftsmen in those days. Skills supplied the tools to make average people without towering genius capable of competent, predictable performance, and capable of advancing from generation to generation by organized systematic apprenticeship. Skill created the division of labour, and therefore made possible economic performance. By the year 2000 BC or so, our ancestors in the irrigation civilizations of the Eastern Mediterranean had developed every single one of the basic social, political, and economic institutions of society, every single one of our occupations, and most of the tools man had at his disposal until two hundred years ago. The discovery of skill created civilization.

Now we are about to work another major move. We are beginning to apply knowledge to work. We are not yet much further ahead, I submit, than were those remote ancestors of ours who first made hunting a specialized occupation with its own special tools, and with a skill to be learned in long arduous apprenticeship. But even the first faltering steps we have taken have shown that applying knowledge to work is a big idea, and an exciting one. Its potential may be as great as was the potential of skill when first discovered. The development may take as long. But the impacts already are very great – and the changes they imply are indeed tremendous.

As great and as profound as any of these impacts *of* knowledge are the impacts *on* knowledge. Above all, the shift to knowledge as the foundation of work and performance imposes responsibility on the man of knowledge. How he accepts this responsibility and how he discharges it will largely determine the future of knowledge. It may even determine whether knowledge has a future.

Conclusion

THIS BOOK, despite its length, reports only on one dimension of our experience and existence: the social one. It probes for the discontinuities in technology and economy, in society, politics, and education. It pays, at most, passing attention to science and the arts, and virtually none to the emotional and spiritual life of man.

It is, therefore, a superficial book. The social is the surface of human existence, the skin, so to speak.

What has happened, and what it means in tasks and opportunities ahead, is the book's concern. It looks for the cutting edges of the future. It looks for what is clearly visible, but is not yet being perceived. Disciplined observation rather than powers of prophecy is what its author would like to claim for himself.

But precisely because the events reported are accomplished facts, they are unlikely to disappear. The tasks will remain and will become increasingly urgent. While the discontinuities described here do not predict what will happen, they do indicate, with high probability, what we will have to concern ourselves with. They also indicate what is not likely to happen. If there is substance to this report on our changing society, it is unlikely that the trends of the last sixty years will dominate the rest of this century, as most predictions of 'The Year 2000' assume. Instead we can expect different and new trends to emerge and different and new concerns to claim our attention.

If this report is valid, the expectations of the 'New Left' are equally improbable. We will not see technology and economics become irrelevant or secondary. We will not see

461

concern with production become obsolete. Rather we can expect a rapidly changing technology and a new concern with production and productivity. Nor are we likely to see a society that repudiates organizations. Rather the concern will be with making organization fully effective as a major instrument and tool of man and as a central organ of human society.

Self-limitation to the social dimension and to reporting on events that, while not yet perceived, are still accomplished facts, restricts both the time span with which this book deals and its scope. Surely the arts rather than social events are the true harbingers of tomorrow. And no matter how perceptive a reporter is, and how keenly he analyses what has already happened, he is no more capable than the next man of predicting great events of tomorrow, whether catastrophes or blessings, or the great men, whether heroes or villains.

Yet the future that the artist's vision foretells we only recognize after it has become fact, and yesterday. Who, for instance, a hundred years ago, would have been able to show that the Impressionists in France, rather than the Pre-Raphaelites in England, were the harbingers of tomorrow? Who would have been able to show that Louis Sullivan's first toll buildings in Chicago foreshadowed the architecture of the twentieth century rather than that most admired Victorian monument, the St Pancras Railway Station in London? And would even knowledge of the right artistic trend enable one to divine the society or the environment the trend embodies in advance? Like all oracles, the artist's vision can only be understood after the forecasted event.

Similarly the great events and the great men can be predicted only after they have occurred. Whether history has logic and laws has been debated for thousands of years, but neither, all our experience proves, can be foreseen. They only come into the focus of hindsight. In prospect the logic and laws of history are possibilities only, all equally probable and equally improbable.

The discontinuities are, however, certainties – precisely because they are on the surface, precisely because they have already happened.

No one needs to be told that our age is an age of infinite peril. No one needs to be told that the central question we face with respect to man's future is not what it shall be, but whether it shall be. If we do not survive, the concerns of this book will, of course, perish with us. But if we do survive, its concerns will become our tasks.

They are humdrum tasks, tasks of patching the fabric of civilization rather than of designing a new garment for a 'New Adam'. They are tasks of today, and not tasks for 'The Year 2000'. But they are the tasks to which we have to address ourselves to deserve tomorrow.

Index

Index

Adams, Henry, 135, 171
ADELA, 162
Adolescence, 394, 395–8
  among physicians, 397
  extended by years of schooling, 396–7
Advertising, 205
Aeroplane, economic impact of, 19
Agriculture, 25–31
  business research into, 225–6
  'contract-growing', 165–7
  failure of US farm programme, 281
  in developing economies, 37, 137–8, 142–4
  nineteenth-century 'bread baskets', 140
  production efficiency throughout world in, 142
'Alliance for Progress', 163
Aluminium,
  as a competitor to steel, 32
  establishes itself, 46
American Can Company, 50
American Capitalism, 305 *n.*
American Challenge, The, 122, 323, 433
Anarchism, 299, 300
Andean Indians, 103, 132 *n.*
Anglo-Dutch Shell Oil Co, 121
Asian Drama, 132 *n*, 168
Austin, John, 307
Automation, 360–1, 362
Automobile industry, 35–7

and employment, 362
automotive saturation, 37
in developing economies, 37–8

Barchester Towers, 233
Becket, Thomas à, 315
Bell Telephone Co, 18, 69
  as innovator, 76
Big Business, 218 *n.*, 233 *n.*, 260 *n.*
Black Power, 294
Boston University, 224
Brahe, Tycho de, 178–9
Brazil, 153
  automobile industry in, 36
  development pains in, 171
  economic emergence of, 17
  racial cleavage in, 132 *n.*
Breton Woods Conference, 112–13
Brown, Lester R., 137–8
Bryan, William Jennings, 115
Bunge & Born, 125–6
Business,
  extending into education, 224–5
  extending into research, 225
  test of performance and, 292

California Institute of Technology, 224
Canada,
  'American domination' in, 126–7
  obsolete government activities in, 240

467

Index

Index

Index

MANAGEMENT SERIES

MANAGEMENT DECISION MAKING 30p
A symposium of five international experts – British and American – stress the importance of scientific decision making in modern business administration.

MARKETING MANAGEMENT IN ACTION 60p
Victor P. Buell. A guide to successful marketing management by a former national vice-president of the American Marketing Association.

THE PRACTICE OF MANAGEMENT 50p
Peter F. Drucker. An outstanding contribution to management theory and practice.

MANAGING FOR RESULTS 40p
Peter F. Drucker. A what to do book for the top echelons of management.

THE EFFECTIVE EXECUTIVE 35p
Peter F. Drucker. How to develop the five talents essential to effectiveness and mould them into results by practical decision-making.

THE AGE OF DISCONTINUITY 60p
Peter F. Drucker. The author presents numerous practical examples from Central Europe, Britain, US and Japan to produce 'A major work of great brilliance.'

CYBERNETICS IN MANAGEMENT 40p
F. H. George. Introduction to the ideas and methods used by cyberneticians in the running of modern business and government.

PLANNED MARKETING 30p
Ralph Glasser. A lucid introduction to mid-Atlantic marketing techniques.

FINANCE AND ACCOUNTS FOR MANAGERS 30p
Desmond Goch. A vital and comprehensive guide to the understanding of financial problems in business.

INNOVATION IN MARKETING 37½p
Theodore Levitt. A brilliant exposition of original and stimulating ideas on modern approaches to marketing.

MANAGEMENT SERIES (cont.)

THE ESSENCE OF PRODUCTION 40p
P. H. Lowe. Explains the components, diversities and problems of production within the general framework of business management.

MAKING MANPOWER EFFECTIVE. Part 1 37½p
James J. Lynch. The techniques of company manpower planning and forecasting.

A MANPOWER DEVELOPMENT SYSTEM 40p
Part 2 of MAKING MANPOWER EFFECTIVE. Shows the need to integrate manpower forecasting, compensation planning and career development into a manpower development system.

CAREERS IN MARKETING 30p
An Institute of Marketing Review. A guide to those seeking a job in the exciting field of marketing.

THE PROPERTY BOOM (illus.) 37½p
Oliver Marriott. The story of the personalities and the companies that emerged enriched from the commercial property industry in the years 1945–1965.

SELLING AND SALESMANSHIP 30p
R. G. Magnus-Hannaford. A clear, concise and forward looking exposition of practical principles and their application.

MARKETING 37½p
Colin McIver. Includes chapters by Gordon Wilson on the Years of Revolution and Industrial Marketing.

EXPORTING: A Basic Guide to Selling Abroad 37½p
Robin Neillands and Henry Deschampsneufs. Shows how smaller and medium-sized companies can effectively obtain and develop overseas markets.

DYNAMIC BUSINESS MANAGEMENT 30p
Harold Norcross. A simple guide to the rudiments of successful business management.

FINANCIAL PLANNING AND CONTROL 40p
R. E. Palmer and A. H. Taylor. Explains the nature of the assistance which levels of accounting can provide in the planning and control of a modern business.

MANAGEMENT SERIES (cont.)

COMPUTERS FOR MANAGEMENT 30p
Peter C. Sanderson. A timely appraisal of computers and electronic data processing – their basic concepts, potential and business application.

GUIDE TO SAMPLING 30p
Morris James Slonim. A fine exposition of sampling theory and techniques.

MANAGEMENT INFORMATION – Its Computation and Communication 40p
C. W. Smith, G. P. Mead, C. T. Wicks and G. A. Yewdall. Discusses Education in Business Management, Statistics for Business, Mathematics and Computing, Operational Research, Communicating Numerical Data.

MANAGERS AND THEIR JOBS 35p
Rosemary Stewart. Helps managers to analyse what they can do, why they do it, and whether they can, in fact, do it better.

THE REALITY OF MANAGEMENT 35p
Rosemary Stewart. Compass bearings to help the manager plot his career.

HOW TO WIN CUSTOMERS 45p
Heinz M. Goldmann. A leading European sales consultant with unique experience of British, Canadian, US and European markets examines the sixteen areas of creative selling.

These Management Series titles are obtainable from all booksellers and newsagents. If you have any difficulty please send purchase price plus 5p postage to Claude Gill Books, 481 Oxford Street, London, W.1 where the whole series is on display.

While every effort is made to keep prices low, it is sometimes necessary to increase prices at short notice. PAN Books reserve the right to show new retail prices on covers which may differ from those previously advertised in the text or elsewhere.